CW00945324

RIFLE GREEN
IN THE
PENINSULA

*Badge of the Rifle Corps*
*on its formation in 1800*

Dedicated to Derek and Kate Haighton

# Rifle Green
## in the
# Peninsula

# Volume III

An account of the 95th Foot
in the Peninsular Campaign of 1808–14.
Volume III covers the sieges of Ciudad Rodrigo, Badajoz
and the battles of Salamanca and Vitoria,
together with the Military General Service medal official entitlement
and actual entitlement as proven by the paylists.
Fully illustrated throughout with
maps, photographs and scene reconstruction.

## by

# George Caldwell and Robert Cooper
## Illustrated by James Dann

## BUGLE HORN PUBLICATIONS

*Correspondence: 49 Cromwell Road Great Glen Leicester LE8 9GU England*
*Tel/fax: +44 (0)116 2593124 Email: info@buglehorn.co.uk Web: www.buglehorn.co.uk*

### Rifle Green in the Peninsula
### Volume III

In preparation
*Rifle Green in the Peninsula*
*Volume 4 in a series of 4*

By the same authors
*Rifle Green at Waterloo*
*Rifle Green in the Crimea*
*Rifles at Waterloo*
*Rifle Green in the Peninsula Volume 1*
*Rifle Green in the Peninsula Volume 11*

Designed and Produced by
Citrus°
www.citrus.co.uk

Printed and Bound by
CPI Group (UK) Ltd
Croydon CR0 4YY

British Library Cataloguing in Publication Data:
A catalogue record for this book is available from the British Library.

**ISBN 978-0-9516600-5-8**

# Contents

# Introduction

## by John Sly

This is the third volume of the history of the 95th Rifles in the Peninsula and it deals with one of the most militarily important and significant episodes of the entire war. The years 1812 and 1813 were a turning point, and although this book concentrates on the story of the 95th, it also illustrates clearly the overall military history of these years.

From a personal point of view, reading the book brought back memories of my visit, a few years ago, to some of the towns mentioned in the text. It is difficult to imagine now that my pleasant walk around the walls of Ciudad Rodrigo would have been impossible 200 years previously because at that time several thousand men were attempting to kill each other there, in hand to hand fighting. Whether any of those men were particularly aware of the strategy and tactics conceived by their respective generals, or whether they were remotely concerned with the political questions that had led to them being in this place at this time, can only be a matter of pure speculation.

The walls of Badajoz that are still standing continue to bear the evidence of the cannon shot that was directed against them, and looking towards this fortress from the height of the town of Elvas stimulated sobering thoughts about the efforts that had to be expended by all arms of Wellington's force in order to achieve the required results.

Again, it is almost sacrilege to visualise the beautiful city of Salamanca, a jewel of modern Spain as it was in 1812 and has been for several centuries, witnessing one of Wellington's most famous victories. However, even standing on the Greater and the Lesser Arapile on a sunny summer's day, viewing the towers of Salamanca in the distance, I found it totally impossible to recreate in my mind the masses of men comprising the French and Allied forces, fighting and dying on the rolling country around the Arapiles on that July afternoon and evening in 1812. Even though I had read Roger Robinson's eloquent account of the part played by 6 Division in general, and 1/11th Foot in particular [1], and even though the whole battlefield was more or less laid open in front of me, I personally could not 'see' the thousands of soldiers engaged in what was clearly a truly desperate physical struggle.

In these circumstances the description by John Keegan, in his seminal work, *The Face Of Battle*, [2] inevitably came to mind. Although Keegan was writing in the context of Waterloo, his remarks are appropriate for any engagement between formed units of infantry, in the age of 'black powder warfare', and it was infantry to which William Napier referred on the famous occasion of Albuera as 'the pith and strength of battle', in his *English Battles And Sieges In The Peninsula*.[3] Keegan saw the 'clash of heavy infantry, in close order, over levelled musket barrels,' as something totally incomprehensible to researchers and historians of the twenty-first century: 'What makes episodes of this sort so difficult for the modern reader to visualize, if visualized to believe in, if believed in to understand, is precisely this nakedly face-to-face quality, their offering and delivery of death...their letting of blood and infliction of pain in circumstances of human congestion we expect to experience only at cocktail parties or tennis tournaments.' Whenever we read or talk about the warfare of the Napoleonic period, indeed of all periods until the twentieth century when long-range death-dealing became routine, it is the intensely personal aspect of the fighting that should be borne in mind if we are fully to appreciate the cost in human terms of what was achieved by thousands of individual soldiers on all sides. The men fighting at Ciudad Rodrigo, Badajoz, Salamanca and Vitoria could easily see the faces of the individual enemy troops at whom they were aiming their muskets. For them it was truly up close and personal.

In his introduction to Volume II of *Rifle Green In The Peninsula*, Richard Rutherford-Moore in part explored this aspect of the military life on a very personal level of his own, as he was closely involved in the dramatisations for television of Bernard Cornwell's *Sharpe* novels over a period of sixteen years. Rutherford-Moore played an active part in the programmes as a Rifleman, and thus had to wear the full uniform of the period. He made the important point that 'unless you "do it" in a recreated form, you never get the full experience from reading history books'. He was absolutely right, of course, but very few students of the Peninsula War have the chance or inclination to do this, so we have to rely vicariously on what the original surviving participants have left for us in their writing.

Philip Haythornthwaite, who wrote the introduction to the first Volume of *Rifle Green In The Peninsula*, mentioned that 'of all the many published memoirs of the Peninsular War era, more emanated from the 95th than from any other regiment: the works of, for example, John Kincaid, Edward Costello, Benjamin Harris, Jonathan Leach, Harry Smith, William Surtees and William Green include some of the great "classics" of the genre...'. Once again attention is drawn to the individual soldier and his personal experiences, each of which was an intensely felt microcosm of the war. In this third Volume the authors make many references to these memoirs, as well as those of contemporaries in other regiments, because each adds to the picture of the war lived as a personal event, even if the various authors occasionally disagree about exact details of time and place.

The writing of military history concerning the Napoleonic period is so often confined to the strategy and tactics of a particular attack or siege, rarely delving deeper than battalion level; the effect of the decisions made by senior commanders on individual soldiers is usually ignored, unless the written evidence provided by the relatively few of those individuals who could write is used for source material.

Several of the individual memoirs of the period covered by this volume relate to the taking of Badajoz on 6th April 1812 and its dreadful aftermath, when the British Army seemed collectively to go mad. Napier described it thus: 'Now commenced that wild and desperate wickedness, which tarnished the lustre of the soldiers' heroism...Shameless rapacity, brutal intemperance, savage lust, cruelty and murder, shrieks and piteous lamentations, groans, shouts, imprecations...and the reports of muskets used in violence resounded for two days and nights in the streets of Badajos.' These appalling travesties were carried out in the most part by the survivors of the assault who only a few hours before had shown such bravery in action. These days we would probably ascribe it to post-traumatic stress: the sheer bloodiness of the assault and the loss of life had created a rabble out of a disciplined army. Elizabeth Longford [4] reported that Wellington, on seeing the British dead lying in heaps, wept, an emotion completely at odds, apparently, with that of his fellow generals and other memorialists, who would have expected nothing other than that the town should be plundered. If innocent inhabitants died in that process, it was what might now be called 'collateral damage'. Perhaps that was why Wellington took no firm steps to put a stop to it until 8th April.

Although Wellington was not in the least concerned with the respective careers of individual soldiers in his army, he was concerned with their overall well-being, and he deplored losing men unnecessarily. Experienced soldiers were not easy to replace, and he had few enough of them. Elizabeth Longford recorded that after Albuera, Wellington visited the battlefield and saw the men of the 29th Foot lying dead where they had stood; after he had commiserated with the wounded of that regiment in respect of there being so many of them in that state, one of his wounded veterans replied that there would not have been so many had Wellington been in command.

A large number of incapacitated veterans who survived the war were given Chelsea or Kilmainham pensions, and those records fortunately exist through The National Archives for military researchers and family historians alike to uncover. There is a wealth of detail in these classes of documents, and it is sometimes incredible how many times these pensioners could be wounded, or be inflicted with disease, and still live to what even today would be considered a ripe old age.

One such soldier was Thomas Plunkett, 95th Rifles, about whom one of the authors of this Volume has published a monograph. Plunkett was an Irishman, born in Newtown, County Wexford, who enlisted for 2/95th at Dublin 10th May 1805. He served with the Rifles in South America in 1806, then later with Sir John Moore's army in the retreat to Corunna, during which he became a legend for shooting dead the French cavalry General Auguste François-Marie de Colbert-Chabanais at a greater distance than would have been thought possible. Badly injured after having been ridden over by a French Dragoon, he was back in Spain in 1812. After more than 12 years with the Rifles, including the battle of Waterloo, he served for some time in the 41st Foot, Militia and Veteran Battalions, finally being discharged from military service on 4th November 1824. He died sometime in the 1830s.

All three volumes of the history of the 95th by these two authors have concentrated on the individuals who served with the regiment. Many personal names of the Riflemen are recorded, sometimes with allusions to their history. No general can fight a war without being able to trust in the quality of the soldiers under his command. Wellington knew this only too well, although he did complain, after the looting following the battle of Vitoria, that 'We have in the service the scum of the earth as common soldiers'. However, he did remark later, before Waterloo, when pointing out a British infantryman, that 'it all depends on upon that article whether we do the business or not. Give me enough of it, and I am sure'. The rest is history.

John Sly

1   *The Bloody Eleventh.* RER Robinson, Exeter, 1988
2   *The Face of Battle.* John Keegan, London, 1976
3   *English Battles And Sieges In The Peninsula.* Lieutenant General Sir William Napier KCB, London, 1879
4   *Wellington—The years of the Sword.* Elizabeth Longford, 1972. The Chaucer Press

# Foreword

by Alan Harrison

As the Peninsular War drew towards its climax, the Duke of Wellington, (as he was to become in 1814), wrote a rare reflection on the qualities of his army, by informing Earl Bathhurst, in November 1813, that in his opinion, 'the army was never in such health, heart and condition as at the present time, and that it is probably the most complete machine, for its number, now existing in Europe.'

This was a bold assertion, but when the question is considered, there is every reason to believe that his statement was correct. Within that 'most complete machine' were components of complete competence. Amongst the acknowledged elite of the army, was the Light Division, which had forged into a remarkable fighting contingent by a number of innovative and forward-thinking officers, and led, for much of its time until his death at Ciudad Rodrigo, by the formidable 'Black Bob' Craufurd.

Within the strength of the Light Division, arguably the finest element was the 95th Rifle Regiment, the tactics of which, developed over a few years and refined in battle, were the forerunner of all modern infantry service.

During the period covered in this volume, the Light Division, with the 95th in particular, had become hardened by the experience of seasoned campaigning, as even the best intense training and the high calibre of both officers and other ranks, were not enough alone, to produce the highly efficient force that they had become.

This point was made tellingly obvious, by an account on the baptism of battle of the 2nd Battalion 43rd Light Infantry at Vimeiro!

'Landed from England but a few days before—a finer, more robust and healthy-looking body of soldiers it would be difficult to find, but poor fellows! The pipe clay was soon shook out of their jackets, for getting somehow exposed to a galling range of fire, they were most severely handled, with whole sections of them lying, as they fell, in the dykes and hollows where they had been stationed. With scarcely anything beyond sundry evolutions at the double-quick, their military education was supposed to be complete, but the men knew nothing of the business of a rifleman—firing, in the usual manner, at the clouds, they did little execution, while they were peppered in the way before described.'

Yet this was a regiment (though a second battalion) that subsequently became one of the pillars of the Light Division. Experience was crucial during the war, and Wellington had an engaging battle with the commander-in-chief and the Horse Guards in order to retain the units made efficient by long and hard campaigning, rather than to send them home on recruiting duties. Only to be replaced by unseasoned and inexperienced raw recruits, which was the preferred policy of those in authority. An experienced cadre was essential, so that drafts of new recruits could be absorbed and learn from the veteran. None were more experienced—and thus more valuable—than the 9th, by their own assertion, 'the first troops into action, on any battlefield, and the last to leave'—their training and expertise, making them ideally suited to serve as the van guard or rear guard of the Army.

They were possessed not only of battle experience but also the specialist individual skills of sharp shooting and skirmishing, tactics not generally practised by most of the other regiments, and they formed Wellington's most valuable asset, a fact that was proved in all of the actions recounted in this volume. Alongside their skill, and arising in part from it, was a level of morale and courage not exceeded by any other regiment. Nowhere were these factors more needed, or more demonstrated, than at the twin sieges of Ciudad Rodrigo and Badajoz, the successes of which, opened the way for Wellington's thrust into Spain, which enabled him to switch his objective from the defence of Portugal to the ultimate objective of driving the French from the Iberian Peninsula.

The enormity of the trial, represented by these actions in exemplified by a comment by one of the 95th's best known memorialists, John Kincaid, 'as respectable a representation of hell itself as fire and sword, and human sacrifices could make it' that were the breeches of Badajoz. It is not possible to recount the exploits of any particular regiment, without acknowledging the fact that each unit was essentially a group of individuals, every one of whom was a small, but a vital leg in the smooth running of a very well oiled, whole machine. This was emphatically true of the 95th, their tactics of which depended upon the initiative of every individual soldier, more than for any other corps.

This was expressed effectively, once again by John Kincaid, who remarked that in battle, soldiers 'are apt to have feelings that they are but in significant characters, only a humble individual out of many thousands, and that his conduct, be it good or bad, can have little influence over the fate of the day. This is a monstrous mistake, for in battle, as elsewhere, no man is insignificant unless he chooses to make himself so.'

The truth of this assertion in demonstrated within these pages. Individuals are named and identified, and their actions are described for good and occasionally for ill, which brings to life many remarkable men, who served in a very remarkable regiment, which was a vital part of a remarkable army.

Alan Harrison

# Acknowledgements

It is rare to find a book that has been written without some kind of help or input from others, often unsung heroes, whose contributions have been overlooked, mostly by accident. Therefore, it is with great pleasure that we direct due praise to all those who have helped to make this volume, which we believe to be our best to date.

John Sly and Alan Harrison, besides sharing their expert research knowledge, consented to pen an introduction and foreword, for which we are most grateful. Major Ron Cassidy, always an ever willing pillar of support, who pushes us in the right direction to extend our knowledge on such a remarkable regiment. Derek Haighton and his late wife Kate, I could never thank enough, from a personal point. Their confidence and faith in turning me into an established regimental historian author, I hope, will never be diminished. Keith Webster, always willing to chase our requests, especially on the 5th Battalion 60th Regiment.

Philip Haythornthwaite, 'our' very own evergreen military oracle, who has come up time and again with facts we could never have dreamed of finding and his support has always gone far beyond the call of duty.

James Dann, who is now a permanent part of the team, has once again brought our text alive with his own brand of illustration and is fast becoming a sought after addition to the military world.

Stephen Bufton, for bringing to our attention John Lowe of the 2nd Battalion 95th's personal account of his service. The late Tony Mullin, who gave us such sound advice, along with his encyclopaedic knowledge of the Napoleonic era, he would have loved this volume. Andrew Black, was most helpful with research on Spanish recruitment into the 95th.

James Cooper, who once again has turned our research into such a quality publication and, last but not least, Barbara and Carol our supportive wives. Their contributions are too numerous to mention.

If we have omitted anyone please accept our apologies but feel proud to be linked with this publication when reading through its pages and recognise your personal piece of help.

George Caldwell/Robert Cooper, 2012

# Sentries at Barba del Puerco
# 19th March 1810—Vol II Revision

Historians writing on the combat at the bridge, have possibly referred to and used George Simmons' account of the affair. Simmons, who was present at the bridge, mentions that the double sentries were Riflemen Maher and McCann. Our initial research, using the Muster Roll for 25th September to 24th December 1810, showed:

R'man John McCann Prisoner of war, 24th July Coa, returned 3rd June 1814.
R'man Thomas Mahar Prisoner of war, 20th March, returned 16th May 1814.
R'man Alexandre Moore Prisoner of war, 20th March, rejoined 1811.

From this it would clearly indicate that the two sentries were Mahar and Moore. Further research into the three Riflemen produced more complications. This may be in part due to the Clerk's inaccurate entries in the "remarks" column.

John McCann 1/95
Dec.–24 Mar. 1810 Foreign Service. "wounded and taken" 24 March
Mar.–24 June 1810 Foreign Service. "prisoner of war"
June–24 Sep. 1810 Valle near Santarem. "prisoner of war since 20 March"
Sep.–24 Dec. 1810 Valle. "prisoner of war 24 July." Prisoner of war to 1814

Alexandre Moore 1/95
Dec.–24 Mar. 1810 Foreign Service.
Mar.–24 June 1810 Foreign Service. 25 March transferred to 3rd company
June–24 Sep. 1810 Valle near Santarem. "prisoner of war 24 July."
Sep.–24 Dec. 1810 Near Campo Maior "prisoner of war 20 March" Prisoner of war to Dec. 1811 to Mar. 1812

Thomas Mahar 1/95
Dec.–24 Mar. 1810 Foreign Service. "wounded and taken 24 March"
Mar.–24 June 1810 Foreign Service. "Prisoner of war."
June–24 Sep. 1810 Vale near Santarem. "Prisoner of war since 20 March"
Prisoner of war rejoined from French prison 16 May–24 June 1814

Research can be quiet confusing at times but the one 'casting' vote in support of George Simmons could be that McCann and Mahar were both paid to 20th March 1810, whereas Moore was paid to 24th July 1810.

# Calender of Events

8–19th January 1812  Siege of CIUDAD RODRIGO.

8th January 1812       Storming the convent of SAN FRANCISCO at CIUDAD RODRIGO, Lieutenant Hawksley killed in action.

19th January 1812      CIUDAD RODRIGO, MGS clasp 'CIUDAD RODRIGO'.
Eight companies of the 1st Battalion, two companies of the 2nd Battalion and three companies of the 3rd Battalion were engaged.

27th January 1812      Death of General Robert Craufurd from the wounds he received on 19th January.

17th March 1812        Second siege of BADAJOZ begins.

22nd March 1812      Riflemen pick off French gunners at BADAJOZ and at the fort of SAN CHRISTOVAL.

26th March 1812      BADAJOZ, MGS clasp 'BADAJOZ'.
Storming of fort PICURINA.

6th March 1812         Storming and capture of BADAJOZ. Eight companies of the 1st Battalion, two companies of the 2nd Battalion and five companies of the 3rd Battalion were engaged

11th March 1812        All three Battalions leave BADAJOZ for MADRID.

12th July 1812         Captains Duncan and Fergusson join the Light Division and the 2nd Battalion now up to four companies.

22nd July 1812        SALAMANCA, MGS clasp 'SALAMANCA'.
The 95th was only slightly engaged. Six companies of the 1st Battalion, four companies of the 2nd Battalion and five companies of the 3rd Battalion were engaged.

| | |
|---|---|
| August 1812 | One wing of the Light Division marches to GATAFE and the other to MADRID. |
| 29th October 1812 | Marching to join Wellington from CADIZ and TARIFA the two 2nd Bn. companies of Captains Cadoux and Jenkins with Skerrett's force were engaged at ARANJUEZ. |
| 31st October 1812 | Rifles evacuate MADRID, force march to PORTUGAL with Wellington's Army. |
| 18th November 1812 | The last day of the retreat into PORTUGAL, all three 95th Battalions in action. |
| 25th November 1812 | 95th go into winter quarters at ALAMEDA and ESPEJA. Joined by the two 2nd Battalion companies from CADIZ. |
| 21st May 1813 | All three Battalions break up from winter quarters and march into SPAIN. |
| 11th June 1813 | The 1st and 3rd Battalions cross the PISUERGA in pursuit of the French. |
| 15th June 1813 | All three Battalions cross the river EBRO. |
| 18th June 1813 | Skirmish of SAN MILLAN, 1st, 2nd and 3rd battalions were all engaged. |
| 21st June 1813 | VITORIA, MGS clasp 'VITTORIA'. All three Battalions in action. |
| 23rd June 1813 | Pursuit of the French, some Riflemen mounted behind Royal Dragoons. 95th engaged at ECHARRI ARINEZ. |
| 24th June 1813 | Pursuit of the French, all three Battalion in action near LA CUENCA and captured the last gun of the French Army. |

# Chapter One

# Preparation for the Campaign of 1812

The year 1811, it would be safe to comment, was one of mixed emotions and fortunes for Wellington's Allied Army and especially so in the Light Division. The beginning of the year had seen General Robert Craufurd, their commander, slink off in a fit of pique and depression to England to visit his family, with Wellington's displeasure ringing in his ears. Returning in May just in time to command the Light Division at Fuentes de Onoro, his handling of the division before and during the battle went a long way to restoring his credibility and prestige, not only with Wellington but throughout the whole army whatever else could be said against the man, the truth he was a master at handling light troops.

The reputation of the 95th Rifles during this period was still increasing in popularity, especially amongst the officer classes. Back in England new officers and volunteers could not join quickly enough, hoping to share in their glory and fame. The down side for the Rifles during this year however, was the loss of their colonel and father figure, Beckwith, who had left for England due to ill health; at least that was the official reason. His dislike of Craufurd's erratic behaviour and explosive temper was well known throughout the division and probably a major factor in his leaving the Peninsula. During Craufurd's absence Beckwith had excelled in command of a brigade of the Light Division, even under the hapless Erskine who had been placed in temporary command until Craufurd's return. The division had not only lost Beckwith but the death of Colonel Drummond deprived them of their two most respected brigade commanders. Beckwith's replacement Colonel Barnard, of the 3/95th, was an equally able replacement, who in time became an accomplished commander of light troops. He still, however, had to fathom out the unpredictable and complicated Craufurd. The latter months of 1811 were quite a challenge for Barnard, the trying conditions, lack of food, overworking of the men and of course, Craufurd with his black temper tantrums, who irritated the regimental officers with what they thought as petty and pointless exercises, all of which was gradually affecting the ordinary Rifleman. Some men took drastic steps against such treatment by deserting to the enemy, causing Wellington some concern about his elite division. One can sympathise with the men and in particular those in the 95th. The Light Division was considered a light or beacon for the commander, which in effect meant they were his eyes and ears. Even in winter quarters it was their duty to provide security for the whole army, patrolling and watching the border being of paramount importance, while at the same time they were still required to be employed in the general duties of the army. It is no wonder that the men felt they were being treated unfairly. Craufurd's moods had taken on a more menacing phase during the latter months of 1811. In today's parlance he would be described as a classic manic depressive. Once again he was considering returning home but this time quitting the army altogether. His brother, however, all too familiar and aware of his condition and shortcomings, persuaded him to remain. The fact that Wellington was preparing for a full scale attack on the frontier fortresses of Ciudad Rodrigo and Badajoz was a timely step in the right direction for the restless Craufurd, who found this stage of 1811 most boring!

While Craufurd was complaining of boredom and inactivity, the Light Division was suffering from endless picquet and siege preparation duties, but it is surprising to hear that men in other divisions, in far more comfortable conditions, were still not happy with their existence. Private Wheeler of the 51st Regiment in the 7th Division complained about the want of new clothing and a fresh supply of necessities and the house he was billeted in was not built for comfort! Even the luxury of being quartered in the comfort of a house out of the elements, sleeping in a bed every night was cause for complaint.

During the autumn of 1811 Wellington's army suffered terrible sickness; at one time he had 17,000 men on the sick list. This also affected the Rifle battalions the 1st Battalion had 142 men listed as sick in September, 162 in October, while in December out of a total strength of 702 men only 578 were listed as fit for duty. The ill-health in the Regiment caused some deaths; those we have been able to confirm were: Sergeant William Hipkiss, Riflemen Robert Paterson and Francis McNamara all died in August, Rifleman Edward Ellis in September, Sergeant William Fenton in October, Riflemen Murray Doyle, John Jizon and John Thomas in November, Riflemen John Brewin, George Hunter, David Hunter and Corporal Hector Paterson all in December. Lieutenant Bartholomew Keappock also died in August, Captain M. Pratt in September and 2nd Lieutenant Henry Moore in November. Another notable absentee from the ranks of the 1st Battalion was Rifleman Thomas Plunkett, of the retreat to Corunna fame. Plunkett was invalided to England in December after spending some time in the General Hospital due to having been ridden over by a French dragoon. His internal organs were damaged and he did not return to the Peninsula until 1813 with a detachment from the regiment having transferred into the second battalion.

Lieutenant John FitzMaurice, whom we met as a volunteer in volume two and received his commission quite quickly in the Rifles, was probably now wondering what he had let himself in for. Though when he looked about him and saw the likes of John M'Cullock who had been captured at the Coa, making his escape disguised as a peasant with the help of a lovestruck Spanish damsel, role models were not hard to find. New officers and volunteers were often targets for the senior officers to play practical jokes upon and how they reacted often told them a lot about their fellow Riflemen. Lieutenant Sarsfield, [1] was singled out as a target for this treatment, though for how long it continued is anyone's guess when it became common knowledge that he slept with a brace of pistols close to hand, proving he might not be such an easy target after all. One officer who joined their ranks in January 1812 would have raised an eyebrow or two for the single curiosity of being an American! Gairdner, however, was not one to fall pray to their jokes and his loyalty was soon tested when Britain declared war on America in 1812. His father was happy enough with the situation as long as he never came into conflict with his fellow countrymen. This bizarre situation was brought about by Gairdner's father living in America and his sister, the Rifles Lieutenant's aunt living in England; it was quite obviously a family of divided loyalties. There was little chance of another new officer recruit being made a fool of; William Hamilton joined them having seen action in a couple of campaigns as a Lieutenant, then retired only to volunteer into the Rifles a couple of years later. He was a bit of a fire eater as we will see in later sections of this history.

Wellington during this time was suffering with his own demons and starting to lose government support back home, May had been the last occasion he sent to England news of a British Allied victory. Since then the costly Battle of Albuhera had taken place. Its severe casualties deprived Wellington the equivalent in strength of a division all to no avail, for it ended in a costly stalemate, the only consolation being that the French suffered equally severe losses of manpower. A satisfying and worthwhile victory would have kept Wellington and the army on good terms with his paymasters and the Prince Regent. During this period of inactivity, however, the focus of those back home had changed to something more entertaining, the erratic behaviour of the Prince Regent, who might have tried to influence the Duke of York at Horse Guards, making Wellington's position, at best, uncomfortable. An example of the Prince's unpredictable and unhelpful comments came about when a member of the Prince's privileged inner circle was heard praising Wellington's achievements. He countered this with, 'Damn the north! Damn the south! and Damn Wellington! The question is how am I to be rid of this damned Princess of Wales?'

The Prince Regent had separated from Caroline of Brunswick, the Princess of Wales, as soon as she gave birth to their only child Princess Charlotte, but he never divorced her. She had as a result become a constant thorn in his side, which only served to upset the already fragile state of the Prince's mind inflaming his temper even further. Wellington was now one of those feeling the backlash of such tantrums, [2] the Prince was even turning against his ministers, who of course held the purse strings to Wellington's military chest! To show what depths he had sunk one only has to quote the example of when the Prince gave a grand fête but did not invite a single minister from his government, but encouraged every blackguard and whore in London to attend! This had been reported back to Wellington by his brother William, but should not be taken literally, though no doubt it made the Duke feel it was not only himself in the firing line of the Prince's rants.

It was during this climate of uncertainty at home, that Wellington was struggling to come to terms with the unrest in the army. Craufurd brought to his attention the number of desertions in the Light Division, placing the cause firmly at his door, blaming the conditions, lack of food, clothing and equipment for his men's actions. Wellington inspected the Light Division and dismissed this claim out of hand, putting the blame solely down to Craufurd's administration.

From a Rifles' perspective, the men we are sure, would have been quite happy to dismiss all this rhetoric, if it had meant seeing some action with regard to their welfare taking place. Some desertions had occurred amongst the Riflemen; those extracted from the muster rolls for this period are: Joseph Almond, William McFarlane, Malcolm McInnes, Miles Hodgson and Alan Cummings, the latter man in fact deserted much earlier, therefore the conditions of 1811 could not be blamed. There would always, of course, be men who required only the right opportunity or circumstance to crop up to abandon their commitments to regiment and country, any excuse to get away from soldiering, which in some cases had been forced upon them, the lesser of the two evils, prison or the army. But the Riflemen listed above had in the main been of reasonably good character, so it is not so easy to dismiss their actions or find any plausible reason for it. It would be hard, therefore, to find any single event that could be attributed to such a course of drastic action, the likelihood has to be it was a combination of events. Of course there could always be the possibility of a hidden agenda that has been lost in the sands of time being responsible. Some writers have put it down to Craufurd's liking for the use of the lash. On the retreat to Corunna, Craufurd was at his harshest with the men, but this never affected the mindset of the brigade and in many cases amongst the Riflemen they thought it was warranted. If this was the cause, then why was Craufurd received with such enthusiasm on his return to the division just prior to Fuentes de Onoro? Numbers of men did desert at the end of the Peninsular War rather than return to England. In this instance circumstances were different probably mostly down to the men having either Portuguese, Spanish or even French wives, whom they were not prepared to abandon.

So far, our research has not unearthed an officer of the Rifles openly complaining about their lot during this period. Captain Leach of the Rifles was always one of the first to have a dig at Craufurd, but is deafeningly silent during this period. Though as we will see later, he could have been otherwise distracted! Harry Smith, that well known Rifles' officer, has this to say, 'As the winter approached we had private theatricals. The Duke of Wellington appointed so many days for horse races and grey hound matches etc;'

this gives the impression that off duty the officers had an easier life. Captain Leach, who chased anything in a skirt, found time to visit as many villages he could during off duty periods, taking his fellow company officers with him. All enjoyed being entertained by, and able to dance with, the local females. No effort was spared; they took every possible comfort they could find which even went as far as commandeering the piper from the regimental band [3] to provide the music. For General Craufurd life was becoming boring, which is plainly clear from a letter he wrote to his wife, 'There is such a sameness in our life here, and such a uniformity in my feelings and state of mind, and such a settled desire of getting out of this horrid scrape that I am entangled in, that at the end of each week I have only to repeat what I told you at the beginning of it. I can not say that Wellington and I are quite so cordial as we used to be. He was rattled at a report which I made of the wants of the division.' It is plain to see Craufurd didn't have the slightest inkling of when he upset people yet was so sensitive to criticism himself. Craufurd was obviously missing his wife and family, for he also states that he hoped to be reunited with them by the end of the year. While Craufurd complained of boredom, activities were encouraged to help while away this bleak period, Wellington himself even taking part and the officers seem to have had little to complain about when it came to food, clothing or choice of shelter.

It is easy to see how the ordinary Rifleman was feeling less than enchanted with his lot; the lack of decent food, shelter and the ability to keep warm was enough to try the stoutest hearts, especially when the winter snows covered their outposts. Being constantly on the move patrolling the border to make sure the French did not catch them wanting, and always pressed by Craufurd to remain at their best, it is with little wonder that men chose the easy option. At the same time, the rest of the army was oblivious to the Light Division's plight on the front line, quartered in fairly relevant comfort, safe in the knowledge that their security was in good hands.

Sickness was still a problem but not as bad as it had been during the latter months of 1811; even Wellington fell ill for two weeks. It was during this problematic period he had the sad task to inform Major Hercules Pakenham, an ex-Rifleman, that his brother Captain William Pakenham had been lost at sea with all hands when his ship foundered. The Pakenhams were Wellington's brothers-in-law.

During all of this Wellington was required to keep a clear head so as to plan and organise the logistics of the approaching siege of Ciudad Rodrigo. It is well known he never left anything to chance. The troops in their divisional cantonments had not been idle during the winter for he had them making gabions, fascines, hay bags and ladders ready for action. To move all his guns and bring up the ammunition, entrenching tools and equipment to undertake such a bold plan required Wellington to be at his best. He was never more so than when preparing to engage the enemy. The roads had also been put in good order so as to carry any amount of traffic required of them. Hundreds of a new form of bullock carts were manufactured, with iron axle trees and brass boxes; this was to aid easy movement of this mass of equipment. Mules were acquired in numbers never seen before, allowing one in proportion to every six infantrymen and two for each cavalry trooper. It was calculated that the commissariat would require 10,000 mules to transport supplies and provisions for the army alone. Each animal had been expected to carry a 200lb load; Wellington's precision to detail worked out that they would also have to carry a further 30lbs of corn to last each animal six days. Having replaced the inferior Portuguese carts with the new model meant easier movement; it would, therefore, only require two animals to pull them. Every 25 carts formed a brigade with 50 allocated as a division. What is more intriguing is that all these preparations were kept in isolation, each army division unaware of the part the other was playing. With his own men kept in the dark there was little chance of the French discovering his plans.

By 1st January 1812 Wellington's preparations were practically complete; he had 38,000 British and 22,000 Portuguese troops present fit for duty. A bridge had also been constructed across the Agueda at Marialva where he was now able to bring up his siege-train and equipment.

The strength of the 95th Rifles for the coming campaign was:

1st Battalion
No 1 Company, Captain Hon. J. Stewart
No 2 Company, Captain J. Leach
No 3 Company, Captain J. Uniacke
No 4 Company, Captain J. MacDiarmid
No 5 Company, Captain W. Balvaird
No 6 Company, Captain C. Beckwith
No 7 Company, Captain A. Cameron
No 8 Company, Captain J. Crampton

2nd Battalion
No 1 Company, Captain S. Mitchell
No 2 Company, Captain J. Hart

3rd Battalion
No 1 Company, Captain W. Percival
No 2 Company, Captain C. G. Gray
No 3 Company, Captain J. Diggle
No 4 Company, Captain J. Travers
No 5 Company, Captain J. Kent

# The Siege and Capture of Ciudad Rodrigo

*Panorama of Ciudad Rodrigo*

The campaign of 1812 now started in earnest, its timing catching out Captain Jonathan Leach and his merry band of officers, who at the beginning of January had ventured to Robadilla, a large village tucked away in one of the deepest and most secluded valleys of the Sierra de Gata. These intrepid Riflemen were not going to let the thick blanket of snow put them off for their reward; spending many an hour in female company was far better than boring cantonment life and well worth the trek. It also helped their cause that in the village resided a family who had become good friends of the Riflemen during the previous year. On arrival they gathered together a number of the most eligible females in the village to entertain them—however to be on the safe side, they enlisted the services of some of the local priests to act as chaperones. The priests soon showed their dislike for the attention-seeking young Riflemen. Leach, his mind always set on the fairer sex, was probably one of the main attractions, a strikingly handsome man, who no doubt was in great demand. The attitude displayed by the priests had not gone unnoticed by the Riflemen, and when the evening's activities concluded these clerics still hung about the streets with their lanterns, obviously as a deterrent to any after dark trysts that might have been arranged. The Riflemen, true to their devil-may-care nature, were not going to let this incident pass without some retribution and amusement, and attacked the unsuspecting clergymen with a hail of snowballs! A number had been especially hardened to produce the right effect and smashed their lanterns; the priests cursed the godforsaken heathen Englishmen as they raced for the cover of their respective quarters. Hearing that the Light Division had moved against Ciudad Rodrigo and that the Rifles were on the march to El Bodón, Leach and his party immediately made all haste to join up with the battalion, arriving late that same evening. These Riflemen were now about to swap snow balls for lead balls and face a much more robust enemy.

The Allied Army had moved off on 4th January 1812 to take up their allotted positions for the investment of Ciudad Rodrigo and the Light Division was soon on the move. The Rifles crossed the Agueda via a ford during a storm of the bitterest driving rain, the swirling icy waters coming up nearly to the shoulders of many of the men. To keep their ammunition dry they fixed their pouches to the top of the knapsacks and, to prevent being swept away by the torrent of water, were forced to link arms with each other for support. Safely on the opposite bank the Light Division was ordered to occupy quarters at Pastores, La Encina and El Bodón. Arrangements had not been made in anticipation for the arrival of the Riflemen, no quarters having been prepared. Wearing soaking wet, freezing clothing with no means to get dry or to warm themselves, they spent a most miserable night in the bitter cold. Officers and men huddled together wherever they could find shelter to while away the night. The frost was so severe during the whole of the siege that when the men covered themselves of an evening with their blankets during trench duties, they found by morning that they had frozen to such a degree it was possible for them to stand up on their own! Conditions thankfully improved the following day when the Riflemen were housed individually by company. The weather was so severe that five men in the 3rd Division died from exposure, while at the same time a hardy Irish woman belonging to the 88th Regiment, gave birth to a baby at the road side and continued the march with the child in her arms! The 4th Division occupied San Felices El Chico, the 3rd was at Manthago and Zamarra, with the 1st at Espejo and Gallegos. Meanwhile the 5th and 6th Divisions were concentrated closer to the front line by crossing the Coa near Almeida, the 7th moved to Fuente Guinaldo. Wellington recalled Hill's Division after its earlier successes against the French in Estremadura, where he had been since 27th December 1811, spreading alarm and confusion amongst d'Erlon and Soult's forces. Wellington posted Hill's division between Portugal and Castello Branco, from where he could observe every movement made in Lower Beira.

*Map of Ciudad Rodrigo*

Ciudad Rodrigo, the object of all this attention, was in the view of virtually every chronicler who wrote about it, a considerable obstacle, though not without its weak points. The French had strengthened this fortress town quite considerably since its capture and occupation in 1810. Ciudad Rodrigo stood on a low hill close to the right bank of the Agueda, some 150 feet above the river. The actual town was the usual maze of narrow streets protected by ramparts built along an ancient wall, some 32 feet high. Outside of this wall the French had built a more modern style 'fausse-braie', which was a low continuous outwork, of bastion-trace along the eastern side, with indented lines forming its northern and western sides. In fact the fausse-braie had been built rather too low down the hill side to afford much protection and had no covered way! The glacis was very steeply sloped, while the ground on the southern side fell sharply away to the river bank. Outside the fausse-braie was a ditch with a masonry counterscarp, some 12 feet high. 200 yards north of Rodrigo a low ridge ran parallel to the walls. This was known as the little Teson or Teso, (Teso meaning the brow or crest of a ridge) and a small stream ran parallel with it at the foot of the glacis. About 400 yards north of the little Teson and separated from it by another small stream was a second much larger and higher ridge, 'The Great Teson'. This was of great strategic importance to the French; it stood some 13 feet higher than the ramparts of the town! To prevent it becoming an advantage to the British, the French built on it a redoubt, in the form of a redan. This they protected by a seven foot deep and eight foot wide ditch. The rear had been closed off by a brick-built wall, which had been loop-holed. The foot of the counterscarp had been palisaded, while the rear wall was defended by chevaux-de-frise. The redoubt had been armed with a howitzer and two guns. To give further protection to this vulnerable advance work, two guns had been established on a flat roof in the San Francisco suburb, east of the fortress, at about 400 yards' distance and covered its right. 200 yards' west of the town in the fortified convent of Santa Cruz another two guns were positioned at a range of about 700 yards. Across the river and connected by a bridge of boats to the fortress was a second suburb and, like San Francisco, had been strengthened. All were solid defensive positions and covered by the guns of the fortress. (Sir John T. Jones his Journals of Sieges, volume one p107–109.) [1]

Marmont left the garrison within the walls of Ciudad Rodrigo, not only with the normal armament for defensive warfare, but the whole of the siege train belonging to the Army of Portugal. This meant it was more than capable of defending itself; the downside however, was the shortage of supplies to feed the 2,000 strong garrison.

Wellington knew that Marmont was still with the main part of his army in the Tagus valley, while Dorsenne was in the north. Parts of Marmont's forces were also in support of Suchet. Reports, however, now reached him that the Imperial Guard was marching from Valladolid towards France and being joined by numbers of other troops. Napoleon was busy gathering a force together to extend his campaign of European dominance towards Russia. This then gave Wellington a small window of opportunity in which to attack and capture Ciudad Rodrigo, before aid could reach it from an over-stretched French Army corps. Some 60,000 men were in effect on the march to join Napoleon's force from various parts of Spain. In addition to these troop losses Soult, who was also in Andalucia towards the end of 1811, detached a force to besiege Tarifa.

Due to the condition of the ground, Wellington chose to attack the northern side of the town which meant attacking the advanced work, the San Francisco Redoubt, established on the Great Teson. If this could be taken it would advance his cause by several days, the only advantage he had being in the speed and surprise in which the attack would be conducted. For the assault to be carried out without any previous bombardment would be unheard of during this period of military history. Therefore it was a calculated risk by Wellington who obviously had the fullest confidence in the troops being mustered for this task. Wellington had arranged a number of horse races and greyhound matches, amongst other activities, around this time and to mask the troops' movements; the final of the races had been organized for the day of the assault. On 8th January 1812 the Light Division paraded before daylight, forded the Agueda this time at the ford at Cantarrenas three miles north of Pastores, close to the convent of La Caridad. The water was still bitterly cold, but, at least came only roughly up to between knee and thigh height, a blessing to the personal comfort of the Riflemen. At one stage the cavalry had been ordered to form up across the river in line so as to break the impact of a number of large chunks of ice that came swirling down with a force that could carry off a man. They marched east of the suburb of San Francisco and once out of range of the guns halted behind a hill north of the town.

The French, seeing the Light Division come to a halt, convinced they still held an impregnable position, combined with the activities taking place in the British lines, all added to their feeling of wellbeing, full of bravado, came out from the security of the redoubt protected by its wall and approached to within 50 yards of the Riflemen. To attempt such an action tells us these men were either plain fool-hardy or had never been confronted before by the deadly Baker rifle, the specialist arm of these marksmen. The French officers and their men began bowing, taking off their hats and saluting the men of the Light Division, in effect, plainly taking the Mickey!

Colonel John Colborne of the 52nd Regiment had been given the distinction of commanding, organising and assaulting the redoubt. The force to complete this task was drawn from the Light Division; two companies from the 43rd Regiment, four from the 52nd Regiment, two from the 95th Rifles and one from each of the Caçadore regiments. [2] Captain Crampton's 1st Battalion and Captain Travers' 3rd Battalion companies were the two allotted this task in the Rifles. Four companies from the stormers were selected to form the advanced guard and occupy the crest of the glacis, from where they would open a severe fire on the redoubt. Behind these came a party with ladders, under the command of Lieutenant Alexander Thompson of the Royal Engineers. Their job was to rush forward and put the ladders in position ready for the stormers who would be following closely. Each company in the assaulting force was under the direct command of the senior captain(s) of its particular regiment; it was in this formation under the cover of darkness that Colborne's force advanced. An officer of the 95th, along with two sergeants, had been previously instructed before it became dark to advance to the brow of the hill from where they could mark out the angle of the redoubt. This was to be the focus of the attack, using the steeple of a church in Ciudad Rodrigo as a guide; its silhouette in the half light now showed the direction to make the attack. Colonel Colborne on checking the numbers as they arrived, stated to his Brigade Major, Harry Smith of the 95th, that there were not enough men and ordered him to go and bring up another company. He duly arrived with Lieutenant MacNamara who was in temporary command of one of the 1st Battalion 95th companies. [3] Colborne ordered the force to advance in total silence, [4] each captain having already been given instructions where he would exactly post his men. On reaching the 95th guides, they were pointed towards their allotted positions and in this manner the first assault company covered the front face of the redoubt. As the second company arrived it took the right face, the third company the left, and so on. Captain Mulcaster of the Engineers, who had just arrived, suggested to Colborne as he dismounted from his horse that it would be better to wait for the lighter ladders. Colonel Colborne aware that timing was of the essence to the success of his plan, proceeded with the heavy ladders, [5] which had only been made that day. About 50 yards from the redoubt Colborne gave the order to double quick towards the redoubt. As soon as the men burst forward their canteens and equipment started rattling, which immediately alerted the defenders who had time to fire one round from each of their guns. Captain Crampton's company, forming on the crest of the glacis, was soon joined by Travers's and MacNamara's companies, from where they returned a telling fire. The ladder men on arriving placed them in the ditch. The next moment Captain Mein of the 52nd arrived with his escalading companies and immediately descended the ladders and then placed them against the walls of the redoubt. Captain Mein on mounting the rampart was accidentally shot and wounded by one of his own company.

The attacking force suffered only minor casualties, for once it reached the walls of the redoubt, it was shielded from the defenders who, under a constant fire from the covering Rifle companies, were limited to throwing shells and grenades blindly over the walls. Lieutenant Gurwood of the 52nd, moving to the rear of the redoubt, immediately informed Colonel Colborne, that it would be possible for a company to gain access via the gorge using ladders. Colborne told Gurwood to take whatever ladders he could find and to attempt it. On reaching the gorge they started escalading the walls until the gate was unexpectedly blown open! A French artillery sergeant shot dead just as he was about to throw a lit explosive onto the stormers, caused the shell to fall amongst the defenders who, in their panic, tried to kick it clear but only succeeded in knocking it towards the gate. Gurwood's force was now able to enter the redoubt via the ladders and the open gate.

The defenders, seeing it was impossible to continue the unequal contest or escape the wrath of the determined Light Division stormers, surrendered; those who refused felt the cold steel of the attacker's bayonets. However this did not mean those who survived were immune from further harm, for the Portuguese Caçadores had an agenda all of their own with one or two scores to settle with any Frenchman who fell into their hands. This became all too evident when one of the French officers arrived before Craufurd, stripped of everything but his trousers, with blood flowing from his nose and mouth. He was later joined by one of his sergeants in a most distressed state who was completely naked, showing equal signs of mistreatment. Craufurd expressed his pleasure however at the attitude of Rifleman Tom Crawley who offered the officer the temporary use of his greatcoat, while Harry Smith stepped in and tied his handkerchief around the sergeant to shield his modesty. [6]

With the redoubt now firmly in the hands of the Light Division, working parties set to reversing the works and opening the first parallel. The gunners in Ciudad Rodrigo, seeing the redoubt was lost immediately sent a heavy fire against the captured works.

Colborne, his task complete, left the redoubt to the engineers with their working parties. Assembling his attacking force he marched them down to the rivulet near the base of the glacis; here he placed them in positions best for protecting the redoubt against a possible sortie to recapture the works. The working parties continued under the supervision of the engineers until the moon came up, by which time they had made good progress fortifying a length of trench some 600 yards long. Colborne's success meant that not only had he secured a most valuable position for Wellington but also added two cannon and a howitzer to the British cause.

Two captains and 48 men were taken prisoner. The losses of the French garrison were reported as three killed; 68 captured, nine including officers, with four 'survivors'. The Light Division returned to their quarters that morning having been relieved by the 1st Division who took their place in the trenches, only to have to cross the Agueda once more to their camp tired, cold, hungry and wet. [7]

The Rifles had Second Lieutenant Rutherford Hawksley and one Rifleman killed, with seven Riflemen wounded in this action, roughly a third of the Light Division casualties, which amounted to six killed and 20 wounded. Riflemen William Roland and John Wicks, both serving in Crampton's company, are shown as being killed in action on 8th January. It isn't easy to pick out those who were casualties in this action but some of the following could be those who were wounded: Rifleman James Harvey General Hospital (GH) from 9th to 21st January and deceased 14th February; Rifleman Thomas Payne (GH) 9th to 11th January; Rifleman William Lovack (GH) 9th to 21st January; Rifleman John Marshall died 9th January; Rifleman George Potter died 17th January; Rifleman Samuel Stubbs died 12th January; two Riflemen, William Chappell and John Swaine are both shown as being killed in action but no date is given. Rifleman Thomas Rice died on 9th January at Coimbra but he can be ruled out because he had been in the (GH) since the 5th; and Rifleman Thomas Price was in the (GH) 10th to 21st January; of course some of these men could have been sick.

With the siege now firmly in progress a system was established whereby four of the army divisions provided the troops to man the trenches. This was done by having one division at a time on 24 hour duty, which meant half were working for six hours in the trenches, while the other half covered them; they swapped over every six hours to alternate the duty. Wellington had issued instructions at Gallegos on 8th January 1812 to all general officers that the troops were to have with them a day's cooked provisions and they were to be followed by two days' spirit but no baggage. Also that the chief engineer would require daily, from each division, 20 miners, 30 artificers or persons accustomed to this work, with a proportion being non-commissioned officers. They would be placed under his directions, with a list of their names and the regiments to which they belonged.

The French, observing the change over between the Light and 1st Divisions, seized the opportunity to exact some revenge for their loss during the night. Though the working parties had been fired upon during the night, daylight meant the French gunners could pick out their targets much easier; they had spotters in the Cathedral tower from where it was easy to make out any movement in the British siege lines. With so many men in the trenches at once, the barrage sent against them was relentless and bound to have some success.

General Craufurd had his horse killed under him by a round shot! The distance between El Bodón and Ciudad Rodrigo was nine miles, which had to be marched each tour of trench duty. The musket and rifle ammunition attached to the Light Division was taken to the front on the first day and had to remain there. The 9-pounder guns attached to the 4th Division were likewise ordered to the front the same day. On 12th January, under the rotation system, it was once again the turn of the Light Division to take up the trench duties. Lieutenant Kincaid was ordered to take 30 of his Riflemen with shovels and, under cover of a thick fog, they advanced from the trenches closer to the walls of the town where they dug a number of pits. Secure in their advanced position they took on their more conventional role of sharpshooters from where they were able to pick off the enemy gunners. Even under such a deadly fire the French still kept up a brisk bombardment which slowed down the progress of the working parties in the trenches. Without the contribution of the Riflemen it would have been much worse. However, these advanced Riflemen had to suffer the bitter cold, for in their cramped position they could not warm themselves, which made loading all the more difficult. Captain John Uniacke, a most active (he was the fastest runner in the regiment) and well liked officer amongst the Riflemen, had recently received a new second lieutenant in his company; this was the American John Gairdner. This was the ideal time to blood the new arrival and test his mettle. During this spell of trench duty he sent Gairdner with a piquet of 30 Riflemen to lie out on the glacis, a sloping rampart surrounding Ciudad Rodrigo. This proved productive; Gairdner gained invaluable experience under fire which would not have gone unnoticed amongst the Riflemen who were all seasoned veterans. His piquet got off lightly, with only three men being wounded, which he proudly reported back to his father. Uniacke was not the only Rifles' officer to sound out the American; Captain Leach informed him that the fortress was to be stormed by the Royal Wagon Train supported by the mounted 14th Light Dragoons! Gairdner was no fool and took this in good form as part of the ritual of becoming a Rifleman. Riflemen John Gillespie and Patrick Rigney both 2nd 95th men were killed in action on the 12th, with Rifleman Robert Needham, 1st 95th in hospital from 12th to 21st January; Rifleman Robert Stephens 2nd 95th in hospital from the 12th and died on the 15th.

On the 13th the Light Division was relieved by the 1st Division to their great relief. The hard work of digging was detested by the Riflemen though it kept them warm and they had been greatly hampered by the French gunners. It didn't help matters that the tools sent out from England were of inferior quality, the contractors commissioned to supply them profiteering at the expense of the British Army, much to the Commander-in-Chief's disgust. [8] Wellington's meticulous planning seems to have fallen short here, for there was not enough transport to bring up the numerous stores and ammunition to the front line. Only a third of the native carts had arrived and their local drivers were proving to be most difficult, much of the ammunition for the 24-pounder guns being still at Villa de Ponte. To add further to Wellington's problems intelligence had been received that Marmont was rallying to the plight of Ciudad Rodrigo and preparing to attempt a rescue. Wellington had no choice but to advance his plans, going against all the rules set out for such an undertaking. He ordered the counter-batteries, which were only some 600 yards from the curtain to open a breach in the main wall. To attempt an assault without lowering the counterscarp, meant those chosen to storm Rodrigo were going to be sacrificed for the sake of time, which was running out. The unpredictable Agueda River could also flood at any moment and that would only assist the French in any attempt at relieving the fortress. Wellington now set about concentrating his force closer to Ciudad Rodrigo by posting them around the villages of the Coa.

During the night of the 13th a gallant band of King's German Legion troops with a company from the 60th Rifles belonging to the 1st Division stormed and carried the convent of San Francisco in the suburbs. This deprived the French of two more precious pieces of artillery with which they had been successfully enfilading the trenches. On the morning of the 14th, 500 French soldiers made an equally gallant sortie from the town undetected, but were eventually repulsed by the 24th and 42nd Regiments at the point of the bayonet and forced to return, having almost succeeded in entering the batteries where the battering cannon had been placed the night before. These 24-pounder guns were quite recognizable, made of iron and mounted on smart looking carriages which had been painted a lead colour. The following day the derelict convent of Santa Cruz was assailed most gallantly by the 40th Regiment, which was able to advance under cover of darkness and gained entrance to the convent, much to the surprise of the garrison, who were quick to make good their escape into the town. The guns here had been positioned in the tower of the convent; a group of men including William Lawrence, volunteered to go to the top of the tower to disarm the guns. Once at the top, they found that they were already damaged. The guns were then pushed out of the tower to further their destruction. The 40th Regiment took up residence in the convent, which now became the target of the French gunners. [9] William Lawrence must have led a charmed life, for he was struck in the chest by one of their cannon-balls which had bounced off the convent; he received nothing more than severe bruising! At 4 o'clock that same afternoon the British batteries opened on the town for the first time, firing upon the walls against the same point the French had previously breached in 1810. The 3rd Division doing duty in the trenches also kept up a heavy fire against the town.

*Convent of San Francisco*

Wellington summoned General Barrié to surrender the town, he refused saying that he and the garrison would rather perish in the ruins rather than yield! At the same time he had already started building barriers, leaning against the interior wall which formed the escarpment. His engineers and fatigue parties were clearing away the rubble at the foot of the breach and building up the terre-plaine and fausse-braie.

On the 16th it was the turn of the Light Division to take up their duties in the trenches, the Riflemen once again continuing to pick off the enemy gunners from the advanced rifle pits. This was quite necessary, since the Riflemen had last been in the trenches the French gunners had worked out the exact range and were literally dropping the shells right into the trenches. Lieutenant John Kincaid was sent to take command of the Highland company in the left wing of the 1st Battalion of the Rifles, which was under the command of Major Cameron, the other wing being under the command of Major Gilmour. Kincaid joined the piquet belonging to the company situated between the right trenches and the river. Half of the company was posted in a mud cottage, with the rest in parts of the ruined convent, close under the walls. Travelling to this point in daylight, was rather precarious, for only a stone's throw from the walls was the French infantry, manning the ramparts, who delighted in firing at anything that moved.

After it became dark, Kincaid went into the cottage for some welcome rations, which were cooking and almost ready, when a round shot passed through both walls of the dwelling and dumped a mound of earth and rubble onto the eagerly awaited food, greatly to the officer's disgust. The fact that they had escaped with their lives was only secondary! Lieutenant John FitzMaurice in another section of the trenches was doing duty with another young officer (Gairdner?) and their captain, in an exposed position, picking off the enemy gunners. As soon as a flash of a gun was observed it was the duty of the captain to give the warning to the men and they would take cover. The two junior officers noticed that the captain was rather too quick, for the credit of the regiment, in taking cover himself. The next time a shell was spotted and the captain gave the warning and jumped for cover, they hit him in the back with a couple of frozen clumps of earth. When the danger had passed he jumped up and exclaimed, 'Boys what an escape, I have had two bits of shell struck me and I am not killed.' The two officers congratulated him on his good fortune and tried out the jest a couple more times during the night, of course not letting any of the men see what they were up to. The bombardment continued against the fortress; the ramparts were so vigorously fired upon that they started to crumble quicker than expected and a second, smaller breach was opened at a turret further along the walls, some 300 yards to the left of the large breach. During the night five more guns were brought up and at daylight the besieging batteries continued even more fiercely, however around 8 o'clock, a thick fog came up and they had to call a halt. During the night the parallel on the lower Teson was extended, the division was relieved on the 17th by the 1st Division. The fire from both sides now continued very heavily. Rifleman James Horroux 2nd 95th was killed in action on the 17th. It had by this time been agreed that their relief would be undertaken in small groups rather than by a full scale exchange which was causing untold casualties. The allies lost some 500 men doing duty in the trenches during the days leading up to the storming of Ciudad Rodrigo. It was therefore rather remarkable that on this particular change over, the men of the Light Division chose to disregard their personal safety for an early return to camp. Instead of crossing the Agueda via the long route behind the San Francisco convent, they chose to cross near to where they were and risk running the gauntlet of the enemy gunners, saving themselves three miles of marching. By the 18th, two breaches in the walls were reported as being practicable for storming; the small breach had been made the easier, due to a tower collapsing outwards into the breach and ditch.

Wellington ordered the Light Division to advance to Ciudad Rodrigo on 19th January; this being out of sequence with their normal tour of duty in the trenches, it was quite obvious to the officers and men therefore that something of consequence was about to take place. The 3rd Division was on duty in the trenches at this time and when the men were relieved they too were ordered to remain in the area. (It has been suggested that Picton on hearing that the Light Division was to be part of the assault, demanded that his division should also take part.) In an attempt to deceive the French as to what was taking place, the Light Division marched for some distance along the Salamanca road, ready to return under cover of darkness. The same afternoon they were ordered to advance closer to the siege trenches. They spent most of the day behind the convent of Norbortins, a magnificent ruin situated close to the right bank of the Agueda, this was three miles southeast of Ciudad Rodrigo. Here the men were able to cook their meals. Shortly after 3 o'clock they moved off and headed for the ground occupied by the Foot Guards a mile and a half from the suburbs of the town. The previous stealth tactics seem to have been forgotten for the bands struck up the popular tune 'The Downfall of Paris' as they marched along. With the Light Division having taken up a position closer to the town, it was time for them to be officially told what their specific tasks would be; the storming of the lesser breach. Wellington then informed the 3rd Division they were to attack the large breach. The colonel of the 40th Regiment volunteered for the forlorn hope, but of course was refused. General Pack's Portuguese were to make a diversionary attack against the eastern part of the town. Wellington ended his order, 'Ciudad Rodrigo must be stormed this evening.' The men therefore were left in no doubt that this was going to be a desperate night's work which would have only one outcome, whatever the cost!

Once the nature of their duty was known groups of officers and men could be seen congregating and conversing on what their fate might be that night. Friends shook each other by the hand and wished one and another success, promotion and to finally meet up in one piece in the town. Major Napier of the 52nd Regiment immediately confronted General Craufurd and asked for the command of the storming party, to which he agreed. Brigade Major Harry Smith, equally animated in wishing to shower himself with glory, was, however disappointed. Craufurd denied his request to command the Forlorn Hope, 'Why! You cannot go, you a Major of Brigade, a senior Lieutenant, you are sure to get a company, No, I must give it to a younger officer,' had been his reply. Lieutenant Gurwood of the 52nd was given the honour to lead this gallant band of 25 volunteers.

The official order of attack in the Light Division was:

Vandeleur's Brigade,

Four companies of the 1st Battalion 95th Rifles under the command of Major Cameron to advance and line the crest of the glacis, from where they were to keep down the fire of the defenders. The Portuguese Caçadores were to bring up the ladders and hay-bags, the latter to be thrown into the trenches. Then the forlorn hope, under Gurwood, followed by the storming party under Major George Napier, then behind these the remainder of the brigade. Colonel Barnard's brigade was in reserve to support the main attack. Craufurd would advance with the main attack.

When about a mile from taking up their final positions, Napier was ordered to get his 100 volunteers together from each of the British regiments in the Light Division, along with the appropriate number of officers and non-commissioned officers (NCOs). Addressing the 43rd, 52nd and 95th Rifles, Napier said, 'Soldiers I have the honour to be appointed to the command of the storming party which is to lead the Light Division to the assault of the small breach. I want 100 volunteers from each regiment; those who will go with me come forward.' Instantly almost half the division stepped forward, forcing Napier to select them by chance.

100 volunteer stormers 43rd under Captain James Fergusson, Lieutenants John O'Connor, Alexander Steele and John Bramwell.

100 volunteer stormers 52nd under Captains Joseph Dobbs and William Jones.

100 volunteer stormers 95th under Captain Samuel Mitchell, Lieutenants William Johnstone, John Kincaid and William Hamilton.

For the Rifles this meant one wing of the 1st Battalion: Gilmour's, with Barnard, was to be part of the storming column and the other, Cameron's, as we have seen, providing covering fire, each four companies' strong. We have been unable to find any specific task being allotted to the 3rd and 2nd Battalion companies. There is no doubt they played an equally important part in the action. Three companies of the Rifles were detailed to cover the left flank of the 3rd Division stormers, logic suggests they came from the 3rd Battalion, we know the two 2nd Battalion companies were also in the thick of the action. John Lowe, a Rifleman in this battalion had been wounded in the head by a shell splinter while manning the trenches prior to the storming. With his head now heavily bandaged he took part in the main assault and at one stage was in sight of Craufurd when he received his fatal wound. This further points out how important it was to the men not to miss out on the final act of the siege, unless of course they were completely incapable. Proof that the 2nd Battalion was at the sharp end, is further borne out by the number of casualties received in these two single companies.

*Outer walls of Ciudad Rodrigo*

Captain Jonathan Leach is quite specific in pointing out that Captain Uniacke was sent to keep up communication between the two divisions along the glacis and to keep down the fire of the French Infantry behind the ramparts. It is clear that the Light and 3rd Divisions would need to establish how well each other's attack was faring. Leach says Uniacke was to keep down the enemy fire which meant he had to have his company with him, so his task was more than just as a fast communicator. The 3rd Division had the harder of the two tasks to perform, therefore it would be important for them to receive help from the Light Division, as much as Picton would have loathed this. The fact that Uniacke was reported as being the first officer in the small breach to reach the ramparts closely followed by William Johnstone, also of the Rifles, tells us he did not cover the 3rd Division attack with his company as stated by Leach. The more likely scenario was that the three (3rd Battalion) 95th Companies sent to cover the 3rd Division assault were given this task and maybe Uniacke was to keep up communication once through the breach and on the ramparts, which he tried to do.

Lieutenant John Cox [10] of the Rifles tells us that the 3rd Battalion 95th covered the left of the 3rd Division attack and kept up the communication with this division. They advanced by moving along the ditch to their right, the enemy threw out several fireballs as they were moving into position which illuminated the whole of the ground to be crossed by the stormers.

Lieutenant Cox was wounded in the attack, a musket ball having broken the bone in his upper arm.

Regarding Lieutenant Gurwood and his 25 volunteers from the Light Division, it has been impossible to find any evidence as to who took part in this group. One would think they were drawn from all the three main British regiments similar to the stormers. Volunteers were most likely chosen by ballot or given to individuals for previous good conduct. We would therefore expect that it contained its fair share of Riflemen but not to the extent given by Cope. [11]

Volunteers for the Forlorn Hope 2nd Battalion 95th:

| | | |
|---|---|---|
| Sergeants | Bowley | wounded |
| | Comerford | ” |
| | Derby | killed |
| | Ecke | |
| | Fairfoot | wounded (serving with the 1st Battalion rank corporal) |
| | Spencer | |
| | Tuite | |
| Corporals | Larkins | wounded |
| | Nesbit | ” |

If these nine non-commissioned officers did take part, that would have meant the remaining 16 volunteers came from the 43rd and 52nd.

By 6.30 p.m. the Light Division was formed up behind the convent of San Francisco, which was almost opposite the small breach roughly 300–400 yards to their front. For once all was quiet with both sets of guns, but the French artillery was ready waiting to wreak havoc on the storm about to break against the towns walls. The moon appeared from behind the clouds and picked out the bayonets of the French infantry manning the battlements. Captain Uniacke of the Rifles turned to his friend Lieutenant FitzMaurice and said, 'Look Fitz, what would our mothers say (they were both widows) if they saw what was being prepared for us?' 'Far better they should not know,' he replied. 'But what an extravagance to put on a new pelisse for such a night as this,' 'I shall be all the better worth taking,' Uniacke replied. [12] The moonlight picked out the determined features on the faces of the men of the Light Division, as they waited for the order to start the night's work. A little earlier General Craufurd had addressed the volunteers of the forlorn hope and stormers under Napier. 'Soldiers!' he said, in his clear distinctive voice, 'the eyes of your country are upon you. Be steady, be cool, be firm in the assault. The town must be yours this night. Once masters of the wall, let your first duty be to clear the rampart, and in doing this keep together.'

The Light Division on their way to take up their position at the San Francisco convent passed where the 3rd Division had halted, Grattan of the 88th Regiment describes them thus: 'They were in the highest spirits, but without the slightest appearance of levity in their demeanour on the contrary, there was a cast of determined severity thrown over their countenances that expressed in legible characters that knew the sort of service they were about to perform, and had made up their minds to the issue. They had no knapsacks their firelocks were slung over the shoulders their shirt collars were open.'

Brigade Major Harry Smith finding that the engineers had not brought up the ladders or hay bags approached a group of officers standing around a fire and stated that one of their number must come and collect some ladders and bring them to General Craufurd. Lieutenant George Simmons of the 95th in his eagerness to be active immediately gathered a number of Riflemen together and followed Lieutenant Smith to the engineers' camp, where he received the ladders. On reaching Craufurd, he was instantly taken to task for bringing only 'short' ladders! Simmons returned deflated, his pride dented with the short ladders and on passing a Portuguese captain with his company, handed over the ladders to him without any orders or authority and returned to his own battalion company, who was now at the head of a column ready to advance. Had circumstances not intervened Craufurd would probably have had Lieutenant Simmons court martialed. In hindsight these short ladders would have been better than no ladders. This could well be the source of the ladder problem that later evolved in the storming and why so many chroniclers pointed out that the Portuguese failed to bring up the ladders in time. The ladders passed on by Simmons were the ones that did make it in time to be used.

Suddenly a signal rocket burst from one of the batteries and Lieutenant Cooke of the 43rd reports he then heard a clock strike seven in the town. 'Now lads, for the breach,' Craufurd called out. The Portuguese, with the hay-bags and ladders, had still not arrived; [13] the stormers, however, carried a number of these bags with them. Cameron with his four rifle companies burst from the cover of the convent and headed straight for the glacis; once they reached it, the men threw themselves down and opened a severe fire against the ramparts. The stormers and the forlorn hope were following close behind; they were all soon rushing across the open ground. It had been ordered that Captain Ellicombe, Royal Engineers, was to guide the troops to the descent of the ditch and that Lieutenant Alexander Thompson, of the same corps, was to guide the stormers. On reaching the fausse-braie, the stormers, who had hay-bags, threw them into the void to lessen the impact of jumping some 11–12 feet into the ditch. As soon as the signal rocket was fired, the French lit the area with numerous fireballs. Their cannon fired burst after burst of grapeshot, which swept the open ground, while their infantry sent volley fire into the mass of men making their way towards the outer walls. The French were well prepared and met this rush of humanity with equal guile; fireballs and explosives of all description were thrown or fired from the ramparts. Having bravely crossed the open ground under this intense barrage, the men reached the glacis, from where they continued onto the fausse braie. The ditch being dark and intricate the troops entered opposite a ravelin which they mistook for the point of attack. The forlorn hope, in their confusion, veered to the left, on the wrong side of the tower and came up against the solid wall of the ravelin. The men started banging the butts of their weapons against the walls in frustration, thinking the French had some how blocked up the breach. Two men moving to their right accidentally stumbled against some rubble and knew it had to be part of the breach and called out to Gurwood, their commander. Lieutenant Theodore Elliott of the Royal Engineers, meanwhile, was at the edge of the ditch and, seeing a party of the stormers take a wrong turn, shouted to them pointing out the direction of the breach, saving the loss of further valuable time. The stormers having gone straight ahead, were starting to climb the rubble of the breach, which they found was surprisingly steep and here they were joined by the forlorn hope. The breach was very narrow at the top, about five yards wide, which had enabled the French to position a large gun sideways across it, practically barring the opening.

A gap of only about a yard separated the muzzle of the gun from the wall; the mass of men now being funnelled towards the narrow opening could only squeeze past the gun and wall one or two at a time while others scrambled over the gun. The attack having lost its impetus meant the assault was in jeopardy of grinding to a halt. Under a constant fire from the walls the men instinctively attempted to fire back forgetting the order that had been given not to have their weapons loaded during the storming. Major Napier fell at this point, struck by a grapeshot which shattered his arm; Rifleman Edward Costello caught hold of him as he fell and enquired if he was badly hurt. Napier told him not to worry but to continue and called out to the men to use their bayonets. Captain Dobbs 52nd, on reaching the head of the breach, fell shot in the chest, when the French sent a crashing volley into the stormers. The fire also wounded General Vandeleur and Colonel Colborne, both being hit in the shoulder.[14] Craufurd meanwhile having advanced to within shooting distance of the walls, stood on the glacis, about 60 yards left of where the stormers had entered the ditch. He began shouting directions to the column from this exposed position, screaming out his orders in a high pitched voice, in an attempt to be heard above the terrific barrage of noise emanating from the town and breach. The ditches of the fausse brae and the main breach being quite narrow, meant Craufurd was isolated and totally exposed, within easy shooting range of the French infantry manning the walls.

*Death of Craufurd*

While in the act of directing his division, a musket ball passed through his arm, broke his ribs and punctured the lungs before lodging in the spine. Craufurd dropped and rolled down [15] the glacis. His aide de camp Shaw, managed to drag and half carry his stricken general from out of the immediate line of fire. Meanwhile, Cameron, with his Riflemen along the length of the glacis, kept up a heavy rifle fire against the rampart walls and the troops manning it, much to the relief of the storming brigade, who had been joined by the columns from the two brigades. Brigade Major Smith, who had been refused the command of the forlorn hope by Craufurd, was in no mood to miss out in storming the town and he wasn't the only one wishing to cover himself in glory. The Earl of March, who was then a Lieutenant in the 13th Light Dragoons, had volunteered with the stormers of the 52nd Regiment. Two other would-be heroes who attached themselves to the Light Division assault were the Prince of Orange and Lord Fitzroy Somerset. (The latter to become better known as Lord Raglan of the Crimea). All three of these junior officers serving on Wellington's staff would be taken to task for their actions at breakfast the following morning, by the Commander-in-Chief. On ascending the fausse braie Smith climbed on top of a ravelin, ahead of the 43rd and 52nd, who were advancing in column, only to be pulled down by Colonel Colborne; so he could ascend the correct breach. Smith had been able to see that the 3rd Division was in the process of storming the great breach, with the French holding a line behind the works. If the Light Division gained the lesser breach and rushed along the ramparts towards the great breach they would be in a position to enfilade the whole enemy line opposing the stormers of the 3rd Division. Who, once they gained the top of the great breach, would have had very little room to continue, as they would have been boxed in. The defenders had dug retrenchments in the rear of the breach to protect it and once the stormers were through the main breach they would be attacked from in front and both sides, by the fire directed at them from the ruined houses only a short distance from the breach. However, the French, in their haste to escape the assaulting British troops left the planks of wood in place by which they had made good their escape across the ditches.

Bugler Green, who was in Uniacke's company, was lucky to escape unhurt, when a six-pounder gun was fired into the midst of the men he was advancing with. The survivors continued and Green came face to face, once more with the very same gun fully loaded, with a French gunner about to apply the match. However, one of his comrades reached it just in time and knocked the Frenchman down with the butt of his rifle.

Lieutenant Kincaid, one of the storming party, was equally disorientated by the darkness and confusion. On reaching the fausse braie, he entered the ditch with a group of men opposite a ravelin, which was mistaken for a bastion and tried first one side then the other. Captain Uniacke met up with Kincaid at some point. Kincaid seeing that one corner of it had been knocked about, thought it to be the breach and placed a ladder against it. Uniacke disagreed and moved on leaving Kincaid to mount the ladder, a pistol in one hand, and his sword in the other with a face like thunder, ready to meet whatever fate awaited his ascent and called to the men to follow him. On reaching the top he was expecting an instant challenge, only to find the place clear apart from the bodies of two Riflemen slumped across the top of the ladder. Climbing on top he could see from this position that they had entered the wrong section of the ravelin and was just about to go back down the ladder when a shout came from the other side, claiming the breach was there. Kincaid dropped from the ravelin, landing in the ditch opposite the foot of the breach, just as the head of the storming party was fighting their way in. On jumping into the ditch, Kincaid tried to avoid what he thought were the bodies of fallen Light Division men, only to find they were the hay bags thrown for the very purpose of breaking their fall.

The sprightly Uniacke, though not part of the forlorn hope or stormers, was soon clearing the top of the breach followed by Lieutenant William Johnstone and a number of men from his company. Lieutenant Gurwood had been up with these two officers but was knocked back as they reached the top of the breach. They immediately turned to their right along the ramparts towards the great breach which was being attacked by the 3rd Division. (Could this have been what was meant by Uniacke keeping open communication with this division?) Brigade Major Harry Smith ordered a company of the 43rd to follow him much to the annoyance of their Captain Duffy and some sharp words were exchanged, but the men obeyed Smith and they all raced after Uniacke. Edward Costello, also in Uniacke's company, along with some of his fellow Riflemen, turned left out of the breach, and continued in the dark along the ramparts. Once through the lesser breach, there were no defensive trenches to tackle, as the French had not built extra defences here as they had at the great breach. Costello in his hurry to be one of the first into the town ahead of his comrades, was suddenly brought up short, having run smack into a howitzer. He fell on top of a wounded French officer who was being attended to by a gunner. Being taller and heavier than Costello the gunner immediately tackled the shocked Riflemen and was able to overpower him. By this time his comrades had arrived. His friend Wilkie, [16] knocked the gunner down to join his officer, but before Costello had time to thank him, Wilkie fell to the ground mortally wounded, probably shot from one of his own side. Wilkie died holding Costello's hand. The French officer, sensing he could be in for a rough time, offered the Rifleman his gold watch. There never seems to have been much time for sentiment amongst these tough hard-drinking Riflemen. There being no reason or point in remaining, this little band was soon making its way towards the town. By this time most of the Light Division had reached the breach and were pouring through the gap, many of them in the process of heading into the town. Lieutenant Kincaid, like Costello, had also turned left out of the breach with a number of men and continued to follow the ramparts around the town, which the enemy had abandoned. He eventually reached the point opposite to where the Portuguese troops were storming, they were cheering for all they were worth, as they gained the walls not realising that the town had fallen.

Uniacke and Harry Smith meanwhile, were both advancing along the ramparts in the direction of the 3rd Division, who had been attacking the main breach in two separate brigades under the command of Generals Mackinnon and Colville. Their storming party was under Major Russell Manners of the 74th Regiment. Picton, also, gave them some encouraging words before the attack commenced. Mackinnon's brigade was to storm the breach while two regiments in Colville's brigade had been singled out for some special tasks, while the rest of the brigade acted as cover and support to the main assault. The 2nd Battalion 5th Regiment had been selected to advance between the river and the fortress, where they were instructed to cut through the gate into the main ditch. Once through they were to mount the outer wall with scaling ladders, pushing any French troops before them and clearing the ditch of any obstructions they should come across. The 2nd Caçadores, along with the Light companies from the 2nd Battalion 83rd Regiment, were to cross the bridge over the Agueda and in total silence escalade the outwork in front of the castle to capture the two guns covering the main wall. Colonel Campbell of the 94th, was directed to take his regiment in double columns of companies from the left of the convent of Santa Cruz and enter the ditch. Turning left, carry the breach at the fausse braie and to remove all obstacles placed there and then join the stormers. Prior to setting off the 94th was issued from the engineers' stores with a number of knotted ropes to assist in descending the ditch and felling axes to break down and remove whatever impediments that were believed to be blocking the breach. It was planned so they would reach the breach ahead of the stormers, that way it would be clear for them.

The remaining companies of the 2nd Battalion 83rd Regiment manned a section of the second parallel from where they fired on the main wall, the 77th was to remain in reserve but somehow joined in the attack. [17] Once Mackinnon's brigade left the trenches, their place was to be taken by a Portuguese brigade. Three companies of the 3rd 95th, after clearing any French infantry occupying the ravelins in this area were to continue to provide covering fire, the same as the 83rd, only at a much closer range.

The French were falling back under the fierce assault from the Grenadiers of the 88th Regiment. Seeing that it was impossible to hold them back any longer a mine which had been hidden was sprung for just such a scenario. The mine exploded with such violence and power it blew up friend and foe alike. General Mackinnon was amongst those sent into the air by the force. Uniacke had just reached the rampart above the breach when it exploded, Brigade Major Smith also felt its blast. Being slightly more sheltered he was thrown some distance, scorched black, but not wounded; he landed on a number of primed shells! Lieutenant Patterson of the 43rd was also caught up in the explosion and blown over the wall, his face and one hand severely burnt. He then received a deep cut from a shell splinter or musket ball in a buttock. Uniacke, apart from being blasted into the air and burnt black, received a number of serious wounds from splinters of ammunition cases. These injuries turned out to be mortal, although he was still able to walk back to camp. Harry Smith looking now even less like a staff officer was about to jump down into the main breach when Sergeant MacCurrie of the 52nd stopped him and lent him his cat-skin forage cap. There was no easy way into the town from the breach stormed by the 3rd division and Sergeant MacCurrie's intervention saved Smith a lot of wasted effort. The men gathered at that part of the rampart, now looked for an easier route to descend into the town. Smith's strange cap combined with his burnt black clothing was nearly his undoing. When they came up with the men of the 3rd Division, he was confronted by Lieutenant Stewart, a giant of a man in the Grenadier Company of the 88th, with one of his men.

Stewart grabbed Smith by the throat almost choking the breath from his body exclaiming, 'You French..!' Smith had just enough breath left to blurt out a string of damnations for his rough treatment in time to prevent Stewart's man from running him through with his bayonet.

Meanwhile, back at the lesser breach, the Light Division had taken full control; all resistance in this area had ended with the French falling back into the streets in a running battle with those who followed. Colborne, though severely[18] wounded, ordered the officers to concentrate the men. Lieutenant Johnstone, of the Rifles, had, prior to the assault, worked out a position from where to enter the fortress. As a result, he was the first man into the city, followed by a few of his men. When Gurwood arrived, he found Johnstone and his men had already beaten him to it. Though fractionally missing out at being the first through the breach, he still had an agenda of his own to complete. Gurwood was soon making for the citadel, where he took General Barrié, the governor prisoner.[19] Lieutenant John FitzMaurice of the Rifles, couldn't have been far behind, for he also entered the citadel and took a snuff box from Barrié's desk as a souvenir.[20]

*Barrié's sword.*

The French conceding defeat, threw down their arms in droves. The two storming divisions, having become severely fragmented in the action, some kind of order was immediately required. Lieutenant Colonel McLeod of the 43rd Regiment, was soon carrying this out, along with a number of his officers.

They were eventually able to gather around 200 of their regiment on the ramparts and the colonel demanded they keep together. Lieutenant Cooke, also of this regiment, advanced towards the main breach where he was met by an officer walking slowly between two men. Not able to recognise him asked, 'who is it!?' A faint voice replied, 'Uniacke' and walked on. That Cooke was unable to recognise Uniacke tells us how severe were his injuries, only an hour or two earlier they had drunk chocolate together. Uniacke had an eye blown out, one arm hung limply by his side, while the flesh had been torn from his arms and legs and besides this he was burnt completely black. McLeod getting something near to order in his regiment, instructed Lieutenant Madden to take 25 of his men and descend into the breach and to remain there for the rest of the night. This was to prevent anybody leaving the town through his position with plunder of any kind. The Lieutenant, knew he was bound to be in for a hard night's work, immediately ordered his men to build a large fire so they could pick out any would be escaping plunderers, while at the same time keeping themselves warm. McLeod also sent a number of officers into the town in command of sections of men, with the specific task of securing any stores they could find. These groups gradually disintegrated as the men slipped away in the dark to take part in the growing chaos.

Lieutenant Cooke returned to McLeod's position and finding he was free of any duty went to inspect the breach. There he came upon the body of Captain Dobbs of the 52nd, lying on his back stripped of his uniform. It is amazing how quickly the camp followers and peasants from the outlying villages, descended to scavenge through such horrors, with little regard for the dead or wounded. Cooke lifted up Dobbs and the blood flowed from his fatal wounds, a ball having gone clean through his chest and out his back.

Soldiers were now entering the town from every direction and, as a result, many fired upon each other; what has since been erroneously declared as friendly fire! Costello of the Rifles and his party on entering the town found themselves in a large square, where they were soon joined by men representing every regiment that had taken part in the assault. Everywhere there was chaos, until a regiment from the 3rd Division (the 77th) marched into the square, still in some semblance of order under the command of their officers, and order began to be restored. [21] The regiment's colours were placed in the centre of the square, declaring the town was taken, three rousing cheers were then given. The men started firing into the air, then at the windows and in no time chaos reigned once more, as the men went in search of drink and plunder. In no time locked doors were smashed in, stubborn locks blown open by rifle or musket fire. The reins were off, no amount of coercion by their officers could stop them and in a short space of time the victorious troops had become hordes of uncontrollable men roaming the streets, out for whatever they could find. With the vast quantities of wine and raw spirit now being consumed, the beast suppressed in a large number of the men's breasts was unleashed. The taking of a fortress was a new experience to these men and they soon became a law unto themselves; soon the ugly side of the drunkard was in plain evidence all around. [22]

Costello joined one of these groups as they stumbled down the dark streets of the town; they were suddenly brought up short by those leading crying out in pain. They found that they had got amongst a pile of discarded muskets which still had their bayonets attached. The men at first believed they had stumbled on to a chevaux-de-frise. But it was just a pile of discarded muskets that the French had thrown down in haste to escape the wrath of the invading force. Close by they found a wounded French soldier from whom they gathered, in their limited Spanish, that they were close to the French barracks. The thought that they could be confronted by a large force of French infantry panicked Costello and he was soon retracing his steps towards the square, only to run into another party of looters. They were feeling their way down the dark street with the aid of a candle. On hearing a noise ahead of them they began firing in Costello's direction, he instantly took shelter in a near by doorway. As they advanced and came level with Costello's hiding place, he implored them that they were firing upon their own men. This second group now joined forces with the original group and having sufficient numbers guided by the French soldier, entered the barracks through a large gate. On mounting a stone stair case they found they were in the French hospital, full of sick and wounded men. Those able to move and sit up were now quite agitated, in the half light, by the sight of this group of ferocious looking men, lucky for them they were not yet the worse for wear with drink and still had some compassion for their enemy. They tried to comfort and reassure these poor souls that they would come to no harm, when suddenly a shot rang out and the man holding the candle fell with a ball through his head. A third group of plundering rogues seeing the light fired through the window, they then all opened fire on the hospital. Costello and his comrades had little choice but to take cover. Eventually, one of their group went to the window and shouted that they were firing upon their own men.

In many other parts of the town, once the cellars had been located, the wine and brandy flowed quite freely and the men soon became possessed. Some in sheer devilment, but others, in some cases, with serious intent started shooting from the windows at anything that moved. Lieutenant Cooke had unwisely entered the town and came face to face with the regimental barber in the square and while talking to him, Private Evans suddenly fell dead at his feet with his brains running out over the floor, shot no doubt by one of these lunatics. Cooke immediately scampered for shelter, on entering a large house came across his colonel, McLeod and some officers doing the very same!

They all now had to wait until morning came to save them from their uncomfortable and dangerous situation.

Lieutenant John Kincaid who we left earlier circumnavigating the ramparts with his men, was confronted by a large group of French soldiers, who immediately threw down their arms as they approached. At the same time pleading that they were not French but Italians, this was the wrong thing to have said. The Riflemen, for some reason unknown to Kincaid, had an instant dislike for Italians and any who declared themselves from that race were shot![23] They continued on, around the ramparts until they came to the breach stormed by the 3rd Division. Here they climbed down to enter the town and joined the flow going in the same direction. At the entrance to the first street Kincaid was accosted by a French officer who begged his protection giving him his sword, at the same time telling him there was another officer inside. He now followed the Frenchman into the building and up a flight of stairs where a violent scream rang out from another room. Kincaid pushed open the door to find the lady of the house struggling with a British soldier. The Rifles' officer grabbed hold of him and threw him head first down the stairs. Leaving the house he followed the throng to the main square and here he found Colonel Barnard and Major Cameron berating the Riflemen they could find, while trying to knock some sense and order into them. Those who continued to load and fire were hit about the head with broken musket barrels! They gradually gained some order, collecting a number of the Riflemen together and ushered them out of the town, finally getting them as far as the ramparts where they settled down for the rest of the night. Lieutenant Simmons having previously positioned himself on the ramparts, close to a fire, to wait out the rest of the night, was greeted by some of his own men who had been forced out of the town. They offered him ham, eggs and wine from their nights foraging, for which he was most grateful.

Costello and the men in the hospital, now joined forces with the group who had attacked them, and they all went off confident that the size of the group gave them the strength to face any force they might encounter. They were still searching for what every other soldier in Ciudad Rodrigo seemed to have already found. Eventually they arrived at a large house that had doubled as the French commissaries stores; there was, however one problem, it had been put under the protection of a determined single German guard. He was adamant they could not enter and, while his sense of duty was admirable, under the circumstances was not very wise. The men were in no mood to be denied, especially after what they had experienced so far, shrugging off his warning they rushed the door breaking it in, the German was knocked aside and run through with a bayonet! Inside the men found they had hit the jackpot and it was easy to see why a guard had been placed over it.

The rooms were full of casks of spirit. Rifle and musket butts soon set to work, smashing in the heads and any vessel that came to hand was pressed into service to scoop up the nectar of life that meant everything to these men. Those who could not find anything to drink from plunged head first into the liquid. In no time they were raging drunk, unnoticed in the haze of intoxication a couple of individuals fell into the large casks and drowned, others lay about incapable of moving. (Reminiscent to some of the scenes depicted in our volume one on the retreat to Corunna.) This would prove to be their undoing, for at some point during this Bacchus drinking party a light was dropped into a barrel of spirit and soon the place was on fire. Taking hold quickly, it soon engulfed the house and a number of the worst cases were burnt to death. During the night, at least another two houses were set alight; but thanks to the efforts of some officers and men the fires were prevented from taking hold in the town.

The situation could have been much worse, however, but for an incident that received very little attention. Captain William Jones of the 52nd, when in the town, with his company, was approached by a French Officer who surrendered to gain his protection. Before handing him over, Jones decided he would use him to his advantage, making him guide them to some comfortable quarters, this ended at a large store where he quartered the largest part of his company. He then followed the officer to a church. A number of Portuguese troops were already in the area and they had lit a fire on the pavement just out side of it. On entering, the French officer threw up his hands and ran back outside in panic. Jones could not speak a word of French and had no idea what was the matter with him until he came across some loose powder on the floor not far from the fire. The powder trailed back through the church to a number of barrels full of gunpowder. Jones immediately called to his men and they helped him carry the barrels to safety and out of harms way. [24]

Picton finally put in an appearance and in his usual no nonsense manner, his voice booming out above the din, was easily recognised cursing all and sundry, damning every soldier he came across. That morning the 5th Division marched into the square and took control of the town. It was now time to count the cost of the night's work. Lieutenant Cooke says he saw numbers of men lying dead in the streets, no doubt victims of the night's unpleasant chaotic carryings on. The French prisoners were being escorted out of the town amongst whom were found a number of deserters from the British Army.

Wellington's choice of the Light and 3rd Divisions as stormers of the city was probably a calculated gamble, the assault had to succeed at all cost. What better way of insuring that this would end in a victory than by pitching these two arch rivals, Picton and Craufurd, against each other! There was equal rivalry between the two sets of troops, the Light Division was already ahead on points with the capture of the redoubt under Colborne at the beginning of the siege.

The casualties in the Light Division:

1st Battalion 95th
Captain Uniacke died of wounds.
Lieutenants John Cox and William Hamilton wounded.
1 Rifleman killed, 1 sergeant and 15 Rank and file wounded.

2nd Battalion 95th
Captain Mitchell, Lieutenants Bedell and M'Gregor wounded.
8 Rank and file killed and 22 rank and file wounded.

3rd Battalion 95th
2 sergeants and 7 rank and file wounded.

1st Battalion 52nd
Colonel Colborne wounded in shoulder, Major George Napier wounded
in arm later amputated. Captain Dobbs killed. Captain William Mein and
Lieutenant John Woodgate wounded, 8 rank and file killed 1 sergeant and 33
rank and file wounded.

2nd Battalion 52nd
1 sergeant and 3 rank and file killed, Lieutenant John Gurwood and 5 rank and
file wounded.

The casualties extracted from the pension rolls for Ciudad Rodrigo in the 95th:

John Edwardstaff gun-shot wound of the head.
William Wallace wounded in thigh and arm.
Sergeant Edward Cassidy 3rd Battalion gun-shot wound left foot.
James Farmer gun-shot wound right knee.
John Rowse injured right foot.
William Haig 3rd Battalion gun-shot wound right foot.
George Coeman received a severe injury on the rampart and gun-shot wound
to right thigh.
William Sperry injured by an explosion.
Hugh Monks gun-shot wounds to back and both arms when storming.
Thomas Kinslow wounded.

While their fellow Riflemen of the 60th Rifles casualties amounted to:
Captain Livingston and 4 rank and file wounded
1 sergeant killed and 2 rank and file wounded the previous day.

49

Costello seems to have remained reasonably sober during his escapades with his gang of looters and eventually ended up spending the night with a fellow Rifleman in a house that was the home of a doctor. The poor man and his beautiful young niece were petrified by the presence of these two rough looking characters. As a result they were offered the best of hospitality and wallowed away the night in relative comfort.

The next morning Costello's first thoughts were to look for the body of his friend Wilkie, which he found stripped naked as the day he was born, in the lesser breach. He was able to pick him out easily enough, for Costello thought he resembled his sister; it would seem that Costello was on favourable terms with Wilkie's family. (One therefore has to question Costello's motive for inventing Wilkie's death as happening at Ciudad Rodrigo. Of course Costello was not expecting to be questioned when relating his narrative of service, first aired in the pages of the United Services Journal of 1839. Eileen Hathaway remarks in her book [25] on Costello, that he might have embroidered the truth for the sake of Wilkie's family, so that they could picture him having a hero's death. One would have thought they would have learned of his death in the returns of the previous month. How would Costello have been able to inform them for at this time he could not write and he did not return to England until 1814? Costello also gives us two locations of his death, first in detail on the ramparts then in the breach the following day. Those members of the regiment who left accounts of the storming of Ciudad Rodrigo, such as Leach, Costello, Simmons, Gairdner and Cooke of the 43rd all seem to have a morbid curiosity in wanting to view the death scenes of both breaches. Maybe this was a way of feeling thankful it was not themselves lying there. All seem to confirm the sight of the larger breach was most shocking, the bodies of the opposing forces were badly burnt and mutilated by the explosion, with bits of bodies everywhere.

Lieutenant Madden, who we left guarding the small breach from would-be escaping plunderers, while at the same time preventing men entering the town via the breach, seems to have had his work cut out during the night. Numerous piles of clothing and objects of all description taken from the escaping hordes now covered the area in testimony to his endeavour. Dresses, clergymen's clothing and all manner of household goods were removed; the mind boggles at what they expected to do with half of what was taken. Colonel Barnard collected what he hoped were the last of the stragglers from the town about 9 o'clock on the morning of the 20th. The 1st Battalion Rifles formed up and quit the town marching out through the gate leading to the bridge over the Agueda. The sight they presented was quite amusing to all who witnessed it, for the men were represented by every conceivable manner of dress one could imagine, from female attire to the vestments of the clergy.

They were likened to the participants of a country fair with rifles slung over the shoulder, sword bayonets fixed, adorned with all kinds of cooked meats and bread. The funniest was seeing Riflemen; many of course still the worse for wear, with the mother of all hangovers, trying to keep step with their more sober comrades in large jack boots, which had previously been the property of the garrison in Rodrigo. Others were wearing necklaces made of various types of ladies' footwear, carrying birds in cages with some even reported as having tame monkeys on their shoulders! This sort of dress in different degrees was probably worn by many in the Light Division and not just the Rifles.

*Spoils of Victory'*

It was here they were met by the 5th Division, who had been ordered to take over the town, repair the breaches, bury the dead and round up the last of the Light and 3rd Divisions' delinquents. They halted to let the Light Division pass; forming up they presented arms in honour of their splendid victory, no doubt with many a smile on their faces. Wellington riding towards the town on passing the Riflemen enquired from one of his staff, 'who the hell are those fellows?' Proof if ever it was needed to the array of costumes being worn, the Rifles normally being one of the easiest of regiments to recognise due to their distinctive dress. The 52nd Regiment was similarly attired and on coming up with General Picton had the cheek to ask him for a cheer! 'Here you are you drunken set of rascals,' he laughed, 'Hurrah! We'll soon be in Badajoz.' [26]

On reaching their former camp site, it was back to soldiering and reflecting on the losses in the battalion. None more so than Captain Uniacke, who died of his wounds on the 27th, a young athletic man and the most likable of officers, a credit to his rank and the regiment. He was idolised by the men of his company who had previously served under that other wise old goat Captain Peter O'Hare. The whole of Uniacke's company attended his burial, though according to Costello, this did not pass without mishap! Those carrying his coffin were still the worse for wear and as a result succeeded in dropping it, spilling out the remains of their beloved Captain on the cold, hard earth. Fairfoot, one of the corporals in his company, who had been slightly wounded himself, wanted his Captain to be interned in a Christian plot. He convinced the local priests that Uniacke was befitting such an honour as he was an Irishman, which established him as a Catholic in the eyes of the clergy. Uniacke was therefore buried beneath one of the finest trees in the church yard.

*Burial of Craufurd*

Craufurd had died three days earlier, his mortal wounds eventually bringing his distinguished life to an end, although he had been attended by Wellington's own Surgeon, Gunning. Even under the constant care of his staff, he deduced that nothing could save him. Craufurd died in his sleep around 2 o'clock in the morning of 24th January. Plans were immediately made for his funeral. The best account of the proceedings comes from the pen of Subaltern Gleig, 85th Regiment;

'The morning of Craufurd's funeral the sky was clear and bright and a bracing frost covered the ground. The roads the day before a quagmire were now frozen solid, the whole of the Light Division had been ordered to parade to show their last respects to their late general. They marched under arms to Craufurd's house, (in the suburbs of the San Francisco Convent) then advanced with their arms reversed, between a double row of soldiers of the 5th Division with their arms pointed to the ground who were lining each side of the road. Craufurd's coffin was born by six sergeant majors from the Light Division with six field officers as supporters. Stepping off, several bands started playing mournful airs. The coffin was immediately followed by General Stewart and Craufurd's ADC Shaw, then Wellington, General Castanos and Marshal Beresford. They in turn were followed by a long train of Staff and General officers. The coffin was born to the lesser breach and deposited in an area that had been specially prepared for his remains, close to it.' According to General Stewart, Lord Wellington decided he should be interred by his own division near the breach which he had so gallantly carried. [27]

An incident, on returning from Craufurd's funeral, quoted by Harry Smith, sums up the mood and spirit of the Light Division at this time in relation to the respect they had for his discipline. Marching back to camp they marched straight through a large area of water that was on their route rather than go around it. Over the years this had been one of Craufurd's pet maxims and was considered harsh by all ranks, whenever they were on the march. If ever an officer or man was seen by him to deviate from his march he would command, 'Sit down in it Sir, sit down in it.'

Wellington wrote to the Earl of Liverpool, the Secretary of State informing him of Craufurd's death; 'Major General Craufurd died on the 24th instant, of wounds which he received on the 19th, while leading the Light Division of this army to the assault of Ciudad Rodrigo. Although the conduct of Major General Craufurd on the occasion on which these wounds were received, and the circumstances which occurred, have excited the admiration of every officer in the army, I cannot report his death to your Lordship without expressing my sorrow and regret that his Majesty has been deprived of the services, and I of the assistance, of an officer of tried talents and experience, who was an ornament to his profession, and was calculated to render the most important services to his country.'

A few days after the siege Wellington was at dinner when he learned of the fate of a number of the sick and wounded soldiers. They had been dumped out of doors, so he rode 30 miles that night to where they had been quartered to see the situation for himself. On arrival he ordered the men to be carried into the officers' quarters. The following day he returned to find they had been placed out side again, after ordering them inside again, he had the officers involved cashiered from the army!

The British deserters were to be tried by their respective divisions; seven of these men belonged to the Light Division and three were Riflemen. Costello calls one of these deserters Cumming of the 52nd Regiment, but he was being a little economical with the truth as he was a Rifleman. He was the Rifleman who had deserted in 1810, a member of the Regimental Band. Alan Cumming had six brothers serving in the 1st Battalion along with himself, either in the band or as buglers. General Kempt having arrived from England took over the command of the Light Division and presided over the courts martial, Alan Cumming rather unfairly was pardoned. The excuse trotted out by those who had deserted was the lack of wages; this was thought of as a poor reason for such action by their fellow Riflemen.

A general court martial was held at Nave de Haver on 12th February 1812, this was to accommodate the deserters of the Light Division, they were: William Mills, Miles Hodgson and Malcolm McInnes belonging to the 95th, Corporal Robert Fuller, Privates William Robinson, Patrick O'Neil and John Maloney 52nd Regiment, Private Thomas Price 43rd Regiment, George Cameron Royal Horse Artillery.

Deserters were not soley confined to the Light Division; others also tried by court martial were: Privates John Curtain and Luke McGann 88th Regiment, Thomas Jones 23rd Welsh Fusiliers, Riflemen Joseph Lambrecht, Conrad Eylich and John Engle 60th Rifles, Charles Knierim Kings German Legion and Joseph Ball 7th Royal Fusiliers. All these men were found guilty and sentenced to be shot in the presence of their own particular division.

The Light Division deserters were kept in confinement at the village of Ituero on the banks of the River Azava. Quartermaster William Surtees of the 95th was present at the executions and his description of the event probably is one of the most accurate. Seven men of the division were actually listed as being for the firing squad and of the eight men listed above, one Rifleman was pardoned. This seemed rather harsh on the remainder, though not one of the men attempted to plead not guilty having been captured in Ciudad Rodrigo, it virtually put the seal on their fate. No sympathy for their predicament seems to have been expressed by any of their comrades; they thought the excuse for their desertion of poor rations and conditions, rather lame. Especially as they were all in the same boat, it was accepted that at times they were short of food and that the clothing was stretched to its limits of service. This probably was the root cause of so many; the division wearing whatever came to hand in the looting of Ciudad Rodrigo. It hadn't helped their cause when it was reported by some of the stormers that their cries could be distinctly heard with comments such as, 'Now here comes the Light Division; let us give it to them, the rascals.' The Light Division was formed up on a plain in front of the village, as part of a three sided square, the open side facing the freshly dug graves of the condemned.

Harry Smith as Brigade Major had the task of assisting the provost during the executions. A firing party from each regiment had been formed up in the centre loaded and waiting to perform their solemn duty. The provost conducted the prisoners to the place of execution and each man knelt down in front of the pile of earth that marked his last resting place, facing the division and firing squad. With their arms tied to their sides, blind-folds were placed over their eyes, the Assistant Adjutant General read out the sentence of the court, so that the whole division could hear and take in the enormity of their crime.

*Shooting of deserter*

The firing party was instructed by the provost to each fire at the man from their own particular regiment; they advanced to within ten or twelve paces of the condemned and after a short pause, so they could reflect in what little time they had left on this earth to consult their maker, the signal was given and the men fired. After the volley echoed away one poor wretch was still kneeling unharmed while some of the others had not been killed outright. One Rifleman begged Brigade Major Smith to put him out of his misery, he at once ordered one of his Riflemen to reload and placing the muzzle of the rifle to his breast fired, at the same time the provost did the same to George Cameron of the artillery who did not have a squad designated from his corps to perform the duty of executioner. The division was then formed up in column and marched past the bodies of the deserters, to affect a lasting imprint on their minds as what to expect should they ever think of committing such an act themselves. Just prior to this event on 10th February, the 1st Battalion 95th received 50 reinforcements from the depot companies in England and their first introduction into life in the Peninsula was to witness the execution of these deserters.

It would seem that it was easy to be coerced into such an act; McGuinnis of the Highland Company had been of previous excellent character. Rifleman Almond a notable absentee from those caught in Ciudad Rodrigo seems to have been behind McGuinnis's desertion. Almond was eventually caught and also executed by firing squad.

In General Orders a change was now announced to take place in the Light Division on 23rd February 1812. That would affect its strength, an extract is shown here:

No3 The commander of the Forces having received orders to draft the 2nd Battalion 52nd Regiment into the 1st Battalion, the following arrangement is made for that purpose.

No8 The commander of the Forces begs the 2nd Battalion 52nd Regiment will accept his thanks for their very distinguished services. Since they have been in the Peninsula they have had various opportunities of displaying their gallant and good conduct, and the Commander of the Forces has had reason on every occasion to be satisfied with their behaviour.

As a result, ten sergeants, seven buglers and 487 rank and file were in consequence transferred from the 2nd Battalion to the 1st Battalion and ten sergeants, five buglers and 85 rank and file being unserviceable, were transferred to the 2nd Battalion. On 25th February the skeleton of the 2nd Battalion marched for Lisbon on its way to England.

The 1st Battalion 52nd Regiment marched on 26th February under the command of Lieutenant Colonel Hunt from Guinaldo to Badajoz via, Aldea de Ponte, Sortellia Escarigo, Alpedrinha, Alcairo, Casel Branco, Niza, Castello de Vide, Portalegre, Monches and Elvas, where the regiment arrived on 16th March. The Rifles left their cantonments on 26th February via Castello Branco and Villa Velha headed for Badajoz at the village of Povo das Meadas, near Niza they took up quarters. From here Quarter Master Surtees was sent to Lisbon, where he was to collect the newly arrived regimental clothing. However, because of the lack of transport returned arriving back at the camp before Badajoz on 25th March empty handed, no doubt to the annoyance of the regiment. On the 27th, the Light Division formed on the glacis of Elvas, before starting off to take part in the siege of Badajoz.

# Siege of Badajoz

The Light Division left Castelo de Vide on 14th March and marched the ten miles to Elvas, which they reached on the 16th, marching out on the 17th for Badajoz to the tune 'St Patrick's Day' played by the bands. On crossing the Guadiana River by a bridge of pontoon boats chained together, they found the 3rd and 4th Divisions already in position. The Light Division took up residence on the Spanish side of the river, where they set up camp on a small hill; where they enjoyed the comfort of Portuguese tents. That same night, detachments from the Light, 3rd and 4th Divisions set to work breaking ground before the outwork fortress, Picurina. The working party in severe, wet, stormy conditions was concealed in hollow ground some 300 yards from the salient of the outwork, while 2,000 men were held in position as a covering party. By daylight 600 yards of the parallel had been opened up, some three feet deep by three and a half feet wide, together with over 1,000 yards of communication trenches, parts of which were within 160 yards off the covered-way.

Riflemen detailed for the working party carried a skip and a spade to the trenches. They filled the skip with the sodden earth and once completed placed it in front of them, to be replaced by another which was then filled and placed in front on top of each other. Gradually a protective screen was built up in front of the excavated trench. They detested such work. At daylight, the French, on seeing the efforts of the besiegers' night time labours, countered this by firing some field-guns and a howitzer into the works. This they accompanied by a heavy musketry fire from the parapets and covered-way. On the morning of the 19th, the guns on the town's ramparts opened on the working parties, luckily with little effect. This prompted Governor Philippon into taking immediate action and at 1 o'clock the same day he ordered a vigorous sortie against the British working parties. Some 1,500 infantry with 40 cavalry, burst from the Talavera gate, forming up in the communication trench between the San Roque Lunette and Picurina fort. Rushing forward they entered the first parallel before the British had time to stand to arms. The cavalry galloped round the right flank of the parallel and reached the artillery field-park, a thousand yards in rear of the British trenches. Here they caused confusion and alarm amongst the unarmed men until eventually rallying some 50 yards behind the British trench they charged the French, driving their gallant enemy attackers back to the town. Not, however, before they were able to seize around 200 most needed entrenching tools and were able to fill in a portion of the trench. This surprise attack cost the British dearly, with 150 Officers and men killed and wounded, none as far as we know, belonging to the Rifles.

Wellington, however, was not going to be caught out a second time and ordered some squadrons of the 14th Light Dragoons, plus a brigade of field guns, to be kept in readiness on the heights of San Miguel. Two batteries were eventually completed to take four 24-pounders, three 18-pounders and three five and a half inch howitzers. On 20th March, Sergeant John Power of the Rifles was killed. The works continued to make steady progress until the morning of the 21st, when the French opened with two field-pieces, positioned on the hills close to San Christobal, from where they were able to enfilade the British right battery. To counter this a detachment of the 95th Rifles was sent down to the banks of the river, where they fired upon the guns killing or wounding a number of those working them, causing them to be withdrawn. For some nights prior to this, a Rifleman named Brooks had had the same recurring dream, in which he saw a Rifleman without a head. On the day the Rifles attacked the two French guns, Riflemen Costello, Treacy and Brooks jumped out of the trench having accomplished their task and ran back to the next parallel immediately coming under fire from the French. Costello was ahead of his two comrades when he heard the familiar whooshing sound of a cannon-ball in full flight, as it passed, something then splashed all over his jacket. Jumping into the parallel he then looked behind where he saw the headless, quivering body of Brooks before it fell to the ground. Brooks' dream was the very premonition of his own death, the cannon-ball had smashed his head completely from his body. Costello's jacket was splattered with Brooks' brains and Rifleman Treacy had been wounded by a splinter of bone from Brooks' skull which embedded deep into the skin behind his ear! The musters confirm Brooks' death on the 21st, along with Corporal William Skinner and Riflemen John Beddie both killed in action.

On the 22nd the French renewed their attack using the same guns close to their previous position, but this time they were under cover. They gained some success, for they were able to send their shot some 1,600 yards into the parallel. To help counter this Wellington ordered General Leith to advance his 5th Division from Campo Mayor and invest San Christobal on the same side of the river as the guns. Meanwhile a detachment of Riflemen was ordered to Elvas the same day, their task to help bring up some of the badly needed heavy artillery. The weather was really bad, the conditions only allowing the guns to be pulled by some 12 bullocks to each gun on improvised sledges. Arriving at the pontoon bridge, close to Badajoz, they found that due to the constant downpour, it had been swept away by the ferocious torrent that was now the river. They had to spend the night in some tents which had been provided for the use of some sappers who had been sent to repair the bridge. With an advanced piquet being provided for by the Riflemen, the remainder now settled down for some well earned rest out of the rain. The French, however, had other ideas, seeing the bullocks grazing at leisure, sent some shells amongst them. One of the round-shot went clean through a tent full of Riflemen, who seconds before were all sound asleep, it took the centre pole with it, bringing the tent down on their heads. Two Riflemen, Green and Lea were wounded, one had his thigh broken and the other a leg taken off at the calf. On the 23rd, with the bridge repaired, the Rifle detachment was able to cross and return to their camp. Later that day Riflemen Paul Conray and John Shortes were killed in action.

By the night of 24th March, the British batteries were in place and had been completed to accommodate 28 guns and their ammunition. They opened up a heavy bombardment on the Picurina Fortress at 11 o'clock on the 25th. This fire was kept up at a brisk pace all day and also, at the same time, directed their attention on the supporting batteries. Picurina Fort was built in the form of a Redan protected by a deep gorge, which had been closed off with three rows of palisades. The parapet was some 30 feet above the base of the ditch, the scarp however was only 15 feet high but had a line of fraises along the top, behind which was a steep earth slope. The counterscarp was nine feet high and splinter-proof retrenchments had been built inside the work, defended by 230 men and seven guns. The bombardment had managed to dismount the fort's guns, knocked in parts of the salient of the work and smashed up some of the fraises. As a result Wellington ordered a force under General Kempt, who was at that time in command in the trenches, to attack and take the place that night. The attack was to be made by the 3rd Division in three columns, the first two with 200 men in each column, were provided by men of the 77th and 88th Regiments, with 100 men of the 83rd Regiment forming the third column as a reserve. A further 100 men provided by the working parties of the Light division carrying axes, crowbars and ladders, preceded the storming columns. (Jones in his sieges p187–189 says these parties were provided by the Sappers and Miners, 24 to each column, and that the reserve column had ladders) While it is accepted there would be Sappers and Miners involved it is also clear that the Light Division provided ladder parties at the very least. Lieutenant Stokes of the 95th, was in command of a ladder party tasked with advancing to the walls ready for the stormers. Captain Ewart of the 52nd, also, had 100 men under his command with orders to advance ahead of the storming parties, with axes, crowbars and ladders. There was always a competitive edge to any action involving the men of Light and 3rd Divisions, much of it encouraged by their respective commanders, Picton and the late Craufurd.

This came to the fore in this action. The Riflemen placed their ladders ready for the stormers and having completed their allotted task ready for the arrival of the 3rd Division, who on coming up, told them, 'Come, stand out of the way.' Sergeant Brotherwood of the Rifles, inflamed at their manner replied, 'Damn your eyes, do you think we Light Division fetch ladders for such chaps as you to climb? Follow us.' and raced up the ladders with some of his men, before the stormers had a chance to mount them. A number of them being instantly knocked down by the defenders. Lieutenant Stokes of the Rifles is likewise reported to have ascended the ladders and been the first man to enter the fort.

The 74th and 88th Regiments' columns divided so that half of each went right and left around the fort, while the remainder attacked the palisades in the ditch. They were unsuccessful as they had no means of breaking them down and suffered accordingly. Captain Ewart's men on arriving had problems in the deep ditch, for the escarp was strongly defended by fraises, and were having difficulty with the strong, three deep lines of palisades which enclosed the gorge. Ewart fell wounded and Lieutenant Nixon continued on until falling severely wounded himself with the axe men who eventually broke through the gate of the palisades. The men struggled to gain entrance through the narrow interior, but success was finally assured due mainly to the defenders' attention being diverted, at this point, against the men of the 83rd and 88th Regiments. The fort of Picurina was eventually captured by the point of the bayonet. The 52nd had two Officers, Captain John Ewart and Lieutenant William Nixon wounded, with 34 rank and file killed and wounded. Captain Madden of the same regiment was lucky not to have joined them, for prior to the storming he had been out shooting game. As a result he was still dressed in non-regulation clothes; hearing of the attack on his return, he immediately joined in with the attackers and in the heat of battle became a target for both French and British, for no one could make out who he was! He must have led a charmed life for he escaped the night's work uninjured, though his luck was to run out in the main assault on Badajoz. The known Rifles casualties in this successful action were: Sergeant William Kenderine killed in action, Riflemen Edward Evans (KIA) Joseph Gibbons and Peter Lavasey killed. Of the defenders, the Commandant, with two officers and 80 men were taken prisoner, while one officer and 31 men managed to make good their escape. The rest were either killed or drowned in the inundation, Philippon was inflamed by the loss of this important work and censured the troops of the fort's garrison for not firing the mines and other combustibles they had prepared for just such an attack. If they had, the losses of the force would have been even more severe than they already were. The British lost four officers and 50 men killed and 15 officers and 250 men wounded, a total of 319 out of a strength of under 600.

The constant bombarding of the trenches by the French guns meant that many body parts of the killed and injured were scattered around the area. This was pretty unnerving to our Portuguese allies and it was decided to collect them as soon as the occasion allowed, so not to give them the slightest excuse to quit the field. A group of Rifleman on piquet duty, observed one day, a party of Portuguese carrying in a blanket one of their own wounded officers to the rear. Before they could reach safety however a cannon-ball whizzed between them and cut the poor unfortunate officer in two. They instantly dropped the blanket and ran for the cover of the trenches. Undaunted, one of the Riflemen on trench duty rushed forward, tipped what was left of the Officer on the ground and returned with the blanket. Observing the look on his comrades faces said, 'It's an ill wind that does nobody any good.' On 26th March, Rifleman John Horn of No. 2 company 3rd 95th was killed and Rifleman John Knight, killed in action.

The French wasted no time in countering the capture of fort Picurina, for the next morning they set their guns against it and destroyed part of the reversed defences built up by the new garrison, which that night were repaired once more. At the same time, the 2nd parallel was advanced, two old batteries filled in and three new ones built. The one on the left of Picurina was armed with twelve 24-pounders, with the task of breaching the south face of the La Trinidad bastion which was only some 580 yards distance. The other two were constructed in the gorge of the Picurina, so as to reduce the Santa Maria bastion from their three 24-pounders and eleven 18-pounders at 500 yards distance. A fourth battery was constructed in the 1st parallel, containing four howitzers, whose task it was to enfilade the ditch in front of the La Trinidad, so as to prevent working parties of the enemy completing a counter guard. However, the French sharpshooters on 30th March, were able to pour a destructive fire into one of the batteries erected in the gorge of the Picurina, from their covered way. A party of the 95th was sent into the trench in front of the battery and, from ranges of 250–350 yards was able to keep down the fire of these French marksmen.

It was around this time that a party of convalescents arrived from hospital just as the Rifles were being formed up on parade, amongst them was Sergeant Jackson, who had been absent from Captain Harry Smith's No. 3 company for some two years. Major O'Hare who had previously commanded this company called him out, 'Is that you Sergeant Jackson?' he said, 'And pray where have you been for the last two years? The company have seen a little fighting during your absence.' Jackson having found himself a nice comfortable safe job looking after stores in Lisbon, replied rather sheepishly, 'The Doctors would not allow me to leave the hospital, sir.' 'I am sorry to hear that, well all I can do is give you the choice of a court-martial for absenting yourself from duty without leave, or I can have your stripes taken off.' Jackson was no fool, forfeited his stripes, which were cut off by the Sergeant Major. Major O'Hare turned to the men, 'By God, I will not have these brave fellows commanded by skulkers.' Taking Jackson's stripes and sash, he handed them to Corporal Ballard, 'You will not disgrace these.'

The most hazardous duty for the Riflemen was reserved for the best shots, who had the unenviable task of running out in separate files to occupy a number of rifle pits that had been dug at night between the British batteries and walls of Badajoz. Each man had a rifle-pit to himself, from where he was to pick off as many of the enemy gunners, foolish enough to show themselves at the embrasures on the walls. As a result the French lost many a man during the siege by this method, due to the deadly accuracy of the Baker rifle. The Riflemen though didn't always have it all their own way. Some of the relieving Riflemen, on occasion, found the pit still containing its former occupant either dead or wounded. This was a problem, for the area excavated being too small for two men, increased the odds of the newcomer becoming a casualty. The known casualties during this time were: 27th March, Rifleman James Desbury No 5 company 3rd 95th killed; 28th March, Sergeant Bernard Sands No 2 company 3rd 95th and Rifleman William Wallby No 5 company also 3rd 95th both killed; 29th March Rifleman George Potts No 4 company 3rd 95th killed; 30th March, Riflemen Joseph Emees and John Gibson both No 5 company 3rd 95th are shown as being killed. It would appear from these casualties that the 3rd Battalion was providing men for the more risky duties at this time.

However, for all their success, trench duty of any sort was still loathed by the Light Division and in particular the Riflemen, who likened it to a cross between being a gravedigger and a game keeper, preferring their natural roll of keepers of the outposts. Working in the trenches was no picnic, whoever you were, for death, or injury, could come so swiftly out of the blue, working under a constant barrage of musketry from the French sharpshooters on the city's walls and the constant shelling. It is strange therefore, to note that those not directly involved in the siege were at times unable to resist visiting the trenches! Captain Thompson of the 88th, fitted into this category, having already survived a visit with another officer decided to return a couple of hours later, for which he paid the ultimate price, falling dead with a musket-ball to the head.

On 4th April, Lieutenant George Simmons of the 1st Battalion 95th was in command of a group of Riflemen with the specific task of reducing the fire of the enemy guns. They had the satisfaction of seeing their deadly fire inflict such severe casualties on the French gun teams, to such a degree, that at least three or four guns were prevented from firing a single shot all day!

During this duty, a French officer who was evidently a good shot, placed his huge cocked hat in the long grass near the covered way. By leaving it there he had hoped to fool the Riflemen into thinking that was where he was firing from, having moved a little distance from it. As he fired he had his men load for him. Simmons, also used to firing a rifle, found out where the Frenchman's shots were coming, called to one of his own men, telling him to rest his rifle upon his shoulder, so as to get a steadier aim. Pointing him in the direction of the concealed French officer, he told him to bide his time. Eventually the

Rifleman fired and no more was seen of the officer, but Simmons suffered a scorched ear from the flash of the rifle's pan. There was no doubting that their would-be assassin, was either killed or wounded, for his cocked hat remained in position for the rest of the day.

During the progression of the siege Majors Squire and Burgoyne, of the Engineers, had to report daily to their wounded commander, Colonel Fletcher, informing him of their progress, or lack of it. Philippon meanwhile was using similar tactics as in the siege of Ciudad Rodrigo, by placing men in the tower of the Cathedral, from where they observed the movements of the British working parties in the trenches. As soon as they observed the troops changing over, they alerted their artillery by ringing the bells, as they knew there would be double the men in the trenches and the more chance of inflicting casualties. Immediately a tremendous barrage would be directed at the siege trenches. William Lawrence witnessed first hand, the results of such an attack when a shell fell amongst the two working parties, which on exploding, killed or wounded around 30 men. The aftermath of such a successful bombardment, was most trying for the men, with legs, arms, heads and torn bodies scattered everywhere. James MacCarthy tells us in graphic detail, an injury to one of his men. 'On the working party returning to make way for the relief, the last man stood by my side waiting his turn to pass out of the trench, this was done alternately. I desired to let him through, at that instant a cannon-ball fell on him. It tore out his intestines entire from his right breast to his left hip and they hung against his thigh and legs as an apron, instantly he lost his balance and fell.' Captain Mulcaster of the Engineers, was struck in the neck by a round-shot that removed his head and part of his back and shoulders.

The only answer to countering this fire from the artillery was to have a man posted upon the outer part of the battery. Every shot fired in their direction was reported back to those digging in the trenches and they would immediately dive for cover. A large proportion of the allied artillery men were Portuguese who under their British officers, provided an excellent service to their comrades. Lieutenant John Kincaid of the Rifles, has given an amusing description of a Portuguese 'look-out man' at work in one of our big batteries. This man knew exactly the position of all the enemy's guns which could bear on the battery and when they fired, due notice of what was coming, whether a shot or a shell, by calling 'balla,' or 'bomba,' as the case might be. Sometimes the French fired a salvo from all arms, upon which 'he would throw himself down screaming out "Jesus! todas, todas," meaning everything.'

At the same time the trenches being worked by the men were at least knee deep in water. It was under such conditions that Major William Nicholas of the Engineers was able to swim across the inundation, formed by the French damming the Rivillas at the mill and inspect the ground. It built up to such an extent that it was gradually flooding the area of the proposed storming; close to the walls being breached.

*San Roque*

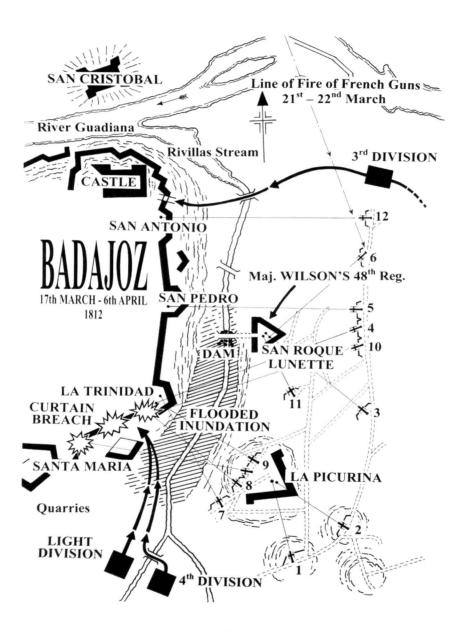

*Map of Badajoz*

Throughout all this activity the French continued to strengthen the fortress city ready for the inevitable attack. They completed a communication trench from the La Trinidad bastion, to the San Roque lunette. However, instead of digging it out, for time was against them, they cleverly masked their movements by the use of a screen which they made by fixing canvas to stout poles placed along the side of the road. As a result, men and equipment were able to pass behind this curtain unnoticed. The dam at the San Roque was further strengthened to enable the inundation to spread even wider and deeper, creating a formidable obstacle, with very little effort involved. The continuing rainfall added to this growing lake by the day. Had the siege continued for another week, it would have grown into such a formidable obstacle that it would have reduced the chance of the assault on the breaches ever taking place. New embrasures were cut in the castle walls to take additional guns, 24-pounders, which enabled them to fire into the British batteries and trenches.

Gradually, the walls of La Trinidad and the Santa Maria bastions gave way under the incessant pounding from the British siege guns, of which no less than 38 guns were brought into action enlarging the breaches. It became all too apparent to the defenders that this was to be the point of the assault and they countered this with a number of surprises of their own. On the morning of 5th April 1812 it was reported that an assault was now practicable.

# Assault and Capture of Badajoz

On 5th April 1812, after an intensive day long bombardment, it was declared that by evening the allied artillery would have successfully reduced the two breaches in the Santa Maria and La Trinidad bastions. Wellington inspected the works, and having already received the news that Soult had reached Llerena and, therefore, in a position to make a move against Badajoz, sent Hill's Division to delay him. A far more pressing scenario, however, concerned Marmont, whose present position meant he could advance against Ciudad Rodrigo. Wellington left the city under the command of General Carlos de Espana, with only temporary repairs having been made to it before advancing against Badajoz. He was not sure how reliable the Spanish General would be in holding out against Marmont, even though the latter had no siege train. Given ample food and funding to resist such an event, Espana, to Wellington's consternation had already started distributing the food for general use! This forced Wellington into ordering an all out assault on the breaches that night, though it was against his wishes. He would have much preferred to continue the siege, in the hope of eventually forcing Philippon, the Governor, to surrender, avoiding the severe loss of life and the further reduction of his army a storming would inevitably have brought. There would have been little chance of this happening, even if time had been on his side. Napoleon's orders were quite specific and to the point, no fort was to surrender without a fight to the bitter end, no matter what the consequences! The French troops knew this all too well and the inevitable retribution that would follow should they fail. Wellington's men on the other hand were elated by the news, this soon changed when around 4 o'clock word was circulated that the assault had been called off. Colonel Fletcher, Wellington's Chief Engineer, had recovered enough from an earlier wound to inspect the breaches to be stormed and was not happy with what he found. He recommended that a third breach should be made in the curtain, the wall linking the two reduced bastions. The men were livid at being denied the chance to avenge their comrades, who had been killed or wounded during the siege. They took their frustration out on the engineers, who were mercilessly abused for the change of plan. When the reason for the delay was eventually explained and that it would take place the following night the mood thankfully changed. Wellington postponed the assault until 6th April and under the cover of darkness ordered 14 howitzers to be moved to a position right of the first parallel. Here they could concentrate their fire on the curtain which was reported to be a weak spot. The following morning, the artillery with every available piece of ordnance at their disposal bombarded the curtain wall. This third breach was going to be of vital importance. If successful the attack would allow the stormers to take the defenders of the two breached bastions in the rear. Though the thinking behind this delay was sound, it would also be of equal significance to the defenders, for they were given a further 24 hours to repair and strengthen what they knew was obviously going to be the main point of the attack. The breach made in 1811 by the British, had been repaired and strengthened and it was now believed to be the strongest part of the towns' defences, while the castle had also received extra guns.

Wellington had originally ordered that the Light and 4th Divisions would storm the breaches on the 5th, now kept to the same format for the rearranged assault on the 6th, even though the 4th Division was on trench duty. The paragraphs in his orders relating to the Light and 4th Divisions are transcribed as follows:

No 13 The advance of the divisions must be formed into firing parties and storming parties. The firing parties must be spread along the rest of the glacis to keep down the fire of the enemy while the men of the storming party who (carry bags) will enter the covered way at the Place d'Armes under the breached face of the bastion of the Trinidad those attached to the 4th Division on its right those to the Light Division on its left looking from the trenches or the camp.

No 14 The storming party of the advance of the Light Division will then descend into the ditch and turning to its left storm the breach in the flank of the bastion of the Santa Maria, while the 4th Division will likewise descend into the ditch and storm the breach in the face of the bastion of the La Trinidad. The firing parties are to follow immediately in rear of their respective storming parties.

No 15 The heads of the two Divisions will follow their advanced guard keeping ready together but they will not advance beyond the shelter afforded by the quarries on the left of the road, till they will have seen the heads of the advance guards ascend the breaches. They will then move forward to storm in double quick time.

For Wellington to have altered the orders, this would only have caused further delay, and no doubt upset the men of the 4th Division who were fired up ready for action. General Colville's division would have to assault the La Trinidad bastion on a narrow front, west of the Rivillas stream, as well as the new breach being made in the curtain, to its left, which had not been in the original orders. The Light Division was to concentrate their attack solely on the Santa Maria bastion, but unforeseen circumstances would cause great confusion in the ditch. Each division was to provide 500 [1] men for the storming party, with 12 ladders, along with a party carrying hay-bags. The counterscarp was still intact, so it was quite clear that the men would have a long drop into the ditch and the hay bags would be a great benefit in breaking their fall. Wellington's orders were for the two divisions to advance in columns of brigade, with a Portuguese brigade placed between the two British brigades. Colonel Andrew Barnard of the Rifles, was given the command of the Light Division in place of General Vandeleur, who had still not recovered from the wound he received at Ciudad Rodrigo. Colonel George Elder the commanding officer of the 3rd Portuguese Caçadores, an ex-Rifleman, was appointed second in command of the division.

Lieutenant Harvest, of the 43rd Regiment had been given the honour of commanding the forlorn hope [2] of the Light Division, Lieutenant William Johnstone of the 95th Rifles having failed in his quest for the same duty. However, to offset Johnstone's disappointment, he was given the command of a rope party of six men. Their task was to precede the forlorn hope with ropes that had been looped so they could throw them over the chevaux-de-frise so as to pull it from the top of the Santa Maria breach! This mission was no more than a mini forlorn hope in all but name. It is obvious from the start that it was only a token measure to placate Lieutenant Johnstone, otherwise, three rope parties would have been required to confront each breach. [3] Lieutenant Johnstone's group, being the sole representatives of any rope party, and the fact he was given only six men for such a dangerous undertaking it is plain to see it was nothing more than a suicide mission. However, Lieutenant Johnstone would have had no problem attracting volunteers to join him in such a dangerous task, for he was one of the most popular officers in the Rifles.

It has been impossible to find any specific evidence, or facts, as to the actual break down or numbers involved for the forlorn hope, or indeed how they fared in the assault. Taking into consideration the numbers involved for the same duty at Ciudad Rodrigo and that Badajoz was by far a bigger nut to crack, we have come to the conclusion it numbered between 25 and 40 men. We found that Riflemen who left an account of their service during the war and stated they were part of the forlorn hope clearly were not, but instead, members of the storming party. There seems to be very little to distinguish between stormers, forlorn hope or rope party, the expected survival rate for all these duties was pretty slim, as they were all equally fraught with danger. As things turned out, nearly every attack made on the breaches throughout that terrible assault, was a 'forlorn hope' in its own right.

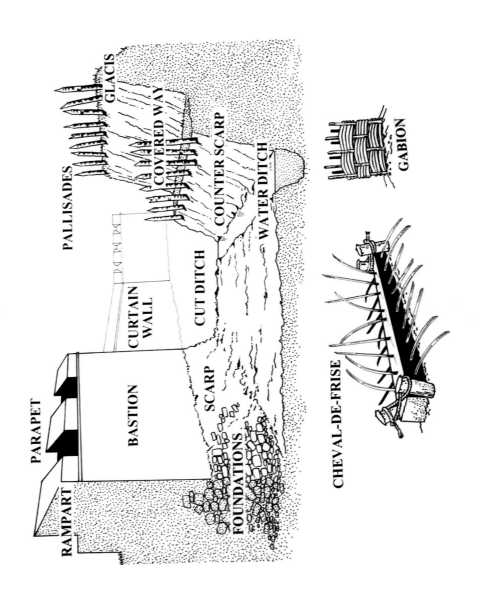

*Glossary of siege warfare*

Bugler William Green and Rifleman Edward Costello both of the 1st Battalion 95th Rifles and Rifleman John Lowe of the 2nd Battalion, all state they volunteered to serve with the forlorn hope, but as we will see this is not true. Bugler Green put his name forward for this duty and lots were drawn as to who would go, only two buglers were allowed from the '100' volunteers from each Regiment taking part; this confirms he was with the 'storming party'. Green's name came out of the hat but his success was short lived, for Bugler West, not satisfied at having been on the forlorn hope at Ciudad Rodrigo, offered Bugle Major Daniel Kelly two dollars to be allowed to take Green's place. The Bugle Major foolishly accepted the bribe, much to Green's annoyance and he challenged the Bugle Major's decision. Kelly reacted by threatening to confine him to the guard tent. William Green was not going to take this lying down and reported Bugle Major Kelly's action to John Kincaid the Acting Adjutant. Buglers came under the direct jurisdiction and authority of the Adjutant, so it was not out of place for him to be confronted on such a matter. Kincaid took the Bugle Major to task for taking bribes and left him in no uncertain terms as to the seriousness of his action and, that if such an act was ever brought to his attention again, he would have his stripes removed. Kincaid restored Green to his rightful position in the storming party.

Such an action could have back-fired on Green, for he would have been at the Bugle Major's mercy for years to come; circumstances however came to his rescue. Bugle Major Kelly was discharged the following year due to length of service and the events, as we shall see that night, altered the whole outcome of Green's army career. The 100 volunteers for the Rifles storming party, would have been chosen from all three battalions present in roughly similar numbers. The 2nd Battalion therefore with only two companies present, would have been significantly decreased in strength, though all Rifle companies were under strength at this time, with on average, of 90 men to a company.

Prior to moving off the Riflemen received a double allowance of rum, no doubt this was most welcome, the raw spirit helping to steady the nerves. Rifleman Costello was positioned on the right of the front section of the stormers when Major O'Hare arrived with Captain Jones, a most distinctive sounding Welshman of the 52nd Regiment, the commander of their stormers, Captain Fergusson being in charge of the 43rd men. Costello was standing close enough to hear O'Hare and Jones talking, observing at the same time that they were two of the ugliest men he knew, but a better pair of soldiers never stood before the muzzle of a Frenchman's gun. Captain Jones said, 'Well O'Hare, what do you think of tonight's work?' The Major seemed in rather low spirits. 'I don't know. Tonight I think, will be my last!'

'Tut, Tut, man!' retorted Jones, 'I have the same sort of feeling, but keep it down with a drop of this,' and handed his calabash to the Major. It is clear as fearless a character as O'Hare was, he was resigned that night to his fate, for earlier he had stated to Lieutenant Simmons of the Rifles that he would be, 'a Colonel, or cold meat in the morning!' While Captain Jones had declared to a fellow officer, Captain Dobbs, that he would be, 'a man or a mouse that night!' It was at this point Sergeant Patrick Fleming of the Rifles, a faithful supporter of O'Hare, who was still serving in the major's old company, came up and informed him that a ladder party was wanted. O'Hare ordered Sergeant Fleming to take the right file from the leading sections. Fleming immediately tapped Costello and his front rank man on the shoulder and four other Riflemen for the ladder party. The delay with the ladders at Ciudad Rodrigo, was not going to be allowed to repeat itself, this time; they were going to be under the direct supervision of British troops. As each division was to have only 12 ladders it would appear that the 43rd and 52nd Regiments were allotted this duty for the Light Division stormers. For some unknown reason, the 43rd ladder party was short of men: was it with one of its ladders that the Riflemen were issued?

These Riflemen besides carrying a ladder also had a hay bag and a rifle, while on either side of Costello's ladder party, two men were carrying hatchets, their task being to cut down anything that might bar the way, or delay them from reaching the ditch. This is the only time in the whole of our research that we have come across the mention of a 95th Rifles' ladder party, therefore it stands to reason they had not been previously tasked to such a duty. If they had, then they would have moved up much earlier with them and not waited until the last minute. It is strange that they also carried a hay bag, though it seems to have been the case with the other regiment's ladder parties. The ladders were reported as being much longer and heavier than at Ciudad Rodrigo, having been made from green timber. Freshly felled trees would be full of moisture adding considerably to their weight. Each man in the storming party had been ordered, prior to reaching the point from where they were to launch the attack, to collect a hay bag from a pile made ready for the assault. [4] On reaching the ditch they were to throw them into the dark void in an attempt to break their fall and prevent possible broken legs when jumping into the unknown, while at the same time covering some of the obstacles in the ditch. To assist with the main assaults on the breaches two diversionary attacks were also to be made; Power's Portuguese Brigade would threaten a movement against the fort at the bridge-head at the Oliveca Gate. Leith's 5th Division, who up to this point had not been involved in the siege, had been ordered to try and escalade the river bastion of the San Vincente, [5] positioned at the extreme north-west part of the town defences, an area that had received little or no attention during the siege. The Portuguese Brigade belonging to this division would attack the Pardaleras Fort, which was connected to the town by a trench protected by high earth banks.

Picton was not happy at being left out of these arrangements and in his usual brusque manner made his feelings known to Wellington. The problem was how he could be expected to make a worthwhile contribution to the diversionary attacks made for the benefit of the 4th and Light Divisions? The latter's involvement would of course be a sore point. The rivalry between these two divisions was legendary, though Picton would have expected to gain the upper hand now that Craufurd was out of the picture. Picton inspected the ground on which the Castle had been built observing that it would be possible to mount an attack. He now made a strong case for his division to be allowed to attempt an escalade, arguing that while the defence of the breaches would be taking up most of the defender's force, they would be further depleted by opposing the false attacks. The castle was already thought of as a naturally strong position and would therefore not have required such a large a number of men to defend it. Picton had not taken the risk involved for such a task lightly, his reconnaissance had singled out that the walls were lower in places, due to being built on the natural rock formations, conforming to the irregularities these produced. This attack also had the advantage of being a complete surprise, for it had not been considered before. Picton's division however would have to cross the Rivillas stream near the ruins of a mill that spanned it. No action had been directed at this position during the siege, as it was protected by the San Pedro bastion and in easy range of the numerous cannon positioned in the castle which overlooked it. Wellington finally conceded to Picton's request, either to keep him from the constant badgering or because the argument made sense; whatever the reason, it was a victory making decision.

The 4th Division, besides being given the task of attacking the Trinidad, was also to attack the new breach, but they had also been providing the working party and guard in the trenches. This duty consisted of about 800 men each night working in the trenches while a large number provided a covering party. The 48th Regiment, of their division, also provided a detachment 300 strong, under the command of Major Wilson to storm the San Roque Lunette. This gave the 4th Division a total force for the assault of around 3,500 men, while the Light Divisions strength was nearer 3,000. Wellington produced, an overlong, but detailed order on 6th April running into some 26 paragraphs for the assault on Badajoz, down to the very last detail. The timings were to be staggered, to allow the separate forces enough time to arrive from the various distances they were camped, to enable them to reach the point at which they would move off to their position of attack.

*Outer walls of Badajoz*

For Wellington to get the mass of his troops in place and at the right time without showing his hand too soon, needed careful planning. Therefore, the distances between the starting points of each division to its objective, had to be taken into consideration. Wellington's calculations worked, to a degree, although Picton's Division was compromised, as we shall see, before the rearranged assault time of 10 o'clock. The 5th Division would be over an hour late in starting their attack. The French were aware of what was happening as they had seen the siege ladders being brought up.

The stage was now set to assault and capture Badajoz. Wellington was confident his plan would succeed, while Philippon, the commander of Badajoz, was equally determined that it would not. It was because of the full focus by both commanders in concentrating on the breaches that the brilliant success of the diversionary assaults was allowed to take place resulting in total defeat for the French. Nothing can be taken away from both attackers or the defenders' resolve to achieve their aim, the ingenuity of the French was a master plan for the age, while the determination of the assaulting divisions was glorious, stubborn and brave.

Captain Alexander Cameron and Lieutenant Kincaid were assigned the duty of covering party to the stormers of the Light Division, they were to be positioned on the glacis to give essential covering fire to the attack. They had already performed this duty at Ciudad Rodrigo and were in no doubt as to its importance and the difficulties that it would involve. These two officers reconnoitred, in the cold light of day, the ground that they would be expected to cross. By not leaving anything to chance they were able to reach the exact spot on the glacis in total darkness without being discovered. Captain Shaw 43rd Regiment also walked the route prior to the evening's events, so as to be familiar with the ground the 43rd would cover.

The night of 6th April 1812 was dry and cloudy, with a thick mist coming up from the river and stream. The ramparts and trenches were unusually quiet, while in Badajoz lights flittered here and there, the sentinels could be heard proclaiming from time to time, 'Sentinelle, Garde a vous.' More, one suspects, in assurance to the inhabitants and defenders that the defences had not been compromised under cover of darkness. Which the men translated as, 'All is well in Badahoo!'

By all accounts and reports Badajoz was considered to be one of the strongest and impregnable defensive works in the Peninsula. But, it would not be until after the fall of the city, that the full extent of Philippon's defences could be appreciated, for he had used the expertise of his Chief Engineer, Lamare, to the full. What a hopeless and futile task it turned out, that Wellington had set the Light and 4th Divisions! Besides cutting off the breaches on both sides by entrenchments, parapets of earth and sand bags, woolpacks [6] had been placed behind them. The engineer had also concealed numerous mines and barrels of powder at the foot of the counterscarp, [7] these then connected at some considerable distance to the ramparts by covered trains, ready to be ignited when required. The mines were hidden on the near side of the ditch in the dead ground that Wellington's artillery had been unable to reach. At the bottom of the ditch and the foot of the breaches, the engineers put in place all manner of obstacles to delay and break up the assaulting formations, from up turned barrows, to broken carts and wood staves sharpened to deadly points. Even a damaged boat had been pressed into service, dangerously linked by rope entanglements and piles of broken gabions and fascines. The slopes of the breaches had been covered with crows feet, lethal metal spikes which the blacksmiths could easily manufacture in a way, that however they were thrown, always left at least one spike sticking up. The breaches were also protected by heavy planks of wood, studded with numerous six inch nails and spikes. They were not solidly fixed, but hung by one end from ropes under the chevaux-de-frise. This allowed them to move about on the rubble of the slope preventing the attackers from gaining a firm footing. In some places, harrows had been fixed into the ground along side doors, studded with deadly spikes, all set into the slope. At the top of the breach was the ultimate obstacle of death mentioned previously, the 'chevaux-de-frise,' [8] formed of razor sharp cavalry sword blades set in foot square beams of wood and chained down into a ridged, impenetrable barricade, one observer comparing them to a porcupine. These swords originally belonged to a large body of Spanish cavalry who surrendered in March 1811. After having navigated all these obstacles Lieutenant Johnstone and his six Riflemen were then expected to pull this formidable structure free with their ropes! The French flooded the centre of the ditch and unbeknown to the British, had deepened its centre to some six or seven feet and if this was not bad enough, let the contents of the town's sewer system run into this channel. Besides all these delaying devices the assaulting troops had to survive the torrent of shot, shell, grenades and all other manner of missiles and combustibles hurled down from the walls. [9]

To defend the breaches, Philippon had placed 700 men from the Light and Grenadier Companies of each Battalion, in the garrison, plus four Fusilier Companies of the 103rd Line Regiment to man the curtain and bastions of Santa Maria and La Trinidad. [10] This meant the troops defending the breaches, amounted to around 1,200 men, as a reserve a battalion of the French 88th Regiment was placed behind in the cathedral square from where they could easily rush to the support of the defenders whereever a weakness was reported. Two Hessian battalions had the task of holding the Castle, lunette of San Roque and the San Pedro bastion. The bastions and curtains from San Juan to San Vincente were occupied and defended by another three French battalions. Due to the number of French casualties sustained throughout the siege, the total available force to defend Badajoz was around 4,000 men. With practically half this number involved in defending the breaches meant that the positions being defended by the remaining troops would be rather sparse in places. The castle, a formidable obstacle, had as Picton thought, only a small garrison of some 250 men with which to defend it, two Hessian companies and one French.

Originally the assault had been ordered to take place at 7.30 p.m., but was put off until 10 o'clock, as Wellington's force would not be ready in time, which meant the siege batteries slackened their fire after dark. It was reported they were firing blanks by the time the Light and 4th Divisions were marching to their positions. [11] This delay allowed the defenders time to repair and strengthen the areas damaged by the allied bombardment. But what was more significant, the final fixing of the trains to set the mines off, along with a number of items which could only be placed on the slopes at the last minute and the final fixing of the chevaux-de-frise. A concentrated bombardment, even in the dark, on these defences would have greatly disrupted the defenders ability to put their final preparations in place. The daylight bombardment would have given the gunners a rough idea of what to aim for and if nothing else it would have kept French heads down.

*The walls near the Trinidad breach*

The Light Division marched in silence to their allotted positions of assembly. Through the ravine to the left of the Pardaleras hill, they assembled near a small bridge over a stream where they ate a final meal from their haversacks. The order of dress was; without stocks and packs and with trousers rolled up to the knee. [12] It was here that the roll was called and an unexpected incident occurred in the Rifles. Lieutenant Bell [13] of the 1st Battalion, who only hours before had been the example of a strong and healthy officer, suddenly reported he was ill. Major Cameron, all too aware to what had happened gave him an ultimatum that if he was to return to camp he might as well resign his commission. Undaunted, Bell returned to the camp and lay on his bed. This is the first time in all our research that we have come upon such an open and shut case of cowardice in the Rifles. This only came to light because Lieutenant Gairdner of the same battalion reported the incident in a letter home to his father. [14] Colonel M'Leod chose this time to address the 43rd, being one of the main columns of the Light Division; he expressed his greatest confidence in the outcome of the attack and finished by repeating, 'that he left it to the honour of all persons present to preserve discipline, and not to commit any cruelty on the defenceless inhabitants of the town!' Each Division had been ordered to leave 1,000 men in the quarries as a reserve; all indications are that for the Light Division this was provided by the two regiments of the 1st and 3rd Caçadores under Colonel Elder and some companies of Riflemen from the 95th.

The two attacking brigades of the Light Division were formed in close column of companies, with the left hand companies in front; this was about 300 yards from the ditch under the command of Colonel Barnard. The covering or firing party as Wellington styled it, consisting of Major Cameron's four 1/95th companies, the left wing of the battalion, formed up in front of the stormers. They were to be the most advanced troops at this stage, with orders upon reaching the edge of the covered-way, to extend to the left, along the glacis where they were to keep down the fire from the ramparts. The storming party was made up of 100 volunteers from each Regiment of the Light Division, under the command of Major Peter O'Hare of the Rifles. The Rifle Officers volunteering for this duty were: Captain Crampton, 1st Battalion, Captain Hart; Lieutenants Bedell, Manners, Coane and M'Gregor, 2nd Battalion and Captain Diggle of the 3rd Battalion.

Sir William Cope in his History of the Rifle Brigade states that volunteers from the 95th for the forlorn hope came from the 2nd Battalion, all non-commissioned officers (NCOs). This is questionable but not impossible; the second battalion only had two companies present at Badajoz. Those listed by Cope as being in the forlorn hope were: Sergeants Cairns, Fairfoot wounded, Taggart wounded and Kennedy wounded. Corporals Coward wounded, Derby killed, Cordell wounded (the paylists only show a Corporal McCardle as killed) and Nesbit (the musters show he was killed). Sergeant Fairfoot, [15] was serving with the 1st Battalion. The fact that only one of these NCOs escaped injury is an indicator in their favour to being part of the forlorn hope, but of course they are just as likely to have been wounded or killed during the storming. Fairfoot eventually reached the rank of Quarter Master. His statement of service mentions he was part of the forlorn hope at Badajoz. He was certainly in and around the area at the time.

It is hard to fathom the logic behind the employment of so many senior NCOs of the 2nd Battalion being allowed to take part in such a dangerous duty. The command structure of the two companies would be severely disrupted, as the odds favoured them either being killed or wounded. [16] The only practical reason we can come up with for this undertaking is, being virtually two independent companies and not attached to either of the other two battalions, they were out on a limb with no specific duty being allocated to them for the assault. It is also questionable why Wellington chose to risk so many lives from the Light Division. That was his most accomplished and specialist Division in the whole of the army and to replace his light troops was not a simple matter as it would be for line regiments, unless he depleted the light companies from the other divisions. We have already seen how he had originally spared Picton's 3rd Division, due no doubt, to the severe casualties received at Ciudad Rodrigo, though this fact was lost on Picton.

Even the Rifles were surprised to find the division was singled out to be part of the storming, as they had performed this service at Ciudad Rodrigo. They would have expected to be excused the duty at Badajoz and that it would, therefore, be the turn of one of the other divisions.

The 3rd Division on the night of 6th April, was under the command of General Kempt, as according to Napier, Picton had fallen in camp or had not been warned in time as to the changes. According to other accounts though, it is also reported as, 'having received a wound in the foot' at the beginning of the action. Colonel Williams was assigned the duty of covering their advance, with seven light companies of the division, which included the three Headquarter companies of the 60th Rifles [17] under the command of Lieutenant Colonel Fitzgerald. Colonel Williams, having taken the circuitous route, pressed on quietly till he reached the Rivillas stream. To add further strength in defence of these vulnerable bastions, the French had flooded the approaches by damming the Rivillas stream. The bridge at the San Roque gate had also been built up; here the accumulation of water resembled a small lake which lay below the bastions of San Pedro and La Trinidad. It had also been allowed to over flow into a ditch in front of San Pedro, here a deep channel had been cut which allowed a narrow but deep water course to form in front of the La Trinidad bastion. This gave the broad dry ditch, a narrow wet one sunk below the counterscarp. [18] By crossing the mill dam, one by one and wading through the water, which here was only knee deep, the men were able to reach the opposite bank. In rear of the 60th Riflemen followed the Light Companies, with Colonel Williams and behind them came in succession the brigades of Kempt, Campbell and Champalimond. Just after the 60th had crossed the stream a French sentry on the covered way discharged his musket and the Riflemen, believing they had been discovered, returned fire. The garrison now alerted, sent a number of fireballs into the night and at the same time returned the 60th's fire with a vengeance; some of the men shot near the stream fell in and drowned. This action caused Kempt to abandon the previous plans and so he ordered a full scale assault, some 15–20 minutes before the cathedral clock struck ten, zero hour for Wellington's plan to begin. After the French opened fire on the 60th, the Light Companies and the rest of the 3rd Division advanced led by Captain MacCarthy, their guide, who was actually unsure of the ground and had to keep advancing ahead of the brigades to convince himself he was on the right track. It was around this time Picton is reported as having been wounded in the foot and General Kempt continued in command of the Division. Major Burgoyne, of the engineers, brought up the stormers and ladder men prior to Kempt's advance. On Captain MacCarthy reaching the palisades he found the ladders had been left there and that this obstruction was still in place.

He shouted, 'Down with the paling!' The men and officers rushed to the wooden stakes, rocking them back and forth to loosen them, pushing them over and picking up the ladders headed for the walls of the castle.

First, the ladder party had to ford the Rivillas stream under a blazing fire from the castle and San Pedro bastion. The palisades on the opposite bank of the stream were broken down in the general rush of men, who eventually arrived at the castle. Here the stormers found it most difficult, due to the steep slopes and struggled with their 30 feet ladders, but eventually they put them against the castle walls. MacCarthy's ladder men however, had put them in the wrong place for escalading and to their astonishment found they were too short. They were also open to a most severe fire from the castle. MacCarthy fell at this point on top of another man who had been shot at the same time, sustaining a compound fracture of his right thigh. This movement twisted the bottom part of his leg, so his heel was now facing to the front! A private picked him up and placed him on his back, carried him out of the direct line of fire, only to place him in a position that was even more exposed! The men of the 94th now came storming up the ladders, all eager to get into the castle, but not all of these could hold their weight and snapped, hurling them onto their comrades below, many landing on the bayonets of the raised muskets. The French were able to push some of the ladders back from the walls with poles and they came crashing down into the ditch, a consequence of which the assault failed. What was meant to have been a surprise attack in concert with the main assaulting divisions was now a complete disaster. General Kempt had been wounded and was being carried back to the camp, passing Picton, who was rushing to take command. He reached the castle just as the men were falling back from the failed attack.

Private William Brown of the 45th Regiment, who was part of this attack, considered because his Regiment formed up on the right of the division, that they should be called the forlorn hope, highlighting the enormity and importance such men put on this duty. It would seem from this statement, that a forlorn hope from the 3rd Division to escalade the castle was not thought of as necessary.

The Light and 4th Divisions, hearing the 3rd Division go into action, remained silent waiting for the allotted hour. Major Wilson with his 300 men of the 48th Regiment jumped the gun, due, no doubt, to being carried away by hearing Picton's division going into action. Leith's Division, also due at 10 o'clock, stalled, for they were still waiting for the arrival of their ladder and hay-bag parties. The officer in charge had lost his way along the bank of the Guadiana. Leith, therefore, had little option but to wait patiently for them to arrive. As a result it was over an hour before they were able to go into action. If they had attacked at the given hour there was a good chance that many of the casualties in the Light and 4th Divisions would have been greatly reduced.

Wellington's plans were starting to unravel around him, confirming that even the best laid plans can go wrong. He was still confident that the two divisions about to go into action against the breaches would succeed. The outcome was that only the main attack on the breaches by the Light and 4th Divisions actually took place at the allotted time. Major Wilson's 300 men of the 48th Regiment, having rushed the San Roque lunette ahead of schedule, cheering for all they were worth, attacked it with such gusto and violence that they were able to take the place with very little opposition. It might not have proved as easy had they attacked at the right time. The French who made good their escape, now swelled the ranks of the defenders in Badajoz.

The 1st Brigade of the Light Division followed their storming party, less the four companies of the 1st Battalion 95th Rifles, under Cameron. All indications are that these four companies remained positioned on the glacis throughout the assault. [19] Their specific task was to reduce the defenders' fire as much as possible, to give the stormers any chance of success. To abandon this duty and advance to the ditch would have caused greater casualties and be a complete waste of valuable covering fire, though it went against Wellington's strict orders. Some historians, however, have suggested they became part of the general attack. Cameron, on moving to his position, was able to bring the head of his wing of Riflemen to the very spot required on the edge of the glacis, where they then extended without making a sound. As each man came up he silently lay down pushing the muzzle of his rifle through the palisades [20] which had been fixed into place along the outer edge of the glacis and covered-way. From here it was possible for the Rifleman to see the silhouetted figures of the French, each man now able to pick out his intended target, no more than 60 yards away. Cameron returned to Barnard and said, 'Now my men are ready shall I begin?' 'No certainly not,' said Barnard. 'I am still waiting for the ladders to come up.' The sound of the 3rd Division going into action probably caused Cameron to think he should open fire. The first the enemy knew of the Rifles' position on the glacis, would be when they fired upon the defenders, after the signal for the assault was given.

The 52nd Regiment's ladder party was under the command of Ensign Gawler, who was being escorted to the ditch and breach by Lieutenant de Salaberrey, an Engineer officer. They had a number of crowbar men with them; whether this was as well as axe men is unclear, though we would believe there was probably only a handful to each division, for according to the list of tools and equipment issued for the siege, there were only ten, six-feet and ten, five-feet-six inch, crow levers (crow-bars). The Light Division ladder party had only proceeded a short distance, when they heard voices coming from their right. Thinking it was the enemy they halted; putting down his end of the ladder, Rifleman Costello immediately cocked his rifle in readiness. 'It's alright!' came a muffled cry, 'It is only the stormers of the 4th Division coming to join us.' Colonel M'Leod of the 43rd was incensed by the amount of noise coming from the direction of the 4th Division. The Light Division arrived behind the large quarry only 300 yards from the breaches, in total silence, with only a small stream separating it from the 4th Division. A voice could be heard coming from that direction giving orders about the ladders; so loud they were sure the enemy was bound to have heard. Colonel M'Leod sent an officer immediately to them, to say he would report this lapse in orders to Wellington. This took place around 9.30 p.m. and was probably the reason why Barnard had to wait for the ladder men to arrive. The Light Division stormers expected that, at any minute, the French would make a move against them and crept quietly through the broken palisades of the covered way. The 52nd ladder men were the first to arrive and slid their six ladders down into the ditch against the counterscarp just in front of the salient. This was actually part of the proper right face of the unfinished ravelin. One ladder had been put into a large hole making it considerably shorter, while one or two of the other ladders were actually placed in the water, which at this point was only about a foot deep. The 43rd ladder men only managed to put three of their ladders into the ditch when all hell broke loose; they were exactly opposite the centre breach. The positioning of these ladders was probably the reason why so many of the Light Division stormers made for the centre breach first of all. In the dark and mayhem they joined the 4th Division stormers who had been given the task of assaulting this particular breach. Ensign Gawler and Lieutenant de Salaberrey with about a dozen men had already descended into the ditch when suddenly a blinding blaze of light illuminated the whole of the approaches. The French Colonel Lamare, remarked how dark it was and that it favoured the stormers. As a result the attacking columns were able to arrive on the glacis without being seen. The head of the columns managed to leap into the ditch and arrive at the foot of the ruins before the clinking of arms gave them away. The French threw a number of fireballs into the ditch; one of these the 52nd men was able to put out by shovelling some earth over it. They were soon followed by many more and a number of explosions of all description was the signal for the enemy to spring their surprise attack. Three of the Riflemen, carrying the ladder with Costello, were instantly killed. The weight of the partially supported ladder knocked him backwards and pinned him to the ground with the hay-bag on his chest. This severe fire prevented the 43rd men from getting all their ladders in place; this confirmed that Costello and his fellow Riflemen had to have been with them.

For Costello to be knocked backwards and trapped by the ladder, meant that he would have been carrying the ladder at shoulder height, which seems logical considering he was also carrying a hay-bag and rifle.

The ladder men in the ditch, were now joined by Lieutenant Harvest's forlorn hope and Lieutenant Johnstone's rope party. They all rushed forward and on reaching what they believed to be the breach, stormed up it, only to find that a sheer drop was before them. This mistake was to prove fatal, as they were instantly swept away. Johnstone fell severely wounded and Lieutenant Harvest was killed, how many of the forlorn hope men survived we will never know. Johnstone, though severely wounded, managed to drag himself clear out of the immediate line of fire to a sheltered spot in part of the ruined ravelin. From here he could only witness the hopeless struggle that was taking place all around, now that the stormers had arrived.

As soon as the forlorn hope rushed to the ladders Barnard shouted, 'Now Cameron' and his four companies of Riflemen sent a terrific rifle fire against the French, many of their rifle balls finding a target. Major O'Hare, advancing with his 300 strong storming party, headed for the same position as the forlorn hope. They came charging past Costello and then instantly started falling all around him from the hail of shot and shell that was sent against them. A couple of these men fell on Costello, adding to the weight of the ladder, which pinned him down even further. The blood pouring from these dead men soaked the trapped Rifleman, who cried out for assistance to get free of the ladder. Bugler Green who advanced with Major O'Hare and his comrades in the Rifle section of the storming party, when nearing the wide ditch, could see those ahead of him throwing their hay bags, then disappear into it themselves. It was only at this point that the enormity of what he was about to do hit home, his immediate thought being, 'You will be in hell before daylight!' Coming to the edge of the ditch holding his bugle in his left hand, he was in the act of throwing his hay-bag when a French musket-ball entered his left thigh, Green dropped like a stone; this was just short of the edge of the ditch. The ball had gone clean through, causing him very little pain but had continued into his left wrist where it embedded itself into the bone.

The 4th Division, consisting of the 7th, 23rd, 40th and 48th Regiments, having made similar arrangements for their own advance, met with disaster as soon as they entered the ditch. Private William Lawrence, of the 40th Regiment, had volunteered with his comrades for the ladder party; they had been quartered in Badajoz after the Talavera campaign and knew the layout of the town and where to go for plunder. They had a specific jewellers already in mind. The thought that they might not survive the assault was the last thing to cross their minds. The 4th Division ladder party, according to Lawrence, was also required to carry a hay-bag.

On reaching the ditch, a French sentry hearing some movement, called out a couple of times, and receiving no reply, a shower of canister and grapeshot, along with a number of fireballs, was sent at random in their direction. Private Harding, Lawrence's comrade, was killed and he lost contact with Private George Bowden, his other friend. Lawrence received two small shrapnel shots in the left knee and a musket shot hit him in the side, but he was saved from mortal injury by it passing through his water canteen. His wounds were not enough to impede his progress and he continued on towards the ditch, putting the ladder into place and descended, with men falling all around him. The leading sections of their storming column had jumped into the ditch without waiting for the ladders and found it had been flooded to a depth far greater than expected. Around 20 men of the Fusiliers were immediately drowned, while others on falling into the water where it was less deep, got trampled into the mud, and some 30 from their Portuguese Brigade were also drowned. This water obstacle caused the 4th Division stormers to turn to their left where it became shallower and join up with the men of the Light Division. All were soon mixed together and making for the same objective, the earthwork to their front, and in the dark, like the Light Division stormers, thought it was the breach. Swarming up this, they were immediately struck by a fierce volley of French musketry and canister shot, which caused what was left of the Light and 4th Division stormers to fall back in total confusion, behind the unfinished ravelin. The officers called out to continue moving towards the walls by coming around the side of the ravelin. Rushing the breach, they were then halted by the chevaux-de-frise and were instantly fired upon from the deep entrenchment behind it. Many, in an adrenalin fused frenzy, tried in vain to remove this obstacle with their bare hands. Private Lawrence, as a result, received a severe cut from the sword blades. From this we can see that the 4th Division did manage to reach the top of the breach, which we assume was in the curtain wall, before moving onto the Trinidad bastion with no mention of any rope men.

The 4th Division stormers, and those men belonging to the Light Division who had joined them were eventually forced to retreat. With his battalion now coming up, Lawrence joined them and continued making charges at the La Trinidad from the ditch. Lawrence, with his wounds bleeding so badly, now began to feel weak from the loss of blood. His comrades urged him to go to the rear, but this was easier said than done. It was with great difficulty that he scrambled over the numerous dead and dying bodies of the stormers. The ladders were a tangle of dead and dying men, with many caught up in the rungs, which made climbing out of the trench with his lacerated hands most difficult. Finally Lawrence reached the edge of the ditch and up onto the glacis, but was only able to crawl away on his hands and knees from the carnage.

It was in this manner that he came upon the Duke of Wellington and his staff, who seeing his condition, asked what Regiment he belonged to. Lawrence, told them the 40th and that he had been part of the forlorn hope. (Another reference of a stormer stating he was a forlorn hope man.) Sergeant Hamilton of the 43rd, is another to state that he volunteered for the same duty, but it is also clear that he was a stormer. Did these ladder and hay bag men regard their duty equal to the forlorn hope?

From this position, the men could clearly see the enemy, who had massed numerous shells at strategic points along the wall, which they lit, dropping them into the ditch where they exploded amongst the massed ranks below, taking ten or twelve men at a time to meet their maker, and many more an appointment with a surgeon. Pinned down in the ditch, the men were desperately frustrated at being in such a hopeless position, full of anger at not being able to repay the defenders for their predicament and the death of so many of their comrades. Once the ditch was full of men the French set off their mines, which caused sheer carnage amongst the stormers. Those who survived were galvanised into continuing to assault the breach time after time, as soon as an officer or NCO gathered a large enough group to climb it again. Bugler Green, by this time, feeling faint from loss of blood, was joined by Sergeant Robert Fairfoot, a friend of his, and one of the forlorn hope who was on his way to the ditch. He asked, 'Are you wounded Bill?' 'Yes!' he exclaimed 'and cannot get up.' Sergeant Fairfoot offered him some rum from his flask saying, 'I cannot carry you out of the reach of the shot,' then left Green to his fate, while he went on to meet his.

John Lowe, of the 2nd Battalion, stated that he was one of six volunteers from his company for the forlorn hope who, upon reaching the lowest rung of a ladder, when descending into the ditch, was brought to the ground at the same time as Lieutenant Manners, by a severe wound in his left shoulder from a shell splinter. Lieutenant Manners was part of the storming party; it therefore stands to reason that Lowe was on the same duty and not part of the forlorn hope. Lieutenant Manners was regarded as a gallant young officer by his men, a leader not a follower, a trait in officers that Thomas Plunkett, a famous Rifleman, due to his specialist shooting exploits during the Corunna campaign, observed equally well. It was hopeless for Lowe to continue with his left shoulder disabled, so he now headed back the way he came. Lieutenant Manners also tried to continue but fell, due to the wound in his leg which he cursed in no uncertain terms. Both men made for some rising ground from where they could hear the forlorn hope and storming parties trying to gain access to the breach. They had remained in this position for a short time when part of the 4th Division came by and a comment from one of these, probably in jest, inflamed Lowe, 'Well Light Division, never boast any more, since your can't take the town.' Lieutenant Manners growled his displeasure. This man, no doubt, would have regretted these words once he saw what was in store for his own regiment. Some of the survivors of the storming party, on returning, helped Lieutenant Manners and John Lowe out of the ditch, from where they then made their own slow and painful way back to the medical tent. It was on reaching the surgeon, that the true character of Lieutenant Manners came to the fore. Lowe reached the medical tent first, due to him being only a walking wounded, when Lieutenant Manners finally arrived the surgeon came to him after a short delay saying, 'Now Lieutenant Manners, I am ready to attend upon you sir!' The Lieutenant replied, 'My turn is not yet come, this man has been waiting longest!' and he insisted Lowe was to be treated first. [21]

Barnard, seeing the storming parties had been repulsed, now advanced with his 1st Brigade of the Light Division. Ordering Bugle Major Kelly to sound the call to advance, in 'double quick' time they charged forward as Wellington had laid down in his orders. Green having fallen on his side, hearing the bugles sounding rolled onto his back; frustrated at being of little use to his comrades, he believed by repeating the call, he was doing them some service. This was to be the last time he would blow the bugle. An officer from the 4th Division came scrambling towards him with his sword drawn and demanded he stop, for he was drawing fire from the walls onto his men. Green feeling rather deflated and crestfallen declared, 'I was only doing my duty.'

With the fire now concentrated against more important areas than the ground where Green lay, he chanced moving out of the line of fire and back towards the camp. Supporting his damaged left wrist with his right hand, for it was more painful than the wound in his thigh, he gradually hobbled to the rear.

A number of the 52nd attackers in the 1st Brigade were deceived by the depth of the inundation, including Lieutenant Colonel Hunt, who was severely shaken after jumping into the ditch with some of his men, instead of using the ladders. Most of his battalion however, descended via them, while a few of the more active men actually scrambled down the remains of one of the narrow ramparts which the enemy had not completely destroyed. It is easy to see how this delayed practically the whole brigade. The companies of Riflemen were all trying to descend some nine ladders, any alternative means of entry into the ditch, being more attractive and worth trying than waiting amidst a hail of shot and shell. Therefore, it is with little wonder that as each mass of men came up to descend the ditch they never got further than the glacis. The leading sections of the brigade made the same mistake as the stormers and charged up the unfinished ravelin in the hope of finding a way through to the centre breach. This attack had little or no chance of success, for field-guns had been placed on the flanks of the Santa Maria and La Trinidad bastions, from where they were able to pour volley after volley of grapeshot across the ravelin, along the covered way and towards the La Trinidad bastion that was being attacked by the 4th Division. All these problems combined to prevent a full-blooded attack from taking place on any of the breaches. This was due purely to the lack of space and the ability to mass enough men at any one time. The constant barrage they received in attempting such assaults can only be imagined; with large numbers of officers being struck down, many of the attacks lacked any co-ordination. As each man entered the ditch, he could, in effect, make for the easier option. Captain Dobbs of the 52nd, descended a ladder stating that the ditch was at least 24 feet deep and found he was standing in a foot of water; moving to his right he found it getting deeper. Therefore, he returned to the ladder and moved to his left, in the direction of the Santa Maria breach which was the true objective of the division. Due to the confusion and circumstances, the Santa Maria bastion [22] received far less attention than the other two breaches. Every new desperate rush was greeted by lighted fireballs, tar barrels, explosions of numerous shells and powder barrels, along with large logs of wood and broken cartwheels. Very few men actually reached the chevaux-de-frise and those who did were soon knocked over. Only one desperate Rifleman was reported as having gained this barricade of death. He fell, and then crawled underneath it, in an attempt to get through; the French rushed at him and crushed his skull smashing it to a bloody pulp with the butts of their muskets. It is hard to see how the French could have reached this point behind the chevaux-de-frise, due to the deep trench protecting the inner defences. The only access was via the use of planks placed across the void. The more likely scenario for such an horrific mangling of the head would be an explosion. As we have seen earlier William Lawrence was able to get close up to the chevaux-de-frise with some of his comrades, but this was at the La Trinidad bastion?

Captain Currie, of the 52nd, seeing what a hopeless situation the whole attack had become, advanced to his left and examined the counterscarp beyond the Santa Maria breach. There he found a narrow ramp that had only been partially destroyed, ascended it and was then able to make his way out and get clear of the bastion and ditch. Here he came upon Wellington with his staff, who were positioned on some rising ground a short distance away. He immediately inquired, 'Can they not get in?' Currie replied, 'Those in a confused state in the ditch could not, but a fresh battalion might succeed by using the descent he had discovered.' One from the reserve was instantly dispatched to be guided by the Captain. Using the broken ramp, these men, as soon as they entered the ditch, immediately became mixed up with those already in it, who were either retiring or rushing the breach, ending what could have been a crucial attack. [23]

Barnard, with great effort, could be seen everywhere encouraging the men to attempt one more valiant charge at the breach. With the help of some of his officers, he managed to separate a large part of the Light Division from the men of the 4th Division and for a relatively short period of time a degree of order was preserved in the Light Division. The noise however was so great, hardly a command could be heard distinctly, except by those close at hand. All the while the mutilated bodies of men, who minutes before were in the prime of life, kept piling up on top of each other, with the wounded struggling to avoid being crushed or trampled to death. The formations soon disintegrated and order became impossible. Nevertheless, officers of all rank, followed by their men, would suddenly start out as if struck by an uncontrollable urge or madness and rush into the breach. Napier likened this to, 'the yawning mouth of some huge dragon, belching forth smoke and flame.' [24] There was no shortage of gallant leaders, or desperate followers that night, but the La Trinidad remained impregnable. Although the breach in the curtain was less strong, the approaches were impeded by deep holes the enemy had skilfully constructed, along with deep cuts in the ditch, making it just as formidable an obstacle as the main breaches and impossible for the men to enter. Gathering in frustrated sullen groups they could only lean on their muskets or rifles looking up in desperation at the La Trinidad and Santa Maria bastions, while the enemy stepped out onto the ramparts, taking aimed shots aided by the light of the burning fireballs. They then goaded them into trying one more time. Rifleman Thomas Meabry, having received several wounds, was ordered to return to the rear by one of the officers; he refused stating, 'There is no going to the rear for me, and I'll restore myself to my comrades' opinion or make a finish of myself altogether.' [25]

Major O'Hare's premonition had come true, for he had already fallen at the head of his stormers with numerous musket balls to his body; his comrade Sergeant Patrick Fleming, lay dead close by. Captain Jones of the 52nd, was also amongst the pile of dead bodies, as was Captain Diggle of the 3rd Battalion Rifles, along with Captain Morphen of the 3rd Caçadores, who had also volunteered as a stormer. Scores of others lay badly wounded, amongst them Captain Crampton and Lieutenant Bedell of the Rifles. The initial storming had proved costly, but the final butcher's bill for this night's work was set to rise dramatically.

The weight of the ladder and dead men on Rifleman Costello was becoming unbearable; if it hadn't been for the protection of the hay-bag, he would probably have been crushed to death. Eventually he was able to free himself; having lost his rifle he now drew his sword bayonet from its scabbard and moved towards the breach, where he found four men putting one of the 43rd ladders down into the ditch. The fireballs, on burning out were soon replaced by fresh ones illuminating the stormers, giving the enemy muskets plenty of targets to aim at. Costello joined the men sliding down the ladder, and on reaching the bottom, was instantly knocked down by the bodies of two of the men who had been shot in attempting to follow him. Costello extricated himself from underneath the men and rushed forward, but went to the right and immediately fell into the flooded part of the ditch, that had already proved fatal to a number of 4th Division men. The water came up to his neck, but being a strong swimmer, he made for the other side of the ditch, which he reached without rifle or sword bayonet, though he was still wearing his shako, having tied it under his chin by the cords. Undaunted, he still attempted to ascend the breach! Costello only managed to get about halfway up, when he was knocked over and rolled senseless to the bottom. Here he joined the numerous dead and wounded piled at the foot of the breach, forming a human barrier for those still trying to storm up the steep incline. Eventually, Costello regained consciousness; whatever hit him in the chest was only a stunning blow. Coming to his senses, he could see that the stormers and their supports were still attempting to gain the breach. Finding to his great relief that the blow to his chest had done no lasting damage, Costello's first thought was to try and seek shelter from the deadly onslaught raining down with no intermission. Feeling weak, and with all the original enthusiasm for the attack all but lost, he, like many men in similar circumstances, prayed for his deliverance and safety. Costello still couldn't believe his luck at being in one piece, though the same could not be said for the poor souls still falling all around him, especially those who had been lying injured for some considerable time. Their groans and screams of agony muffled by the shouts of the attackers and defenders, were accompanied by a symphony of crashing stones, splitting timber and the endless report of muskets, cannons and exploding grenades, unnerving to even the stoutest of hearts. Many of the obstacles in the ditch had been set alight and some of those trapped were burnt to death where they lay.

Harry Smith, a company Officer in the 1st Battalion Rifles, with the 1st brigade, presented an unusual sight for a Rifleman for he was wearing a red coat. One, therefore, can only assume he was still wearing the coat he had worn previously, when acting as Brigade Major. He still held his staff position at Badajoz, though also shown as a company commander, in the 1st battalion, his senior lieutenant, however, would have been in command during his absence. Rushing down a ladder, he headed immediately towards the breach with his men but they soon became a broken force and their assault had no impact. At the breach Captain Smith joined Lieutenant Taggart of the 43rd, one of the remaining survivors of the storming party: they had to hold on to each other for support in ascending the breach because it was so difficult and steep.

They could see a Rifleman stood amongst the sword blades on top of one of the chevaux-de-frise, and they made every attempt, along with some men, to follow him. But the courageous Rifleman was knocked over, dreadfully wounded. The only place offering the slightest bit of shelter was at the revetment of the bastion near the breach, where those wounded and able to move, tried to escape the death raining down from above.

*Thickness of walls*

Colonel Barnard, seeing that his 1st Brigade was making little progress against the centre breach and that very few men were attacking the Santa Maria bastion, retuned to his 2nd Brigade. He now brought up the 43rd Regiment under Colonel M'Leod and the five 3rd Battalion 95th companies under Captain Percival, also part of this brigade. The fresh troops he hoped to channel towards the Santa Maria forcing them to go to their left away from the ravelin and centre breach, that had caused such chaos during the earlier assaults.

The ladder parties had done their duties, but how many survived was anyone's guess. Lieutenant Gurwood, of the 43rd, was still in the ditch, but severely wounded and the rope men had been wiped out almost to a man. Lieutenant Johnstone, too badly wounded to escape this scene of hell, was still trapped behind the ravelin. Pockets of the 52nd and Riflemen, some mixed up with the 4th Division, continued to make futile attempts at gaining the breaches of La Trinidad and the curtain.

Lieutenant Oglander, of the 43rd, was advancing to the ditch with his company in the 2nd Brigade of the Light Division, when a large shot, coming from the direction of the Pardeleras advance work, demolished his whole section. The cannon ball went through left to right and knocked them down like a set of skittles.

Lieutenant Simmons, of the 1st Battalion, originally volunteered for the storming party, but had to concede to those senior to him who demanded this honour. Captain Gray of the 3/95th, was shot in the mouth when attempting to tear down the palisade on the glacis with Lieutenant Simmons. Here, the men were being mown down like grass from a continuous fire of grapeshot; many 95th officers fell at this point. Lieutenant FitzMaurice was one of them, a musket ball having broken his thigh bone. Lieutenant Stokes, a known firebrand in the Rifles, who always went into action with a rifle, was also killed. Simmons eventually descended the ditch by the ladders that were still resting against the counterscarp from within the ditch and from the walls, fireballs and lights of all sorts were still raining down upon the men. Lieutenant Simmons, at one point, was attempting to stamp out one of these lights, when another officer grabbed hold of him telling him to leave it, as there was a live shell beneath it!

The officers of the 2nd Brigade were now falling as fast as those in the other brigade. Colonel M'Leod, the idol of his men and still only the tender age of 27, advanced against the breach with his regiment, who were all eager to succeed where so many had failed, rushed to join their colonel. One of them slipped on the rubble and plunged his bayonet into M'Leod's back by accident. He continued on with the men, until mortally wounded. He tried to force an entry into the left hand corner of the breach, only a couple of yards from the sword blades.

Captain Fergusson, the leader of the 43rd storming party, had already done more than his fair share for king and country, suffered from two wounds received at Ciudad Rodrigo and another in the trenches, prior to the assault. These had now burst open by his exertions in gaining the ditch. He was hit in the head, wounded for the fourth time and fell to the right of the ladders. It was here that Lieutenant Cooke, also of the 43rd Regiment, found him trying to staunch his wounds. Cooke took the handkerchief from him and bound it around his head. It was at this point the French illuminated the area even further, by hanging fireballs from the walls; giving them the appearance of revolving lights. Having assisted Fergusson all he could, Cooke moved off and upon reaching the foot of the central breach, a position that continued to attract the majority of stormers, found around 80–90 men with no one left to command them. A voice cried out 'who will lead us?' Lieutenant Cooke immediately advanced and they moved off to join him, instantly many were killed, while many more fell wounded, only to be impaled on the bayonets of their comrades close behind. Cooke fell when only a yard from the death trap of sword blades. Stunned, he rolled down the slope and into the water flooding the ditch, the cause of many deaths already that night. He would have been added to the list, if it had not been for one of the men pulling him out. Looking up Cooke could see the top of the wall lit by numerous fireball, with the French cheering and goading their attackers into trying once again. Those not knocked down were eventually driven back to the ladders. At the foot of one of these, Captain Harry Smith found Colonel M'Leod, who had managed to make his way back from the breach, his hands clutching at his breast. He told Smith he was mortally wounded and would he help get him up the ladder. Smith managed to drag him out of the ditch repaying M'Leod for saving him at the Coa [26] then returned, where he was joined by Lieutenant Freer of the 43rd. With so many men trying to leave the ditch, Smith and Freer decided that they would throw down the ladders forcing the men into returning to attack the breach. This could well have been at the point when the alarm was raised that the French were making a flanking movement, which, could just as easily have been Captain Currie coming up after his encounter with Wellington, with some reserve troops from a part of the ditch that was unexpected. Smith and Freer, however, soon decided discretion was the better part of valour when the soldiers cursed them and told them if they tried to prevent them gaining the ladders they would bayonet them! This forced the two officers to ascend the ladders with all speed, closely followed by the men. Harry Smith's sash had worked loose, one end caught in the ladder causing him to delay. A bayonet, brought too close for comfort, however, was all the motivation he needed to pull it free. On reaching the glacis, a fresh brigade of Portuguese came up and immediately started to descend the ladders, turning the tables on the men who threatened Smith and Freer, forcing them back down the ladders.

Colonel George Elder, Barnard's second in command, had under his direct command two regiments of Caçadores and a detachment of the 95th Rifles, probably from the 1st Battalion, for it is known that at least one of their companies was with Elder. When Barnard led the second assault with the 2nd Brigade, he ordered Elder to follow at a respectable distance, but not to enter the ditch. An officer of the 95th volunteered to follow the 43rd Regiment and once he saw them enter the ditch, was to report back to Elder. He then advanced with his force to the edge of the glacis, from where he was able to witness first hand the confusion and carnage taking place amongst the troops below. He immediately descended into the ditch to gain an idea what was needed to rectify the confusion. At the bottom of the ladder, he came upon Major Brooke of the 7th Regiment, who was severely wounded, but able to confirm that nearly all the field officers were either killed or wounded. Brooke was trying to make his way back to Wellington to report that the attack on the breach at the La Trinidad bastion had failed. Elder immediately pushed forward his Caçadores and Riflemen and started forming them up in sufficient numbers to make an attempt at assaulting the Santa Maria breach, which he knew to be the original objective. It was while organising his men, that he was struck down and severely wounded. In this condition he managed to climb back up one of the ladders to the glacis, where he was wounded a second time. From the glacis he was eventually carried on the shoulders of some men back to the camp, to receive immediate medical treatment. Lieutenant Gairdner, who was with Elder's 1st Battalion 95th companies, was slightly wounded in the right leg when he advanced against the breach. He was still able to continue with his men, until he was wounded twice more from a burst of canister in the left arm and the chin. A Sergeant from his own company pulled him out of the ditch and with the assistance of some Bandsmen from the 52nd Regiment carried him back to the hospital tent on a stretcher. [27] The attack made by Elder's Portuguese and detached Rifle companies was eventually repulsed.

Barnard meanwhile, was still in the thick of the action. He must have lead a charmed life, for how he managed to escape injury, was nothing short of a miracle. He clambered out of the ditch and collected what was left of the men and urged them to try and succeed where all others had failed. It wasn't until about 11.45 p.m., that any meaningful attempt was made against the left breach of Santa Maria. This was due to the confusion and mix up of the 4th and Light Divisions.

Lieutenant Kincaid was close to Colonel Barnard, when, just after midnight, he observed him receiving repeated messages from Wellington to withdraw from the breach and to reform the Light Division, for a renewal of the attack at daylight. But Barnard could still see fresh attempts being made and that troops were still pressing forward into the ditch. He couldn't find it in his heart to retreat, while a chance of success still remained. Once again he joined his men and lead repeated attempts at assaulting the breaches until about 2 o'clock in the morning. He finally conceded it was hopeless and reluctantly gave the order to fall back some 300 yards from the ditch. Here he reformed what was left of the division. Prior to this, however, with the dead lying everywhere and more falling by the minute, the wounded crawled about trying to find any form of shelter from the merciless shower of death from above. The sickening stench of burnt flesh, acrid smoke and gun-powder filled the nostrils of those still alive. Captain Nicholas of the Engineers, who had originally been tasked to guide the 52nd ladder men, was observed by Captain Shaw of the 43rd, making incredible efforts to force his way, with a few men, into the Santa Maria. Collecting 50–60 soldiers of all regiments, he joined him and passed a deep cut made along the foot of this breach. These two young officers, at the head of their band, rushed up the slope of the ruins. They had reached about two-thirds of the ascent, when a concentrated fire of grapeshot and musketry, struck down practically the whole force, leaving only Captain Shaw and Sergeant Nichols, also of the 43rd, still left standing. Captain Nicholas had received a grapeshot through his lungs, and it would take him three days to die. This attack was worthy of a forlorn hope of its own, and no doubt many more such actions carried out during that desperate night were equal in valour but went unrecorded. Sergeant Nichols though miraculously escaping the first attack on the chevaux-de-frise, was determined to tear the sword-blades from their fastenings. He continued his attempt, despite a continuous stream of musket-balls poured out against him by the defenders. After this, however, hardly any further effort was made against any part of the defences. The troops remained passive, resigned to the situation, unflinching before the enemy's shot, which continued without remission.

Captain Shaw finally admitted failure and decided against any continued attack on this bastion and retired with a few men back to the ruined ravelin in the ditch between La Trinidad and Santa Maria bastions. This was one of the few places within the defensive systems, which afforded a small degree of shelter for the attackers. Here, he found the wounded Johnstone, of the rope party, who had crawled there at the very beginning of the attack. He remained here throughout the whole of the assault, for he was incapable of getting clear on his own. Also taking shelter was another Rifle officer and two officers from other regiments, together with a small group of men. It was agreed that they should try and hold this position until daylight. It could prove significant in providing a point from where further attacks could be made, should Wellington want to resume the assault. It was at this time that a general alarm was given, that the French were making a sortie into the ditch. This caused blind panic amongst the men still massed in the ditch! It never entered their heads that this would be a rash move on the part of the enemy, who were causing untold casualties from behind their defences. At this point, logic was the last thing to cross the minds of these men and any chance of escaping certain death in the ditch or breaches was welcome. It was a case of every man for himself and they rushed to the ladders to get out of the ditch. Captain Shaw, not prepared to leave the stricken Johnstone to the mercy of the French, pleaded with the right hand man from his own company, Private Norton, to help assist him. After much effort, they succeeded in dragging and pushing Johnstone up the ladders and out of the ditch. Unfortunately, Norton then fell dead from the ladder, having been shot in the head by a musket ball.

As previously mentioned the panic may have been caused by Captain Currie with his men, entering the ditch from the flank of the Santa Maria bastion.

The buglers, probably from Cameron's companies, were sent to the crest of the glacis to sound the retreat. This did not go down well with those still desperate to succeed in the ditch and who could not believe their ears. Any bugler, who attempted to repeat it was actually struck down. Eventually there was little else to do other than scramble out of the ditch. The thick clouds of smoke helped to conceal their withdrawal. Lieutenant Gawler, who commanded the 52nd ladder party, was too severely wounded to get out of the ditch. He was now resigned to remaining behind when one of his men told him to hang on to his accoutrements so that he could drag him up a ladder. He succeeded in getting Lieutenant Gawler to safety, only to be killed himself, falling back into the ditch. Time after time, the four companies of Cameron's 1st Battalion 95th continued to pour a concentrated fire at the defenders. Had it not been for this many more men would have been killed in the ditch and breaches. Cameron's men, though, were not having it all their own way and received an intense counter fire. Their position was constantly bombarded with canister and grapeshot and as a result they received their fair share of casualties, which is confirmed in the casualty returns.

Even though the fire had slackened, Rifleman Costello remained in the breach and could hear cheering coming from within the town. Attempting to stand, he found he was unable to do so because he had, without realising, been wounded and had no idea when he had been hit! Adrenalin and fear are a strange mix, which can overcome the most severe pain. A musket ball had passed through the lower part of his right leg. Two others had perforated his shako, which he would have lost had he not secured it before starting out. Men were moving towards him and he feared it was the French, coming to dispatch him; he was relieved to find they belonged to the Rifles. One of them was William O'Brien of his own company who, on seeing Costello, exclaimed, 'What! Is that you Ned? We thought you ladder men all done for.' He then helped him to get up, and with the use of O'Brien's rifle as a crutch and the Rifleman's shoulder to lean on they headed towards the breach and town. They could not pass the chevaux-de-frise until more men coming up removed it from its fastenings. At the top of the breach, they found another trench barring their way, although a plank of wood laid across it enabled them to get to the other side; it led them into the town. Blood had started trickling down Costello's face and it was only then, that he found one of the balls passing through his shako had actually torn the skin from his head. Crippled as he was, he and O'Brien, accompanied by a few other Riflemen, hurried from the breach as quickly as possible, for they were in fear of the French exploding a mine.

Lieutenant Fitzroy Somerset, one of Wellington's staff, came up to where the Rifles had retired and remained halted with the division. Meeting Harry Smith he said, 'Where is Barnard?' 'I don't know,' Smith replied but he assured him he was neither killed nor wounded. Somerset then said, 'The Duke desires the Light and 4th Divisions to storm again.' 'The devil!' said Smith, 'Why, we have had enough, we are all knocked to pieces.' 'I dare say you are,' came back the reply, 'but you must try again.' Smith gave a wry smile saying, 'If we could not succeed with two whole fresh divisions, we are likely to make a poor show of it now. But we will try again, with all our might!'[28]

*Inside Badajoz near the castle*

Before the remaining men of the Light Division could be put in motion, bugles could be distinctly heard sounding in the town, heralding the success at the Castle and Puerto de Olivenca. Colonel Ridge of the 5th Regiment, with a number of his men of the 3rd Division, had earlier advanced with ladders. Many historians repeat the often misguided notion that Colonel Ridge picked up one of these ladders and single handed placed it against the walls of the castle. This only serves to point out their lack of understanding of the practical situation involved, as no one man could lift one of these ladders on his own, let alone scramble up a steep incline and place it against the castle. Ridge and his men placed the ladders at a point on the wall not previously attempted, which was considerably lower than the earlier attempts, probably the part Picton originally pinpointed as being accessible.

Ridge was the first to ascend the ladders, followed by Grenadier Canch of the same regiment and these two officers were soon followed by a number of men. The speed with which they climbed the ladders took the French on this part of the defences, completely by surprise. Both gained the ramparts and beat back their attackers, until, eventually, they were joined by a large group of their men. The all important foothold Picton's Division needed had been achieved, the few soon swelled to a mob. Seeing them established on the castle walls was great encouragement to the men below and a general rush took place. Other ladders were brought up and the red tide of frustrated and heaving humanity soon made a strong presence on the castle walls, nothing was going to move them now. Colonel Ridge gathered a group from his own regiment and set off to seize the governor. Those climbing the ladders now came face to face with the defenders for the first time. Lieutenant Kingsmill of the 88th had struggled to gain access from a ladder as it was lower than those placed by Ridge. However, one of his men, by lying flat on the wall with his legs held by a comrade, reached down and pulled Kingsmill up by the scruff of his collar. He then found himself standing amongst a group of French soldiers, who were around one of their artillery pieces, with one holding a slow match in his hand. For a moment time stood still, a French Grenadier leant against the gun, bleeding severely from a head wound. The others were sitting in despair, their huge bushy moustaches and mouths blackened due to the constant biting of the cartridges, added to the fearsome, bronzed faces, striking a picture which would last his life time. These men however were all dejected and caused them no further concern.

Ridge's party encountered a group of French soldiers, who they fired at and on returning fire, a musket-ball hit Ridge in the chest and he fell; dying soon after. Nothing could stop the 3rd Division now, the success of the night all hinged on their securing and holding the castle, an action the army had been waiting for far too long. By the time the men of the 3rd Division reached the castle gate they found the French who, upon retreating into the city, had closed and locked it. They were therefore confined to the castle and the only access into the city was via a small gate which as soon as any attacker showed his face the French protected with volleys of musketry.

Philippon and his staff were informed that the British had captured the castle, much to their total astonishment. Everything they coveted, the extra supplies of food and ammunition were now locked up in the castle with their enemy, their last bastion of defence in which they had expected to make a last stand. The French Governor lost valuable time trying to come to terms with this turn of events, before eventually deciding to send some troops against them. The 5th Division meanwhile had gained the walls and it was due to their efforts and success that the French had been forced to abandon the two breached bastions the 4th and Light Divisions had been attacking; leaving the way now open for them to advance without any opposition. Philippon collected his men and retreated across the bridge of boats, from where he was eventually to concede defeat and surrender.

*Fort of San Christoval from Badajoz*

# Aftermath of Badajoz

The firing ceased and with the confusion of battle subsiding, a ghostly presence now descended over the ditch and breaches that had been attacked by the Light and 4th Divisions. Choking smoke hung thickly over the prostrate bodies of the dead and dying, surrounded by the chaos and destruction which only a short time previous was the animated scene of such despair and desperation. It was only now that the cries of the wounded could be distinguished from the noise of battle, many crying out for water, fear and pain causing their mouths to be parched. Broken bodies, many beyond repair, their owners crying out in excruciating pain for assistance while others screamed out with their last dying breaths for mothers or wives for some sort of comfort. Bandsmen could be seen picking their way through this sickening scene of gut-wrenching carnage. Those men with little or no chance of survival, sadly, had to be left in favour of the less seriously wounded. It was hard to make such a choice, especially if they knew the men as friends or more intimate colleagues. Their first task was to deal with the men of their own regiments, but later it became the case of saving any man who still had a reasonable chance of reaching the surgeons alive. At the regimental hospitals the tents resembled abattoirs, as surgeons removed limbs with great speed, which soon started piling up; while the dead were laid out in rows, many beyond recognition as being part of the human race.

The assaulting divisions headed reluctantly back into the ditches but were relieved to find all opposition had ceased, the men however still found it a difficult and dangerous task to gain the summit of the city walls. The fixings to the chevaux-de-frise had to be hacked away so they could be dragged free and allow easier access, and even without these obstacles, it was still dangerous even unopposed. Major Cameron gathered his wing of the 1/95th together and placed them as piquets to the entrances to all the narrow streets leading from the walls into the city. At the same time he gave strict orders that any man who left the ranks without permission would be shot on the spot. The cheering, erratic gun fire and screams coming from the inner city was a magnet to these men, who had already sampled the freedom of sacking Ciudad Rodrigo and knew what was awaiting them in Badajoz. Any thought for their comrades lying in the ditch or breaches in agony was forgotten by the need to get into the city. A few hours of uncontrolled freedom could make a man his fortune, if he was wise enough to retain his wealth.

Prize money would eventually be shared out amongst the troops, but they knew their share would be a pittance when compared to that of the officers and especially the generals. It is hard to censure their plundering when weighed up against the excesses over the years by the French. It is also a fact that had they not taken away whatever they could carry, the peasants from the surrounding countryside would. They were equally on a mission to take advantage of a life changing opportunity to become extremely wealthy. The cruelty in how this was obtained, however, was another matter! The root cause of the night's shame was the unlimited availability of such enormous amounts of wine and spirits. Human nature being what it is, we have all witnessed the shocking scenes due to drink that taint our modern society, therefore, it is easy to identify with the despicable activity displayed during the occupation of Badajoz. All sense or reason was lost as men and women lost their inhibitions, their heads turned by drink, some becoming most barbaric, minds poisoned beyond all recognition and control. The chaos and mayhem taking place in Badajoz gradually grew louder as the regiments of the 3rd and 5th Divisions disintegrated into a baying uncontrollable rabble. Cameron knew he was holding onto a powder keg of resentment from his Riflemen, so promised they would be allowed their turn to fall out and enjoy themselves, once he was certain the city was completely in the hands of the British Allied Army.

The wounded, many unable to move from the scene of battle, were now at the mercy of those with any compassion to their plight, which in essence meant the officers. The regiments, once dismissed from any immediate duty, just scampered off into the night, all thought for their fallen comrades gone. The regimental and divisional camps were soon deserted, apart from the hospital tents, for everybody wanted to be part of the victory in Badajoz. The camp followers were joined by the local peasants who poured through the city gates once they were forced open. Meanwhile, wives searched through the heaps of dead in the ditches and breaches for their husbands. In daylight the task would be made all the easier for the wives of the Riflemen, for they would be able to pick out their distinguished uniforms. The Spanish peasants, who thought it unwise to enter the city, found less dangerous sources of wealth awaited them by descending on the dead and dying in the breaches; stripping them of everything of value, including their clothing. By the time the first rays of daylight illuminated the scene of carnage many men were already lying naked, their horrific wounds exposed for all the world to see, testament to a valiant death or a prolonged agonising death for the wounded. Once the full heat of the day played across the breaches, these lifeless forms swelled into bloated and blackened carcasses, which somehow never seemed to put-off the scavenger or curious.

Adjutant Kincaid was detailed to post the piquets, and while organizing one of these a Rifleman brought a Frenchman to him who claimed he was the Governor. On confronting Kincaid, the Frenchman immediately declared this was untrue and he had only said it to secure his protection and that he was in fact a colonel. His surviving officers were sheltering in a house close by and would be prepared to surrender to an officer who could guarantee their safety. Kincaid took a group of Riflemen with him and found some 15 or 16 officers assembled. They still could not come to terms with the unexpected turn of events, repeatedly asked how they had managed to get into the city! On returning to the half battalion, with his jabbering group of Frenchmen, Kincaid was challenged by a piquet drawn across the street. It was still very dark, and as a result, Kincaid had taken a different turning. His little band of officers had since swelled to around 100 men as French soldiers began attaching themselves to his party. To the approaching piquet, this had all the signs of a French rally, or reinforcement against their position. They were just about to fire a volley into them when Kincaid shouted out for Colonel Barnard. They relaxed, realising just in time that they were their own men with a number of French prisoners.

Captain Dobbs of the 52nd, on entering the city, found it impossible to keep his company together before they crept away under the cover of darkness. Dobbs continued into the city and while walking down one street, he saw at the other end, coming toward him, a group of men crazed with drink chasing a bull. They sent a volley after the poor beast. The musket balls came flying close to Dobbs in all directions as they ricocheted off the walls of the houses. Deciding this was no place to be at this time, he returned to the camp. The livestock in the city was being used by the soldiers as targets, except those who were using the French or Spanish, making for better fun!

A number of Riflemen did get into the city, before their comrades in Cameron's wing received permission to fall out. The wounded Costello, supported by Rifleman O'Brien, reached the inner city without any mishap and joined up with another couple of Riflemen. These men must have looked most fearsome in their appearance. Costello limping along with a rifle for a crutch, his trousers rolled up to the knees, and blood pouring from the bullet hole in his lower leg. His uniform was soaked and caked in mud, a battered shako on his head with the cords tied tightly under his chin, framing a face contorted in pain and anger, with blood pouring down it from a scalp wound. A most frightening sight to the inhabitants. Making their way down a street they came upon some men, where a light shining from a window picked them out as being French. On seeing the Riflemen they soon fled, except one, who made a rush at them with his musket. Rifleman O'Brien leapt forward and wrestled the firelock from his grasp.

Costello, his anger at its peak, said to O'Brien, 'let me have the pleasure of shooting the rascal!' Pointing the rifle to the Frenchman's breast, the thought crossed his mind that this could have been the very man who had wounded him. Costello was ready to pull the trigger, when the Frenchman fell upon his knees begging for mercy. This was a sobering moment for Costello, who now felt ashamed of his action and instantly dropped the rifle. The Frenchman jumped to his feet and flung his arms around his neck, trying to kiss him on the cheek. The Riflemen now continued on their way with the Frenchman supporting Costello who was now under his protection. This sudden change of heart, probably saved him from receiving a severe wound to his hand, having used the rifle for a crutch, the barrel was more than likely to be damaged or clogged with mud.

This intrepid group of Riflemen, decided it was time they got some refreshment. Knocking on a door, they waited for it to be opened. One of them eventually put his rifle to the key-hole and fired, forcing the lock, sending the door flying open. On entering, they found a young Spanish woman crying in terror, who told them she was the wife of a French officer. O'Brien demanded she brought them something to drink, but she could only produce some spirits and chocolate. Looking around, it was clear to the Riflemen the only thing of note in the house was the poor woman herself! They all moved off in the direction of the market-place, while out of the darkness could be heard the raucous shouts and laughter of drunken soldiers, the firing of muskets and the crashing of doors as they were forced open in the endless quest for drink. A shiver ran down their backs at the appalling shrieks coming from women, who had fallen into the depraved hands of men with more than drink on their minds.

On arriving at the square, the Riflemen were confronted by a sight plucked straight from the jaws of hell, a living canvas that was a true representation of *Dante's Inferno*. To add to the mayhem, numbers of Spanish prisoners had been set free from the city gaol, still wearing their chains, no doubt many with a score to settle, all joining the ranks of the massed allied drunken army. At this early stage, many men were from the 5th and 88th Regiments, who had been amongst the first into the city, having gained an advantage over those just arriving. Men could be seen holding candles to light their way through the houses being looted of everything, whether of value or not, with the inevitable results that some houses were set on fire. Some of the Spanish prisoners, turned into savages, as they took out months or years of imprisonment, on anybody who got in their way.

Costello and O'Brien entered a house in a street just off the square, where they found some men from Picton's Division. One fellow, seeing Costello was wounded, struck the neck off a bottle of wine with his bayonet and gave it to him. The wine was a great relief to Costello, who was feeling faint from the loss of blood. He sat next to a roaring fire that was being fed with a number of chairs, once the prized possession of the owner! Screams, coming from an adjoining room, jolted Costello from his comfortable position. Hobbling over, he entered the room and found an old man on his knees, imploring mercy from a soldier who had his musket levelled at him. With some difficulty, Costello managed to prevent him from being shot, advising the Spaniard that if he did not give up his money, the soldier would shoot him. The old man brought out around 150 dollars, wrapped in a night-cap, from under a mattress on the bed. The men shared them out, Costello stating he received around 25 dollars (a dollar at this time was equal to about five English shillings or five days pay for a private soldier). The front door suddenly burst open and a group of Portuguese soldiers entered, one of them seeing Costello sat by the fire, fired his musket at him, thinking he was a Frenchman. Luckily it misfired! Costello rushed at him and in no time there was a general scuffle between the British and Portuguese, which continued until one of the latter was stabbed with a bayonet. The Portuguese left, dragging their wounded comrade with them. The victors now started ransacking the house and, as a result, discovered the old man's two daughters and their mother, who they then proceeded to rape, while subjecting the old man to further abuse as he tried to help his family.

Hundreds of similar scenes were being acted out throughout the city. Costello, sick of the horror that was taking place in the old man's house, helped by his terrified Frenchman, made for a house on the other side of the street. There he found more men of the 3rd Division, making drinking chocolate with wine! Though these men seemed less drunk, the same shameful acts against the women were taking place in other parts of the house. Costello remained here for the remainder of the night, to rest his wounded leg in an attempt at staunching the flow of blood.

Quartermaster William Surtees, of the 3/95th, serving in Captain Percival's company, had originally remained behind in camp at the time of the storming, deterred from going into action by his fellow officers, who stated it would have served little purpose, especially if he had been killed or wounded! Surtees joined the staff officers of the 43rd Regiment, who were in the same brigade, watched the night's proceedings from the safety of a hill overlooking the breaches. It was in the same area as Wellington;

all were spectators to the events unfolding before them that night. It was here he witnessed Wellington reading by torch light the dispatch sent from Picton, that the castle had been taken. Surtees immediately moved off, with his haversack slung over his shoulder containing a loaded pistol and a few necessaries, to join his division. Meeting up with them near the quarries, he was able to inform them that Picton had taken possession of the castle. At first, it was hard for them to believe Surtees, for they thought Picton's task had been impossible to achieve. The Quartermaster now enquired as to the fate of his two fellow company officers. Lieutenant Crudace he was informed, had been shot through the body and carried to the rear. Lieutenant Cary, who was acting Adjutant of the 3/95th, they knew had fallen, but had no idea of what had become of him. With the Division moving forward to aid in taking possession of the city, Surtees departed, joined by Captain Percival, in search of his friend Cary.

Colonel Barnard, in trying to keep the Division together, after having experienced its disintegration at Ciudad Rodrigo, placed himself in front of the opening into the town. The multitude of men, however, was far too great to restrain and the men would not listen to him or their regimental officers. Major Cameron seems to have been the only senior officer able to command any sway over his half battalion. Barnard tried to wrench the musket from a 52nd soldier who just forced his way passed him, falling in the process and was nearly thrown at the same time into the ditch. Having escaped the whole night's work without injury, Barnard was nearly crushed in the final hour of victory. Seeing what a hopeless task it was, stepped back before the horde, and then set off with several officers of the division, to try and restrain the men in the city.

Surtees and Percival, on entering the ditch, seeing so many men lying wounded and helpless, immediately set to work getting as many as possible out and back to the hospital tents. This they found most difficult, without the help of a number of men. Captain Percival used his stick, to compel a few men into lending a hand in getting some of the wounded into the town, where it would be easier to establish some form of hospital. It was a case of extracting those who looked the most likely to survive. These two officers, continued with this task until noon, by which time they were too exhausted to continue. Surtees, undaunted, went in search of his friend Lieutenant Cary, which had been his original quest. He eventually found him beneath a ladder, stripped naked except for a flannel waistcoat. Cary had been shot in the head, but was still breathing. Surtees managed to coerce some drunken men into carrying Cary back to his tent, though they dropped him a few times on the way. In spite of all Surtees' efforts, the young Lieutenant died of his wounds. One sight which astounded Surtees and Percival when extracting the wounded, was seeing an officer with yellow facings to his uniform come out of the town with a frail fair haired female on his arm, carrying a bird in a cage and stepping over the mangled remains of numerous naked men without the slightest concern!

During this time, the excesses in the city were growing worse. Once the city gates had been opened, the Spanish peasants and hordes of camp followers rushed in, adding further mayhem and chaos to what was already taking place. By 10 o'clock that morning, amongst the chaos, the garrison was marched away as prisoners to Elvas. Major Cameron finally rewarded his wing of Riflemen, by dismissing them from duty. The men, kept begrudgingly in check,

were itching to be let into the city and knew Cameron would have been true to his word, in shooting anybody who left the ranks. Before their final departure, he told them that he expected them all to be back in camp for roll call at tattoo! Of course, once the genie was out of the bottle, there was no getting it back in; events would have to run their course. The men of Cameron's wing had a lot of catching up to do and in no time this was achieved and soon were as drunk as everybody else. One Rifleman managed in that short space of time to get hold of a hogshead of brandy.

This would confirm the state that the rest of the army must have been in. He placed it in the street, where he sat astride of it and filled his mess-tin, forcing everybody who came by, including his company commander, to have a drink. The first thing Major Cameron did, on arriving back at the camp, was to confront Lieutenant Bell about his conduct prior to the assault. He found the Lieutenant lying on his bed in his tent, where he had remained the whole night, while his comrades in arms struggled to gain access in the death traps at the breaches. As a result, Lieutenant Bell was forced out of the regiment. It would have been hard for him to face his fellow officers, especially after so many had fallen that night.

Captain Harry Smith and Lieutenant John Kincaid, leaving the men to enjoy their free time, retired to the practically deserted Rifles' camp. It was while standing at the opening of their tent the next day, that they noticed two females making their way towards them from the direction of the city.

They were both quite young and their dress told them they were ladies of the highest order. The elder of the two, on reaching them, pulled back her mantilla, exposing the most striking of features to these battle-worn heroes, telling them she was the wife of a Spanish officer who was serving in another part of the country and at the present time was not sure if he was still alive. Their house in the city, once a dwelling of some considerable standing and wealth, at one time having entertained a high ranking officer of the British Army, now lay in ruins. They, therefore, were prepared to put themselves at the mercy of the first British officer they met, in order to escape the brutal excesses of the soldiers in the city, who, earlier had treated them so harshly and with contempt, by savagely ripping the rings from their ears tearing the flesh. Her main concern, however, was for her younger sister. To save themselves from further outrage, and the wholesale raping and butchery taking place only a short distance away, they implored Kincaid and Smith to be placed under their protection! As the younger woman removed her veil and revealed her face to the Rifleman, the blood on her torn ears provided evidence to what had taken place earlier; Captain Harry Smith and Lieutenant Kincaid were instantly struck by cupid's arrow and captivated by the girls' beauty.

Harry Smith immediately placed her under his personal protection. As a result, this 14 year old girl, in a short time became his wife. Smith was some ten years older than his prospective bride, Juana Maria de Los Dolores de Leon, who hailed from one of the oldest and well known families in Spain. Had these two ladies remained in the city, there is no doubt they would have fallen victims to the drunken mob, disgracing the noble name of the British Army, normally known for its restraint and compassion. Throughout the second day of occupation, the city continued to be stripped of its wealth amid the mindless destruction. The daughters of Governor Philippon had to be personally protected by Lord Fitzroy Somerset and another officer who, with swords drawn, warned off the rabble who tried to drag the women from their grip. They all, thankfully, returned safely back to Headquarters. No one was spared the attentions of the uncontrollable men. Nuns who tried to conceal themselves in some of the most obscure and out of the way places, fell into the clutches of the rampaging mob. The narrow streets, wide enough for only a cart to pass down were blocked, filled with the broken contents of the houses and shops, from furniture to beds, ripped open in search of treasure. Some houses were set on fire and by this time even a convent was in flames.

Major Nevill, of the 30th Regiment, entered Badajoz in search of his servant. When finally meeting up with him, he found he already had his haversack well filled with plunder. He asked his servant where the rest of the regiment was, but he said he had no idea. Seeing that his Major was bleeding from wounds to the head and leg he told him he had better conduct him back to the camp.

Major Nevill, up to this point had been unaware of his injuries, for the events of the last few hours had masked the pain; it was only now when they were brought to his attention that he felt rather weak. Taking the advice of his servant, they began making their way out of the city. Passing what appeared to be a religious house, two soldiers came from it, dragging an unfortunate nun, with her clothes all torn: in her agony she knelt and held up a cross. Remorse seized one of the men, who appeared more sober than the other and he swore that she should not be further outraged. The other soldier, in a matter of fact way, stepped back and coolly shot his comrade dead. Whilst taking in this despicable scene, they were suddenly surrounded by a group of Portuguese soldiers, who, raising their muskets at them, menacingly ordered them to halt. Nevill told his servant to throw them some of his plunder, taking off his haversack he threw it at the Portuguese, some silver coins rolled out and they let them pass. Had he not done so they would certainly have become just another couple of victims to the night's horrors, with no-one any the wiser. They finally reached the safety of a bastion, from where Major Nevill, due to the loss of blood, was carried on the back of his servant to the camp. On receiving a draught of water, Nevill instantly fell asleep and did not waken till after midday.

Whenever an officer appeared in the streets, the inhabitants would flock round him with terror and despair, embracing his knees to supplicate protection. But it was impossible, let alone dangerous, to oppose the soldiers. There were 10,000 of them, crowding the city in all directions; it was difficult to escape them unhurt. The whole problem was made even worse, when a large number of their women came in from the camps and poured into Badajoz before it was properly secured. They were all eager for their share of the plunder and drink. They were, in a number of instances, worse than the men. Major Nevill likened them to so many tigresses in the shape of women. He had been sickened to watch them being so matter of fact towards the dying by coolly stepping over them, indifferent to their cries for a drop of water, and then deliberately search their pockets for money, or even strip them of their blood-soaked clothes.

Some soldiers, meanwhile, had taken over the shops they had looted and upon becoming the new owners, began selling off the contents to anybody who was prepared to pay. When they felt they had made enough money, they left, or in some cases were forced out by stronger more sober groups of men, who then carried on in their place. One officer, wandering the town, reported being accosted by a soldier of the 88th, the worse for wear due to the amount of brandy he had consumed, waving his loaded musket at him, but luckily he eventually allowed him to pass. This was not always the case during these dark days, which would take many years and hard won victories to eradicate.

The same officer, was then accosted by a young girl of about nine years of age, who implored him for protection for her mother. However, on reaching the girl's house, he found the mother was already beyond his help, for she was now a prisoner in her own home, providing the entertainment for a gang of armed drunken men who had fought hard and long for just such an occasion. Moving on, another 88th man passed him, dragging a peasant by the collar with the intention of shooting him, because he could not provide him with necessary funds. The officer pleaded for his release and the soldier relented. The city, was now full of wives and camp followers who, by now, were just as drunk and in as uncontrollable a state as the men. They were forced into providing the carnal pleasures demanded by the men, whether they wanted to or not, many in such a terrible condition they would have been unaware what was happening to them! The excessive drinking had created such a crazed soldiery, that even the meekest and normally most mildest of men, sank to the same depths of depravation as their more evil-minded comrades. Many of those who had only joined to escape prison as the lesser of two evils, soon reverted to type!

In one house, a group of seriously wounded British officers was being cared for by the female inhabitants, who were sympathetic to their plight. A rampaging gang of drunks burst into the house and began trashing and plundering the place of whatever they could find. Their final act was to systematically rape all the women, in front of their officers, who minutes before they had been treating with such compassion.

Rape is a heinous crime, but it cannot be viewed in these times, through the eyes of our modern-day world and expect to be understood. As late as 1825, in England, two men were each given three years' imprisonment: one for raping a ten year old girl and the other a mature woman; while stealing something as mundane as a cheese could result in transportation for life to Australia, property far outweighing the sanctity of the life of a human being. To put it into some perspective, it would be equally hard for men from Wellington's Peninsular Army to come to terms with how we view our so-called modern world, when we give a shrug of the shoulder to genocide, ethnic cleansing and the mass murder, that has become a part of life for numbers of people throughout the world.

Gradually, the men started heading back to their camps, which soon represented the most unbelievable of sights. They were dressed in all manner of costume, carrying all kinds of plunder taken from every house, shop, store, or church in Badajoz. Much of what was carried away had little use or value whatsoever to a soldier, so the camps soon resembled a village fair and carnival rolled into one. These items were eventually either sold or exchanged for a pittance. Many soldiers comically could be seen dressed as priests, or wearing the broad brimmed hats of monks, some even in nun's habits, others dressed as grandees and even more hilarious, ladies of rank. Others in a combination of them both, mixed with their uniform. Dowdy camp-followers suddenly became imitation ladies overnight though their manners were as coarse as ever.

The empty camps had been ransacked of stores and equipment for there was no one to protect them. If ever there was a time to inflict a severe crushing and lasting defeat on the British Army it was now, for half of it was incapable of any resistance. Wellington finally decided enough was enough and on 9th April ordered General Power's Brigade of Portuguese into the city. The Provost Marshal erected a gallows in the grand square, from which he hung three nooses. Wellington's orders were to hang anybody continuing in the excesses that so shocked the officers over the last three days. Johnny Castles of the Rifles, normally the most meek of characters, was seized and placed in a cart. One of the ropes was placed around his neck, a most sobering moment if ever there was one, but he was later released! This was probably done more for its visual effect than to punish him and to act as an instant deterrent to those still in the city. It worked; by the end of the day only the comatose and dead remained in Badajoz. It was only then, that it was possible to count the terrible cost of victory, as the casualties were assessed. The inhabitants of the city were left to reflect to what the cost had been evicting the French from occupation. Woe betide any drunk straggler they discovered, on whom they could take out any retribution.

On 8th April, Captain Dobbs of the 52nd, who we originally left returning to camp, was ordered on command to take the wounded from his regiment to the General Hospital at Elvas. Reporting to collect the men at the regimental hospital, he saw Surgeon Maling in action, still busy cutting off arms and legs. Maling was first class at his profession, though rather rough in his manner. The Surgeon had his coat off, with his sleeves tucked, with a knife in his hand and a patient stretched out upon a table. After making a sweeping cut around the limb, he placed the knife between his teeth, so as to leave his hands free to tie up the arteries! Maling was well known for throwing off his coat in an emergency and rolling up his sleeves, which inevitably gained him the nickname of 'Short Sleeves'. The same day, the Rifles lost Sergeant Hugh McKay, dying from the wounds he received in action during the storming.

The excesses that took place after the fall of Badajoz were firmly placed at the door of the British Allied Army and rightly so. The events, however, were not viewed with the same degree of shock and horror by the Spanish authorities. The following month, they agreed to allow 5,000 Spanish volunteers to join Wellington's army, to be recruited into the individual regiments, as opposed to forming Spanish Regiments. Wellington, of course, welcomed this move, because of the severe losses at Ciudad Rodrigo and now Badajoz.

He desperately needed reinforcements to bring his divisions up to strength; these losses, added to those at Albuhera the previous year, had seriously depleted his force. 5,000 Spanish recruits would go a long way to rectifying this shortage, especially as they would be incorporated into his under-strength regiments. Reinforcements from England were only arriving at a trickle. Walcheren, that disastrous campaign of 1809, was still having an effect on the health of the men serving with the Peninsular army, who had taken part in that campaign. Many were constantly breaking down and out of action for long periods, due to the malarial disease, contracted in Walcheren.

The Spanish recruits, however, would still have to conform to the strict criteria and standard that was demanded by the Commander-in-Chief. As a result, a number of regiments were singled out to start enlisting up to 100 Spanish recruits, all volunteers. They had to be over five feet six inches in height, strongly built and between the ages of 19 and 27. They were to enlist with the understanding that if any regiment in which they were serving left the Peninsula, they would be immediately discharged with a month's pay to allow them to make their way home. All recruits would be allowed to follow and attend Divine service in accordance with their Roman Catholic beliefs. Recruits would be fed, clothed and paid the same as a British soldier, posted to companies in the same manner as any other reinforcement or recruit. They would be placed on the payroll from the day they were recruited but receive no bounty; the captain of their company was allowed eight dollars to supply each man with necessaries which included a knapsack, two pairs of shoes and two shirts. Thereafter, shoes would be issued at the usual rate by the Commissariat. It was stressed that the volunteers should be treated with utmost kindness and indulgence and brought by degrees to the same system of discipline as the army.

This idea had first been put forward in a dispatch in August 1811, while another previously sent in July had been for the enlistment of Portuguese. By July 1812, it would appear the recruiting of the Spanish volunteers was not going well. Wellington writing to Horse Guards, after receiving criticism of the methods used to recruit them, pointed out; 'The fact is, that I adopted it because any other that was preferred might be adopted in lieu of it; and I suspected what has turned out to be the case, that we should get but few or no recruits. We have not got enough in the whole army to form one company; and I am sorry to add that some have deserted.'

The scene at the breaches meanwhile, was still one of stark contrast to what was happening in the camps. Many of the dead still lay where they had fallen, their bloated, blackened, naked bodies, tainting the air for miles around. The engineers, undaunted, were busy repairing the damage to the breaches, that only days before were receiving such constant attention to reduce them to rubble.

The casualties for Badajoz were given as follows:

Light Division    977 plus those in the Caçadore Regiments
4th Division      925
3rd Division      500
5th Division      500

The total losses 62 officers and 744 men killed. 251 officers and 2,604 rank and file wounded. The Light Division suffered the highest casualties and not the 4th Division quoted by Oman and subsequently by other historians. He omitted to include the losses incurred by the two 2nd Battalion companies of the Rifles or the casualties received in the 1st and 3rd Caçadore Regiments. The 40th Regiment suffered the worse casualties in the 4th Division, 236, with a divisional total 925 all ranks, the 4th Foot in the 5th Division 230. The total casualties in the 95th Rifles was 305 all ranks. The losses in officers were quite devastating to the regiment:

1st Battalion
Major Peter O'Hare, killed
Lieutenant James Marshall Stokes, killed
Captain Jeremiah Crampton, died of wounds
Captain William Balvaird, wounded
Captain Charles Gray, wounded
Captain John MacDiarmid, wounded
Lieutenant William Johnstone, wounded
Lieutenant John Gairdner, wounded
Lieutenant Donald M'Pherson, died of wounds
Lieutenant Gustavus Forster, wounded
Lieutenant John FitzMaurice, wounded
3 Sergeants and 24 rank and file killed; 15 Sergeants, 3 Buglers and 136 rank and file wounded.

2nd Battalion
Captain Thomas Diggle, killed
Lieutenant Walter Death Bedell, wounded
Lieutenant Henry Herbert Manners, wounded
1 Sergeant and 20 rank and file killed; 3 Sergeants and 31 rank and file wounded.

3rd Battalion
Lieutenant Tarlton Hovenden, killed
Lieutenant George Marcus Cary, killed / died of wounds
Lieutenant William Allix, killed
Lieutenant Christopher Crudace, killed

Lieutenant MacDonald, wounded
Lieutenant Thomas Taylor Worsley, wounded
Lieutenant Duncan Stewart, wounded
Lieutenant William J. G. Farmer, wounded
Volunteer Samuel Humble Lawson, wounded
9 rank and file killed, 2 Sergeants and 45 rank and file wounded.

It can be seen from the casualty list that the two 2nd Battalion companies were as heavily engaged as the other two battalions! The following men of the regiment have been extracted from the muster paylists by company as possible casualties at Badajoz.

## Casualties Badajoz

### 1st Battalion 95th Rifles

Captain Stewart's No 1 Company

| | | |
|---|---|---|
| Sergeant | William Niven | GH 10–24th April 1812 |
| Corporals | Thomas Bancroft | GH 9–24th April |
| | Joseph Clemons | KIA 6th April |
| Riflemen | John Bandick | GH 11–19th April |
| | Nathaniel Booty | GH 10–24th April |
| | John Bushfield | GH 15–24th April |
| | John Collum | GH 19–24th April |
| | John Davies | KIA 6th April |
| | Miles Farlane | GH 16–24th April |
| | Edward Fitzsimons | GH 9–24th April |
| | David Foulkes | GH 10–14th, 16–24th April (lost left arm) |
| | Thomas Hague | GH 10–21st April |
| | William Hinde | GH 10–21st April |
| | Hugh Jones | GH 12–24th April |
| | James Kennedy | GH 10–24th April |
| | James Masterson | GH 12–24th April |
| | Patrick Newall | GH 9–24th April |
| | Oliver Peacock | GH 12–24th April |
| | Thomas Robinson | GH 6–20th April, Leicester Rearsby |
| | Thomas Robinson | GH 11–16th April, Buckingham Malyshire |
| | Hamilton Rose | KIA 6th April |
| | Robert Seath | GH April. Died 18th April |
| | John Thomas | GH 9–24th April |
| | Joshua Thomas | GH 11–24th April |
| | Andrew Wilson | GH 10–24th April |

Captain Leach's No 2 Company

| | | |
|---|---|---|
| Corporals | Francis Dransfield | GH 11–24th April |
| | Micheal Sparkett | GH 12–24th April |
| Riflemen | James Adderly | GH 10–24th April |
| | Isaac Bradbury | GH 12–22nd April |
| | Thomas Buchannon | GH 9–24th April |
| | Robert Collins | GH 8–13th April |
| | John Donovan | GH 15–24th April |
| | Micheal Harrington | GH 12–16th, 19–21st April |
| | Thomas Hay | GH 12–24th April (wounded left leg) |
| | Lawrence Hurely | GH 13–24th April |
| | William Jones | GH 11–16th, 11–14th April |
| | William Langley | GH 7–16th April |
| | Jacob Mutchinson | GH 16–24th April |
| | William Ridgley | GH 10–24th April |
| | James Ridings | GH 10–24th April |
| | Samuel Roystone | GH 6–24th April |
| | James Thompson | GH 10–24th April |
| | Isaac Whitman | GH 10–11th April |
| | William Winterton | GH 7–17th April |
| | James Wright | GH 10–24th April |

Captain Harry Smith's No 3 Company

| | | |
|---|---|---|
| Sergeants | Patrick Fleming | KIA 6th April (Stormer) |
| | James Lawson | GH 10–24th April |
| | Thomas Morgan | GH 10–14th April |
| Corporal | John McNaughton | GH 10–16th April |
| Bugler | William Green | GH 10–14th April (wounded thigh and wrist) |
| Riflemen | Willaim Butterfield | GH 10–24th April |
| | Thomas Dailey | GH 15–16th April |
| | Christopher Davies | GH 13–14th April |
| | Robert Deacon | GH 9–24th April |
| | John Emmerton | GH 17–24th April |
| | Cornelius Gollougher | GH 10–24th April |
| | Daniel Howard | GH 11–19th, 22–24th April |
| | William Johnstone | GH 9–24th April |
| | James McLaughlan | GH 9–10th April |
| | Alexander McLeod | GH 10–24th April |
| | Emmanuel Mattershaw | GH 10–24th April |
| | John Murphy | GH 7–18th April |
| | John Palmer | GH 10–24th April |
| | John Thomas | GH 13–24th April (lost left arm) |

## Captain MacDiarmid's No 4 Company

| | | |
|---|---|---|
| Sergeants | Anthony Hutton | GH 9–24th April |
| | Charles Masling | GH 10–24th April |
| | Alexander Sutherland | GH 10–24th April (wounded through both shoulders and body) |
| | William Thornton | GH 9–24th April |
| Corporals | Joseph Wall | GH 10–16th April |
| | John Tatt | GH 11–24th April (gun-shot wound) |
| Riflemen | John Alsop | GH 10–24th April |
| | Henry Berry | GH 10–11th April |
| | Robert Bowen | GH 9–24th April |
| | John Crampe | KIA 6th April |
| | John Dent | GH 10–24th April |
| | Williams Dilks | GH 9–15th April |
| | John Fisher | GH 10–24th April. Peter Fisher (wounded left leg) |
| | John Fitzgerald | GH 11–14th, 16–24th April (wounded right shoulder) |
| | Richard Fletcher | GH 10–17th April (wounded right leg) |
| | Joseph Goddart | GH 9–24th April (wounded right arm) |
| | Robert Liston | GH 16–24th April |
| | Lawrence Maher | GH 10–23rd April |
| | Thomas Quinn | GH 10–24th April |
| | William Reynolds | GH 9–24th April |
| | William Smith | KIA 6th April Leicester Thringstone |
| | William Smith | KIA 6th April Hertford Royston |
| | James Warberton | GH 9–19th, 22–24th April |
| | Francis Wolridge | KIA 6th April |

## Captain Balvaird's No 5 Company

| | | |
|---|---|---|
| Corporal | William Browne | GH 9–24th April |
| Riflemen | Robert Burns | GH 9–20th April |
| | William Cotton | GH 10–24th April (wounded left leg) |
| | Evan Ellis | GH 10–19th, 22–24th April (wounded left arm) |
| | Thomas Gardner | GH 10–11th April |
| | David Goodchild | GH 9–24th April |
| | John Griffith | KIA 6th April |
| | William Guscott | GH 10th April Elvas |
| | William Hall | GH 10–21st April |
| | James Hulett | GH 10–21st April |
| | William Lincoln | GH 10–11th April |

| Michael Molloy | GH 10–24th April |
| Dennis Moore | KIA 6th April |
| William Parkinson | GH 10–24th April |
| William Payne | GH 10–24th April |
| George Piggott | GH 11–24th April (lost right arm) |
| Ellis Williams | GH 9–24th April |
| Charles Allen | wounded but not on paylist |

### Captain Beckwith's No 6 Company

| Riflemen | John Butler | GH 11–24th April |
| | William Butler | GH 10–24th April |
| | Joseph Fuller | GH 9–24th April (wounded left arm) |
| | Thomas Lawrence | GH 10–24th April (Lost left leg) |
| | Patrick McGovern | GH 9th April. Died 9th April Elvas |
| | John Montgomery | GH 9–24th April |
| | John Rouse | GH 7–24th April (wounded right shoulder) |
| | Edward Ryan | GH 8–24th April |

### Captain Alex Cameron's No 7 Company

| Sergeant | Hugh McKay | DOW 8th April |
| Corporals | James Gilchrist | KIA 6th April |
| | Thomas Uttley | GH 9–19th April |
| Riflemen | John Banks | GH 12–24th April |
| | Andrew Bowe | GH 9–20th April |
| | John Polson | GH 15–24th April |
| | James Dutton | KIA 6th April |
| | Charles Kettles | KIA 6th April |
| | John McDonald | GH 16–20th April |
| | | (John McDenough shown as wounded) |
| | Donald McGregor | KIA 6th April |
| | Robert McKenzie | KIA 14–24th April |
| | Hugh McMaster | KIA 6th April |
| | John Malloch | GH 10–19th, 22–24th April |
| | Jacob Mills | GH 9–24th April |
| | John Mills | KIA 6th April |
| | Robert Moon | GH 12–22nd April |
| | Thomas Reston | KIA 6th April |
| | William Richmond | KIA 6th April |
| | Archibold Sparrow | GH 9–24th April |
| | Henry Turner | GH 6–24th April |
| | Thomas Young | GH 22nd April Died |

## Captain Crampton's No 8 Company

| | | |
|---|---|---|
| Sergeants | Charles McPherson | GH 10–16th April |
| | Thomas Weston | GH 10–24th April |
| Corporals | John Courtney | GH 12th, 16–24th April |
| | Robert Watt | GH 10–14th, 16–24th April |
| Riflemen | Thomas Bunton | GH 13–24th April |
| | Andrew Crawley | KIA 6th April |
| | James Darcey | GH 10–24th April |
| | Joseph Dodd | GH 12–24th April. Wounded right shoulder |
| | Christopher Dowland | GH 6th April. Died 17th April 1812 |
| | John Hewitt | KIA 6th April |
| | John Hogan | KIA 6th April |
| | Thomas McDermott | GH 10–17th April |
| | Samuel Matthews | GH 10–24th April |
| | James Miles | GH 6–24th April |
| | George Pardo | GH 19–24th April lost right thigh |
| | William Price | GH 10–24th April |
| | John Rearder | KIA 6th April |
| | John Reynolds | GH 11–24th April |
| | Isaac Shoebridge | GH 12–24th April |

## 2nd Battalion 95th Rifles

### Captain Samuel Mitchell's No 1 Company

| | | |
|---|---|---|
| Corporals | Luke Derby | KIA 6th April, forlorn hope man? |
| | John Nesbitt | KIA 6th April, forlorn hope man? |
| Riflemen | Johm Adcock | Died 10th April |
| | John Ashwell | Killed 6th April |
| | John Baxter | Killed 6th April |
| | Thomas Key | Killed 6th April |
| | Robert Manton | Killed 6th April |

### Captain Hart's No 2 Company

| | | |
|---|---|---|
| Corporals | William Carmichael | sick absent, died in GH 24th April |
| | Charles Cavanagh | Killed 6th April |
| | Lawrence McCardle | Killed 6th April, forlorn hope man? |
| Riflemen | William Crick | Killed 6th April |
| | Thomas Finan | Killed 6th April |
| | David Jones | Killed 6th April |
| | Josiah Loder | Killed 6th April |
| | Thomas Meabry | Killed 6th April |
| | Samuel Shadwell | Killed 6th April |
| | John Simpkin | Killed 6th April |
| | Patrick Karrigan | Killed 6th April |

In the paylist around 55 men are listed as sick absent and there is no doubt many of these are casualties for Badajoz.

### 3rd Battalion 95th Rifles

Captain Percival's No 1 Company

| Rifleman | Samuel Wood | died 8th April |
|---|---|---|

Captain Gray's No 2 Company

| Riflemen | James Martin | KIA storming 6th April |
|---|---|---|
| | John Springate | " |
| | George Whiteman | " |
| | James Walwork | GH died 14th April |

Captain Diggle's No 3 Company (we think he must've exchanged with Mitchell)

| Corporals | Michael Mason | KIA 6th April storming |
|---|---|---|
| | William Offer | " |
| Riflemen | Thomas Calnan | " |
| | John Cole | " |
| | Arthur Donnoley (1st) | " |
| | Isaac Ward | " |

Captain Travers' No 4 Company

| Riflemen | Thomas Hadkiss | KIA 6th April storming |
|---|---|---|
| | George Lang | " |
| | James McCann | " |
| | John Spence | " |
| | Colson Hamilton | GH died 20th April |

Captain Kent's No 5 Company

| Rifleman | William Frost | KIA 6th April storming |
|---|---|---|
| Corporal | Peter Murtock | GH died 23rd April |
| Rifleman | Richard Gough | GH died 10th April (Goff?) |

Again there are a number of men listed as sick, absent and general hospital. It is, therefore, not possible to distinguish true casualties. Captain Kent was serving on the staff, therefore, his company would have been under the command of the senior Lieutenant.

How the other regiments went about choosing to enlist Spanish recruits, we have been unable to confirm, but if the figures we have extracted are anything to go by, they had very little, or, in fact, no success. In the Rifles this duty was given to Captain Gray of the 3rd Battalion 95th Rifles. To obtain some badly-needed replacements, he headed the regiment's recruiting party and set off for Alicante with a Corporal and six Riflemen, all Spanish volunteers who were already serving in the Regiment. It would seem, by what Wellington had written to Horse Guards, that most of those recruited chose to join the 95th Rifles. Rifleman Edward Costello of the 1st Battalion, has a different outlook on the addition of Spanish recruits, 'We were joined by a sufficient number of Spaniards to give 10 or 12 men to each company in the battalion. This we found surprising. The mystery was soon unravelled by the recruits themselves, who gave us to understand that they had but three alternatives, to enter the British service, Don Julian's service, or be hanged!'

This seems at odds with Wellington and the Spanish authorities, for introducing them into the British Army. By September 1812, we have been able to confirm that 41 Spanish recruits joined the 1st Battalion 95th, 10 for the 2nd Battalion and 35 for the 3rd Battalion. These men were the only Spanish recruits to join the Rifles for the remainder of the Peninsular Campaign. Costello further adds, 'Many proved themselves worthy of their new comrades, whom they rivalled in courage and determination in every undertaking; some were even made corporals.' We found that Jose Bajon was the only Spaniard ever promoted to the rank of corporal!

Around this time, a number of men in the Light Division were feeling a bit put out because they saw their comrades in the 52nd Regiment, who had taken part in the storming party, being given the distinction of a badge. This was sewn to their coat sleeves and had the letters VS on an oval backing cloth, which represented that they were a Valiant Stormer!

Edward Costello of the Rifles did, later in life, receive a Regimental medal for the storming of Badajoz but its style goes against the accepted type of regimental medal of this period. This would seem to suggest that it was manufactured long after the Peninsula War for which it represented!

Due to the severe casualties in the ranks of the Rifles, the 1st Battalion companies were reduced from eight to six and the company commanders of all three battalions were numbered as follows:

1st Battalion
No 1 Company Captain Hon J. Stewart
No 2 Company Captain Jonathan Leach
No 3 Company Captain Harry Smith
No 4 Company Captain John MacDiarmid
No 5 Company Captain William Balvaird
No 6 Company Captain Charles Beckwith

2nd Battalion
No 3 Company Captain Samuel Mitchell
No 6 Company Captain John Hart
No 8 Company Captain John Duncan
No 10 Company Captain Donald Fergusson

3rd Battalion
No 1 Company Captain William Percival
No 2 Company Captain Charles Smyth
No 3 Company Captain William Hallen
No 4 Company Captain James Travers
No 5 Company Captain John Kent

# Salamanca

With the fall of Badajoz, the French had to urgently rethink their plans and continue Napoleon's original orders. Marmont in Northern Portugal, had already ordered Soult to advance and join him with as many men as he could spare from Cadiz, without breaking the blockade. Soult eventually joined d'Erlon at Llerena on 4th April; their combined force amounted to around 25,000 men. The news of this junction had been the catalyst which forced Wellington into an all-out assault on Badajoz a couple of days later. Soult and d'Erlon's combined force, however, was still no match for an Anglo-Portuguese Army of some 55,000 men, especially after they learned that their communications with Malaga, Granada and Cordoba had been severed by that constant thorn in their side, the Spanish guerrillas. [1] Leaving d'Erlon at Llerena, with two infantry and one cavalry division, Soult then made his way in all haste to Seville.

*French officer handing over sword to a Spanish Guerrilla*

General Cotton, in command of a brigade of light cavalry and two of heavy cavalry, engaged the French horse at Villa Garcia, some four miles from Llerena. They succeeded in routing the enemy horsemen in a sharp encounter, pushing them back on to a defensive position held by their infantry who were protected by d'Erlon's guns. Soult, believing the British would now invade Andalucia, withdrew d'Erlon to Seville. Wellington, however, still had the tricky situation of dealing with Marmont, whose force armed with bridging equipment, scaling ladders and enough supplies to last two weeks, had reached Ciudad Rodrigo on 31st March. Leaving a force to blockade the fortress, Marmont then crossed the Agueda and advanced into Portugal. With the approach of the French, the 1st German Hussars, under Victor Alten guarding the Salamanca road, abandoned the ford across the Agueda; while Carlos de Espana fell back with his small force on Almeida. The position became critical for Wellington until Trant, with around 6,000 Portuguese, arrived at Guarda from Lamego, where he joined forces with Wilson and his 6,000 Portuguese. It was from there that they were able to afford some protection to the British magazine and hospital in Celorico. Marmont retreated on this position with his combined force giving Trant no option but to retire. It was on crossing the Mondego that Trant's force was caught by the French cavalry and badly cut up. Only at this point was Wellington assured there could be no chance of Soult and Marmont joining forces. Reinforcing Hill with another cavalry brigade, he left him to watch over d'Erlon.

The Rifles broke up from their camp before Badajoz on 11th April 1812 and marched north, returning to the area they knew so well around Ciudad Rodrigo, not, however, before having all the plunder from Badajoz confiscated. This was collected into piles and burnt; all packs were searched so nothing would impede their march. Moving off on the 12th from Campo Major their first halt wasn't until they reached Arronches, where they bivouacked in a wood. Crossing the Tagus at Villa Velha on the 15th, the 1/95th then made for Monte De Senhora and the 3/95th, Sernadas; before advancing to Castello Branco on the 16th. It was quite evident the effect the French foraging parties had made on the land, but none more striking than on reaching Castello Branco where there was total devastation. Then, on reaching Sabugal, the Riflemen found it had suffered a similar fate. The French had been using it as some sort of supply depot. On all sides of the town, the entrails and offal from the slaughtered sheep and bullocks was scattered about, poisoning the air for miles around, while myriads of vultures and other birds of prey swarmed all around. Unfortunately they had to halt here to allow the supplies to catch up with them. Baron Charles Alten now took over command of the Light Division from Barnard of the Rifles, who had filled the vacancy at Badajoz. On reaching Loisa they came up close to the French rearguard.

Here the locals informed them that the enemy was in force only a short distance to their front, which caused the Light Division to advance with caution, for they had no supports with them on this side of the Tagus.

The Rifles reached Ituero on 24th April, occupying cantonments on the Agueda for two days, the 1/95th between Ituero and Castellejo De Azarava and the 3/95th at La Encina with the 43rd Regiment. It was now that every effort was made to bring the Rifles up to a fighting and serviceable condition. With no new uniforms being secured, the clothing and equipment was repaired the best way possible, though new shoes were issued. On 27th May, with Wellington's Headquarters positioned close by, he reviewed them between Guinaldo and El Bodón. Even though their uniforms were patched with numerous multi-coloured pieces of cloth, the officers faring little better, he looked beyond their flawed appearance declaring, 'They looked well and in good fighting order!' Meanwhile back in England, the country was in a state of flux after the shock assassination of Prime Minister Spencer Perceval on 11th May in the lobby of the Houses of Parliament, by an insane bankrupt, Francis Bellingham. The good news for Wellington over this sorry episode was that Lord Liverpool was appointed Prime Minister, who gave him a sympathetic ear. It was to Liverpool that Wellington wrote concerning the severe casualties received at Badajoz due to the lack of a proper Engineer Corps, which led to the formation of a Sappers and Miners Corps. [2]

*Fuente Guinaldo*

The 1/95th moved to El Bodón on 6th June, with the whole regiment moving from their cantonments on the Agueda on the 11th. Here they all bivouacked in a wood near to Ciudad Rodrigo, moving off again on the 13th to advance on Salamanca, via various marches, through Alba de Yeltes, Sancuo Bueno and on the 15th to Matilla. This brought them now within five miles of Salamanca. Meanwhile on 14th June, two French divisions, with some cavalry and 20 guns, had forded the river close to Huerta, and threatened to cut Wellington's line of communication. General Graham, with two divisions and the cavalry, promptly put an end to this notion, forcing Marmont to withdraw his force back across the river.

On the 17th, the Rifles moved even closer to Salamanca but due to the strong defence of the bridge over the Tormes by the French, they were forced to cross the river using a deep ford a mile further up the river. Eventually they bivouacked on a plain a short distance from the crossing, finally moving onto Aldea Seca, a distance of about a league and a half from Salamanca. The British cavalry made contact with the French, forcing them to retire. The Rifles were called to arms the following day due to the French making an appearance in force, but nothing came of it and they moved to Monte Rubio.

Wellington meanwhile, entered Salamanca on the 17th, where he received a warm reception from the ecstatic Spanish, who had been under the oppressive rule of the French for some three years. Unfortunately it was to be short lived!

Marmont on 22nd June, after much surveillance of Wellington's position decided to abandon the forts at Salamanca, leaving them to their fate, purely as an obstacle to be conquered, for he realised his army was not strong enough to attack Wellington in his present position. Wellington, as a result on the following day, changed formation and occupied with his centre the village of Aldea Lengua, his right the ford of Santa Marta, and with his left in the village of Moris Cos. The outposts of the Light Division having made contact with the French cleared them from Alder Lengua. The forts abandoned by Marmont were solid works of masonry, which the French had plenty of time to construct during the last two years. It was only after they surrendered, that it could really be appreciated as to how formidable an obstacle it represented. The forts were protected by strong ditches and palisades with very sturdy timbers taken from the roofs of the public buildings belonging to the university. The houses, in an area for around 400 yards, had been destroyed and cleared, a covered way constructed, the parapet of the principle fort was raised and loop-holed along with the erection of a considerable glacis. The forts were armed with 24 guns, including some large howitzers and garrisoned by a force of some 700–800 men.

The British guns, having previously been withdrawn on the 20th, opened fire on the forts on 23rd June. The same night the 6th Division was given the honour of storming them, but unfortunately they failed, with the loss of 120 killed and wounded. The Light Division was now ordered to provide a storming party, consisting of two men from each company, to storm the San Vincente Fort, the strongest of the three. The volunteers marched down to the attack position, only to find the order had been countermanded, which was just as well, as the forts capitulated on the 27th. Marmont retreated that night on Toro and Tordesillas.

Wellington ordered the Light Division off in pursuit, halting on 29th June at Castellanos De Moriscos and bivouacked, before continuing with further marches via Parada de Rubiales, Castriud and Alaejos, until halting at Nava del Rey on 1st July. By this time, the British cavalry had caught up and overtaken the French cavalry, only to be confronted by their infantry at Rueda. They were positioned here so as to cover the withdrawal of Marmont's force as they crossed the Douro at the bridge of Tordesillas. The Royal Horse Artillery coming up, immediately opened fire upon them with shrapnel, throwing them into total confusion. An advanced party of the Rifles now joined them, capturing some French infantry, amongst them a Sergeant Major of cavalry. He was later exchanged for one of their sergeants, the French stating that their man was due to be raised to the ranks of the officers. The Light Division entered the town just minutes after the French had left.

Marmont was now positioned behind the Douro at Tordesillas, his right on Pollos and left at Simancas, on the Piuerga. The Light Division was sent to Tordesillas on the 3rd, with the 3rd Division going to Pollos, but found the fords were too deep to cross. The Light Division, therefore, was withdrawn to Rueda that evening, where it remained for near on two weeks. This was to help combat the sickness that was prevalent in the ranks at this time. It was felt it would also be more beneficial if they were to occupy the buildings in the town during the heat of the day, then every night advance and bivouack a mile in advance of the town. This movement was undertaken so that in the event of the general alarm sounding, the men could fall in more quickly than if in cantonments. The remainder of the Army was halted in rear of Medina del Campo.

For the Rifles' officers to be quartered in houses made a welcome change, Lieutenant Simmons much preferred them to the two blankets he had stitched together to form a sort of sleeping bag! It is interesting to note how the system was applied for the distribution of houses throughout the division. It was all down to the Regimental Quartermasters of each regiment, who were given a number of dwellings to allocate between the officers and men. Though it didn't always go to plan, as Quartermaster Surtees of the 3rd Battalion Rifles confirms, due to the action of a senior officer with a grudge against him! Surtees' block of dwellings had a number of stables attached to it which was a bonus when on campaign.

Without checking inside each dwelling individually, he marked up the houses in the usual custom of giving what he thought as the better accommodation to the senior officers and so on down through the ranks. One Rifles' officer, having been given one of the best houses on offer was put out because it did not have a stable attached, whilst the Quartermaster moved into a lesser house, which also had no stable. He put his horses and mules into a house with some of the men and then went off to continue with his duties. On his return, he was informed by his servant, that the officer in question, senior to him, having no stables turned all his baggage animals out of the house and replaced them with his own, leaving the Quartermaster's running about loose, while all his saddlery and mule-apparatus had been cast out into the yard. Surtees had to bear this indignation with clenched teeth.

Life, as we can see, was not always harmonious amongst the officers of the Rifles; there were a number of occasions when all was not well within their ranks. Lieutenant Gairdner, the American, was often at odds with Major Cameron, due to the fact he was often biased in favour of his fellow countrymen, this being a similar gripe voiced by Irish officers. Surtees was pleased, no doubt, when ordered to Salamanca to bring up the rations for the battalion; away from such petty complaints made amongst the officers. Then he moved onto Abrantes to arrange for the badly needed clothing and various goods and equipment to be brought up to the regiment. However, he and the regiment were to be disappointed, for there was no transport available for him to carry out this task. At Abrantes, he was joined by a detachment of the 2nd Battalion 95th Rifles, the two companies of Captains Duncan and Fergusson, fresh from England, who were proceeding up country to join the Light Division.

There was a down side for the Rifles' staff being stationed so long at Rueda, as it contained a large number of huge wine vaults set in the sides of the surrounding hills, for which it was well known. This was a great temptation and it took all the guile of the officers and senior NCOs against the cunning of the men to keep the two apart. It was when, on entering some of these caves for the first time, that the Rifles found the bodies of a number of French soldiers who had been severely mutilated by the Spaniards. It was also while here on another occasion, that a prominent Rifleman, by the name of Taylor, who had been given the nickname of 'Sir Arthur' for his likeness to the Duke of Wellington, met with an unusual end. One of the Riflemen, on taking a drink from a large open cask, came in contact with the 'nose' of Sir Arthur, who no doubt had sampled more than was good for him and slipped into the vat and drowned! Rifleman Taylor was the servant to Charles Eeles and on completing his duties he would then, each night, as circumstances allowed, go on a drinking binge; probably his sole pleasure in life.

These two weeks were treated more like an unofficial truce by the men of both armies who bathed with civility at the same spots, and even went as far as sharing rations. It wasn't without incident, however, for one Rifleman was drowned while bathing. What was ironic about the whole episode, was the fact that this Rifleman had already survived a most serious wound in 1811. A ram-rod fired by the enemy, had gone straight through his body and lodged in his back bone and it could only be removed by knocking it out with a stone!

Around this time Quartermaster Surtees of the 3rd Battalion Rifles was sent recruiting for Spanish volunteers. This must have been a separate duty from Captain Gray of the same battalion, for he states, his party did not gain a single Spanish recruit! An incident involving a sergeant of the 3rd Battalion Rifles caused some sadness in their ranks at this time. A grenadier of the 61st Regiment, Private Dennis Farrell, travelled from his quarters on a quest to seek out a Rifles' Sergeant serving with the Light Division. This involved the delicate situation of his wife's desertion in favour of the Rifleman, leaving him with the impossible task of caring for two children. Why she chose such drastic action can only be guessed at, though it was implied that he treated her rather roughly. The grenadier, however, was hell bent on a reconciliation, confronted his wife and persuaded her to go with him some distance from the camp so they could settle their difference in private, away from outside intervention. Ann, his wife, was still adamant however, that she was going to remain with the Rifle Sergeant, as her life had changed for the better in these harsh times, especially as she had established herself as an agreeable addition to the wives and camp followers of the Light Division. She had become quite a favourite amongst the men with her dancing and gay presence, which even touched the heart of high command, as she had danced on a number of occasions with old General Vandeleur, well he appeared old to the younger Riflemen, though in fact he was only 49! The grenadier saw his task was hopeless and burst into a jealous rage; withdrawing his bayonet he plunged it into his wife's breast. The Riflemen, hearing her chilling screams rushed to her aid, but on arrival found she was beyond all help. The grenadier was eventually arrested at Fon Castin on 8th July 1812 for the murder of his wife and found guilty of manslaughter and received 12 months' imprisonment in custody of his regiment. He would eventually end his days later in the year killed in an action on the mountain slopes of the Pyrenees. His wife's remains were buried by the Riflemen, who could only regret her passing, for she was sorely missed.

Marmont's request for further troops, up to this time, had brought only the arrival of Bonnet's Division. Marmont, however, was still in too strong a position for Wellington to attack him, even without this additional force. On 16th July, Marmont sent Bonnet's Division across the bridge at Toro to see what sort of a response it would provoke. Wellington immediately obliged, by countering this by sending a force to meet it. Marmont withdrew at midnight and the next day ordered the bulk of his army across the river at Tordesillas, and then made a forced march to Nava del Rey.

As a result, the Light Division advanced with the cavalry. They had a number of sharp skirmishes with the French horse on 18th July, who had advanced from Nava del Rey. Wellington and Beresford rode off that morning about 7 a.m. to Castrejon, a movement they would soon regret. A piquet of the Rifles, consisting of 30 men under a subaltern with a similar piquet of the 43rd stationed on their right, had been in position in advance all night. It so happened, that at the same time as Wellington's arrival, a French officer decided to make a daring raid on two guns belonging to the Horse Artillery, under the command of Captain Jenkins with Cotton's cavalry. The Rifles' piquet immediately came under fire from round shot, which was flying all about their position. Lieutenant Kincaid, the Rifles' piquet commander, was more surprised, however, by the terrific yell and commotion coming from behind the rising ground to his left front. Realising that his men were in immediate danger he ordered them to take cover in a deep, wide ditch a hundred yards to their rear. In the next instant, Lord Wellington and his staff were followed by a cloud of French and English dragoons, all intermixed with the Horse Artillery. They came bursting into view over the same hill on which they had previously been stationed. The cavalry were furiously chopping and stabbing at each other's heads with their swords in a confused, animated mass. Wellington and his staff took up a position with the guns behind the Riflemen, safe from the cavalry as they swept past. Neither Riflemen nor 43rd, were able to fire a shot for fear of injuring their own men. The British dragoons were reinforced by more of their own cavalry and turned the tables on the French horsemen, sending them scurrying back to their own lines. The air was blue with outrage and condemnation by Wellington's staff, especially General Bock and his huge German dragoon orderly. Cotton arrived with his cavalry brigade, on the right, this meant the piquets could be withdrawn and Kincaid and his Riflemen rejoined the Light Division.

Marmont now brought up his infantry from Alaejos, turning Wellington's left flank. This caused him to order the three divisions he had with him, to fall back on Torrecilla. This they completed by each battalion moving in close column of companies, so that they could form square if attacked, while the cavalry guarded their flanks. The French pressed on, thinking they could turn Wellington's left, but the British divisions were able to continue their movement unhindered. This made for a splendid, but odd military spectacle, with both armies marching in parallel lines around 500 yards apart across a level plain, all eyeing each other just waiting for the slightest break of formation to instigate an attack. The Light Division brought up the rear.

The French had in position a large force of cavalry, ready to pounce in an instant, should the opportunity arise.

The two armies continued in this manner for some ten miles, avoiding any village or ground that could disrupt their formation, making them vulnerable to a cavalry attack. In the heat and dust, the men were suffering terribly from the lack of water as they made for the high ground on the other side of the River Guarena. Every now and again the Royal Horse Artillery unlimbered and sent a couple of rounds into the enemy, the French cavalry would then dash at them and on one occasion succeeded for a short time in taking possession of the guns. At one stage a group of French infantry rushed forward and caused the Light Division to veer off the road, forcing them to continue their advance through fields of standing corn. At last the Guarena was reached and the 5th Division immediately halted to drink. The Light Division bringing up the rear, rushed into the river with every man and beast eager to quench their parched throats. This was just the opportunity the French had been waiting for and they fired a number of guns into this mass of men. Captain Leach of the Rifles said, 'while trying to get a mouthful of the lukewarm muddy water the enemy round-shot came smashing into our position.' On the opposite bank, Wellington took up a position on high ground. The 4th Division going to the left close to Castrillo, the Light Division formed the centre and the 5th on the right near to Canizal; while the other divisions formed to the right at Vallesa.

A French column consisting of a brigade of dragoons, with an infantry battalion and three guns crossed the ford near Castrillo, but Victor Alten soon drove them back to their own side of the river, with the loss of their brigadier and around 100 men. The British cavalry now attempted a counter-attack, but they failed to achieve anything. The 27th and 40th Regiments were also ordered forward and sent a volley into the French infantry, who were soon in retreat. The British cavalry captured around 150 prisoners, with the loss of 145 of their own force, in killed, wounded and captured. The total allied loss for the day was 442, a third belonging to 27th and 40th Regiments. The firing ceased once it became dark and the British Allied Army now bivouacked for the night.

The following day, with the heat again most oppressive, the French fired round shot and shells at Wellington's position, just to keep them on their toes. The Light Division was stood to arms when a round shot took the head completely off a Rifleman who had only just arrived from England. Late afternoon, Wellington sent the 1st and Light Divisions to counter a move being made to the south by the French. With night falling, both armies settled down in formation, the British on the heights of Vallesa, and the French at Tarazona.

During the night, Marmont tried to cross the Guarena at Cantalapidra, to reach the extensive plateau that stretched towards Salamanca. At daybreak, on 20th July, Wellington found the French were nowhere to be seen. The cavalry now informed him that the French had turned his right flank, by keeping to the lower ground. The Light Division was sent in that direction and the Rifles soon came in sight of the French, who had been hidden by the undulating ground. The companies of Captains Stewart, Leach and Smith of the 1st Battalion 95th, along with the battalion Staff, were attached to the Light Division's 1st Brigade, while those companies of MacDiarmid, Balvaird and Beckwith remained with the 2nd Brigade. Both armies, as a result, were once again marching parallel to each other as they had done a couple of days earlier. With this martial stalemate taking place once again between the two armies, the British baggage, camp followers and supplies, were stretched out for quite some distance behind the divisions. Wellington had planned to cut the French off at Cantalpino, but they had out-marched the British force. Ordering the 5th Division to protect the baggage and supply line, Wellington inclined more to the west towards Aldea Rubia and as a result, the gap between the two armies widened, and gradually they lost sight of each other. The heat was now so unbearable, that a short halt had to be made to let the men and animals escape the choking dust which engulfed them on the march. The column continued until late in the evening halting close to Cabeza Vellosa, from where they could see the French camp fires around Babila Fuente, confirming Marmont had out-manoeuvred them again.

On the 21st, Wellington marched to San Christobal, as it was now clear to him that Marmont was trying to cut his communications with Ciudad Rodrigo. He conceded that he could not continue with an offensive campaign and the defence of Portugal had to be the greater priority. However, Marmont's indecision and resulting movements, changed the situation completely from one of advantage over the British and their defensive-minded commander, into what would become a catastrophic turn of events for the French Army. With the French commander holding Calvarrasa de Arroba as an advance post and another division posted on the heights of Babila Fuente, he started to take up a position with the rest of his corps, between Alba de Tormes and Salamanca. Wellington, having crossed the Tormes near Salamanca, took up a position facing east, with his left on the Tormes near Santa Marta and right near the village of Los Arapiles. The 3rd Division (now under Packenham) and the Portuguese cavalry, were entrenched at Cabrerizos, from where they were able to watch the fords to the west of Barila Fuente, the main army having crossed by the bridge at Salamanca. The Light Division, meanwhile, had crossed by the deep ford of Santa Marta further down stream. On reaching the opposite bank, they pitched their bell tents on ground that had been marked out for them and settled down for the night. A terrific storm broke with torrents of rain accompanied by the most frightening thunder and lightning ever remembered, startling the horses of both armies. Some of the horses in the Light Division broke from their piquet lines and galloped through the camp causing chaos and confusion. This disturbance continued until it was established that the French cavalry had not attacked them!

The following morning was one of complete contrast and brilliant sunshine. Wellington's plan, at this stage, was still to fall back on Ciudad Rodrigo and as a result he sent all his baggage off in advance of his divisions under the protection of D'Urban's cavalry, at the same time placing his remaining divisions under cover of the heights. Only the 7th Division being visible to Marmont, the French commander was still under the impression Wellington was about to retreat along the Trejares to Ciudad Rodrigo road and the 7th Division was his rearguard. He therefore ordered his troops to march around the southern flank of Wellington's force with the intention of out-flanking them and cutting their line of communications.

The events that now unfolded, meant that the Light Division and the Rifles in particular, played very little part. Their only consolation was that two companies of the 2nd Battalion mentioned earlier joined them here. The four 2nd battalion companies were now under the temporary command of Major George Wilkins, who would be replaced by Major Amos Norcott, when he joined from Cadiz, with the remaining two companies of this battalion.

*Lesser Arapile or Arapile Chico*

Wellington had a mixed force of 50,000 men, of which half were British with 60 guns, opposed to a French force with 47,000 men, all veteran seasoned troops and 78 guns.

To cover his out-flanking movement, Marmont ordered Bonnet to occupy both the greater and lesser Arapiles. Wellington, however, beat him to the lesser Arapile by sending a contingent of Caçadores to occupy it. Foy and Ferey's Divisions of some 10,000 infantry and 1,300 cavalry, held Calverrasa de Arapil, while a 20,000 strong force of four divisions marched to the south-east of the great Arapile, with Thomières' division pushing on to some heights south of the village of Los Arapiles.

Wellington countered these movements by occupying the village of Los Arapiles and forming a defensive line facing south and east, using the lesser Arapile as the salient. The Light Division was ordered to hold the ground west of Cawarrasa de Arriba, with the 7th Division in support, and with Bock's German Hussars on its flank. Pakenham, with the 3rd Division was to cross the Tormes and occupy a position at Aldea Tejada, three miles south of Salamanca.

The clouds of dust raised by the movement of the 3rd Division, led Marmont to believe Wellington was retreating on Ciudad Rodrigo. He then made the fatal mistake of ordering his divisional commanders to reinforce his left, who were under the misapprehension that they were going to continue the parallel marching of the previous days.

Wellington couldn't believe his luck. From the lesser Arapile, he now witnessed half the French force marching away from his centre. Marmont, as a result, was suddenly confronted by three British divisions coming from behind the shelter of the hills, which were now all making for his weakened centre. Frantically, he ordered Ferey and Sarrut to join him. Wellington galloped over to Pakenham, ordering him to advance and seize the heights some two and a half miles to his front. This movement, at first, went undetected by the French. Thomières' Division at this point, was stretched out for at least a mile across the very front of the advancing 3rd Division. This gave D'Urban's cavalry the ideal opportunity of charging amongst the straggling division before it had a chance to form up properly, causing much confusion. Pakenham's infantry, advancing under a storm of grapeshot, arrived with the leading brigade formed into three lines, charged, and broke up the French columns. The 5th Division was also on the move advancing from Los Arapiles, Wellington's centre, attacked the heights to the south, under an equally strong artillery fire. Their determination overwhelmed the French and in the confusion the leading brigade pushed too far in advance and became mixed up with it. As a result there was some anxiety in the division, but Cotton's heavy brigade of cavalry came up and charged three separate formations of the enemy, with the sad loss of Le Marchant.

They were followed up by the light dragoons who drove the French horse from the field, leaving their infantry unprotected.

In an unbelievably short time Marmont's left, consisting of three divisions, had been put out of action with both Marmont and Bonnet being wounded. The command devolved on Clausel, who gained some success against Cole's division which had been checked. Pack's Portuguese failed to capture the greater Arapile. The French now made a determined counter-attack with Sarrut's Division, supported by parts of Bonnet's and Ferey's. They were having some success until the 6th and then the 1st Divisions arrived, forcing the French to retire. Clausel ordered Ferey to hold the British advance; he made a desperate stand with seven battalions formed in line. Eventually they were forced to fall back to the edge of a forest, where Ferey was struck by a round shot.

The only French Division still intact was Foy's which engaged the Light Division. Just before sunset, Clausel ordered him to cover the flank of his retreat. Wellington immediately followed up with the 1st and the Light Divisions, but Foy was equal to this and was able to retire to Alba de Tormes. Wellington thought he now had Foy trapped, for Carlos de Espana, with 3,360 Spaniards, were holding the castle which commanded the bridge and ford. For some inexplicable reason, de Espana, without orders, abandoned his post, which allowed the scattered French army to escape!

The Light Division had remained as spectators for the greater part of the day, their presence enough to keep the French in check in this part of the battlefield. Some companies of the Rifles did get detached around noon to aid the light troops of the 7th Division, fighting with Foy's voltiguers. It wasn't until around 5 o'clock in the afternoon that they were actually ordered up to attack the French right flank. Before they could engage with the enemy, the light faded, allowing them to escape under the cover of darkness. It was because of this, that part of the Rifles met with an unexpected opposition; their officers leading them on came suddenly upon the French without warning due to the blackness of the night. Foy was able to keep the Light Division at bay by posting a strong rearguard of light troops, even though Ross's battery engaged them. Foy wrote later; 'night alone saved my division, without it the enemy would have arrived at Alba de Tormes before the units of our seven routed divisions got there' (Foy, *Vie Militaire*, p 176), though Foy was unaware that had the Spanish commander, de Espana, held his position with some conviction, the French would have been completely destroyed. Marmont reported that his losses at Salamanca amounted to only 6,000 men and nine guns; Oman was scathing in his being economical with the truth, but who could blame him for not wanting to report to Napoleon that his real losses, according to Oman, were, not less than 14,000 in killed, wounded and prisoners.

This did not include some 10,000 men missing, who dispersed to rejoin later. (Oman Vol V. p469 and appendix xi)

Wellington, in his despatch, reported 7,000 prisoners were taken. The British losses being: 28 officers and 360 other ranks killed, 176 officers and 2,491 other ranks wounded, a total including missing of 3,219. The Portuguese lost around 2,000. The Spanish on the other hand, had two killed and four wounded which, under the circumstances, is hard to see even how these could have occurred. In the Light Division, the casualties were one officer and 27 men wounded; of these, only seven belonged to the Rifles.

We have found Rifleman Isaac Haywood, of two company 2/95th, as sick absent died 9th September and Sergeant George Ecke six company 2/95th, died 26th July 1812, as the only possible casualties in the musters.

The battle of Salamanca was a brilliant victory for Wellington's allied army, described as: 'The Battle where he beat about 40,000 Frenchman in forty minutes!' It was definitely a war changing battle, for it released southern Spain from French oppression. The 44th Regiment captured the eagle of the French 62nd Regiment, while the 88th have often been quoted as capturing the eagle of the 101st Regiment, though there is some doubt as to what happened to the Eagle of the French 101st, when in fact it was only the 'Jingling-Johnny'; a form of band instrument, according to Paddy Griffiths, p35, *A History of the Peninsular War Volume IX, Modern Studies of the War in Spain and Portugal, 1808–1814,* Greenhill books.

During the battle, the Light Division spent the greater part of the afternoon exposed to a cannonade but had to remain in position, advancing only at a very late hour, by which time it was too dark to make any worthwhile contact. The Light Division spent the following morning cleaning their weapons and equipment after the night's heavy storm. About 10 o'clock they were ordered to stand to and move position with their left resting on the Tormes and their right extending along a ridge of rising ground with a sprinkling of trees. Beyond these could be seen the other divisions in continuation of the Light Division formation.

# Advance to Madrid
# and Retreat into Portugal

The battle of Salamanca was felt as an anti-climax for the Rifles, as they had played very little part in the victory. They advanced the morning after the battle in hot pursuit of the retreating French Army.

On 23rd July, the cavalry of Anson and Bock, out in advance, came up with the French at Garcia Hernandez, a village some four miles east of Alba de Tormes. The French rearguard consisted of infantry, cavalry and a battery of Horse Artillery. The allied cavalry immediately attacked the French horse forcing them to retire; their infantry instantly formed square. One of Bock's German squadrons attacked the nearest square and succeeded in breaking it although they received numerous volleys from the determined Frenchmen. The squadron took many casualties in both men and horses, but practically destroyed the French square. Another German squadron attacked a second French square, with a similar result. The third French square of the 69th Regiment was able to repulse the attack made on it. This was due to the ground they had chosen being on an angle of the road that was rising towards higher ground. Foy was in this square and no doubt his presence added to the French resolve.

The Rifles, at the head of the Light Division, came up just as this action had concluded and were able to view the aftermath first hand. The sight that greeted them was one of mixed emotions. A number of horses and men lay dead close to where the squares had formed, some, still on their mounts, gripping their swords, man and beast frozen in a macabre death pact. As the Rifles were passing this glorious but sad scene a German Hussar officer came up looking for his brother, stating he had not seen him for some six years; he found him dead, sword in hand, upon his horse.

On 25th July, a Corporal's detachment of the 14th Light Dragoons, under the command of William Hanley, was out on patrol to ascertain the movements of the French cavalry. The 1st German Hussars and 14th Light Dragoons of the Light Division, had already halted and bivouacked at Arevola. At the small village of Blanchez Sanchez, Corporal Hanley's patrol came upon a group of French Dragoons. Their piquet, on seeing the British horsemen, ran to take shelter in a house with a high wall and out-buildings that enclosed a courtyard, with only a narrow passage for entrance or exit. Corporal Hanley surrounded the building and had some of his men fire along the passageway and then tricked the French officer in command, into surrendering.

He let them retain some honour by keeping their personal baggage. Eventually they emerged and piled arms. Hanley was surprised, as was the French officer, that his little band had captured one officer and 27 dragoons without a single casualty! On making off with his prisoners, they were joined by a French colonel, his servant and baggage animals; coming up to Hanley he slapped him on the back, assuming the British dragoons were the prisoners of the French cavalry. Hanley immediately turned the tables, taking him prisoner along with the servant, making a splendid addition to the success of his patrol. On returning to the regiment they were cheered and praised for their conduct. The horses of the French found fit enough for service, were drafted into the cavalry remount pool and the amount they were valued distributed between the men of the patrol. Wellington later granted each man 12 dollars and double that amount to the corporal, who was mentioned in his despatches.

With Wellington's army advancing on Burgos, the Light Division pushed on after the rapidly retreating French Army, heading towards Madrid. They crossed the Guaderama and reached the area around Escurial and bivouacked in the town's park. As they were taking off their packs in preparation to settling down for the night, two boars startled by all the activity, came rushing out of the undergrowth. Suddenly they were being chased, stabbed and slashed at by the hungry soldiers and in no time they were killed, cut up and distributed amongst the men. The officers of the Light Division took time out here to witness first hand the splendours and last resting place in the famous palace of Escurial, of the Kings of Spain and the royal family. Captain Dobbs of the 52nd Regiment tells us, 'Part of the building contained members of the Royal Family who were in wooden berths, like bunks on a ship. The bodies, embalmed and baked in ovens, their coffins having been opened by the French who left them exposed in full view, still in elaborate dress.' He took two silk buttons from John of Austria's costume as keepsakes! The French had already taken everything of value.

It was around this time that Adjutant Kincaid of the 1st Rifles tried to obtain some extra provisions for his messmates. Seeing a large farmhouse at some distance he made his way to it; on entering the building, he came upon two women belonging to the German Legion in the kitchen sitting smoking their pipes. Looking around, he soon came to the conclusion that anything of value had already been secured by the women. Kincaid therefore, made them an offer to purchase whatever they had; promptly two live chickens were produced. Kincaid, pleased with his purchases, mounted his horse but had only gone about a hundred yards when the hens started flapping about, which instantly panicked his horse into bolting and as a result, it caught its hoof in a rut throwing Kincaid head first into a ditch full of muddy water, while the horse continued in one direction and the chickens in another.

The dazed and soaked Rifles officer, all dignity lost, went running after his horse which came, as luck would have it, to a sudden halt, his heavy boat cloak having slipped with the saddle and hung under the animal, restricting its movement. Rider and horse now returned to the farm, for Kincaid had seen the two German women chasing after the chickens; on reaching them he demanded to have the fowls back. They pretended to know nothing about them. Sensing that nothing would be gained by this approach, Kincaid produced a half dollar and the chickens miraculously appeared from beneath their skirts. The two German women were most formidable; both heavily built and standing six feet or more, which convinced Kincaid that they had probably thrashed a better man than himself on more than one occasion. He now rode away, not sure whether to be pleased or sorry with himself!

In Madrid, all was total confusion amongst the French, who knew how close the British Allied Army was. They abandoned the city leaving behind a garrison of around 2,000 men plus, more significantly, 180 pieces of artillery, 20,000 stands of arms and enormous amounts of stores, along with all the spoils of war that a plundering army had accumulated that could not be taken away. All this would fall into British hands and they surrendered without the firing of a single shot in anger!

On 4th August 1812, the 1st Brigade of the Light Division moved to Pedraja de Portillo, where Captain Balvaird relinquished the command of his company on account of ill health and returned to England. On the 10th, a group of Portuguese cavalry with two guns, who was in advance of the Light Division, was attacked by French Dragoons. Putting up little resistance, the guns were taken before the Light Division could come to their aid. The Rifles eventually arrived at Vilaverde, which was about two miles from Madrid, the 2nd Brigade remaining there while the 1st Brigade moved on to Getafe, a further eight miles from the city.

On 12th August the 2nd Brigade of the Light Division went into the city, and the other brigade remained at Getafe, until the retreat into Portugal. When the Madrid garrison surrendered on 14th August, they were allowed to keep their personal baggage and packs. Many were found to be German and most often blind drunk.

The Division was now able to enjoy what Madrid had to offer in reasonable comfort as it was not required for the siege and storming of Burgos. The 3rd Division was also in Madrid. The only drawback for the officers and men was they had very little money, for they were still six months in arrears with their pay. For the troops stationed in Madrid, this brought on a whole new experience, especially for the Riflemen, being the nearest to a civilised existence the officers had enjoyed since landing in the Peninsula. They were now able to attend numerous dances and enjoy the company of Spanish ladies and reflect in the attention being paid to them by the grateful inhabitants. The officers of the Light Division who had been involved with the theatricals, were able to capitalise on this by putting on a number of their plays. They were so successful that they were able to donate 250 dollars to the poorest families in the city.

On 31st October, Captains Cadoux and Jenkins' companies, under the command of Major Norcott, finally arrived from Cadiz, where they had been serving with General Graham. They now joined the 2nd Battalion companies in the 2nd Brigade. Three Companies of the 1st Battalion, which had been detached to serve with the 2nd Battalion, were able to return to their own battalion in the 1st Brigade. The 20th Portuguese Regiment of line, also part of the force from Cadiz, was placed in the 1st Brigade.

The divisions halted for the night on 2nd November close to a small town. Lieutenant Kincaid, having posted the Rifle piquets, rode into the town to join up with his fellow officers to get something to eat. On entering its large market square, he found it crowded with soldiers of all regiments and nations belonging to the allied army, most of whom were drunk. In the middle of this mayhem was a maddened bull being teased by the soldiers for their amusement. It suddenly came charging past Kincaid, immediately making a lunge at Quartermaster Ross of the 1st Battalion Rifles. It ripped off part of his trousers before continuing on to find another target, which happened to be an unsuspecting Portuguese soldier. Charging into him with great force, he was sent spinning two or three times into the air before coming to the ground with a crash, in astonishment, as he had no idea what had just taken place! Before it had a chance to make Kincaid its next victim, the Rifle officer directed his horse through the first set of doors of the nearest house, thundering into a room full of bullock-drivers who were sitting around a table and just about to eat a meal. Horse and rider crashed into the table and the astonished men, sending the contents and lighting into the air. To avoid becoming the victim of their wrath, feeling it was safer to face the raging bull, he left as quickly as he entered!

With the advance of the French in force and Burgos proving to be too tough a nut to crack, Wellington had to abandon the siege and fall back on Portugal. The Light Division, therefore, reluctantly left the poor citizens of Madrid to reflect on their fate, once the French re-occupied the city. On reaching Salamanca, the Rifles were billeted in the Irish College. Parts of this large building had, more than likely, provided some of the timbers required for the palisading of the forts constructed by the French. On the night of 10th November Lieutenants Simmons and Firman, being orderly officers of their respective battalions, were about to check that the men were present and that all lights were out prior to the companies settling down for the night.

On reaching the stone stairs that accessed the upper corridors of the building, they found them too slippery and dangerous to ascend in the dark, due, no doubt, to this section of the building being exposed to the elements. Parts of the protective balustrade were missing which added to the danger involved. Lieutenant Simmons told Firman he would go and find a candle to light their way. On returning he was surprised to find the Lieutenant had already ascended the stairs. Simmons, with the aid of his flickering candle, only managed to ascend three or four steps when a sudden movement from above alerted him. Firman came crashing through the balustrade, his head hitting the wall on one side and his feet the other, before coming to a sickening thud on the paved floor of the cellar. Rushing to his aid, he could see in the half light that his brother officer was in a terrible state. At the same time he was equally astonished to see close by, a Private of the 43rd Regiment with his Portuguese wife fast asleep, both oblivious to the fatal drama occurring only a few feet away. Lieutenant Firman died of his injuries on 13th November.

*43rd marching through swampy ground*

The army started out on their retreat from Salamanca to Ciudad Rodrigo on 15th November, the beginning of a most difficult period for the men, with the weather turning extremely bad and food becoming nonexistent. As if this was not enough, the French, sensing a chance to turn the tables, pressed the rear guard in earnest. The Riflemen as a result, were continually looking for any opportunity to stave off their acute hunger while in constant contact with the French troops. On coming upon the carcasses of some half-starved bullocks lying dead in their yokes and attached to abandoned baggage carts, they immediately started cutting off chunks. The Riflemen roasted them best way they could on makeshift fires, devoured the half cooked meat, even though it was as tough as the soles of their boots! Men could also be seen scavenging amongst the trees trying to find any of the sweet acorns which fell from the trees in these parts, which they ate after roasting. Herds of pigs belonging to the local peasants normally grazed on these acorns; however, the men from the preceding divisions had shot and eaten most of them. The shooting of these animals at first caused some concern in the Light Division, for it was thought the divisions in advance of them had come under attack. Wellington, instead of being sympathetic to the plight of his army, immediately had two men executed as a deterrent to others, to prevent them killing any more of these animals.

Numbers of men from all the divisions who had been wounded or too sick or exhausted to continue, now fell into the hands of the French advance guard. The rear guard at one point was pressed most severely by the French who, on 17th November, were so close that the 1st Battalion 95th had to move to higher ground commanding both sides of the road to keep the French at bay. Half-starved, cold and wet, they eventually gave way and retired due to the superior enemy force. Rifleman John Himbury, of the 2nd Battalion 95th, was taken prisoner whilst covering the ford at San Muñoz during a snow storm. He later managed to escape and rejoin the battalion on the 18th, minus shirt, shoes and socks. The French troops pursuing them were noted by one of the Light Division as wearing: broad toed shoes studded with nails; wide trousers of Spanish brown cloth; light grey great coats decorated with red or green worsted epaulettes with their belts outside and carrying brown hairy knapsacks; a broad leather topped-shako decorated with a ball; shining scales and fronted by an eagle with extended wings.

Lieutenant Cameron of the 2nd Battalion Rifles, in command of the baggage and sick wagons, was at this point positioned between the rear of the 7th Division and the leading companies of Rifles in the 1st Brigade, Light Division. The French in their advanced position, seeing they were lightly guarded, seized the opportunity and attacked the column. They captured Cameron and after taking his horse and relieving him of his shoes along with the contents of his pockets, set him free. Obviously they had more pressing matters to contend with. As it turned out, this was the capture of General Paget! Colour Sergeant George Baller, of the 1st Battalion 95th, had been ordered by General Vandeleur to take charge of the baggage at Salamanca. Baller was something of a celebrity in the regiment, due to having been captured during the action at the Coa in 1810 with Captain M'Cullock, along with half a company. Like M'Cullock, Baller escaped and joined a group of Spanish partisans and finally made his way back to the regiment. He had also been wounded a couple of times and was now captured for a second time while escorting the baggage. It is safe to assume it was around the same time that Cameron's baggage column came under attack.

On reaching the River Huebra, an important stage on the retreat, an officer who had advanced from where they were waiting for orders, suddenly came riding back shouting, 'the enemy cavalry, fall in, join the ranks!' Immediately some French cavalry, who were wearing bright shinning helmets and distinctive white cloaks, could be seen amongst the trees watching their movements. The 1st Brigade of the Light Division was ordered by General Erskine, [1] whom they knew all too well from his short time in command of the Division when Craufurd was in England, to cover the withdrawal of his cavalry. General Alten was most indignant at having his brigade ordered to such a precarious position. After forming up and halting them in column, ready to form square, he then remonstrated with Erskine in no uncertain terms. Luckily Wellington came up at this moment and immediately ordered the brigade to cross the river. This wasn't a moment too soon, for five minutes later the French infantry with a large force of cavalry and artillery in support, instantly took up the high ground overlooking the river, sent a heavy barrage into the retreating brigade, killing and wounding a number of men. The Light Division's Royal Horse Artillery troop, drawn up on the opposite bank, gave them some badly needed covering fire. The French, on trying to seize the initiative, sent a large body of infantry down towards the river, opposite the Light Division's left. Two companies of the 2nd 95th, Captains MacNamara and Gray, were sent to skirmish with them, while four companies of the 1st 95th, with some companies of the 52nd Regiment, went down to the river and formed line to oppose any thought the French might have had of crossing. Captain Dawson, of the 52nd Regiment was killed during this action. The rearguard remained in this position until dark, the men laying down on the same ground in line, with two Rifle companies on piquet in front. It continued to rain and the men, still without rations, not being able to seek any form of shelter, spent a most miserable night in the open.

Reaching Portugal on 25th November, the Rifles were re-supplied at Villa de Puerco from the stores in Ciudad Rodrigo and relieved to be reunited with their baggage. When the men finally arrived they looked more like a band of beggars than soldiers. [2] The Light Division was now able to spend nearly five months in winter quarters. Lieutenant Firman's possessions were auctioned off; Captain Gairdner bought his pony. When the effects of Captain Crampton were sold off, some months earlier, the American 95th Rifles' officer, bought his 'gun' along with several other items.

It was army protocol to auction deceased officers' effects and the proceeds would then be sent to their wives or next-of-kin. On the retreat into Portugal it was reported in the 1st Battalion that 22 men were missing, most of these were probably overrun around the same time as Rifleman Himbury.

On 28th November the 1st Brigade of the Light Division, less the 3rd Regiment Portuguese which remained in the suburbs of Ciudad Rodrigo, marched off to be distributed at the following locations: 1st 95th Villa de Puerco; artillery and one company 3rd 95th to Sesmirs, remaining four companies 3rd 95th Nartillan, 20th Portuguese Regiment at Sasquilla. When the 1st 95th arrived at Villa de Puerco, they found it rather crowded as the 5th Division, some artillery and squadrons of the 12th Light Dragoons were also billeted there. Later, however, they marched out to other quarters. Around this time, Lieutenant Gairdner had his batman court-martialed for losing his baggage, as he was too drunk to look after it and, as a result, he was sentenced to be flogged.

On 30th November 1812 Wellington issued a General Order which stated: Every non-commissioned officer (NCO) and soldier who was present with his regiment in Spain between 15–19 of November was to receive a free pair of shoes from the commissary. This was just as well for many of the officers and men in the Rifles had to cut their footwear from their swollen and blistered feet!

In December, another General Order was issued stating that due to the weakness of a number of regiments, Provisional Battalions would be formed. Wellington much preferred to keep his seasoned troops rather than have them returned to England to recruit and reform. As a result, four companies of the 2/31st and four companies of the 2/66th became the 1st Provisional

Battalion; four companies of the Queens and four companies of 53rd the 2nd Provisional Battalion; four companies 2/24th and four companies 2/58th the 3rd Provisional Battalion; four companies 30th and four companies 2/44th the 4th Provisional Battalion. The Light Battalion of the King's German Legion was removed from the Light Division and put into the 1st Division. The remaining men of the regiments forming the provisional battalions who were unfit for service, were to return to England. During December, the Rifle Battalions are shown as being distributed as follows: 1st 95th Alameda, 2nd Nava de Haver, and 3rd Espejo.

In the Light Division, now distributed amongst the villages for the winter months, many men were still smarting from the censure levelled at the whole army by Wellington for its conduct on the retreat into Portugal. They felt this was unjustified, and rightly so, having provided the rearguard, being pressed every inch of the way by the French advance guard and covering the army's withdrawal, much of it in appalling weather conditions. Wellington's anger, however, was mainly aimed at the generals of division for the unnecessary loss of so many sorely needed men for the coming campaign, but this hadn't filtered down to the other ranks.

However, when they compared this with the previous winter of discontent, things soon began to brighten up at least amongst the ranks of the Riflemen. Comfortable quarters, regular rations and the chance to fraternise with the opposite sex were all good therapy. The officers of the Light Division combined to make light of their long winter nights by forming a theatrical unit, having commandeered an old chapel at Galegos, which they turned into a theatre. Their first performance, 'She stoops to Conquer' was soon playing to full houses. A second play was then produced, 'The Rivals' and Wellington, after returning from Lisbon, was in the audience on two separate occasions.

Mixing with the local females was certainly an important part of the winter activities for the Rifle officers; Harry Smith however was now content with the company of his young wife, much to the envy of his comrades. If the experience related by Commissary Schaumann is anything to go by, the officers were in great demand! He notes that in one part of Spain, the girls and women of the higher and lower classes were practically all disreputable. Pure virgins were rare, some parents having to resort to using the mediaeval contraption, the chastity belt, while one officer lived in quarters in the town on terms of great intimacy with the wife, the daughters and the maidservant! No wonder Schaumann remarked, 'The life we led here was so heavenly.' Whether this could be said of the other ranks is not recorded, but human nature being what it is, and as the men of the 1st Battalion Rifles did not bring out their wives with them in 1809, it can never be ruled out.

Colonel Barnard seems to have preferred his quarters, as he was noted as being partial to more than the odd cigar, for their distinct aromatic smell and smoke often filled his room. Lieutenant Lawson, having received his promotion from volunteer, returned to England and sold his horse to the American Lieutenant Gairdner, who remarked that on 25th March 1813, it was warm enough to bathe, his first time that year!

On 13th March, a grand fête was held at Ciudad Rodrigo for General Lowry Cole's installation as a baronet. The 17th Portuguese was exchanged into the 1st Brigade of the Light Division in place of the 20th Portuguese, (though it is believed the latter had never joined the Light Division) on 20th March. The companies of Captains Leach and Smith were moved to Castletos.

News had been received at the beginning of 1813, of the severe set back to Napoleon in his disastrous campaign in Russia, which had helped lighten the mood in the camps. A brigade field day was held at Espejo on 19th April, the first signs that their winter recess was coming to an end. Paymaster McKenzie of the Rifles, was ordered to England on 24th April to take over as Paymaster at the depot. Then, on 13th May, General Alten ordered all the mounted officers in the Light Division to drill at points. The campaign of 1813 was about to begin.

# Advance to, and Battle of, Vitoria

By the May of 1813 some 5,000 extra troops had arrived at Lisbon and as a result the army was formed into eight divisions:

Sir Thomas Graham was appointed to second in command of the Army
1st Division under command of Lt. Gen. Kenneth A. Howard

| | | |
|---|---|---|
| 2nd | " | Lt. Gen. Hon. William Stewart |
| 3rd | " | Lt. Gen. Sir Thomas Picton |
| 4th | " | Lt. Gen. Sir Lowry Cole |
| 5th | " | Lt. Gen. Sir James Leith |
| 6th | " | Lt. Gen. Sir Henry Clinton |
| 7th | " | Lt. Gen. Earl George Dalhousie |
| Light Division | " | Lt. Gen. Baron Charles Alten |
| Cavalry | " | Lt. Gen. Stapleton Cotton |
| Portuguese | " | Marshal William Beresford |

The 2nd Division had been detached to Estremadura under the command of General Stewart, while the Great Depot at Belem in southern Portugal had been moved to Santarem, a most significant undertaking for the coming campaign. The British and Portuguese Armies were in good condition after their winter rest. Wellington's Allied Army was at last stirring from its winter hibernation, with the Light Division eager to take the fight to the French. Refreshed and equipped once more, uniforms and arms in first class order, their health better than it had been for quite sometime, the Light Division represented the most perfect and self-contained fighting unit in Wellington's Army. A new sense of optimism was also spreading through the army, Napoleon's disastrous campaign in Russia having lifted the spirits of the officers and men. Wellington's veterans were straining at the leash to be let loose on the French once more, while the reinforcements, fresh from home, wanted to test their mettle in battle. For many it would be the first time. The proud boast of the French Army, that they were the most complete and all conquering military machine dominating the armies of Europe for so long, now looked rather shallow. Wellington's men wanted to challenge this boast and push them out of Spain for good, then defeat them on their own soil. There is no doubt that the French claims were once true, but Napoleon's finest and strongest army now lay scattered in decaying mounds from Moscow to the borders of France and represented only a shadow of its former glorious self.

The Light Division during their time of rest and recuperation reorganised their establishment which now consisted of:

1st Brigade under the command of Major General Kempt
1st Battalion 43rd Regiment Light Infantry, strength five or six companies *
2nd Battalion 95th Rifles strength, six companies under Major Amos Norcott
No 1 Company   Captain Cadoux
No 2 Company   Captain Jenkins
No 3 Company   Captain Hart
No 4 Company   Captain Mitchell
No 5 Company   Captain Fergusson
No 6 Company   Captain Duncan
17th Portuguese Regiment of the Line under Colonel Rolt
2nd Brigade under the command of Major General Vandeleur
1st Battalion 52nd Regiment under Lieutenant Colonel Gibbs
1st Battalion 95th Rifles strength six companies under Colonel Andrew Barnard
No 1 Company   Captain Stewart
No 2 Company   Captain Leach
No 5 Company   Captain Smyth (Smith) **
No 6 Company   Captain Beckwith
No 7 Company   Captain Loftus Gray
No 8 Company   Captain Johnstone
3rd Battalion 95th Rifles strength five companies under Major John Ross
No 1 Company   Captain Percival
No 2 Company   Captain C. Gray
No 3 Company   Captain Hallen
No 4 Company   Captain Balvaird
No 5 Company   Captain Andrews
1st Regiment Portuguese Caçadores
3rd Regiment Portuguese Caçadores
14th Light Dragoons
1st German Hussars
Major Ross's troop of Royal Horse Artillery

*The regiment's strength has been shown as one or the other of these figures during our research. GC/RC

**Not to be confused with Captain Charles Smyth who was killed at the Battle of Waterloo. Though spelt differently it would appear that they sounded the same as Harry Smith's wife was informed it was he who was killed at Waterloo confirming the pronunciation?

17th May 1813, the Light Division was reviewed by Wellington on the plain of Espejo and on 20th May the regiments started assembling near Carpio. When the 1st German Hussars rejoined the Light Division, they rode up smoking their pipes and singing some of their well known aires. The troops lined the road to greet them and cheered as they rode past. Tears began rolling down the cheeks of the Germans' bronzed faces as they shouted back, 'We are always glad to see the old 'Lighty' division who will ever live in our hearts.'

In preparation for the coming campaign great-coats were put into storage, as it was thought with the new issue tent that a blanket would suffice. Each man was to be provided with a reasonable supply of necessaries, including three pairs of shoes and an extra pair of soles and heels in their knapsacks. The daily allowance of rations per man was: one pound of beef, one of biscuit and a small amount of rum or wine.

Most of this was to be carried by the battalion mules under the command of a muleteer, who had five animals in his care. They received five dollars a day, and the reserve ammunition was also entrusted to these men. It is easy to see therefore, why they were given such good rates of pay. These men were also most conspicuous in their dress, wearing either a large hat or a handkerchief of various colours tied tight around the head, with one corner left hanging down their backs, with a red Moorish type of sash around the waist. They wore dark blue or green velvet breeches open at the knee and leather gaiters, with numerous buttons up the side. The mules were equal to their masters, with bells at the head, the hair on their backs closely shaved and their tails tied up in a bunch with coloured binding. The muleteers sat upon the load on the animal's back, singing. These same men were also notorious throughout the war for stealing hundreds of mules from Wellington's Allied Army, once in 1812 going to the extreme of robbing the Light Division of a number of its animals when stationed in Madrid. This was achieved by making a duplicate set of keys to the stable doors where the beasts had been secured. These pack animals were never seen again!

General Graham's force was to form the left wing, and Hill's the right wing of Wellington's advancing army. The Life Guards and Oxford Blues were with the Light Division, who left Fuentes Guinalda on 20th May at the head of Wellington's centre columns. The 1st Brigade lead with the 3rd Battalion 95th forming the advance guard, leaving Alameda on the 21st, crossing the Agueda at Molino Clos Flores by a ford near a mill and moving on to San Felices, where it was joined by the 2nd Brigade. It was only at this point that the whole division assembled, moving off on the morning of the 22nd, crossing the River Yeltsa that same day. On 23rd May, they halted close to San Muñoz on the Huebra, the 1st 95th taking up the same ground they had defended on the retreat the previous year.

They halted on the 24th, marching at daybreak on the 25th, with the cavalry protecting the flanks. The following day they marched to within five miles of Salamanca, where the British cavalry came up against a French cavalry post, forcing them to fall back on the town. The French now withdrew from the town to the heights of Cabrerizos, but were overtaken by Fane and Alten's cavalry. The French formed squares, but were pounded by artillery causing around 400 casualties, in killed, wounded and prisoners, along with seven guns. They continued retiring until reaching the protection of the defiles of Aldea Lengua. The Light Division now camped on the left bank of the Tormes, opposite the village of Villar Mayor, and halted for the day. They crossed the Tormes by a ford on 28th May and marched to Aldea Nueva de Figueroa where they remained until the 2nd June.

Reaching the Douro on 3rd June they found they could not cross the bridge at Toro as its centre arch had been destroyed by the French. However Lieutenant Pringle of the Engineers devised a quick and novel way of crossing the broken bridge by dropping ladders down on each side and lashing them to the stone-work, then placed planks across from one to the other, just above the water line. The men were then able to climb down one ladder, cross the planks in single file and climb up the other side. Though long winded, it worked! They also had the use of a single boat and all the division was across by noon that day. The guns, baggage and cavalry crossed by a deep ford further up the river. The Light and 4th Divisions advanced on 7th June and after a number of marches reached the ancient walled town of Palencia north east of Valladolid. The houses made an odd impression on the Riflemen as they were supported in front by large pillars, causing one Rifleman to comment, 'they looked like a number of old men on sticks.' However, they were warmly received by the inhabitants, who informed them that only the day before, King Joseph had reviewed his rearguard within the walls of the town.

Continuing the advance after the French on 12th June, Grant's hussars and Ponsonby's dragoons were in advance. The Light Division and the heavy dragoon brigade of cavalry reached the villages of Isar and Hornillas on the River Horaza which the French held in strength. They now halted on the heights above the villages, to wait for Hill's Corps to arrive and threaten them. When they did, the enemy promptly abandoned the villages. The Light Division and cavalry, with the Horse Artillery, immediately followed them inflicting considerable casualties before they reached the River Urbel, by which time it was too late to overtake them and so they occupied the villages formerly held by the French.

Just before daybreak on 13th June, a tremendous explosion was heard; it was later confirmed that it was the destruction of Burgos. In their haste to retreat, the French blew up the castle, managing at the same time to include 300 of their own troops into the bargain! This must have given some satisfaction to the troops who had been forced to abandon the siege of Burgos and retreat into Portugal the year before.

On crossing the River Ebro, the 1st Battalion 95th Rifles band struck up with the tune 'The Downfall of Paris' which amused their comrades. They then followed this with some national tunes of Britain, causing many men to reflect on family and friends they had not seen for years. Their nostalgia for home was soon eased by the country they were now crossing, which yielded an abundance of fruit and vegetables. Lush fields and picturesque mountains replacing the parched, waterless, scorched land they had previously traversed. The advance was resumed on the 16th along the left bank of the Ebro, through a narrow pass, the road winding between the cliffs and lofty wooded heights. Camping that night beyond Medina de Pomar, on the River Trueba, the Light Division, now detached from the main central column, marched on the 17th through similar densely wooded mountainous country along the main road to France but it was found to be unsuitable for artillery. King Joseph had reckoned on making a stand here on the rocky heights of Pancorbo, to allow his reinforcements to catch up with him. General Gazan held the front of the pass, Reille was on the right at Espejo to watch the road to Bilbao, while d'Erlon guarded the road from Burgos on the left. However, Wellington had no intention of attacking the French in this fortified pass. Hill, meanwhile, had crossed the Ebro at Puente Arenas, with Graham crossing via the bridges of Rocamunde and San Martin, some 20 miles further up the river. This movement succeeded in cutting off Joseph from the coast, forcing the French to abandon all their sea ports, leaving only one, Santona, which was invested by the Spanish. The British Navy, as a result, was free to enter Santander, which had a dramatic affect on the war. Supplies of munitions, equipment, ordnance and stores could now be brought to the seat of war many days earlier than normal. However, the change for the better in eating arrangements still brought problems and the men were warned when cooking in this part of Spain, not to eat or use any wild vegetables especially the wild onion, that was highly poisonous.

Joseph, meanwhile, on learning of Wellington's flanking movement, ordered Reille to Osma, ten miles south of Orduna; Reille immediately ordered Maucune's division to join him at Osma. This was just as Graham's force, consisting of 1st and 5th Divisions, with a strong cavalry force, attacked him. After a sharp combat, Reille was forced to complete a fighting withdrawal on Espejo.

On 18th June, having been ordered to advance on San Millan, the Light Division continued moving through the hills. The 2nd Brigade was leading and a squadron and a half of the 1st German Hussars were acting as a protective screen out in front. They were followed by Major Ross's five companies of the 3rd 95th, the advance guard to the division this day. While marching along a narrow road, concealed by overhanging woods and mountains, the hussars came upon a French cavalry piquet and succeeded in wounding and capturing around 12 of their number. From the prisoners, they learned that a brigade, belonging to Maucune's division, was in a valley below, towards the village of San Millan and were on their way to join Reille. The French had been overconfident in their position and had no idea that the British were so close. Therefore, they had posted few, or hardly any vedettes, or advance piquets.

A hussar was sent dashing back, to report the enemy position. Wellington, on coming up, ordered the 1st Battalion 95th Rifles under Colonel Barnard, to attack them, followed by the 3rd 95th and the 52nd Regiment, who were in support of the 1st Battalion Riflemen. The Rifles immediately came into contact with the French on a river bank, waiting for their 2nd Brigade to arrive; the delay was due to the baggage train being part of their force. Barnard extended three of his companies into skirmishing order, and they were soon engaged with the French light troops. The French brigade had originally been moving across the path of the advancing British centre when attacked, though having halted, were now rather strung out over a large area. The French skirmishers held the Riflemen back, long enough for the main column to get clear of the rifle fire, then followed their retreating comrades. With a cheer the Rifles charged down the hillside in pursuit of the enemy, treating them to a running fire, causing many casualties in the fleeing French ranks. Maucune ordered a battalion from his brigade to hold the heights, behind the village of San Millan. Wellington, then ordered four companies of Barnard's 1st Battalion Rifles, to turn their right flank. This met with instant success, as the enemy moved off in haste, offering little resistance.

*San Millan*

Colonel Barnard and his Riflemen, having dispersed the French in their front, continued to push them through the villages, taking a number prisoner along the way, capturing their light baggage into the bargain. When Vandeleur's 2nd Light Division Brigade went into action, the 1st Brigade moved off the road to take up a position on higher ground, to form a rallying point for the 2nd Brigade, should it be necessary. It was while in this position, that they were surprised by a second French column coming from between two large rock formations. Their line of march was running parallel to that taken by their under fire advance column and, as a result, was now in rear of the Light Division's 2nd Brigade. The 52nd Regiment, seeing that they were caught between two large enemy forces, turned about, formed line, fired, and then advanced against the French in their rear in double quick time. The 2nd Brigade was now fighting on two fronts. Kempt's, 1st Brigade, advanced against this second French column, who, seeing that they were also being attacked on two fronts, took off their packs and threw them down, so as not to hinder their escape and fled from the area.

The poor baggage guard abandoned and left to fend for itself, could only form into a defensive huddle amongst the rocks, to try and hold off the attack made by the 2nd 95th, 43rd and Caçadores. They were no match for these troops, at the same time, their frightened animals began running loose, giving them no choice, but to surrender.

The 2nd Battalion Rifles and Portuguese continued in hot pursuit of the French. Reille came across these broken men in the hills and valleys, as he struggled to complete his own fighting withdrawal. Barnard's Riflemen continued advancing towards Villa Nueva, where the retreating French were joined by a large body of their troops and taking up a strong position, barred the road. No attempt was made to dislodge them, and later they continued their retreat. The 1st and 3rd Battalions 95th regrouped to count the cost of the day's action, Lieutenant Haggup, who received a severe stomach wound, was the only officer casualty. Casualties among the men were quite light, with 2 Sergeants and 2 Riflemen killed; 13 Riflemen wounded.

The 1st 95th Rifles under Colonel Barnard, now moved off, advancing through the steep wooded ground beyond the left of the town and once the Rifles had made their attack, the rest of the brigade moved forward. The Riflemen continued to disperse any French resistance, pushing them through Villa Nueva to Villanañe. Several of their regiments had formed in column, but became completely cut off. However, they were able to disperse under cover of darkness, though a number were taken prisoner. When advancing through the woods, the leading Riflemen came upon a mortally wounded French aide-de-camp. A lady upon a white horse, probably his wife, had remained with him until the Riflemen came into view. Though they called out to her not to be alarmed, she rode off in great distress, leaving the French officer to his fate. Among the captured baggage-guard, Kempt's Brigade came across a number of Spanish ladies, who had been attached in one way or another, to some of the French officers. However, their relationships couldn't have been too strong, for they soon changed their allegiance to the Light Division, preferring to remain with their captors!

On 19th June, the captured baggage and animals were auctioned off, and the proceeds distributed amongst the officers and men of the 1st Brigade, much to the annoyance of their comrades in Vandeleur's Brigade, who had contributed the lion's share of the fighting that helped secure it. The division now crossed the Camilla at Villamaderme, passing through Salinas. It was here they found the water running crystal clear, which made it so inviting, especially as the weather was very hot. The Riflemen were soon dipping their canteens and mugs into the water, and eagerly gulping it down, then started pulling all sorts of faces. One Rifleman called out, 'the water is damned salty here; we can not be very far from the sea!' The ground in these parts abounded in mineral salt, the reason for Salinas having a very extensive salt works and of course, this was the source of the salt in the water.

*The old salt works at Salinas*

On 20th June, the Light Division halted for the day in a valley close to the foot of a very high ridge of mountains. This was to allow General Graham's column to continue their flanking march, so as to reach its objective, in advance of the main assault on Vitoria. Lieutenant Gairdner, in Captain Leach's 1st Battalion company, was ordered out in front on piquet duty, while the 2nd Battalion 95th and the 1st Caçadores were posted on the mountains, to the left of the Light Division. The 4th Division arrived from Espejo, after a circuitous route around the mountains via another road, where they had fallen in with the French and after a sharp skirmish, caused the enemy to retire towards Vitoria.

Wellington's force had been advancing towards Vitoria in four separate columns, Hill's column, included about 3,000–4,000 Spaniards under General Morillo and the 2nd Division under General Stewart, one of the founders of the Rifle Corps. They advanced on the right, ahead of the centre columns. Wellington's centre two columns, under his direct command, consisted of the 3rd, 4th, 7th and Light Divisions, around 25,000 strong; with them was the main force of artillery and cavalry. Sir Thomas Graham had already been detached 24 hours earlier, to the left, with the 1st and 5th Divisions and some Portuguese, about 12,000 in all. This was to enable him to turn the enemy right flank, and cut them off from the great road leading from Vitoria into France. The 6th Division remained in rear to protect the baggage, stores, spare ammunition and support services.

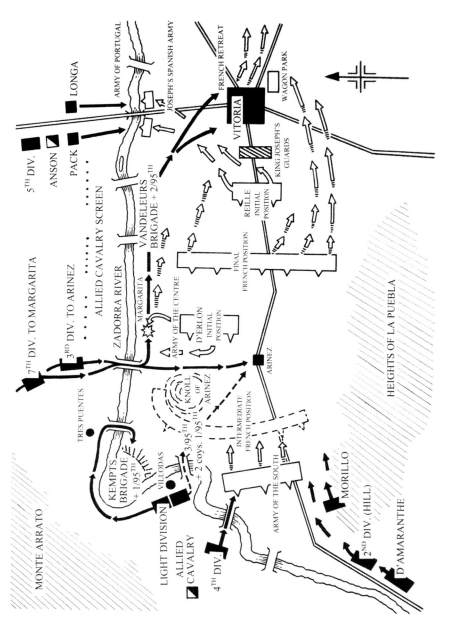

*Map of Vitoria*

In the early hours of the morning of 21st June, the Rifles paraded in total darkness and moved forward, following the same route the French rearguard had taken the day before. It was customary for the Light Division to assemble an hour before daybreak. When passing through the camp of the 4th Division, who were still asleep in their tents, a heavy burst of rain came down and soaked them. This gradually ceased, turning into a misty drizzle, then at daybreak, into a brilliant, sunny morning. The Light Division now formed up and moved up to join the 3rd Division, passing through Subilana-Morillas and a few other villages. On gaining some heights, the Rifles found themselves in position before the River Zadorra, which ran from their left front, east, towards Vitoria. It then turned sharply, roughly south, across their front, to what would become, the British right. A towering steep ridge of mountains rose abruptly from the valley, being the extreme right of Wellington's centre. They could quite clearly see the Spaniards of Morillo's force, followed by part of the 2nd Division, climbing on all hands and knees, up the mountain's steep sides. They had all crossed the Zadorra, via the bridge at the town of Puebla de Arganzon and were now on the enemy side of the river, in a position to attack the French left. In the centre of the French position, rose a lofty conical shaped hill out of an extensive plain, which extended to the left, along with a sloping plain through which the great road ran. This terminated at a long range of mountains that stretched from Puebla de Arganzon, just above the river, to a considerable distance beyond Vitoria. The city was screened from the Rifles' view, by the conical hill, some four to five miles, in their front. The ground along the bank of the river appeared broken and not easily approachable. On the face of the conical hill, however, all the way to its summit there was a mass of troops, clustering like bees, interspersed in places by batteries of artillery and other field-works.

While on the plain between the hill and the long range of mountains, the troops appeared so thick on the ground, that one could hardly find a gap between them. At first there seemed to be no great force on the mountains to their left, or to the right of the hill towards Vitoria, but they did have strong forces there, concealed from view. There were a number of small villages in the plain and on the side of the mountains, but the largest stood to the far right of the plain, Subijana de Alava, with a wood immediately behind it. Along the bank of the river, there were three to four villages, most of them on the British side, with a bridge leading over the river from each village. The French army had not extended as far as the river bank, but was placed at some distance beyond the river. Though it was easily fordable it had steep banks making it impossible for cavalry and artillery to cross. It snaked along the front of the British position, separating both armies from each other.

At this stage, the French commanders were still oblivious of the full scale attack about to take place that would shatter their peace of mind and feeling of well being. Marshal Jourdan and King Joseph set off at dawn at a leisurely pace, to inspect the positions of their armies, which consisted of around 60,000 men, of which 11,000 were cavalry, with 138 artillery pieces. Included among their infantry, interestingly, was a number of enlisted Spaniards, who no doubt, would regret this decision by the end of the day! The French Army of the South, was the first line of Joseph's defence in the plain, with the heights of La Puebla to its left and front, facing the defile, from where the main road ran between these heights and the river. Both flanks had good natural obstacles behind them. Slightly to their right, was the Army of the Centre, again in a natural defensive position, due to the river running along its front, before doubling back via a hairpin bend, protecting their right and rear. In its left centre, was the knoll and village of Arinez, on the main road to Vitoria. The Army of Portugal had been allocated a third defensive line to the north of Vitoria, with a division either side of the river, at Abechucho and Gamarra Mayor, where the road from Bilbao headed south into Vitoria. Joseph had also been reinforced by Acapulco's Spaniards, detached from the Army of the North. At this stage, the Armies of the South and Portugal were separated from each other by a distance of some six miles. The only reserve Joseph and Jourdan could now rely upon, should the situation require, was the Royal Guard less than 3,000 strong stationed, on the Zuazo. Wellington's flanking columns of Graham and Hill,

however, were still on the move, trying to cross difficult, uncompromising terrain to reach their allotted positions, in time to execute their commander's daring plan. The Light Division, in the centre column, was the first to arrive. Now, only a mile from the river, when close to Olbabarre, hidden by the overhanging rocks in this area, they moved left off the road, halted and piled arms, still in close columns. Rifleman however never piled arms, always preferring to keep their rifles close to hand. They were soon joined by the Hussar Brigade, which also moved off the road to the left and dismounted, close to the Light Division. The 4th Division, on coming up, completed a similar movement, but this was to the right of the road. Here they were all able to sit down and relax, until required; this, however, would be sooner than expected for the Rifles!

*Spanish soldier of Napoleon's guard*

At around half past eleven, Wellington personally led the Light Division via a hollow sunken road towards the river, placing them in a position unobserved amongst some woods. This was exactly opposite the enemy right centre and within 200 yards of the bridge that lead to Villodas, which they had been destined to assault. Lieutenant Cooke of the 43rd Regiment, in Kempt's Brigade, while waiting for the action to start wandered to the edge of the woods; from where he could see the enemy guns with their gunners standing by with lighted matches, just waiting to blow their adversaries from the face of the earth. They were well within the range of the rifles of the British Riflemen, who could have played havoc among their batteries from the cover of the trees which concealed them. Wellington was still waiting for the 3rd and 7th Divisions to arrive and take up their positions before making his move, but the rough ground was proving more difficult to negotiate than expected. The enemy gunners were safe for the time being at least.

Wellington, with his numerous staff, advanced towards the river to reconnoitre the enemy position through their telescopes and see if any further dispositions had been made by their enemy, all unaware that the French command had been monitoring their every movement. The position taken up by King Joseph and his staff overlooked the British right centre, who instantly ordered a corps of voltigeurs to rush down to the river and cross the bridge adjacent to the village of Villodas. Here they were able to take possession of a small woody height on the British side of the river, from where they immediately opened fire on Wellington and his aides-de-camp. The 3rd Battalion 95th was the leading battalion of the Rifles at this point and next to it was two companies from the 1st Battalion (probably those of Captains Leach and Stewart), [1] who were ordered to drive the French back over the bridge. In doing so, these Riflemen made the claim of having the honour of commencing the action on what would be a most memorable and glorious day. While this might have been the case in the centre column, the flanking divisions in all probability started the action first. The French light troops were soon driven from the wood, through the village and back over the bridge. This was as far as the Rifles were allowed to venture in accordance with their orders, but from the cover of the village, its gardens and walls, they continued to skirmish with the French voltigeurs. The enemy sharpshooters were only some 40 yards distant across the river, concealed in rock formations and as a result a number of men fell on both sides.

The French artillery near the conical hill, now fired at the Rifles, causing them a number of casualties. One round swept away five or six Riflemen, who were taken in flank as they fired from what they thought was the substantial shelter of a garden wall. This caused the remainder immediately to seek a more stout position to defend. Lieutenant Campbell, of the 3rd Rifles, fell with a musket ball to the forehead, killing him instantly. This was another case of a man foreseeing his own demise. Only the night before the battle, he was full of anxiety for his own safety and believed he would be killed! Major Ross, the commanding officer of the 3rd Battalion now advanced with his staff officers, which included Quartermaster Surtees along with a half company from his battalion and took up a position in a church in the village. Being on higher ground, it gave them a commanding view of what was taking place between the opposing forces in this area. These seven companies remained here for the earlier part of the battle, keeping the light troops opposed to them occupied. [2]

About 12 o'clock, whilst waiting for the remaining centre columns to arrive, a Spanish peasant came up with some welcome intelligence. He was immediately taken to Wellington, to whom he reported that the French had left one of the three main bridges crossing the Zadorra unprotected and intact! The bridge was about two miles from where they were now positioned. He offered to show them the way and also to lead them over it. Wellington eventually came up to where Colonel Barnard was standing with some of his officers, who were using their telescopes to search out the French positions. He asked Lieutenant George Simmons if he saw anything. 'Yes my Lord, I see smoke or dust in that direction.' 'Ah, let me see,' looking in the direction indicated by Simmons, where he had expected Sir Thomas Graham to emerge from the mountains, he turned to Barnard, and said, 'All right get along Barnard.'

Kempt's 1st Brigade of the Light Division formed up into threes, was immediately ordered forward. They set off at a rapid pace, led by Colonel Barnard, with his four remaining companies of the 1st Battalion 95th Rifles. Although they were not part of this brigade, they advanced along a very uneven and circuitous path, but it was well concealed from the French positions due to the woods and high rocks.

Eventually they reached a sharp bend in the river, where they came upon the narrow bridge of Tres Puentes. The 1st 95th, with rifles cocked ready for action, doubled over the bridge, quickly followed by the 1st Brigade, all at a run. They were quite surprised to reach the opposite bank unopposed, and advanced up the road to their front for about 50 yards which gradually became quite steep, all without the slightest challenge from the enemy. The brigade now lined a large bank or earthwork, concealing them from the French.

*Village and bridge at Tres Puentes*

From this position, Kempt could see quite clearly the heavy columns of French, positioned on what seemed to be the principal hill in this part of the field. It commanded a birds-eye-view of the 1st Light Brigade's position and the ground immediately behind them. Kempt's Brigade was fortunately well protected by the bank, as it was convex in shape and formed a valuable bridgehead, large enough to shelter the whole of his formation. It made a formidable defensive foothold on the enemy side of the river. Oddly, the French seemed unconcerned at this British advanced post and left them unmolested, except when the French gunners sent two ranging shots at their position a little after the first crossing of the river, the second of which severed the head from the body of their courageous Spanish guide. The Riflemen and the remaining troops of Kempt's Brigade were so well protected that the gunners gave up. It was now time for Kempt to take stock of his situation. They were posted at the elbow of the French defensive line in front of a hairpin bend in the river, isolated from the rest of the army. At this point, the only way of being reinforced was over the bridge they had just crossed. The way the river meandered and looped either side of them, made it a natural and all round defence. Lieutenant Cooke of the 43rd Regiment, looked rather gingerly over the top of the bank, as there was still no fire directed at their position. He could see, quite clearly, King Joseph and his staff at some 800 yards' distance, surrounded by a mass of troops. It is impossible to guess why

Joseph and Marshal Jourdan chose to ignore Kempt's force at this time; maybe they had more important and pressing matters on their minds, other than this small incursion on their side of the river, isolated from the rest of the British Army and not in sufficient numbers to threaten his massed ranks of troops.

Kempt, entrenched in no man's land with his whole brigade, and feeling rather vulnerable and anxious for their safety, immediately dispatched one of his aides to order the 15th Hussars to cross the bridge to give them some urgent support. Shortly afterwards, the Hussars came galloping over the bridge in single file, with not even the odd artillery shell sent to hinder their progress; dismounting, they fell in behind their comrades. This confirms what a formidable defensive position Kempt had taken up to accommodate such a large group of men and horses. From his elevated position, Kempt was also able to observe what was taking place on the British side of the river. The bridge he crossed was the centre of the three which spanned the river at this point and all were within a quarter of a mile of each other. The bridges either side of the one they had crossed were defended by light troops and also covered by artillery. The left hand bridge, however, had been further strengthened by the building of an earthwork opposite the crossing point, which obstructed access to the enemy side of the river, making an assault a rather bloody and costly proposition. A group of French dragoons was eventually ordered to try and discover the strength of Kempt's force and came slowly down towards them, with much trepidation, not without good reason. When about 50 yards from Kempt's position, the Riflemen sent a few shots in their direction, which had them galloping back to their original position. Joseph was still none the wiser as to the strength of the force immediately to his front.

The French originally believed Wellington would try to turn their right flank. After inspecting the positions of the armies at dawn, Joseph and Jourdan decided it would be a better idea to pull the Army of the South back to the ridge on which they were viewing the whole panorama, now spread out before them. They sent an aide to General Gazan, commander of the Army of the South, with a message asking him to ride back to discuss this movement with them. This, as it turned out, was rather timely for he remained where he was, sending them a reply they hadn't expected—that large columns of British troops were approaching the Puebla defile!

The troops Gazan had seen marching towards the defile, were Hill's column led by Morillo's Spanish Division, which turned off the road to the right and was soon swarming up the hills on his left front, the French piquet stationed there off the heights. The 2nd Division continued through the defile and began to deploy in the plain. Gazan immediately ordered Maransin's brigade from Subilana, being the nearest troops, to recapture the heights. Hill countered this by sending Cadogan's Brigade to reinforce Morillo.

Gazan reacted, by sending Villatte's reserve division to support Maransin. Joseph and Jourdan meanwhile, galloped forward to join Gazan and were now on the knoll opposite the Nanclares bend of the river. Jourdan, however, was convinced that the movements being made by Graham against their right was now nothing more than a feint and should be ignored. The real threat was obviously coming from the south; they had to attack and defeat the troops upon these heights. Immediately orders were sent to d'Erlon to detach one of his divisions along with some dragoons to block the road from Logrono to Vitoria.

It was these movements which weakened the French centre that Wellington had been watching with interest, for they were playing into his hands. The opposition gathered to oppose Hill only aided in advancing Wellington's original plan of attack. The French movements from the centre played a significant part in the eventual outcome of the day's events, especially as regards to the Light Division and in particular the Rifles who were preparing to assault the bridge of Villodas. The 4th Division was to attack the Nanclares bridge to the right of where the 3rd Battalion was keeping the French light troops busy at Villodas, while Dalhousie's column was to make for the bridges of Mendoza and Tres Puentes.

*Villodas Bridge*

Whatever plan Joseph and Jourdan had originally drawn up to defeat the British and gain them a glorious victory, all started to go wrong when they heard the first cannon-shots fired by General Graham's flanking movement

*Assault on the breaches of the Santa Maria and La Trinidad bastions by the Light Division*
*Badajoz, 6th April 1812*

*Kincaid purchasing two chickens from the ladies of the King's German Legion*
*1st August 1812*

*Camp scene of the Light Division in the Pyrenees*

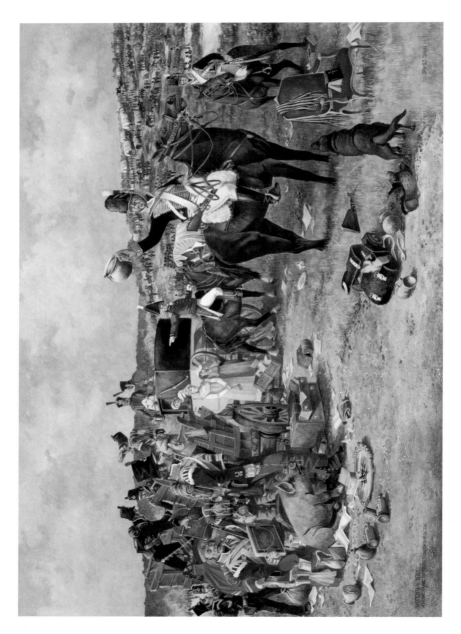

*After Vitoria, the looting of King Joseph's coach*

against the villages of Abechucho and Gamarra. It took them and the inhabitants of Vitoria completely by surprise. The extent of Joseph's confidence in defeating the British can be gauged by his arrogance in having viewing platforms built near the city, so that spectators and followers of his army could see the battle first hand and watch the total destruction and humiliation of the British Army! The cannon fire coming from the Bilbao road behind the city caused instant chaos among its inhabitants. The French court and Army never expected such a turn of events that was about to take place. Baggage, stores and plunder of every description, most of it belonging to the high command, their retirement pensions for life after the army gained from years of the systematic stripping of the wealth of Portugal and Spain, was now on the move and massed with all the encumbrances of a campaigning army. All headed in the same direction and at the same time along the Pamplona road. It was reported that some 2,000 wagons and carriages alone blocked the road leaving the main gateway out of Vitoria towards France. There was nowhere near enough draft animals available to pull such a large quantity of vehicles. A great number of baggage wagons had already been put on the move prior to this mass exodus, but the limited road system available to the French could not cope with such an influx of traffic. The great road back into France was in total chaos. Faster carriages, with ladies of rank, were caught up with much slower and heavier wagons all inter-mixed with the numerous herds of livestock required to sustain such a large army.

Wellington's tactics caught out the French high command, throwing the generals into total confusion. They believed the broken ground with its gorges, ravines, villages and strong rock formations would naturally divide any organized large body of troops sent against them in a concerted attack. Controlling the bridges would have put the British at a great disadvantage. Failing to place a force in position to defend the bridge at Tres Puentes was inexcusable, for this was partly the key to the centre attack's success. This oversight prevented the loss of countless lives that would have been necessary to storm these positions. The destruction of the bridges would have presented the centre attack with a most difficult task in crossing the river. French over-confidence that they would defeat the British, probably prevented their destruction. A victorious army wanting to achieve the ultimate victory, would require swift access in the pursuit of a defeated and routed army. The bridges, therefore, would be an essential strategic part of the French plan to following up their victory.

From his elevated position, Kempt could at last see the bayonets of the 3rd and 7th Divisions. They were still quite some distance from each other, advancing through the standing corn that was widely cultivated in the area around the river and Vitoria. Wellington joined part of the 3rd Division, now advancing from between some rocks towards the bridge and hamlet of Mendoza. This was on the left of Kempt's position. The French battery positioned to cover Tres Puentes immediately opened fire against them and was partly countered by two guns of the Royal Horse Artillery positioned on the British side of the river. The 3rd Division now received a heavy concentration of fire; it would therefore be a most bloody encounter therefore to take the bridge.

*View of battlefield at Vitoria*

Colonel Barnard, seeing the impact the guns and skirmishers were having on the advance of the 3rd Division, gathered his four 1st Battalion Rifle companies together and ordered them forward from their concealed position so as to give immediate covering fire to the 3rd Division. These Riflemen sent a severe fire into the flank of the enemy gunners and the light troops lining the bank. This was achieved at great risk to themselves, for if the French had sent a strong force against them they could have been swept into the river running along the whole of their left flank. The French cavalry was hovering about on their right flank and could so easily have charged them at any moment, causing untold casualties due to such an enclosed and dangerous position. The Riflemen's deliberate fire with loose-ball, soon had the French artillery limbering up their guns to drag them to a safer position back towards their main line of defence. This allowed the 3rd Division to cross, at a run, the bridge of Mendoza cheering for all they were worth, with little opposition.

Once on the other side of the river, they immediately regained their formation.

The advance of Barnard's four 1st Battalion companies came at a price, as they attracted the unwanted attention of the British artillery. Their dark uniform and advanced position, led the gunners to think they were French and they immediately sent a number of rounds into them, causing some unfortunate casualties. The Riflemen could do little to prevent this fire and just had to endure it, until eventually, they were joined by Picton's red coated troops and the gunners then realised their error! Large columns of dense smoke were seen coming from the direction of Sir Thomas Graham's force, confirming his attack was firmly under way. General Hill's Spaniards, previously mentioned, were advancing along the top of the mountain and were causing great concern to King Joseph and Marshal Jourdan. Their staff could be seen highly animated, moving troop formations about, as if pieces on a large chess board. The massed French troops, positioned on the conical hill, started in great numbers to descend into the plain to stem the advance of Hill's force on their left, which if successful could cut them off completely from retreating into France. Some severe and determined fighting now took place in this part of the battlefield and, as a result, Hill's force made very slow progress.

Picton's 3rd Division, joined by the four companies of Barnard's Riflemen, skirmished in advance, with three companies (under 200 strong) of the 5th Battalion 60th Regiment, that was part of his division which advanced rapidly against the formidable village of Arinez, positioned on the main road to Vitoria. The French vedettes to their front, were suffering from the rifle fire, as the Rifleman were picking them off with great ease. Witnessing the fate of their comrades shot from their horses, was most unnerving, for some of those who fell still had a foot caught up in a stirrup iron. Their terrified horses galloped off with the body of the cavalry man dragging behind, bouncing about like a rag doll, hitting the ground with a sickening thud at every bound! Picton, conspicuous in his blue coat and round hat, was at the head of the 3rd Division. Here he was joined by Wellington and the usual profanities issuing forth in the well-worn manner to which his troops had become accustomed, urged the men on. The Rifles cleared the hill of opposing light troops, but were brought up with a jolt when they found the French in force defending a wall that protected the entrance to the village. The remaining troops of Kempt's Brigade had moved out from the protection of the bank and were now following in support of Picton's division.

During the advance, the French guns at times were only 200 yards from the Light Division and the round-shot ploughed up the ground in their rear. Luckily a bank close by gave them desperately needed cover. A Portuguese Regiment, (the 17th Line) in the brigade with the 43rd Regiment, had become detached at one point during the rapid advance and was now marching in close column to join them. This was an easy target for the French gunners and a destructive fire was sent against them. The first salvo ripped into the centre of the Portuguese column knocking down many men. For around ten minutes the dust and smoke made it impossible for the Rifles to distinguish the French positions, other than the odd shadowy figure of the French artillery gunners. The shouts of the troops trying to force their way into the village, however, were most audible even with the constant booming of the guns.

It was around 2 o'clock when the French artillery first started to pull back from their positions, covering the bridges with the larger part, making for the main road into Vitoria. Here they formed up in line across the main road in one massed battery, to pound the British in an attempt finally to stop their advance. Picton's flanking movement had caused his division to march diagonally across the French centre, eventually bringing him opposite to them. Meanwhile, the 4th Division which had been making for the bridge at Nanclares was subjected to a severe artillery barrage; one lucky artillery round had a direct hit on an ammunition wagon, that totally destroyed it along with its two horses and driver. Undaunted, they pushed on and crossed the narrow bridge, the 40th Regiment charging at the enemy, still under this heavy artillery fire, and succeeded in forcing the enemy gunners back over the hill. They then reformed and marched to their left to support Picton's right flank and Kempt's Light Division Brigade.

*The village of Margarita*

On the left of Wellington's centre attack, the 7th Division crossed the bridge leading from Mendoza. Turning to their left, they marched parallel to the river, heading in an easterly direction towards the village of Margarita. They were joined by Vandeleur's Light Division brigade, which had advanced along the same track as Kempt's Brigade earlier in the day, but had remained on the British side of the river. The skirmishers of the 2nd Battalion 95th Rifle companies were providing a protective screen for the column, as it had no other Riflemen in its formation. [3]

Vandeleur sent his Brigade Major, Harry Smith of the 95th Rifles, to report to Lord Dalhousie, who was in overall command of the 3rd and 7th Division column, to see what was required of his brigade. Dalhousie, at this point, was deep in conversation with his Quarter Master General, Drake, an ex-Rifleman. He asked for orders but was ignored. Smith, as ever impatient, overhearing his lordship state to Drake that the village of Margarita to their front had to be taken, seized the opportunity, turned his horse and galloped off, shouting at the same time that it would be achieved at once. Dalhousie and Drake's shouts of protest fell on ears that had suddenly turned deaf. On reaching Vandeleur, Smith reported that Lord Dalhousie required the taking of the village of Margarita. Vandeleur immediately ordered the 52nd Regiment under the command of Colonel Gibbs, to deploy into line, which they did as if on parade at Shorncliffe (the depot of the Light Division). They were preceded by the six companies of the 2nd Battalion Rifles. Smith had previously calculated, by counting their individual fire, that the number of guns protecting the village to be 12. Riding over to the nearest regiment of the 7th Division, he informed their colonel that they had been ordered to support the attack of the Light Divisions at the express wishes of Lord Dalhousie!

The cannon-balls started knocking the 52nd down in files but still they continued their movements much to the admiration of all those watching. The sergeants could be heard shouting out, 'who got that?' then enter their name in his book of casualties. Vandeleur's Brigade now began to move towards the village, following the line of the river. Six guns posted on a hill, only a short distance from them, kept up a heavy cannonade into the advancing brigade. The 52nd stopped to reform their line on rising ground directly opposite these guns. Though the shot slammed into them at close range they carried on regaining their formation with great coolness. Major Mein had been instrumental in these movements being completed, even to the point of making sure the companies kept their dressing. He ordered the companies of Captains Campbell and Currie to clear a copse of French light troops posted there, who were causing unnecessary casualties. After accomplishing this, Campbell returned to join the battalion just as they were advancing against the guns.

Currie, however, continued with his company and on reaching the summit of a small rise, was immediately confronted by a French battalion in close column positioned in a narrow valley. Bravely, Currie rushed at them with his leading skirmishers. The French battalion now extended its two rear companies as cover and moved off. Currie rushed through a low hedge which separated his men from the French and immediately fell in the gap, mortally wounded by a musket ball through the head. Meanwhile the 52nd Regiment, still receiving a severe fire from the artillery, pushed on and took the height, capturing the offending guns. The whole column was now supported by the Hussar Brigade as it advanced and took the village.

An unusual occurrence happened around this time to Brigade Major Smith. He was sat upon his horse watching the proceedings close to Ross's Brigade of Artillery, when his horse dropped like a stone, as if killed on the spot. Freeing himself from the animal, he checked it over but could find no sign of injury, giving it a sharp kick on the nose, the horse shook its head and jumped up none the worse for wear! The artillery men close by told him it had been caused by a current of air produced by an enemy round-shot passing close to the animals head. Lieutenant Northey, of the 52nd Regiment, had a similar experience during the battle, falling to the ground because of a close encounter with a round shot. Some time afterwards his face turned a blue-black colour, making him look as if he had spent a couple of hours boxing. Vandeleur's Brigade was hotly engaged all afternoon, pursuing the French over a number of very broad ditches, until finally nearing Vitoria which was on their left. From here they overlooked a plain that was free from obstructions and they were amazed by the sight that confronted them. So bizarre, one of total and unbelievable chaos, confusion beyond all comprehension, that it was hard to take in. Everybody and anybody, who had been connected with the French Army, were all now trying their best to make a hasty retreat and leave the city, fleeing the scene with all their belongings and ill-gotten goods in whatever mode of transport that could be pressed into service.

The 4th Division, which was in the process of advancing to join Picton's right flank, was suddenly confronted by an enemy column on its right. The 40th Regiment, in this division being the closest formation to this danger, wheeled in its direction and started to advance to meet this new threat. The French column was receiving a continuous cannon fire from the British artillery, which had crossed the river in support of the infantry and cavalry advance. Seeing the change of direction by the 40th Regiment and having no stomach for a fire-fight, the French confidence already shaken by the artillery barrage, followed their centre in all haste and disappeared over the hill immediately to their front. This was completed at such a speed that the 4th Division was unable to catch up with them.

A wounded Frenchman called out to the 40th Regiment as they passed, pleading with them not to leave him to the savagery of the Spanish. It was clear he was beyond all help, having had both legs blown off at the thighs, so the regiment moved on. This was not the time for compassion. With Picton advancing against the hill and village of Arinez, Wellington now returned to the river, crossing by the bridge of Villodas and entered the village still being defended by Major John Ross's Riflemen. He now ordered them to cross the river and join their brigade as the bridge was no longer being defended by the French.

In no time these seven Rifle companies were crossing the river and while negotiating the rocks from where the French light troops had been firing, were greeted with a heavy cannonade. The shells smashed into the rocks sending great shards of sharp stone flying in all directions, causing a number of Riflemen to be injured. Continuing at great speed, they advanced to catch up with Barnard's companies, who were at this time leading Picton's division against the village of Arinez. It was while executing this order, that Quartermaster Surtees of the 3rd Rifles, advancing with the battalion's reserve ammunition mules, reported to Major Ross that he had seen a large body of French troops dressed in blue, wearing white shako covers on their caps obscuring their distinctive eagle badge, retreating along a ravine to their right. This could have been the same force that was moving away from the 40th Regiment's advance. At first it was thought that they were Spanish due to the similarity of their uniforms and the fact that they were so far behind the French rearguard. Wellington, however, had ordered prior to the battle, that all Spanish troops were to tie a piece of white cloth around their left arm

to distinguish them from the French, to prevent what is now commonly known as friendly fire. Major Ross knowing what a stickler Wellington was for having his orders obeyed to the letter, declined to engage them, while the ravine separating both forces would have made their task all the harder. His orders were to rejoin the Light Division. The French, therefore, were left to make their own way unhindered, and the Riflemen pushed on to join Kempt's Brigade. In doing so, they were shelled by a battery of French artillery positioned upon a hill to cover the village, luckily with little loss.

*Spanish soldier*

Barnard's companies of Riflemen, and those of the 60th, were now in a severe fire-fight with the French light troops, separated only by a stout wall that protected the entrance to the village. They kept up a deadly fire at each other's positions for quite some time until, eventually, the British and German Riflemen made a rush at the wall. A fearful hand-to-hand struggle now took place before the Riflemen finally stormed the wall and pushed the enemy back through the village. Two companies of the 95th captured three of the French guns, but this success was short lived when the French infantry made a strong effort in the village and charged up the main street in column. The French artillery sent such a terrible destructive covering fire into the village, that it allowed their infantry to make a successful counter attack and retake the guns. Wellington, having rejoined the centre divisions, once more, coming up to the Riflemen shouted out, 'That's right my lads! Keep up a good fire.'

Kempt's Brigade in rear of the 3rd Division meanwhile had formed lines of battalions and was lying down in some ploughed fields, while the artillery kept up a constant fire against them. The advance against the village by Wellington's centre had outflanked the French line, south of the main road to Vitoria. The defenders in the village of Arinez, however, stubbornly held on. Brisbane's Brigade of the 3rd Division was ordered to take the village. His first line was formed by three companies of the 74th Regiment, with the three companies from the 5th Battalion 60th Regiment, supported by the fire of Barnard's Riflemen. 'Fix bayonets,' was ordered, and with a loud cheer they all rushed from their cover, against the village. They dashed forward with such determination, that they were able to charge through Arinez, and after a very bloody encounter it was carried. The guns were disabled, many of the gunners and their horses having been shot or taken prisoner; the guns were once again in the hands of the Riflemen. The French divisions on the left, opposing General Hill's force, were now under attack from Wellington's advancing centre and they were forced to give ground.

Major Ross's Riflemen eventually reached their brigade just as it was engaging the village and joined the line at a position where the 45th Regiment was posted behind a flimsy hedge. Here its Colonel, Ridewood, was gasping out his last breath surrounded by a number of his men. The Rifles moved on, advancing along the plain and joined their fellow Riflemen, with the divisions continuing to advance by brigades. The two companies of Leach and Stewart, belonging to Barnard's 1st Battalion, were reunited with their comrades. The ground now became intersected with numerous ditches, woods, vineyards and isolated hamlets which dashed all thought of a quick follow-up on the retreating French. It was thought that if the cavalry had come up at this moment the French would have been forced to retire even quicker, in total defeat. It was expected that the enemy would now make a stand on reaching favourable ground, but they succeeded in forming up in excellent order only to move off once they were in range of the British muskets, leaving their light troops to continue the fight. This meant the Riflemen were continually skirmishing with the enemy light troops for the remainder of the battle. The French continued retiring through the villages of Ali and Armentia, these being the last available positions from where they could make a stand in front of Vitoria. Their massed artillery covered the retreat of Gazan and d'Erlon's infantry on Salvatierra, with Picton's 3rd Division taking the brunt of this heavy barrage.

The central divisions advanced by taking the ground alternately as their particular opposition gave way and fell back. No thought had been given to the plight of the wounded, other than by regimental arrangements, for they now lay scattered over a great expanse of battlefield. Many men were left to die who could have been saved if they had received immediate attention. The bandsmen followed up in the wake of their regiments, and had their work cut out trying to find and then convey the wounded to the surgeons. For the Rifles this meant the 1st Battalion band had to provide assistance to the wounded of all three Battalions. They were, however, not immune from the devastating hail of cannon and musket balls fired that day; during the battle the band suffered the loss of a most valued and respected member, Band Master Sergeant William Cumming, whose head was dashed from his shoulders by a round-shot. He was one of the group of brothers of this name that formed a notable part of the band, first brought to our attention by Rifleman Benjamin Harris. One of William's brothers took his place as Band Sergeant, which duty he carried out for the remainder of the war.

It was imperative that Wellington secured victory before nightfall. The 4th Division on the right of the Light Division charged forward against a French formation defending a hill, broke them and caused them to retire in a confused mass. Wellington's artillery was all across the river by this point, and sending a concentrated barrage into the French, while the shells that overshot their targets caused sheer panic and confusion amongst the women, children and non-combatants, trying to flee the scene.

Vandeleur's Brigade, advancing with the 7th Division on the left of Wellington's centre, was moving rapidly after the panic-stricken French infantry, who were withdrawing in droves, when suddenly confronted by a swarm of French cavalry, who burst from among the baggage heading directly for Major Norcott's 2nd Battalion Riflemen. Lieutenant Thomas Cochrane, in command of Captain Jenkins' company, due to his commanding officer having fallen mortally wounded earlier, found they were in the direct line of this mass of animated horsemen. He immediately ordered his company to lie down in rough ground behind a bank, from where they were able to send a destructive fire into the French horsemen.

Seeing their plight, a company of the 1st Battalion Rifles, in which Lieutenant FitzMaurice was serving, came up with Kempt's Brigade and ran to their support. Both sets of Rifleman then gave a concentrated fire at the cavalry, who immediately changed direction and rode off with severe loss. FitzMaurice, from this advanced point, could see French guns placed on a height so as to enfilade the British line. They were beginning to limber up, ready to make good their escape, ahead of the British advance. He calculated that by dashing forward from his position with a section of his men, he could reach a point in the road that would allow him to intercept them. Calling out to his section to follow him, FitzMaurice jumped up and headed for the road, along which the guns were now being hurried. By the time he reached it, five had managed to make good their escape. His men, not being in such light marching order as he was, were unable to keep up with their sprightly young officer. Finding he was alone, FitzMaurice threw himself on the leading horses of the sixth and last gun, which immediately checked them. The French driver, fearing the loss of his gun, took aim with a pistol and fired, the ball passing through the Rifleman's cap. Being unhurt, he pulled the Frenchman from his seat, and at that moment his men came up and he called to them to fire. They shot one of the leading horses, which on falling stopped the progress of the gun; two of his Riflemen and a Portuguese corporal immediately cut the traces and the gun was completely immobilized. Three drivers and four gunners were taken prisoner. Lieutenant FitzMaurice then mounted one of the artillery horses as a prize; it was, however, a powerful animal with a mind of its own, and he had some difficulty controlling it. The horse had only one thing on its mind, to join the French, and FitzMaurice was lucky not to be carried into their lines as they were posted, at this time, only a short distance away behind the walls of a churchyard.

The 1st and 5th Divisions meanwhile had been heavily engaged at Gamarra Major and Abechucho, in front of the respective bridges over the Zadorra. After finally carrying these villages, the French line of retreat along the high road towards France running north-east, was threatened. This caused the French to retire with such speed, it was impossible for the advancing Riflemen in Vandeleur's brigade to overtake them. From their elevated position, however, they were able to view the extensive plain that lay before them. The sight that now presented itself to the advancing brigade of Vandeleur, was one of magnificence, the valley massed with the red ranks of the British infantry pushing before them the dark blue rabble that was the French army. Plumes of smoke from the artillery and volley fire of musketry rolled from every direction, while cavalry probed looking for an opening that would allow them to gallop towards the city. The backdrop to this most animated scene was the lofty white spires of Vitoria, combined with the rising smoke caused by Sir Thomas Graham's advance. General Hill was still heavily engaged on the right, due to the large amount of troops that had been sent against him. A violent and bloody stand had been made by the French at the village and wood of Subijana de Alava, which they had filled with light troops, where the 28th Regiment suffered considerably. It was at this point that the battle had become general, with the British advancing on all fronts due to the French having lost their central defensive position at the village of Arinez. Now and again the two forces made contact, but the cannon of both armies was doing most of the damage.

The centre divisions, on passing the villages of Luazu de Alava and Gnomic, received only a token fire from the French as they continued across the broken ground pushing back any opposition. About 6 o'clock, the 4th Division attacked their left positioned on a hill, which they carried and it was from this point that the French made very little attempt at any further resistance in this part of the field. Their infantry was no more than a mass of fugitives abandoning everything, making for the Salvatierra and Pamplona Road. Between Hill's force and the 4th Division's advance, the ground was being filled by the British cavalry, who filing out of a wood, squadron after squadron, was forming up ready to advance in force. The greater part of the heavy cavalry and dragoons had been held in reserve to secure the area for the centre divisions, should it have been necessary. With Wellington's divisions gaining ground, the French left and centre were driven to within a mile of Vitoria.

Graham's success had come as a result of the hard-won fighting in gaining the heights and village of Abechucho, and all the land in that area which had stalled at the bridges of Ariaga and Gamarra. These two bridges were the key to this position and were strongly defended by two French divisions that had been well posted to resist an attack on these two important crossing points. The advance of Vandeleur's Brigade and the 7th Division, had left Reille's flank entirely exposed; though putting up a most remarkable fight against Graham's force, he had little choice but to fall back on his reserve at Betonia. They then fought their way across country, until reaching the main line of retreat being used by the French. It was only after passing Metanco and reaching some heights, that he was able to make a stand, safe, for the time being at least, from further pursuit. Vandeleur's Brigade pursued him until about 11 o'clock, when they halted and bivouacked on the road some two leagues beyond Vitoria, after more than 18 hours under arms.

In their eagerness to withdraw, the French had abandoned all their artillery pieces by this time, apart from eight guns. The right retired by echelon of divisions and brigades under cover of its left wing. Their last division to quit the field had hardly any ammunition left. Wellington wheeled the greater portion of his army towards the Pamplona road to pursue the defeated French.

The eight pieces of artillery the French managed to salvage were dragged across the fields for nearly a league before they encountered marshy ground. As a result they stuck fast, three rolled into a ditch with the poor mules struggling in the tangle of harness, only two pieces being dragged clear, which they took with them. The roads were so blocked with wagons and carriages of every description that it was impossible for them to be used by the gun teams. With the enemy artillery in the hands of the advancing British columns, the cavalry continued the pursuit, and nearly captured King Joseph.

With night approaching the Battle of Vitoria was practically over and some men now took the opportunity to go in search of plunder. The battlefield had covered an area of around some 20 miles and it was easy for the men to slip away under the cover of darkness; food and drink being their first priority. This soon changed when they came upon the discarded wagons and carts laden with the wealth of Spain and Portugal. Lieutenant Simmons of the 1st Battalion Rifles and his fellow company officers, once halted, settled down for the night beside a large fire. The Riflemen were soon returning with a wide variety of food and drink found amongst the French baggage. In no time, the officers were tucking in to this welcome source of food. They, like their men, had had little time to eat since the early hours of that morning. Simmons having quenched his thirst and hunger now rolled himself in a French officer's cloak, a gift from one of his Riflemen, who had shot the owner earlier that day and soon fatigue was overtaken by a deep sleep.

For Quartermaster Surtees of the 3rd Battalion Rifles, duty didn't end with the close of battle. Being the only Quartermaster present at this point, was sent out to search for the baggage belonging to the Light Division. His quest took him through the city of Vitoria, where he came upon the inhabitants extolling the virtues of a group of Spaniards belonging to Don Morillo's Division, exclaiming that the Spaniards had liberated the city from the French, all on their own! He eventually found the baggage, but the chaos, dark and marauding hordes of men and women meant he was unable to bring it up to the Light Division until the morning. The division, meanwhile, made its camp on the side of a steep hill overlooking the valley of Rosales in an area covered in superb woods.

For the men of Wellington's army a lifetime's opportunity now awaited them. In a small window of unaccountable freedom under the cover of darkness, a vast fortune lay all around them waiting to be swept up as a prize. Many prizes were taken that day along with vast sums of gold and silver coins. The wise found a way of keeping this for their return to England while countless others, who lived for the day, squandered their fortunes long before reaching their homeland. Even though the men had been ordered by their senior officers or company commanders to remain in the ranks and camps, there was little they could do to prevent the men from wandering. At the same time, how could those in any authority know where the treasures lay at that precise moment in time? Whatever the men did not find or take away, their camp followers, local inhabitants or Spanish troops would.

When the 1st Battalion Rifles first halted, the men were ordered to keep in their ranks until they received further orders. Lieutenant Stillwell, not the best Rifles' officer to set an example to the men, decided to jump into an abandoned carriage to see what he might find. A staff officer came up at that moment and demanded to know what he was doing. 'I'm looking for papers, sir,' he replied. 'Go back to your regiment at once, sir,' was the order. Stillwell obeyed, but once the officer was out of sight, he was back inside the carriage and was rewarded with some plunder. Stillwell was known as 'scamp' in the Rifles which probably sums up his nature quite admirably. He was a devil-may-care type of fellow which endeared him to both officers and men alike; his motto seems to have been, live for the day, much along the same lines as appreciated by the ordinary Rifleman. In their line of work, life was cheap, and they could accept his way of thinking. His free spirit and nature, probably came about because it was reported he was an illegitimate son of the Duke of York! An incident recorded during the war sums him up perfectly. A group of Rifles' officers had been invited to dine with a local high-ranking clergyman, Lieutenant Stillwell being one of the party. On entering the room 'scamp' spied a cat sleeping on a chair. Grabbing hold of it by the tail, he swung it around his head a couple of times, then threw it out of an open window to the astonishment of the priest and his fellow officers, saying, 'That showed the fellow!' Stillwell was not the only Rifleman to lay claim to being the result of one of the Duke's extra-marital affairs. Lieutenant John Molloy, in the same company as Stillwell, was known to be the Duke's son, but was nothing like his half brother. His only claim to impropriety at Vitoria was relieving a high-ranking French officer of a treasured award presented by King Joseph, when King of the Two Sicilies. Lieutenant John Stillwell would eventually be killed in action at the Battle of Waterloo.

The 14th Light Dragoons, part of the Light Division, took the silver chamber pot from Joseph's travelling coach, which ever after was held in high regard in their mess. Lieutenant John Molloy, during his wanderings, recalls coming upon a group of Life Guardsmen in a hollow road, helping themselves to the contents of the French military chest. Gold was so plentiful that they did not bother to carry away the silver, which fell into the hands of numerous camp followers. It was reported that some five and half million dollars never reached the public chest, much to Wellington's anger. Vitoria was a great leveller; for the wealth from victory they normally only shared as prize money to the tune of around a week's pay, while many a senior officer was rewarded beyond all fairness. One particular Rifleman, however, did manage to get hold of a large bag of doubloons, which his wife cleverly concealed by sewing them up inside a large Portuguese saddle. This they guarded with their lives and carried about to the end of the war. Lieutenant Molloy tells us that on reaching Dover, where the 1st Battalion Rifles were stationed at the end of the war, he was invited to dine with a local banker. At dinner he was told that a man from his regiment had, that very same day, deposited some £3,000 into his bank, which turned out to be the Rifleman with the Portuguese saddle!

Some men did, however, get caught in the act of plundering. General Kempt came upon one such individual loading himself with money from a captured wagon. He was just about to have him taken away as a prisoner, when the man told the him the wagon was full of boxes of gold. Kempt released him, ordering the boxes to be removed and placed in his tent. He then requested a certain number of men and officers from each regiment to be on parade in the morning. This was in order to reward them for their good conduct and discipline after the battle, by distributing a portion of the gold between them. However, when the boxes were opened all they contained were nails and horseshoes!

Kempt was not the only one to be duped. William Lawrence of the 40th Regiment, remained in camp while his comrade, another corporal, went in search of food and drink. Eventually he returned in the dark with what he thought were sacks of flour but it was not until daylight when they mixed it with water to make dumplings, that they found it was lime! Private Wheeler of the 51st Regiment says their divisional camp took on the air of 'a grand masquerade', with the men dressed in all manner of costume, from generals' uniforms to women's dresses, while much of what was plundered was either being sold or bartered, as if at an English country market.

Numbers of women and children had also fallen into British and Allied hands, but we have not come across any reports in our research of women being ill-treated as at Badajoz. Women of high rank caught up in the pursuit or left in the city, were even escorted back to the French lines. Rifleman Costello, with a comrade, had a memorable encounter in Vitoria when looking for plunder. A French mounted officer, with his sword drawn ready for action, was escorting a carriage out of the city that was being drawn by four horses. They fired at the officer, who immediately fell and the carriage stopped. Inside they found two ladies of high rank, who were most alarmed at the fate of their escort and the sight of the two rough looking Riflemen. They tried their best to assure them they were safe. An officer of the 10th Hussars, coming up at this moment, took them off and later they found that one of the women was the wife of King Joseph and that the 10th Hussar

officer had taken from the carriage Joseph's baton! Though a handsome
trophy, this was lost on the likes of Costello, for he gained something
of far greater value and use to him, in the shape of a thousand pounds in
gold and silver coins during his foraging. The Quartermaster of the 53rd
Regiment could not believe his luck when he found and lost a King's ransom,
when coming upon a treasure wagon abandoned with no animals to pull it
away. While waiting for some of his men to make an appearance, he was joined
by a party of Spanish guerrillas who took immediate possession of the wagon.
They, however, let him take away whatever it was possible for him to
carry in one go; as a result he was richer by 1,500 dollars. Madame Gazan,
the wife of the French general of the centre army, and another lady of rank who
had been left in Vitoria, dined with Wellington before being returned under
escort to their husbands.

On the morning of 22nd June, the regiments rose in damp uniforms
from their night's rest and excesses, for there had been a heavy dew during
the night, ready to continue after the French. It was only now, that the real
cost of the Allied victory over the French could be assessed. The losses in
the whole army amounted to: 33 officers, 19 sergeants and 688 rank and
file killed and 230 officers, 158 sergeants and 3,782 rank and file wounded.
A grand total of 5,914 of which 1,049 were Portuguese and 553 Spaniards.

The 95th Rifles' casualties were:

1st Battalion

1 Sergeant, 3 Riflemen killed
Major Cameron wounded severely (returned to England), Lieutenants Cox,
Hopwood and Gairdner wounded severely, Lieutenant Lister wounded
slightly,
1 Sergeant and 36 Riflemen wounded

2nd Battalion

Captain Jenkins mortally wounded, 8 Riflemen wounded

3rd Battalion

Lieutenant Campbell killed
7 Riflemen killed
16 Riflemen wounded

We have been able to extract the following men as possible casualties in the Rifles at Vitoria:

1st Battalion

Captain Stewart's No 1 Company

| Riflemen | Robert Bowens | General Hospital (GH) |
|---|---|---|
| | Michael Cotter | GH |
| | John Donovan | GH |
| | William Gamage | GH |
| | James Kennedy | GH |
| | Marcus Bentura | GH Spaniard |
| | John Stoughton | GH |

Captain Leach's No 2 Company

| Riflemen | Balthoz Barracas | Deceased Spaniard |
|---|---|---|
| | Pedro Bedero | GH Spaniard |
| | Samuel Chandler | GH |
| | John Connor | GH shot through body taking gun at Arinez |
| | John Fawcett | KIA 21st June |
| | John Fitzpatrick | GH |
| | Thomas Goodman | Died of wounds on 22nd June |
| | Miles Hodgson | GH |
| | William John | GH shot through head |
| | Elegio Mancerrado | GH Spaniard |
| | John Marshall | GH |
| | James Stott | Deceased 22nd June |

Captain Smith's [4] No 5 Company

| Riflemen | Thomas Carter | GH |
|---|---|---|
| | William Carter | GH |
| | Robert Claxton | GH |
| | George Duftey | GH |
| | James Dutton | GH |
| | Nicholas Fowles | GH |
| | William Golding | GH |
| | Maurice Hackett | GH |
| | William Kellum | GH |
| | Edward Longhurst | GH |
| | William Middleton | KIA 21st June |
| | John O'Brien | GH |
| | Thomas Smith | GH |
| | John Spicer | GH |

Captain Beckwith's No 6 Company

| Riflemen | William Bacon | GH |
|---|---|---|
| | John Burns | GH |
| | Robert Gilchrist | GH |
| | Peter Murphy | GH |
| | Thomas Pritchard | GH |
| | Thomas Summers | Died 23rd June |
| | David Thomas | GH |
| | Thomas Thompson | KIA 21st June |

Captain Loftus Gray's No 7 Company

| Corporal | George White | GH |
|---|---|---|
| Riflemen | William Clarke | GH |
| | Reynold Cumming | GH (not one of the band Cummings) |
| | Emmanuel Mathewshaw | KIA 21st June |

Captain Johnstone's No 8 Company

| Riflemen | Augustine Albarez | GH Spaniard |
|---|---|---|
| | Joseph Arms | GH |
| | Charles Coleman | GH |
| | James Fletcher | GH |
| | John Gillespie | GH |
| | Thomas Morris | GH |
| | William Stubbs | GH |
| | James Corcoran | Sick absent, died 12th August |
| | John Gray | Sick absent, died 13th September |

2nd Battalion

Captain Jenkin's No 2 Company

| Riflemen | Robert Fuller | wounded sick absent, no date |
| | Patrick Kelly | wounded sick absent, no date |
| | John Williams (2nd) | wounded 21st June. |

Captain Hart's No 3 Company

| Riflemen | Edward Farmer | wounded sick absent, no date |
| | William Hays | wounded sick absent, no date |

Captain Mitchell's No 4 Company

| Rifleman | Thomas White | wounded sick absent, no date |

Captain Fergusson's No 5 Company

| Rifleman | Jervis Leyland | wounded sick absent, no date |

Captain Duncan's No 6 Company

| Riflemen | James Brice | wounded, no date |
| | William Jones (1st) | wounded sick absent, no date |

3rd Battalion

Captain Percival's No 1 Company

| Riflemen | David Campbell | sick absent since 21st June |
| | John Cubis | sick absent since 21st June |
| | Christopher Martin | sick absent since 21st June |

Captain Charles Gray's No 2 Company

| Riflemen | Francis Hewitt | KIA 21st June |
| | James London | KIA 21st June |
| | Richard Luff | died 21st June |
| | John Wood | sick absent wounded 21st June |

RIFLE GREEN IN THE PENINSULA

Captain Hallen's No 3 Company

| | | |
|---|---|---|
| Corporal | James Johnson | sick absent wounded 21st June |
| Riflemen | John Ashworth | sick absent wounded 21st June |
| | James Beggs | sick absent wounded 21st June |
| | Thomas Dick | sick absent wounded 21st June |
| | Peter McDermid | sick absent wounded 21st June |
| | George Perry | KIA 21st June |

Captain Balvaird's No 4 Company

| | | |
|---|---|---|
| Riflemen | James Buffy | sick absent wounded 21st June |
| | Thomas Daniels | KIA 21st June |
| | James Lord | sick absent wounded 21st June |
| | John McMahon | sick absent wounded 21st June |
| | James Woodley | sick absent wounded 21st June |

Captain Andrew's No 5 Company

| | | |
|---|---|---|
| Riflemen | Samuel Ginn | sick absent wounded 21st June |
| | John Harvey | KIA 21st June |
| | John Johnston | sick absent since 21st June |
| | John Jones (1st) | KIA 21st June |
| | James Wilkinson | sick absent wounded 21st June |

We also know that William Cummings was killed in action on 21st June, but there are blanks in the muster details, as with a number of other casualties, such as Jemmy Copley having both legs blown off, making it impossible to give a definitive casualty list.

Amongst the masses of captured equipment was: 151 brass ordnance and travelling carriages, 415 caissons, 100 wagons and 2,000,000 cartridges amongst immense quantities of ammunition.

# Pursuit of the French after Vitoria

On the morning of 22nd June, Kempt's 1st Brigade of Light Division fell in and started their advance along the Pamplona road in pursuit of the fleeing French army. The fields of trampled corn distinctly showed in which direction the three main enemy columns had moved off. Vandeleur's Brigade, at this time was still on the far side of Vitoria, after their pursuit of Reille. The German Hussars, 14th Light Dragoons and Horse Artillery were leading, and came up with the French rearguard, taking 50 stragglers prisoner.

*From Arinez, the road to Pamplona*

The pursuit continued on the 23rd into the province of Navarre. The 2nd Brigade having joined them, the Light Division found the French posted along the river at a small village. The Horse Artillery fired into the French columns and they were soon moving off. The Light Division with the fast-moving Riflemen out in front, crossed the river by a ford, the bridge, being of wood, had been set on fire, and was soon in action with the enemy rearguard. They pushed them so hard, that they prevented them from destroying any further bridges, but the French did set fire to the villages in the hope that the burning timbers falling into the narrow streets, would delay them. The Rifles came in contact with the French voltigeurs at Echarri Arinez, but they were soon on the run, until drawing up at La Cuenca. Here the Horse Artillery, once again, caused their columns to retire through Huerta. The weather was now very bad. Meanwhile, Sir Thomas Graham's force, originally destined to join King Joseph at Vitoria, was marching towards Bilbao to confront General Foy with a column of some 12,000 men. The 1st and 3rd Battalions were the leading Riflemen; the rain, now heavy and continuous, turned the roads into rivers of mud, which for most part came up to the knees of the men. Though the conditions were quite atrocious, Ross's Horse Artillery showed their worth by performing movements that were admired by the whole Light Division, pulling their guns over ditches and across ground no one would have thought possible to drag them. Their horses were magnificent and were a credit in their quest for success. On reaching the high road from Madrid to Pamplona, the French engaged the 1st Brigade of the Light Division with one of their two remaining guns, sending a few bursts of grape and roundshot into their pursuers. A body of Riflemen was ordered to attack their flank, while the two guns of the Horse Artillery sent roundshot and shrapnel against them, which was followed by a charge from the dragoons. The French panicked and in their haste, overturned the gun, as at this point the road had been cut through a plain leaving high walls on either side, giving them little room to manoeuvre.

The Riflemen were jubilant in following them up; until reaching a position where a number of wounded Frenchmen lay, that had a profound effect on these battle-hardened veterans. The enemy soldiers lay in the thick mud, their blood from broken and lacerated bodies pouring into this quagmire, some with limbs hanging by a thread. Lieutenant Simmons and some men, dragged these pitiful souls to dry ground and gave those able to accept it a little wine. The wounded men, however, requested that the Riflemen shoot them before moving off, stating they were Germans in the French service. The Light Division advanced and occupied a number of villages north of Pamplona, until on 25th June they were ordered to assemble on the great road with the other divisions, in order to cut off all communication with the French and Pamplona, the capital of Navarre, a strong fortress town. The Light Division then moved off along the road and through the mountains, out of range of the town's guns, continuing through Noain on the 26th. Here they were amazed at the splendour of the aqueduct that fed Pamplona, with its 100 impressive stone arches. They now camped at the junction of the roads from Tudela and Zaragoza, where they hoped to intercept General Clausel. As this failed, further marches were undertaken via the Daco, Olite and Aragon Rivers, until the head of their column arrived near to Caseda, but the greater part of the Light Division was still on the march and forced to bivouac along the side of the road as it was so dark. These rapid movements were all made in anticipation of cutting off Clausel's Division. The French general, all too aware of what the British were trying to achieve, crossed the Ebro at Tudela and moved closer to Zaragoza. The Light Division, as a result, halted on the 29th, crossing the Aragon at Caseda on the 30th where they encamped close to Sanguessa.

During this time, due to the severe weather conditions and terrain, the divisions had difficulty acquiring wood to cook, dry their clothes and equipment or keep warm. Timber was especially scarce around Sanguessa. Lieutenant Simmons was sent with a party of Riflemen to forage for it. Their small felling axes, specially bought and issued for such occasions, normally did the trick, but not this time. In the end, authority had to be obtained to level a house, and take what wood could be salvaged back to their divisional camp. Simmons and his Riflemen, loaded with timber, were now making their way back to camp, when they came upon General Picton, whose division was camped just a short distance away. Stopping the Lieutenant he said, 'Well, sir, you have got wood enough for yours and my division, I shall have it divided. Make your men throw it down. It is a damned concern to have to follow you Light Division for you sweep up everything before you.' There is no doubt had Craufurd still been in command Picton would not have even considered such an outrage. Lieutenant Simmons, just as indignant as Craufurd would have been, confronted General Alten, who now commanded the Light Division, and reported what had taken place. Alten, equally annoyed, made this fact known to Picton in no uncertain terms. Simmons ordered his men to load up with the wood, and they all scampered off in triumph to their camp, while the two generals continued to argue each other's point.

Once back at camp Simmons, as mess caterer to his company officers, went in search of provisions in Sanguessa, a reasonably fair size Spanish town with a strong castle. It had been liberated from the French by the Spanish guerilla chief, Mina. Here Simmons had the good fortune to meet with a man of some note who offered him a quantity of quality wine. He offered to pay for this windfall, but the man refused telling his servant to fill a large buckskin container, which held the equivalent of 70 bottles of wine. However, the Lieutenant gave the man's wife five dollars for their kindness and back at camp he delighted his comrades with his good luck.

The Light Division halted on 1st July, then returned to the area around Pamplona the next day, where they then had to supply, on 4th July, a strong working party to cover the siege and piquets. On being relieved by the 4th Division, they then assembled on the 5th from their various villages, and proceeded up a narrow valley to the town of Ostiz, then on to Lanz, situated at the foot of the celebrated Pyrenean mountains, ready to start the final push and campaign of the Peninsular War.

We shall leave the 95th Rifles here waiting in anticipation of climbing the Pyrenees, but before closing this chapter of the Rifles' Peninsula history, we have to retrace our steps to 1811, so that we can chronicle the service of the two 2nd Battalion 95th Rifle companies who should not be overlooked, prior to their joining Wellington's Army in 1812. The defence of Cadiz and Tarifa, Sir William Cope in his epic history of the Rifle Brigade, chronicles in error, saying it took place during 1810. As a result, it is often repeated by fellow historians and members of the regiment as taking place that year. Hopefully by bringing it to the attention of our readers, this will, for once, set the record straight, as well as bringing to the fore the service of these two companies.

# The 2nd Battalion 95th Rifles' Companies in Southern Spain

When Colonel Barnard advanced to join Wellington's army with his four 3rd Battalion companies of the 95th from Cadiz in 1811, Norcott's two 2nd Battalion 95th companies remained behind. As a result, the companies of Captains Cadoux and Jenkins were used in varying degrees as detachments. Cadoux's company, however, seems to have spent their time solely in and around Cadiz, with Major Norcott. Jenkins' company on the other hand, took part in some memorable actions which we will now chronicle.

When Napoleon heard of the recapture of Figueras on 25th August 1811 he sent orders to Suchet to proceed with the subjugation of the province of Valencia. A few weeks later, he ordered Marmont to march into Estremadura and d'Erlon to lay siege to Elvas. Marmont's force was in no condition to undertake such an expedition. In October, Napoleon was once again pressing Suchet against Valencia, with orders that would eventually have a far reaching effect on the whole outcome of the war. The Emperor's strategy was based on the conquest of Valencia; Wellington's army in winter quarters on the frontier of Portugal could wait. Napoleon ordered his brother King Joseph, to send troops to Cuenca to assist Suchet so as to advance on that place and attack its defenders in the rear. This of course, weakened the Army of the Centre. Marmont was also directed to send troops to Suchet and as a result, Joseph was depleted by 3,000 men, while Marmont supplied the remainder amounting in total to some 12,000 men. Soult was not immune from these plans, and was ordered to assist Suchet by advancing from Granada against the Spanish in Murcia.

Suchet moved south in October and laid siege to Murviedro about 20 miles from Valencia. Blake, who had assumed overall command of the Spanish forces, moved up to raise the siege and gave battle to Suchet on the southern part of the Murviedro, but was heavily defeated, even though the force against him was inferior in numbers. Murviedro surrendered, and Blake made for Valencia, only to capitulate on 8th January 1812, with over 17,000 officers and men. Remnants of this force did manage to make their way south into Alicante. Suchet's force never arrived, as they were confronted by numerous Spanish guerrila bands. Montbrun, meanwhile, who had been on the march from Cacus to Alicante, on arriving, found the city to have been too strongly fortified for him to attack and fell back on the Tagus, having achieved nothing in his three week march, other than weakening the Army of the Centre at a critical point in the French campaign. When Soult was ordered to assist Suchet, he was already heavily committed with the attack on Tarifa, and with great difficulty had assembled and detached a force of some 13,000 men to carry this out.

Napoleon only succeeded in compounding the problems and movements for his generals in Spain, by withdrawing some of their best troops to bolster his Grande Armée, destined for his spring offensive against Russia. Soult, therefore, was in no position to carry out Napoleon's orders to make a diversion in Suchet's favour. Though, in fact, he possessed an army of some 80,000 men, many were sick, while the duties he was tasked with, caused these troops to be spread rather thinly over a large area. The blockade of Cadiz alone took up some 20,000 men, while another 5,000 provided the garrison of Badajoz. D'Erlon was watching the movements of General Hill's force of 13,000 men, much as Wellington had planned in Estremadura and Leval, who was in Granada, had more than his hands full. It was under such constraints that Soult had to try and eradicate the region of the unwelcome attentions of the Spanish General, Ballesteros, a constant thorn in the side of the French commander. No matter how he approached the problem, Ballesteros always had two options open to him, to fall back on Tarifa or Gibraltar.

Gibraltar was too powerful a stronghold to contemplate taking action against, for it was impregnable. This left only Tarifa as an option; by attacking and capturing this important fortress town, he could achieve two objectives, denying the Spanish general a refuge, while at the same time disrupting the British supply line. Tarifa was a main point at which supplies from Morocco were landed, besides giving shelter to British shipping and privateers. It had been a great advantage to General Graham in the Barrosa campaign earlier that year.

Ballesteros stopped off with his force at Cadiz, where he requested the addition of one of the Rifle companies and as a result, he was joined by Captain Jenkins' company. They all made for Algeciras where they disembarked in September 1811. The idea was to continue his harassment of Soult's outposts. Jenkins continued with his company to Jimena, an old town with a ruined castle set in the foothills, some 20 miles north of Gibraltar. From this base, he set out with a force of Ballesteros's Spaniards and skirmished with the French near Alcala, forcing them back through the mountains of Jimena. During this period, the Spaniards had a number of minor successes, and Soult ordered Godinot to march west and crush them once and for all. This was easier said than done, for Ballesteros was positioned so that he could choose either Tarifa or Gibraltar as his refuge, depending on the circumstances of the attack.

The French commander had to reduce Ballesteros's options and Tarifa was his obvious target. At the same time, he tried to trap him by ordering Victor from blockading Cadiz, to push him from the mountains near Jimena, while a second force cut him off from Tarifa. The Spaniard, however, outfoxed him and took refuge under the guns of Gibraltar, where he was joined by Jenkins' Riflemen; they then all returned to Cadiz by sea, and then eventually back to Tarifa. On arrival, they found it had been reinforced and its defences strengthened. Lieutenant Colonel Skerrett of the 47th Regiment, had arrived with his second battalion along with the second battalion of the 87th Regiment, a detachment of field artillery and a squadron of the 2nd Hussars of the King's German Legion. These forces now combined to make a garrison of over 3,000 men.

Tarifa was an old, walled, Moorish town with towers positioned at intervals along its length; however it was overlooked by hills and built in the days when the garrison was armed with bows and arrows, making it less than ideal to defend. Captain Felix Smith, of the Royal Engineers, had worked miracles in expending great energy in making it a pretty formidable position, though, its greatest strength he devised, was within its walls. A ravine ran through the centre of the town, which was to allow an immense deluge of water to pass to the sea without causing any damage to the interior during bad weather. It entered through a portcullis below the Retiro tower in the centre of the town. Captain Smith arranged that all the houses on either side of the open space looking onto this position should be loopholed and all the streets leading to it blocked up. Some of the towers were strengthened to carry guns. On the north side of the town, about a hundred yards outside the walls, the San Francisco convent was put in a state of defence as an out-work. The smaller houses adjacent to it, he had demolished. The island of Tarifa is 500 yards from the shore at the end of a narrow isthmus forming a natural defence, that Smith armed with four 24-pounders and two ten-inch mortars. A covered access to the isthmus and a redoubt called the Santa Catalina was thrown up on a sandy hill on which he mounted some 18-pounders.

The French began putting in a serious appearance in the November; Ballesteros, however, was out and about with his force, doing what he did best, harassing the French as they struggled to bring up their siege guns in atrocious weather conditions. On 18th December, he attacked the French rearguard but was driven back and nearly cut off, falling back to San Roque, while the French continued their progress towards Tarifa, at times finding it most difficult trying to cross some of the streams across their path.

Skerrett was anxiously in need of intelligence on what was taking place within the French advance and to their strength. He decided to send a reconnaissance party in force to gather this information.

The men for this mission consisted of German Hussars, a party of mounted Spanish guerrillas and the most odd choice of a group of men drawn from Captain Jenkins' Rifle company, who would be mounted on horses drawn from the artillery. What the thinking was behind this idea we have been unable to uncover or comprehend, other than the skill of the men involved with the rifle, while at the same time, they would have to have had some previous experience of riding a horse.

This is the first instance we have come across where the Rifles acted as independent mounted infantry. They had often been placed behind dragoons to rush them to a forward position when speed was of an essence or advantage. This intrepid group was to be commanded by Captain Bunbury, Skerrett's Brigade Major. Bunbury pushed his force north across the plain, and about noon, came upon the French camped in the woods near Facinad. The Riflemen quickly dismounted and extended into a single line of skirmishers. The French soon realised that they were unsupported, and sent out their dragoons to attack them. The Riflemen immediately remounted to escape from this sudden unexpected turn of events. Artillery horses are not meant to be cavalry mounts, and as such are not chosen with this in mind, but are employed for their ability to pull heavy loads. Under such exertions, and their rider's urgent need for speed, they were struggling to keep up with the rest of their mounted detachment. The Riflemen, not natural horsemen, didn't make their plight any more comfortable, for the Riflemen's sword bayonets, still affixed to their waist belts, jabbed into the animals' backs. This caused the horses to become agitated, and had they not reached the support of their own infantry, who came up at that time, the consequences could have been quite different for this first-time experiment with mounted Riflemen. They all withdrew back on Tarifa safe from injury.

Skerrett advanced again from Tarifa the following day, until coming up with a force of some 4,000 French infantry and about 150 cavalry, he was forced back again on Tarifa. Jenkins' Riflemen, back to their normal mode of transport, skirmished with the advancing enemy troops to give Skerrett's force cover all the way back to the town, while a strong piquet of the 87th Regiment checked the French cavalry at a small river, north of the town. The following morning 20th December, Jenkins' Riflemen, supported by the light companies of the 47th and 87th Regiments with two six-pounders were sent to hold back a large column of French troops, who were advancing along the Algeciras road, making for the east side of the town. They were protected by a long line of voltigeurs, which extended right down to the seashore. The small British force was pushed back to the high ground, north east of the Corchuela tower; a second French column was also advancing at the same time from the north.

The Riflemen and light troops, eventually managed to return to the town after a sharp action, with a total loss of 31 British and about 40 Spanish casualties. Of these, Jenkins' Rifle company had one man killed and 11 wounded. (Rifleman Oliver Peacock is known to be one of these.) The French are reported to have had one officer and three men killed with 27 wounded.

That night, during a severe gale, the fortress was blockaded. The French, however, had to repair the storm-damaged road the following day and began immediately to establish a battery of four 12-pounder guns and two howitzers. At dawn on the 21st, Skerrett again sent out the Riflemen and light companies, who successfully drove the French from the heights some 400 yards north-east of the town. This, they repeated the following day against the enemy posts established on the foreshore north of the town. They had been helped in this by the fire of a number of gunboats. The French siege train guns were now established and positioned with parallels and trenches dug opposite to the Corchuela and Jesus towers. The 12 heavy siege guns now began their work against the defences and were also able to keep the smaller British gunboats at a safer distance.

It was now clear to Skerrett where the impending attack would be targeted, and he started making his own arrangements to deal with this threat. The flank battalion and a Spanish battalion would defend the Isla and outworks of Santa Catalina and San Francisco. The eastern walls, from the Retiro tower to the Jesus tower, were manned by the 87th. The 47th Regiment held the Jesus tower on their right, along with the southern walls. Jenkins' company of Riflemen was posted at the highest point of the town, from the Corchuela tower and along the eastern walls, left of the 87th. From this advantage point, the superior range of the Baker rifles could cause serious disruption amongst the French batteries and working parties, while at the same time when required, they could also rake the flank of any force advancing down the Retiro valley. A number of sand-bags had been obtained previously from Gibraltar, and placed so as to protect the gunners and Riflemen along the wall's defences.

In spite of this, the French were able to push their trenches to within 180 yards of the town's defences, the gales on the 26th, forced the British ships covering Tarifa to seek shelter, much to the relief of the French. But the continuous rain that accompanied the gales, caused just as much a difficulty. The French artillery, in spite of this, successfully silenced the guns on the Jesus tower and knocked out one gun on the Corchuela, causing its other gun to be withdrawn. Later the 18-pounder on the Guzman tower, also ceased firing. The defenders, at this point, were effectively holding off an assault by rifle and musket fire. More alarming to the defenders, however, was what were thought of as strong walls of between six and nine feet thick, proved to be of little resistance to the shot of the French heavy guns. Cannon balls, at such close range, passed straight through the walls in many places. Skerrett was panicked by this sudden change in fortune and decided it would be best to abandon the defence. This loss of such an important anchorage, would then be in French hands and defended by their heavy guns, but this seemed to be lost on Skerrett.

Skerrett's officers were made of sterner stuff and he was overruled by a number of them, Captain Smith and Major Gough of the 87th, being to the fore front of this action. Major King, who was in command on the Isla, sent a despatch by gunboat to his commanding officer, the Governor of Gibraltar, explaining the chain of events. He ordered all the transports back to Gibraltar, denying Skerrett any means of withdrawal. There is no questioning Skerrett's bravery, just his lack of judgement when quick action was required. The remaining large gun in the Guzman's tower he had already had spiked, which only added to his predicament.

The French siege batteries continued on the morning of 30th December 1811 and in no time had opened a breach in the wall to over 30 feet wide. The French then summoned the garrison to surrender, but they refused. They then continued to hammer the walls, and in no time extended the breach to 60 feet, dismounting a gun that had been hoisted onto the Jesus tower to replace those damaged the previous day. To counter the inevitable assualt, Skerrett made his headquarters in the tower of the church. The 87th was pulled back so that its right flank rested on the breach. In rear of the breach he posted a Spanish battalion. The 47th was on the right of the breach, the Rifles remained as before. A company of the 47th held the Jesus tower to outflank any advance on the breach at a distance of only 100 yards. The Riflemen would be able to exact the same effect from their side of the Corchuela, which also had a six-pounder remounted, to command the approach from the sea.

The size of the breach, was of course, a great advantage to the attackers, but while easy to access, on the other side was a sharp drop of some 14 feet. The engineer officer's internal defences now came into their own. The streets had been barricaded with iron window gratings, which are a natural feature in most Spanish towns. The Retiro tower, only yards away with its portcullis closed by an iron gateway, also had palisades fixed on the outside to protect it.

Two hand-picked columns of French troops now came down the valley on the morning of the 31st, advancing on either side of the deep channel in which ran the Retiro stream. The 1,000 strong right column of grenadiers was sheltered to a degree from the trenches of their No 2 Battery, before emerging into open ground. Immediately they made a move to the right to attack the portcullis. It was debatable as to whether this had been planned, occurred naturally, or as a mistake due to the deep winding bed of the stream that would probably have forced their hand.

The second column, 1,000 strong consisting of voltigeurs, advanced along the left bank of the stream again, seeking shelter from the trenches of the left attack. It was supported by a brigade of infantry, who made a feint against the Jesus tower and its adjacent walls. Another brigade repeated this action, by pretending it was to attack from the north side of the Corchuela tower. The rain started to fall in torrents just prior to their attack and the soft soil of the area soon had the grenadiers up to their knees in mud. If this was not enough to contend with, they were struggling under a most tremendous musketry fire and sporadic grapeshot from the Corchuela tower gun. The Riflemen, some 30 feet above them, had numerous targets to aim for at only 200–250 yards distance. The band of 87th echoed the spirit of the defenders, by playing their regimental march 'Garryowen,' much to the delight of their comrades.

The French bravely battled on in spite of the gaps being made in their formation and on reaching the portcullis, were greeted with a shower of hand grenades coming from the walls above. Only a few Frenchmen attempted to ascend the breach and those who did, were instantly shot down. Exposed to such a fire and making little headway against the defenders, they finally fell back.

The British losses were light with two officers and seven men killed and 22 men wounded. Jenkins' Riflemen, had one killed and one wounded. The Spaniards suffered one officer killed with 20 men killed and wounded. Total French casualties are not known, though Leval reported 207 casualties. Oman, however, states the sappers leading the column, lost 43 out of their 50, and four companies of the 51st Ligne, had seven officers and 81 men hit, which suggests the total as being much higher than 207 if the other forces received similar casualties.

The French not only suffered during the action, but also in their living conditions. Their camps were most miserable, the weather meaning they camped in fields of mud with little or no shelter, food or fuel, cold and wet; hundreds of men started falling sick. Leval was all for retiring but Victor insisted that another attempt be made. The night of 2nd January 1812 another bombardment was carried out against the walls nearest the Jesus tower, which had little effect. The following night Victor reluctantly raised the siege and tried to salvage as much of his material, carts and guns as possible. Whatever couldn't be removed was burned; ammunition and stores were destroyed. Four heavy 16-pounder guns had to be rendered useless by spiking and removing the trunnions, because they couldn't be taken away. On their retreat, the French had to abandon four howitzers and a 12-pounder.

Prior to Wellington receiving news of the success at Tarifa, he had written to Lord Liverpool, 'From the accounts I have received of that place, it appears to me quite impossible to defend it, when the enemy shall be equipped to attack it. The utmost that can be done is to hold the island contigeous to Tarifa.' (Wellington's despatches to Liverpool, 9th January 1812) His next despatch to Liverpool was to report, 'I cannot refrain from expressing my admiration of the conduct of Colonel Skerrett, and the brave troops under his command.' (Despatches 21st January 1812)

The retreat of the French, and the movements and actions of Wellington's army at Ciudad Rodrigo and Badajoz, meant the troops in the south could be released to join them. The French outposts at San Lucar la Mayor were finally attacked and driven out on 24th August 1812. Soult abandoned the place on the 26th, undercover of darkness, along with an immense amount of plunder. He was soon followed up by the small Allied force along the bank of Guadalquivir de la Cuesta opposite Seville. The two 95th companies of Cadoux and Jenkins, formed the advance guard, and on approaching the bridge received a heavy fire of grape and musketry, but moved to some covering ground on their left, from where they gave covering fire to the Guards, who rushed the bridge, after the Spaniards had twice been beaten back. They all then crossed over the bridge and after some sharp street fighting, drove the French from the city, who left two guns, 200 prisoners and the greater part of their plunder behind. Skerrett praised the conduct of the Rifle companies during this action, and in particular the conduct and 'great judgement' of Captain Cadoux. These companies now joined their battalion bringing it up to a strength of six companies, ready to take part in the campaign of 1813.

# PART TWO
# MGS Clasp Ciudad Rodrigo
# Ciudad Rodrigo 8–19th January 1812

The beseiging and capture of Ciudad Rodrigo from 8th to 19th January 1812 was the first of the three seiges in which the 95th Rifles were engaged. Present were the eight companies of the 1st Battalion, the same number of companies as at Fuentes de Onoro; two companies of the 2nd Battalion, Captain Samuel Mitchell's Company now joined by that of Captain John Hart; and five companies of the 3rd Battalion, Captain William Percival's Company joined by the four companies up from Barrosa.

Officially the 95th were awarded 286 clasps for Ciudad Rodrigo. We have listed 286 names excluding Lieutenant Dudley Hill, now with the Portuguese army, but including Rifleman Richard Young. From this number we feel that 15 are not entitled and have located a further 33 men entitled but not awarded the clasp. This makes a total of 304 clasps to the Rifles.

We have excluded the following 15 MGS men from the Ciudad Rodrigo clasp:

| | | | |
|---|---|---|---|
| 1 | R'man | William Boyd | 'From 3rd Bn. 95th to 12th R. V. Bn. 22nd May 1811.' |
| 2 | C/Sgt | James Davison | A 2nd Bn. man, in the Peninsula 30th August 1813. |
| 3 | R'man | Thomas Edwards | Joined from England, June 1812. |
| 4 | Corp | Thomas Eggarton | (Eggington) Orderly, Gen. Hosp. 4th to 24th January |
| 5 | Corp | Edward Everard | 2nd Bn. man present at Barrosa, not at Ciudad Rodrigo. |
| 6 | R'man | Anthony Mullins | Not on 2nd Bn. paylist. |
| 7 | Sgt | John Norton | 2nd Bn. man present at Barrosa, not at CR. |
| 8 | R'man | Joseph Piers | 2nd Bn. man present at Barrosa, not at CR. |
| 9 | R'man | Peter Price | 2nd Bn. man who, after Vimeiro, is absent until Salamanca. |
| 10 | R'man | James Saunders | 2nd Bn. man present at Barrosa, not at CR. |
| 11 | R'man | William Sewell | Not at Ciudad Rodrigo, not entitled. |
| 12 | R'man | William Smith | 2nd Bn. man present at Barrosa, not at CR. |
| 13 | R'man | John Standly | In General Hospital. |
| 14 | R'man | William Wellington | 2nd Bn. man present at Barrosa, not at CR. |
| 15 | R'man | William Wells | Not in the the Peninsula until Salamanca. |

## 8th Clasp Ciudad Rodrigo 8–19th January 1812

Reference:  1st Bn. WO 12/9523 25th December–24th March 1812.
2nd Bn. WO 12/9583 25th December–24th January 1812.
3rd Bn. WO 12/9587 25th December–24th March 1812.
Officers WO 17/217.

**1st Bn.**

| Capt. | Hon. J. Stewart | No 1 Co. |
|---|---|---|
| Capt. | J. Leach | No 2 Co. |
| Capt. | J. Uniacke | No 3 Co. |
| Capt. | J. MacDiarmid | No 4 Co. |
| Capt. | W. Balvaird | No 5 Co. |
| Capt. | C. Beckwith | No 6 Co. |
| Capt. | A. Cameron | No 7 Co. |
| Capt. | J. Crampton | No 8 Co. |

**2nd Bn.**

| Capt. | S. Mitchell | No 1 Co. |
|---|---|---|
| Capt. | J. Hart | No 2 Co. |

**3rd Bn.**

| Capt. | W. Percival | No 1 Co. |
|---|---|---|
| Capt. | C. G. Gray | No 2 Co. |
| Capt. | J. Diggle | No 3 Co. |
| Capt. | J. Travers | No 4 Co. |
| Capt. | J. Kent | No 5 Co. |

| Lieut | William Baldock | 4 MGS | Lieutenant 3rd Bn. |
|---|---|---|---|
| Capt | William Balvaird | 6 MGS | Captain 1st Bn. |
| Lieut | Walter Bedell | 2 MGS | Lieutenant 2nd Bn. Wounded. |
| Sub | John Cox | 10 MGS | Lieutenant 1st Bn. Wounded. |
| Lieut | Edward Coxen | 10 MGS | Lieutenant 2nd Bn. |
| Lieut | George Drummond | 8 MGS | 2nd Lieutenant 2nd Bn. |
| Lieut | John Fitzmaurice | 8 MGS | 2nd Lieutenant 1st Bn. |
| Lieut | James Gairdner | 9 MGS | 2nd Lieutenant 1st Bn. |
| Lieut | William Haggup | 8 MGS | 2nd Lieutenant 1st Bn. |
| Lieut | Dudley Hill | 4 MGS | Attached to the Portuguese Army. |
| Asst Surg | William Jones | 12 MGS | Assist. Surgeon 1st Bn. |
| Capt | John Kent | 5 MGS | Captain 3rd Bn. |
| Capt | John Kincaid | 9 MGS | Lieutenant 1st Bn. |
| Lieut | James Kirkman | 8 MGS | Lieutenant 3rd Bn. |
| Capt | Jonathan Leach | 12 MGS | Captain 1st Bn. |
| Capt | John Middleton | 10 MGS | Lieutenant 3rd Bn. |
| Lieut | Thomas Mitchell | 5 MGS | 2nd Lieutenant 1st Bn. |

| 17 | Lieut | George Simmons | 8 MGS | Lieutenant 1st Bn. |
|---|---|---|---|---|
| 18 | Lieut | Harry Smith | 12 MGS | 1st Bn. Major of Brigade. |
| 19 | Lieut | Thomas Smith | 10 MGS | Lieutenant 1st Bn. |
| 20 | Lieut | Thomas Worsley | 9 MGS | 2nd Lieutenant 3rd Bn. |
| 21 | R'man | Thomas Alexander | 10 MGS | Rifleman No 4 Co 1st Bn. |
| 22 | R'man | Charles Allen | 5 MGS | Rifleman No 5 Co 1st Bn. |
| 23 | R'man | John Allsop | 2 MGS | Rifleman No 4 Co 1st Bn. (Alsup) |
| 24 | Sgt | James Anderson | 9 MGS | Corporal No 7 Co 1st Bn. On guard. |
| 25 | R'man | Joseph Arms | 11 MGS | Rifleman No 8 Co 1st Bn. |
| 26 | Sgt | William Armson | 8 MGS | Sergeant No 4 Co 3rd Bn. |
| 27 | R'man | James Ashworth | 7 MGS | Rifleman No 8 Co 1st Bn. |
| 28 | R'man | John Bail | 4 MGS | Rifleman No 2 Co 3rd Bn. |
| 29 | R'man | John Baker | 8 MGS | Rifleman No 1 Co 2nd Bn. |
| 30 | Sgt | George Baller | 4 MGS | Corporal No 2 Co 1st Bn. |
| 31 | R'man | Jacob Barlow | 5 MGS | Rifleman No 4 Co 1st Bn. |
| 32 | R'man | George Barrett | 7 MGS | Rifleman No 2 Co 1st Bn. |
| 33 | Bugler | William Bashford | 9 MGS | Bugler No 5 Co 3rd Bn. (Bashforth) |
| 34 | R'man | James Bateman | 8 MGS | Rifleman No 6 Co 1st Bn. |
| 35 | R'man | David Beattie | 9 MGS | Rifleman No 1 Co 2nd Bn. (Beatie) |
| 36 | Sgt | Stephen Bedford | 6 MGS | Corporal No 1 Co 2nd Bn. |
| 37 | R'man | John Bell | 11 MGS | Rifleman No 7 Co 1st Bn. |
| 38 | R'man | Joseph Bell | 8 MGS | Rifleman No 2 Co 2nd Bn. |
| 39 | R'man | Henry Berry | 11 MGS | Rifleman No 4 Co 1st Bn. |
| 40 | R'man | William Berry | 11 MGS | Rifleman No 4 Co 1st Bn. |
| 41 | R'man | John Bidwell | 8 MGS | Rifleman No 5 Co 1st Bn. (Bedwell) |
| 42 | R'man | Thomas Bloomfield | 3 MGS | Rifleman No 2 Co 2nd Bn. |
| 43 | R'man | John Bool | 6 MGS | Rifleman No 4 Co 1st Bn. (Bull) |
| 44 | R'man | Henry Booth | 11 MGS | Rifleman No 4 Co 1st Bn. |
| 45 | R'man | Edward Bowen | 7 MGS | Rifleman No 5 Co 1st Bn. |
| 46 | Sgt | Joseph Bowley | 10 MGS | Sergeant No 2 Co 2nd Bn. |
| 47 | R'man | Wiliam Boyd | 4 MGS | Not on the paylists. Not entitled. |
| 48 | R'man | Richard Broom | 4 MGS | Rifleman No 3 Co 1st Bn. On duty. |
| 49 | R'man | James Bryce | 9 MGS | Rifleman No 7 Co 1st Bn. Lanark, Newmunklin, Weaver. (2 on 1st Bn. paylist) |
| 50 | R'man | James Buckler | 6 MGS | Rifleman No 7 Co 1st Bn. |
| 51 | R'man | William Buckley | 7 MGS | RiflemanNo 6 Co 1st Bn. |
| 52 | R'man | Philip Bulger | 4 MGS | Rifleman No 4 Co 3rd Bn. |
| 53 | R'man | David Burnet | 6 MGS | Rifleman No 4 Co 1st Bn. |
| 54 | Sgt | Robert Burns | 9 MGS | Rifleman No 5 Co 1st Bn. |
| 55 | R'man | John Burr | 8 MGS | Rifleman No 6 Co 1st Bn. |
| 56 | R'man | John Burrows | 8 MGS | Rifleman No 8 Co 1st Bn. |
| 57 | R'man | William Burrows | 8 MGS | Rifleman No 4 Co 3rd Bn. |
| 58 | R'man | James Byford | 5 MGS | Rifleman No 2 Co 3rd Bn. |
| 59 | R'man | James Cairns | 12 MGS | Sergeant No 1 Co 2nd Bn. (Cairnes) |
| 60 | R'man | Thomas Canning | 6 MGS | Sergeant No 3 Co 1st Bn. |
| 61 | Bugler | William Carden | 11 MGS | Bugler No 8 Co 1st Bn. (Carder) |
| 62 | R'man | Zachariah Cardy | 8 MGS | Rifleman No 6 Co 1st Bn. |

| | | | |
|---|---|---|---|
| Sgt | Andrew Carr | 11 MGS | Rifleman No 1 Co 2nd Bn. |
| R'man | Thomas Carter | 4 MGS | Rifleman No 5 Co 1st Bn. |
| R'man | William Carter | 6 MGS | Rifleman No 4 Co 1st Bn. |
| R'man | Sampson Cartwright | 3 MGS | Rifleman No 4 Co 3rd Bn. |
| R'man | John Castles | 8 MGS | Rifleman No 2 Co 1st Bn. |
| Sgt | Thomas Chambers | 3 MGS | Corporal No 4 Co 1st Bn. |
| R'man | Thomas Chapman | 5 MGS | Rifleman No 2 Co 2 Bn. |
| R'man | Isaac Coats | 2 MGS | Rifleman No 2 Co 2nd Bn. |
| R'man | James Coleman | 12 MGS | Rifleman No 3 Co 1st Bn. |
| R'man | Thomas Coleston | 9 MGS | Rifleman No 4 Co 1st Bn. |
| R'man | George Coman | 10 MGS | Rifleman No 3 Co 3rd Bn. |
| R'man | Andrew Connelly | 5 MGS | Rifleman No 4 Co 3rd Bn. |
| R'man | Owen Connelly | 12 MGS | Rifleman No 6 Co 1st Bn. |
| R'man | John Conway | 7 MGS | Rifleman No 2 Co 1st Bn. |
| R'man | James Cooke | 13 MGS | Rifleman No 2/3 Co 1st Bn. |
| R'man | Thomas Cooper | 9 MGS | Rifleman No 2 Co 2nd Bn. |
| R'man | Thomas Cooper | 5 MGS | Rifleman No 2 Co 1st Bn. |
| Corp | Edward Costello | 11 MGS | Rifleman No 3 Co 1st Bn. |
| R'man | William Cotton | 3 MGS | Rifleman No 5 Co 1st Bn. (Catton) |
| Sgt | Joseph Cowen | 9 MGS | Rifleman No 6 Co 1st Bn. |
| R'man | James Crooks | 6 MGS | Rifleman No 3 Co 3rd Bn. |
| R'man | Edmund Crossley | 9 MGS | Rifleman No 3 Co 3rd Bn. |
| Sgt Major | John Dancer | 6 MGS | Sergeant No 4 Co 1st Bn. On duty. |
| R'man | John Davies | 7 MGS | Rifleman No 7 Co 1st Bn. Carmarthen, Pengboy, Labourer. (Six on 1st Bn. paylist) |
| R'man | John Davis | 2 MGS | Rifleman No 1 Co 1st Bn. Flint, Holywell, Flaxdresser. |
| C/Sgt | James Davison | 7 MGS | Not on paylists. Not entitled. |
| R'man | William Deacon | 8 MGS | Rifleman No 2 Co 2nd Bn. |
| R'man | Thomas Delaroux | 4 MGS | Rifleman No 4 Co 3rd Bn. (Dillerowe) |
| R'man | George Dempster | 9 MGS | Rifleman No 6 Co 1st Bn. |
| R'man | John Dent | 9 MGS | Rifleman No 4 Co 1st Bn. |
| Sgt | John Dickinson | 4 MGS | Sergeant No 5 Co 3rd Bn. |
| Sgt | Tobias Digby | 9 MGS | Rifleman No 1 Co 1st Bn. |
| R'man | John Dixson | 11 MGS | Rifleman No 6 Co 1st Bn. (Dixon) |
| R'man | Joseph Dodd | 7 MGS | Rifleman No 8 Co 1st Bn. |
| R'man | Patrick Downey | 3 MGS | Rifleman No 3 Co 3rd Bn. |
| R'man | John Dyson | 3 MGS | Rifleman No 2 Co 2nd Bn. |
| Sgt | Alexander Eason | 13 MGS | Sergeant No 6 Co 1st Bn. |
| R'man | Thomas Eastwood | 6 MGS | Rifleman No 2 Co 1st Bn. |
| R'man | Thomas Edwards | 6 MGS | Not on paylists. Not entitled. |
| R'man | John Edwardstaff | 8 MGS | Rifleman No 4 Co 3rd Bn. Gen. Hosp. 12–24 Jan. |
| Corp | Thomas Eggarton | 8 MGS | Rifleman No 8 Co 1st Bn. Orderly Gen. Hosp. Not entitled. (Eggington) |
| Corp | Thomas Everard | 2 MGS | Not on paylists. Not entitled. |
| R'man | Bartholomew Fairhurst | 10 MGS | Rifleman No 4 Co 1st Bn. |

| 106 | R'man | Edward Farmer | 5 MGS | Rifleman No 2 Co 2nd Bn. |
| 107 | Sgt | James Farmer | 9 MGS | Rifleman No 8 Co 1st Bn. |
| 108 | Bugler | Richard Farmer | 5 MGS | Bugler No 2 Co 2nd Bn. |
| 109 | R'man | Joshua Farrer | 3 MGS | Rifleman No 5 Co 3rd Bn. (Joseph Farrar) |
| 110 | R'man | Peter Fisher | 4 MGS | Rifleman No 7 Co 1st Bn. |
| 111 | R'man | James Fitzgerald | 5 MGS | Rifleman No 4 Co 1st Bn. (John Fitzgerald) |
| 112 | R'man | David Fortune | 8 MGS | Rifleman No 5 Co 1st Bn. (Daniel Fortune) |
| 113 | Sgt Major | William Fry | 9 MGS | Sergeant Major 1st Bn. |
| 114 | R'man | Joseph Fuller | 6 MGS | Rifleman No 6 Co 1st Bn. |
| 115 | R'man | James Futter | 8 MGS | Corporal No 1 Co 2nd Bn. |
| 116 | R'man | John Gallagher | 2 MGS | Rifleman No 2 Co 2nd Bn. |
| 117 | R'man | John Gardner | 9 MGS | Rifleman No 1 Co 3rd Bn. |
| 118 | R'man | Francis Gibbs | 7 MGS | Rifleman No 1 Co 2nd Bn. |
| 119 | R'man | Alexander Gibson | 7 MGS | Rifleman No 1 Co 2nd Bn. |
| 120 | R'man | Thomas Gilbert | 9 MGS | Rifleman No 4 Co 1st Bn. |
| 121 | R'man | Robert Gilchrist | 9 MGS | Rifleman No 3 Co 1st Bn. |
| 122 | R'man | William Gilmore | 9 MGS | Corporal No 5 Co 3rd Bn. |
| 123 | R'man | Josiah Goddard | 8 MGS | Rifleman No 4 Co 1st Bn. (Joshua Goddart) |
| 124 | Sgt | William Graham | 6 MGS | Rifleman No 2 Co 1st Bn. |
| 125 | R'man | Samuel Green | 10 MGS | Rifleman No 1 Co 2nd Bn. |
| 126 | R'man | William Green | 4 MGS | Bugler No 3 Co 1st Bn. |
| 127 | R'man | Christopher Grimes | 8 MGS | Rifleman No 4 Co 1st Bn. |
| 128 | Corp | William Hall | 8 MGS | Rifleman No 5 Co 1st Bn. |
| 129 | Sgt | William Hall | 11 MGS | Sergeant No 8 Co 1st Bn. |
| 130 | R'man | William Hanley | 5 MGS | Corporal No 4 Co 3rd Bn. |
| 131 | R'man | Thomas Harding | 11 MGS | Corporal No 3 Co 1st Bn. |
| 132 | R'man | Robert Harling | 9 MGS | Rifleman No 2 Co 1st Bn. |
| 133 | Corp | John Hartley | 10 MGS | Rifleman No 2 Co 3rd Bn. |
| 134 | R'man | Israel Harvey | 8 MGS | Rifleman No 2 Co 1st Bn. On guard. |
| 135 | R'man | William Heathcote | 5 MGS | Rifleman No 5 Co 3rd Bn. |
| 136 | R'man | Josiah Heeles | 6 MGS | Rifleman No 6 Co 1st Bn. (Joseph Heels) |
| 137 | Sgt | William Hinde | 11 MGS | Rifleman No 1 Co 1st Bn. |
| 138 | Sgt | Joseph Hindle | 14 MGS | Corporal No 2 Co 3rd Bn. |
| 139 | R'man | James Holden | 8 MGS | Rifleman No 1 Co 2nd Bn. (Holding) |
| 140 | R'man | Thomas Holmes | 10 MGS | Rifleman No 3 Co 1st Bn. |
| 141 | R'man | Elijah Hotley | 9 MGS | Bugler No 5 Co 3rd Bn. |
| 142 | R'man | Patrick Hussey | 10 MGS | Rifleman No 6 Co 1st Bn. |
| 143 | R'man | Robert Hyslop | 3 MGS | Rifleman No 7 Co 1st Bn. (Hayslop) |
| 144 | R'man | Christopher Ingham | 9 MGS | Rifleman No 6 Co 1st Bn. |
| 145 | R'man | John Ireland | 5 MGS | Rifleman No 1 Co 3rd Bn. |
| 146 | R'man | Arthur John | 6 MGS | Rifleman No 3 Co 3rd Bn. |
| 147 | R'man | Charles Jones | 7 MGS | Rifleman No 6 Co 1st Bn. |
| 148 | Corp | John Jones | 9 MGS | Rifleman No 1 Co 1st Bn. |
| 149 | R'man | William Jones | 2 MGS | Rifleman No 2 Co 1st Bn. |
| 150 | R'man | Michael Joyce | 9 MGS | Corporal No 1 Co 1st Bn. |
| 151 | R'man | Samuel Keen | 7 MGS | Corporal No 1 Co 3rd Bn. |
| 152 | R'man | William Kellaugher | 11 MGS | Rifleman No 2 Co 1st Bn. (Kellagher) |

| R'man | John Kelly | 9 MGS | Sergeant No 1 Co 3rd Bn. |
|---|---|---|---|
| R'man | Thomas Kelly | 10 MGS | Rifleman No 1 Co 2nd Bn. |
| R'man | Alexander Kennedy | 10 MGS | Rifleman No 1 Co 1st Bn. On duty. |
| R'man | Edward Ketchlove | 2 MGS | Rifleman No 2 Co 2nd Bn. |
| R'man | Thomas Kilaway | 2 MGS | Rifleman No 2 Co 2nd Bn. (Killaway) |
| R'man | Thomas Kinslow | 3 MGS | Rifleman No 5 Co 3rd Bn. (Kinchlow) |
| R'man | Thomas Knight | 6 MGS | Rifleman No 2 Co 2nd Bn. |
| R'man | John Lamont | 13 MGS | Rifleman No 5 Co 1st Bn. |
| R'man | Richard Lancaster | 3 MGS | Rifleman No 1 Co 2nd Bn. |
| R'man | Robert Lane | 7 MGS | Rifleman No 1 Co 2nd Bn. |
| R'man | Thomas Laurison | 9 MGS | Rifleman No 6 Co 1st Bn. (Lorrison) |
| R'man | David Law | 11 MGS | Rifleman No 6 Co 1st Bn. |
| Corp | George Law | 12 MGS | Rifleman No 6 Co 1st Bn. |
| R'man | Thomas Lawrence | 2 MGS | Rifleman No 6 Co 1st Bn. |
| R'man | James Lennon | 6 MGS | Rifleman No 2 Co 2nd Bn. |
| R'man | Samuel Long | 4 MGS | Rifleman No 1 Co 3rd Bn. |
| R'man | James Lord | 11 MGS | Rifleman No 4 Co 3rd Bn. |
| R'man | Samuel Lovatt | 9 MGS | Rifleman No 5 Co 1st Bn. |
| Sgt | John Lowe | 8 MGS | Rifleman No 2 Co 2nd Bn. |
| R'man | Michael Lyons | 9 MGS | Rifleman No 8 Co 1st Bn. |
| Sgt | William Lyons | 6 MGS | Rifleman No 2 Co 2nd Bn. |
| R'man | John Maher | 5 MGS | Rifleman No 8 Co 1st Bn. |
| R'man | William Mahoney | 10 MGS | Rifleman No 6 Co 1st Bn. |
| R'man | Joseph Marriott | 7 MGS | Rifleman No 2 Co 3rd Bn. |
| R'man | Peter Marsh | 7 MGS | Rifleman No 1 Co 3rd Bn. |
| R'man | John Martin | 8 MGS | Rifleman No 4 Co 1st Bn. |
| Corp | Alexander Masterson | 6 MGS | Rifleman No 1 Co 1st Bn. |
| R'man | Isaac Maynes | 8 MGS | Rifleman No 2 Co 3rd Bn. (Moynes) |
| R'man | George McCann | 7 MGS | Rifleman No 1 Co 3rd Bn. |
| R'man | Robert McKay | 5 MGS | Rifleman No 5 Co 3rd Bn. |
| R'man | William McKay | 5 MGS | Rifleman No 3 Co 1st Bn. |
| R'man | John McKelly | 11 MGS | Rifleman No 4 Co 1st Bn. |
| Sgt | Alexander McLeod | 9 MGS | Rifleman No 3 Co 1st Bn. |
| R'man | Hugh McLeod | 6 MGS | Rifleman No 7 Co 1st Bn. |
| Sgt | Charles McPherson | 6 MGS | Sergeant No 8 Co 1st Bn. |
| R'man | Alexander McRae | 8 MGS | Rifleman No 7 Co 1st Bn. |
| R'man | John McUbby | 11 MGS | Rifleman No 2 Co 1st Bn. |
| R'man | George Michelson | 6 MGS | Rifleman No 4 Co 3rd Bn. |
| R'man | Hugh Monks | 7 MGS | Rifleman No 3 Co 3rd Bn. |
| R'man | John Montgomery | 3 MGS | Rifleman No 6 Co 1st Bn. |
| R'man | Thomas Moore | 6 MGS | Rifleman No 5 Co 3rd Bn. |
| Sgt | John Moran | 11 MGS | Rifleman No 3 Co 1st Bn. |
| R'man | Anthony Mullins | 3 MGS | Not on 2nd Bn. paylist. Not entitled. |
| Sgt | John Murphy | 7 MGS | Rifleman No 3 Co 1st Bn. Wexford, Kilhaven, Labourer. |
| Corp | John Murphy | 12 MGS | Rifleman No 3 Co 1st Bn. Tipperary, Cashel, Mason. (Two on 1st Bn. paylist) |

| 198 | R'man | James Nash | 2 MGS | Rifleman No 3 Co 3rd Bn. Wounded. |
|---|---|---|---|---|
| 199 | Sgt | John Naughton | 4 MGS | Rifleman No 1 Co 1st Bn. |
| 200 | R'man | William Newsham | 6 MGS | Rifleman No 1 Co 3rd Bn. (Newnham) |
| 201 | R'man | William Niven | 9 MGS | Sergeant No 1 Co 1st Bn. |
| 202 | Sgt | John Norton | 9 MGS | Not on paylists. Not entitled. |
| 203 | R'man | Martin Oates | 2 MGS | Rifleman No 2 Co 2nd Bn. |
| 204 | R'man | James O'Neil | 7 MGS | Rifleman No 1 Co 3rd Bn. (O'Neal) |
| 205 | R'man | Charles Ormond | 11 MGS | Rifleman No 2 Co 1st Bn. |
| 206 | R'man | John Palmer | 12 MGS | Rifleman No 3 Co 1st Bn. |
| 207 | R'man | William Parkinson | 5 MGS | Rifleman No 5 Co 1st Bn. |
| 208 | R'man | Oliver Peacock | 9 MGS | Rifleman No 1 Co 1st Bn. |
| 209 | R'man | Samuel Peters | 11 MGS | Rifleman No 4 Co 1st Bn. |
| 210 | R'man | James Petty | 12 MGS | Rifleman No 5 Co 1st Bn. (Pettie) |
| 211 | R'man | Joseph Piers | 8 MGS | Not on paylists. Not entitled. |
| 212 | Sgt | George Piper | 8 MGS | Rifleman No 5 Co 1st Bn. |
| 213 | R'man | William Poole | 6 MGS | Rifleman No 4 Co 1st Bn. (Pool) |
| 214 | R'man | David Powell | 4 MGS | Rifleman No 4 Co 3rd Bn. |
| 215 | R'man | Peter Price | 10 MGS | Not on paylists. Not entitled. |
| 216 | R'man | William Price | 6 MGS | Rifleman No 8 Co 1st Bn. |
| 217 | R'man | Benjamin Pring | 11 MGS | Rifleman No 8 Co 1st Bn. |
| 218 | R'man | Samuel Pryke | 7 MGS | Rifleman No 2 Co 2nd Bn. |
| 219 | R'man | James Rawledge | 7 MGS | Rifleman No 6 Co 1st Bn. (Rowledge) |
| 220 | R'man | Duncan Reid | 7 MGS | Rifleman No 5 Co 3rd Bn. (Reed) |
| 221 | R'man | Henry Reily | 4 MGS | Rifleman No 4 Co 3rd Bn. (Riley) |
| 222 | R'man | John Reynolds | 3 MGS | Rifleman No 4 Co 3rd Bn. |
| 223 | R'man | William Rhodes | 9 MGS | Rifleman No 5 Co 1st Bn. |
| 224 | R'man | Joseph Ripley | 5 MGS | Rifleman No 5 Co 1st Bn. |
| 225 | R'man | Alexander Robb | 6 MGS | Rifleman No 1 Co 3rd Bn. |
| 226 | R'man | Thomas Robinson | 8 MGS | Rifleman No 1 Co 1st Bn. |
| 227 | Sgt | Charles Ross | 7 MGS | Sergeant No 7 Co 1st Bn. |
| 228 | R'man | John Rostrin | 7 MGS | Rifleman No 2 Co 2nd Bn. (Rostrain) |
| 229 | R'man | John Rouse | 10 MGS | Rifleman No 6 Co 1st Bn. |
| 230 | R'man | Richard Rouse | 8 MGS | Rifleman No 6 Co 1st Bn. |
| 231 | R'man | George Rowe | 6 MGS | Rifleman No 6 Co 1st Bn. |
| 232 | Sgt | William Sabin | 10 MGS | Sergeant No 3 Co 3rd Bn. |
| 233 | R'man | James Saunders | 8 MGS | Not on paylists. Not entitled. |
| 234 | R'man | William Sewell | 2 MGS | Not at Ciudad Rodrigo. Not entitled. (W. Sewell 1 & 2 MGS are the same) |
| 235 | R'man | William Sharp | 8 MGS | Rifleman No 5 Co 1st Bn. |
| 236 | R'man | Thomas Sharples | 8 MGS | Rifleman No 2 Co 3rd Bn. (Sharpless) |
| 237 | Corp | Adam Shaw | 9 MGS | Rifleman No 1 Co 3rd Bn. |
| 238 | R'man | William Shearman | 4 MGS | Sergeant No 5 Co 3rd Bn. |
| 239 | R'man | John Sheppard | 8 MGS | Rifleman No 2 Co 3rd Bn. |
| 240 | R'man | Benjamin Simons | 6 MGS | Rifleman No 1 Co 3rd Bn. (Simonds) |
| 241 | R'man | William Slavin | 8 MGS | Rifleman No 1 Co 3rd Bn. (Slaven) |
| 242 | Corp | Michael Smart | 10 MGS | Rifleman No 3 Co 1st Bn. |
| 243 | R'man | William Smillie | 11 MGS | Rifleman No 7 Co 1st Bn. |

| | R'man | Thomas Smith | 11 MGS | Rifleman No 4 Co 1st Bn. |
|---|---|---|---|---|
| | R'man | William Smith | 6 MGS | Not on paylists. Not entitled. |
| | R'man | John Smyth | 12 MGS | Rifleman No 6 Co 1st Bn. |
| | R'man | William Solomon | 9 MGS | Rifleman No 2 Co 3rd Bn. |
| | R'man | John Spencer | 4 MGS | Rifleman No 2 Co 2nd Bn. |
| | R'man | Richard Spencer | 7 MGS | Rifleman No 2 Co 2nd Bn. |
| | R'man | John Standly | 4 MGS | Rifleman No 2 Co 3rd Bn. |
| | | | | In General Hospital, not entitled. |
| | R'man | George Stephenson | 10 MGS | Rifleman No 2 Co 3rd Bn. |
| | R'man | William Stephenson | 5 MGS | Rifleman No 8 Co 1st Bn. |
| | Bugler | James Stevens | 11 MGS | Bugler No 7 Co 1st Bn. |
| | R'man | Jonathan Stubbs | 10 MGS | Rifleman No 5 Co 3rd Bn. |
| | R'man | Edward Sutherland | 8 MGS | Rifleman No 2 Co 1st Bn. |
| | R'man | George Sutherland | 9 MGS | Rifleman No 7 Co 1st Bn. |
| | Sgt | Thomas Tabbutt | 7 MGS | Rifleman No 2 Co 3rd Bn. (Tebbutt) |
| | R'man | Edward Taggen | 10 MGS | Rifleman No 8 Co 1st Bn. (Teagen) |
| | R'man | James Tate | 7 MGS | Rifleman No 4 Co 3rd Bn. |
| | R'man | John Tatt | 6 MGS | Corporal No 4 Co 1st Bn. |
| | R'man | John Thomas | 4 MGS | Rifleman No 1 Co 1st Bn. |
| | R'man | David Thompson | 2 MGS | Rifleman No 4 Co 3rd Bn. |
| | Corp | Edward Tonkinson | 9 MGS | Corporal No 6 Co 1st Bn. |
| | R'man | George Tunnicliffe | 12 MGS | Rifleman No 4 Co 1st Bn. (Toniclift) |
| | R'man | Matthew Turner | 9 MGS | Rifleman No 1 Co 3rd Bn. |
| | R'man | Peter Turner | 6 MGS | Rifleman No 3 Co 1st Bn. |
| | R'man | William Usher | 8 MGS | Rifleman No 3 Co 1st Bn. |
| | Sgt | Thomas Wall | 11 MGS | Sergeant No 3 Co 3rd Bn. |
| | R'man | James Warburton | 8 MGS | Rifleman No 4 Co 1st Bn. (Warbutton) |
| | R'man | John Ward | 10 MGS | Rifleman No 4 Co 1st Bn. |
| | Sgt | James Waterson | 10 MGS | Rifleman No 1 Co 3rd Bn. |
| | R'man | Joseph Watniff | 8 MGS | Rifleman No 4 Co 1st Bn. (Watmuff) |
| | R'man | John Wellbelove | 5 MGS | Rifleman No 1 Co 2nd Bn. |
| | R'man | William Wellington | 6 MGS | Not on paylists. Not entitled. |
| | R'man | William Wells | 7 MGS | A 2nd Bn. man starting at Salamanca, not entitled. |
| | R'man | William Weston | 7 MGS | Rifleman No 3 Co 1st Bn. |
| | R'man | Thomas Whetstone | 8 MGS | Rifleman No 1 Co 1st Bn. (Whitstone) |
| | R'man | William Whitehead | 7 MGS | Rifleman No 6 Co 1st Bn. |
| | R'man | John Williams | 8 MGS | Rifleman No 1 Co 1st Bn. |
| | R'man | Thomas Wilson | 10 MGS | Rifleman No 7 Co 1st Bn. |
| | R'man | Thomas Wilson | 10 MGS | Rifleman No 3 Co 3rd Bn. Perth, Weaver. |
| | R'man | Joseph Witham | 7 MGS | Rifleman No 2 Co 1st Bn. |
| | R'man | Henry Wright | 4 MGS | Rifleman No 5 Co 3rd Bn. |
| | R'man | William Wright | 10 MGS | Rifleman No 3 Co 1st Bn. |
| | Sgt | William Young | 5 MGS | Corporal No 8 Co 1st Bn. |
| | R'man | Richard Young | 6 MGS | Rifleman No 5 Co 3rd Bn. |

## Additional names of MGS men not awarded the clasp for Ciudad Rodrigo:

| | | | | |
|---|---|---|---|---|
| 1 | Lieut | Henry Scott | 3 MGS | 2nd Lieutenant 2nd Bn. |
| 2 | Corp | Isaac Bagshaw | 2 MGS | Corporal No 8 Co 1st Bn. On duty. |
| 3 | Corp | James Britchard | 5 MGS | Rifleman No 2 Co 3rd Bn. |
| 4 | R'man | William Brown | 5 MGS | Rifleman No 3 Co 3rd Bn. |
| 5 | R'man | Thomas Bunton | 3 MGS | Rifleman No 8 Co 1st Bn. |
| 6 | R'man | John Burns | 6 MGS | Rifleman No 6 Co 1st Bn. |
| 7 | R'man | Patrick Casey | 3 MGS | Rifleman No 2 Co 2nd Bn. |
| 8 | R'man | Thomas Daly | 3 MGS | Rifleman No 3 Co 1st Bn. (Dailey) |
| 9 | R'man | Robert Deacon | 5 MGS | Rifleman No 3 Co 1st Bn. |
| 10 | R'man | James Downs | 2 MGS | Rifleman No 2 Co 1st Bn. |
| 11 | R'man | Henry Eldridge | 6 MGS | Rifleman No 3 Co 3rd Bn. |
| 12 | R'man | John Gastle | 1 MGS | Rifleman No 5 Co 3rd Bn. |
| 13 | R'man | John Grant | 1 MGS | Rifleman No 8 Co 1st Bn. |
| 14 | R'man | John Griffiths | 6 MGS | Rifleman No 5 Co 3rd Bn. |
| 15 | R'man | James Hall | 4 MGS | Rifleman No 3 Co 3rd Bn. |
| 16 | Sgt | John McDonald | 7 MGS | Sergeant No 1 Co 1st Bn. |
| 17 | R'man | John McKitchie | 2 MGS | Sergeant No 5 Co 3rd Bn. (McKeckie) |
| 18 | Sgt | John Miller | 1 MGS | Rifleman No 4 Co 1st Bn. |
| 19 | R'man | Henry Nevin | 1 MGS | Rifleman No 4 Co 3rd Bn. Wounded. |
| 20 | Sgt | Robert Nunn | 7 MGS | Rifleman No 2 Co 3rd Bn. |
| 21 | R'man | William Parker | 2 MGS | Rifleman No 3 Co 1st Bn. |
| 22 | Sgt | John Reakes | 10 MGS | Sergeant No 3 Co 1st Bn. Wounded. |
| 23 | R'man | John Riddles | 3 MGS | Rifleman No 1 Co 2nd Bn. |
| 24 | R'man | Thomas Robinson | 4 MGS | Rifleman No 1 Co 1st Bn. Divisional Hospital. |
| 25 | R'man | James Russell | 4 MGS | Rifleman No 3 Co 1st Bn. |
| 26 | R'man | Benjamin Slaughter | 2 MGS | Rifleman No 3 Co 1st Bn. |
| 27 | R'man | William Sperry | 9 MGS | Rifleman No 4 Co 1st Bn. Wounded. |
| 28 | R'man | James Steele | 6 MGS | Rifleman No 6 Co 1st Bn. |
| 29 | R'man | John Symington | 11 MGS | Rifleman No 7 Co 1st Bn. |
| 30 | R'man | Abraham Walker | 9 MGS | Rifleman No 5 Co 1st Bn. |
| 31 | R'man | John Waterhouse | 4 MGS | Rifleman No 3 Co 2nd Bn. |
| 32 | R'man | William Wilkinson | 2 MGS | Rifleman No 1 Co 1st Bn. |
| 33 | R'man | James Woodley | 6 MGS | Rifleman No 1 Co 3rd Bn. |

## MGS Clasp BADAJOZ. Badajoz 17th March–6th April 1812

Shortly after Ciudad Rodrigo the Rifles marched south to Badajoz for the second of the three big seiges. The capture of Ciudad Rodrigo took just 11 days, but the castle at Badajoz with its massive walls prooved, as it can be seen, to take a little longer. The Rifles had present eight companies of the 1st Battalion, two companies of the 2nd Battalion and five companies of the 3rd Battalion.

Officially the 95th were awarded 300 clasps for Badajoz. We have 302 names listed, including Rifleman Richard Young, from which we feel 16 are not entitled to the clasp. In addition we have located a further 26 men entitled but not given the clasp, giving a total of 312 clasps to the Rifles.

We have excluded the following 16 MGS men from the Badajoz clasp:

| | | | |
|---|---|---|---|
| 1 | R'man | William Barker | Not on paylist for Badajoz. In England, "sick at Hythe barracks." |
| 2 | R'man | William Boyd | Not on the paylists. To 12th Royal Veteran Battalion 22nd May 1811. |
| 3 | R'man | Sampson Cartwright | In General Hospital. |
| 4 | R'man | George Coman | In General Hospital. |
| 5 | C/Sgt | James Davison | Not on the paylists until 30th August 1813. |
| 6 | R'man | Thomas Denby | Not on the paylists until Salamanca. |
| 7 | R'man | Thomas Edwards | Not on the paylists until June 1812. |
| 8 | R'man | James Farnfield | Not on the paylists. |
| 9 | R'man | William Giddins | Not on the paylists. |
| 10 | R'man | Isaac Maynes | In General Hospital. |
| 11 | R'man | George Michelson | On command with a sick officer. |
| 12 | Sgt | John Norton | Not on the paylists. |
| 13 | R'man | David Powell | In General Hospital. The 1 & 4 MGS are to the same man. |
| 14 | R'man | Peter Price | Not on the paylists until Salamanca. |
| 15 | R'man | James Saunders | Not on the paylists. |
| 16 | R'man | William Wells | Not on the paylists until Salamanca. |

### 9th Clasp Badajoz 17th March–6th April 1812

| Reference: | 1st Bn. WO 12/9523 25 December–24 March & 25 March–24 June 1812. |
|---|---|
| | 2nd Bn. WO 12/9583 25 January–24 March & 25 March–24 June 1812. |
| | 3rd Bn. WO 12/9587 25 December–24 March & 25 March–24 June 1812. |
| | Officers WO 17/217. |

**1st Bn.**

| | | |
|---|---|---|
| Capt | Hon. J. Stewart | No 1 Co. |
| Capt | J. Leach | No 2 Co. |
| Capt | H. G. Smith | No 3 Co. |
| Capt | J. MacDiarmid | No 4 Co. |
| Capt | W. Balvaird | No 5 Co. |
| Capt | C. Beckwith | No 6 Co. |
| Capt | A. Cameron | No 7 Co. |
| Capt | J. Crampton | No 8 Co. |

**2nd Bn.**

| | | |
|---|---|---|
| Capt | S. Mitchell | No 1 Co. |
| Capt | J. Hart | No 2 Co. |

**3rd Bn.**

| | | |
|---|---|---|
| Capt | W. Percival | No 1 Co. |
| Capt | C. G. Gray | No 2 Co. |
| Capt | J. Diggle | No 3 Co. |
| Capt | J. Travers | No 4 Co. |
| Capt | J. Kent | No 5 Co. |

| | | | | |
|---|---|---|---|---|
| 1 | Lieut | Joseph Austin | 1 MGS | Lieutenant 1st Bn. |
| 2 | Lieut | William Baldock | 4 MGS | Lieutenant 3rd Bn. |
| 3 | Capt | William Balvaird | 6 MGS | Captain 1st Bn. Wounded. |
| 4 | Lieut | Edward Coxen | 10 MGS | Lieutenant 2nd Bn. |
| 5 | Lieut | George Drummond | 8 MGS | 2nd Lieutenant 2nd Bn. |
| 6 | Lieut | John Fitzmaurice | 8 MGS | 2nd Lieutenant 1st Bn. Wounded. |
| 7 | Lieut | James Gairdner | 9 MGS | 2nd Lieutenant 1st Bn. |
| 8 | Capt | Charles Gray | 7 MGS | Captain 3rd Bn. Wounded. |
| 9 | Lieut | William Haggup | 8 MGS | 2nd Lieutenant 1st Bn. |
| 10 | Asst Surg | William Jones | 12 MGS | Assist. Surgeon 1st Bn. |
| 11 | Capt | John Kent | 5 MGS | Captain 3rd Bn. |
| 12 | Capt | John Kincaid | 9 MGS | Lieutenant 1st Bn. |
| 13 | Lieut | James Kirkman | 8 MGS | Lieutenant 3rd Bn. |
| 14 | Lieut | Samuel Humble Lawson | 4 MGS | Volunteer in the 3rd Bn. Wounded. (J. H. Lawson) |
| 15 | Capt | Jonathan Leach | 12 MGS | Captain 1st Bn. |
| 16 | Lieut | John Middleton | 10 MGS | Lieutenant 3rd Bn. |
| 17 | Lieut | Thomas Mitchell | 5 MGS | 2nd Lieutenant 1st Bn. |
| 18 | Lieut | George Simmons | 8 MGS | Lieutenant 1st Bn. |
| 19 | Lieut | Harry Smith | 12 MGS | 1st Bn. Major of Brigade. |
| 20 | Lieut | Thomas Smith | 10 MGS | Lieutenant 1st Bn. |
| 21 | Lieut | Thomas Worsley | 9 MGS | 2nd Lieutenant 3rd Bn. Wounded. |
| 22 | R'man | Thomas Alexander | 10 MGS | Rifleman No 4 Co 1st Bn. |
| 23 | R'man | Charles Allen | 5 MGS | Rifleman No 5 Co 1st Bn. |
| 24 | R'man | John Allsop | 2 MGS | Rifleman No 4 Co 1st Bn. Wounded (Alsup) |

| | | | |
|---|---|---|---|
| Sgt | James Anderson | 9 MGS | Corporal No 7 Co 1st Bn. |
| R'man | Joseph Arms | 11 MGS | Rifleman No 8 Co 1st Bn. On duty. |
| Sgt | William Armson | 8 MGS | Sergeant No 4 Co 3rd Bn. |
| Corp | Andrew Ash | 8 MGS | Rifleman No 4 Co 1st Bn. |
| R'man | James Ashworth | 7 MGS | Rifleman No 8 Co 1st Bn. |
| R'man | John Bail | 4 MGS | Rifleman No 2 Co 3rd Bn. |
| R'man | John Baker | 8 MGS | Rifleman No 1 Co 2nd Bn. |
| Sgt | George Baller | 4 MGS | Corporal No 2&3 Co 1st Bn. |
| R'man | William Barker | 1 MGS | Not on paylist for Badajoz, not entitled. |
| R'man | Jacob Barlow | 5 MGS | Rifleman No 4 Co 1st Bn. On duty. |
| R'man | George Barrett | 7 MGS | Rifleman No 2 Co 1st Bn. |
| Bugler | William Bashford | 9 MGS | Bugler No 5 Co 3rd Bn. (Bashforth) |
| R'man | James Bateman | 8 MGS | Rifleman No 6 Co 1st Bn. |
| R'man | David Beattie | 9 MGS | Rifleman No 1 Co 2nd Bn. |
| Sgt | Stephen Bedford | 6 MGS | Corporal No 1 Co 2nd Bn. |
| R'man | John Bell | 11 MGS | Rifleman No 7 Co 1st Bn. |
| R'man | Joseph Bell | 8 MGS | Rifleman No 2 Co 2nd Bn. |
| R'man | Henry Berry | 11 MGS | Rifleman No 4 Co 1st Bn. |
| R'man | William Berry | 11 MGS | Rifleman No 4 Co 1st Bn. |
| R'man | John Bidwell | 8 MGS | Rifleman No 5 Co 1st Bn. (Bedwell) |
| R'man | John Bivings | 6 MGS | Rifleman No 8 Co 1st Bn. |
| R'man | Thomas Bloomfield | 3 MGS | Rifleman No 2 Co 2nd Bn. Wounded. |
| R'man | John Bool | 6 MGS | Rifleman No 4 Co 1st Bn. (Bull) |
| R'man | Henry Booth | 11 MGS | Rifleman No 4 Co 1st Bn. |
| R'man | Edward Bowen | 7 MGS | Rifleman No 5 Co 1st Bn. |
| Sgt | Joseph Bowley | 10 MGS | Sergeant No 2 Co 2nd Bn. |
| R'man | William Boyd | 4 MGS | Not on the paylists for Badajoz, not entitled. |
| Corp | James Britchard | 5 MGS | Rifleman No 2 Co 3rd Bn. |
| R'man | Richard Broom | 4 MGS | Rifleman No 3 Co 1st Bn. |
| R'man | James Bryce | 9 MGS | Rifleman No 7 Co 1st Bn. Lanark, Newmunklin, Weaver. (2 on 1st Bn. paylist) |
| R'man | William Buckley | 7 MGS | Rifleman No 6 Co 1st Bn. |
| R'man | Philip Bulger | 4 MGS | Rifleman No 4 Co 3rd Bn. |
| R'man | Thomas Bunton | 3 MGS | Rifleman No 8 Co 1st Bn. Wounded. |
| R'man | David Burnet | 6 MGS | Rifleman No 4 Co 1st Bn. (Burnett) |
| R'man | John Burns | 6 MGS | Rifleman No 6 Co 1st Bn. |
| R'man | William Burns | 7 MGS | Rifleman No 6 Co 1st Bn. On duty. |
| R'man | John Burr | 8 MGS | Rifleman No 6 Co 1st Bn. |
| R'man | John Burrows | 8 MGS | Rifleman No 8 Co 1st Bn. |
| R'man | William Burrows | 8 MGS | Rifleman No 4 Co 3rd Bn. |
| R'man | James Byford | 5 MGS | Rifleman No 2 Co 3rd Bn. Wounded. |
| R'man | James Cairns | 12 MGS | Sergeant No 1 Co 2nd Bn. (Cairnes) |
| R'man | Thomas Canning | 6 MGS | Sergeant No 3 Co 1st Bn. |
| Bugler | William Carden | 11 MGS | Bugler No 8 Co 1st Bn. (Carder) |
| R'man | Zachariah Cardy | 8 MGS | Rifleman No 6 Co 1st Bn. |
| Sgt | Andrew Carr | 11 MGS | Rifleman No 1 Co 2nd Bn. |
| R'man | Thomas Carter | 4 MGS | Rifleman No 5 Co 1st Bn. |

| 71 | R'man | William Carter | 6 MGS | Rifleman No 4 Co 1st Bn. |
|---|---|---|---|---|
| 72 | R'man | Sampson Cartwright | 3 MGS | Rifleman No 4 Co 3rd Bn. In Gen. Hosp. not entitled. |
| 73 | R'man | Patrick Casey | 3 MGS | Rifleman No 2 Co 2nd Bn. |
| 74 | R'man | John Castles | 8 MGS | Rifleman No 2 Co 1st Bn. |
| 75 | Sgt | Thomas Chambers | 3 MGS | Corporal No 4 Co 1st Bn. |
| 76 | R'man | Thomas Chapman | 5 MGS | Rifleman No 2 Co 2nd Bn. |
| 77 | R'man | Robert Claxton | 7 MGS | Rifleman No 5 Co 1st Bn. |
| 78 | R'man | Isaac Coats | 2 MGS | Rifleman No 2 Co 2nd Bn. |
| 79 | R'man | James Coleman | 12 MGS | Rifleman No 3 Co 1st Bn. |
| 80 | R'man | Thomas Coleston | 9 MGS | Rifleman No 4 Co 1st Bn. |
| 81 | R'man | George Coman | 10 MGS | Rifleman No 3 Co 3rd Bn. In Gen. Hosp. not entitled. |
| 82 | R'man | Owen Connelly | 12 MGS | Rifleman No 6 Co 1st Bn. |
| 83 | R'man | John Conway | 7 MGS | Rifleman No 2 Co 1st Bn. |
| 84 | R'man | James Cooke | 13 MGS | Rifleman No 3 Co 1st Bn. |
| 85 | R'man | Thomas Cooper | 5 MGS | Rifleman No 2 Co 2nd Bn. |
| 86 | R'man | Thomas Cooper | 9 MGS | Rifleman No 2 Co 1st Bn. |
| 87 | Corp | Edward Costello | 11 MGS | Rifleman No 3 Co 1st Bn. (Costelow) |
| 88 | R'man | William Cotton | 3 MGS | Rifleman No 5 Co 1st Bn. Wounded. (Catton) |
| 89 | Sgt | Joseph Cowan | 9 MGS | Rifleman No 6 Co 1st Bn. |
| 90 | R'man | Edmund Crossley | 9 MGS | Rifleman No 3 Co 3rd Bn. |
| 91 | R'man | Thomas Daly | 3 MGS | Rifleman No 3 Co 1st Bn. (Dailey) |
| 92 | Sgt | Major John Dancer | 6 MGS | Sergeant No 4 Co 1st Bn. |
| 93 | R'man | John Davis | 2 MGS | Rifleman No 1 Co 1st Bn. Wounded, invalided to England. Flint, Holywell, Flaxdresser. |
| 94 | C/Sgt | James Davison | 7 MGS | Not on paylist, not entitled. |
| 95 | R'man | Robert Deacon | 5 MGS | Rifleman No 3 Co 1st Bn. Wounded. |
| 96 | R'man | William Deacon | 8 MGS | Rifleman No 2 Co 2nd Bn. Wounded. |
| 97 | R'man | George Dempster | 9 MGS | Rifleman No 6 Co 1st Bn. |
| 98 | R'man | Thomas Denby | 3 MGS | Not on paylists for Badajoz, not entitled. |
| 99 | R'man | John Dent | 9 MGS | Rifleman No 4 Co 1st Bn. Wounded. |
| 100 | Sgt | John Dickinson | 4 MGS | Sergeant No 5 Co 3rd Bn. |
| 101 | Sgt | Tobias Digby | 9 MGS | Rifleman No 1 Co 1st Bn. (Thomas Digby) |
| 102 | Corp | Michael Dillon | 6 MGS | Rifleman No 1 Co 1st Bn. |
| 103 | R'man | John Dixson | 11 MGS | Rifleman No 6 Co 1st Bn. (Dixon) |
| 104 | R'man | John Dobson | 1 MGS | Rifleman No 7 Co 1st Bn. Wounded. |
| 105 | R'man | Joseph Dodd | 7 MGS | Rifleman No 8 Co 1st Bn. Wounded. |
| 106 | R'man | Patrick Downey | 3 MGS | Rifleman No 3 Co 3rd Bn. |
| 107 | R'man | John Dyson | 3 MGS | Rifleman No 2 Co 2nd Bn. Wounded. |
| 108 | Sgt | Alexander Eason | 13 MGS | Sergeant No 6 Co 1st Bn. |
| 109 | R'man | Thomas Edwards | 6 MGS | Not in the Peninsula until June 1812. Not entitled. |
| 110 | Corp | Thomas Eggarton | 8 MGS | Rifleman No 8 Co 1st Bn. (Thomas Eggington) |
| 111 | R'man | Henry Eldridge | 6 MGS | Rifleman No 3 Co 3rd Bn. |

| 112 | Corp | James Ewart | 6 MGS | Rifleman No 7 Co 1st Bn. |
|---|---|---|---|---|
| 113 | R'man | Bartholomew Fairhurst | 10 MGS | Rifleman No 4 Co 1st Bn. |
| 114 | R'man | Edward Farmer | 5 MGS | Rifleman No 2 Co 2nd Bn. |
| 115 | Sgt | James Farmer | 9 MGS | Rifleman No 8 Co 1st Bn. |
| 116 | Bugler | Richard Farmer | 5 MGS | Bugler No 2 Co 2nd Bn. |
| 117 | R'man | James Farnfield | 6 MGS | Not on paylist. Not entitled. |
| 118 | R'man | Hugh Farrell | 1 MGS | Rifleman No 1 Co 1st Bn. Wounded. (Hubert Farrell) |
| 119 | R'man | Joshua Farrer | 3 MGS | Rifleman No 5 Co 3rd Bn. Wounded. (Joseph Farrar) |
| 120 | R'man | Peter Fisher | 4 MGS | Rifleman No 7 Co 1st Bn. Wounded. |
| 121 | R'man | James Fitzgerald | 5 MGS | Rifleman No 4 Co 1st Bn. Wounded. (John Fitzgerald) |
| 122 | R'man | Edward Fitzsimmons | 7 MGS | Rifleman No 1 Co 1st Bn. Wounded. |
| 123 | R'man | David Fortune | 8 MGS | Rifleman No 5 Co 1st Bn. (Daniel Fortune) |
| 124 | R'man | David Foulkes | 2 MGS | Rifleman No 1 Co 1st Bn. Wounded. |
| 125 | Sgt | Major William Fry | 9 MGS | Sergeant Major 1st Bn. |
| 126 | R'man | Joseph Fuller | 6 MGS | Rifleman No 6 Co 1st Bn. Wounded. |
| 127 | R'man | James Futter | 8 MGS | Corporal No 1 Co 2nd Bn. |
| 128 | R'man | John Gardner | 9 MGS | Rifleman No 1 Co 3rd Bn. |
| 129 | R'man | Francis Gibbs | 7 MGS | Rifleman No 1 Co 2nd Bn. |
| 130 | R'man | Alexander Gibson | 7 MGS | Rifleman No 1 Co 2 Bn. |
| 131 | R'man | William Giddins | 5 MGS | Not on paylists. Not entitled. |
| 132 | R'man | Thomas Gilbert | 9 MGS | Rifleman No 4 Co 1st Bn. |
| 133 | R'man | Robert Gilchrist | 9 MGS | Rifleman No 3 Co 1st Bn. |
| 134 | R'man | John Giles | 1 MGS | Rifleman No 1 Co 1st Bn. Invalided to England 24th August 1812. |
| 135 | R'man | William Gilmore | 9 MGS | Corporal No 5 Co 3rd Bn. |
| 136 | Sgt | Jonathan Glossop | 8 MGS | Rifleman/Corporal No 2 Co 2nd Bn. |
| 137 | R'man | Josiah Goddard | 8 MGS | Rifleman No 4 Co 1st Bn. (Joshua Goddart) |
| 138 | R'man | David Goodchild | 1 MGS | Rifleman No 5 Co 1st Bn. Wounded. Invalided to England 24th July 1812. |
| 139 | Sgt | William Graham | 6 MGS | Rifleman No 2 Co 1st Bn. On guard. |
| 140 | R'man | John Grant | 1 MGS | Rifleman No 8 Co 1st Bn. Wounded. |
| 141 | R'man | Samuel Green | 10 MGS | Rifleman No 1 Co 2nd Bn. |
| 142 | R'man | William Green | 4 MGS | Bugler No 3 Co 1st Bn. Wounded. |
| 143 | R'man | John Griffiths | 6 MGS | Corporal No 5 Co 3rd Bn. |
| 144 | R'man | Christopher Grimes | 8 MGS | Rifleman No 4 Co 1st Bn. |
| 145 | R'man | James Hall | 4 MGS | Rifleman No 3 Co 3rd Bn. |
| 146 | Corp | William Hall | 8 MGS | Rifleman No 5 Co 1st Bn. |
| 147 | Sgt | William Hall | 11 MGS | Sergeant No 8 Co 1st Bn. Wounded. |
| 148 | R'man | William Hanley | 5 MGS | Sergeant No 4 Co 3rd Bn. |
| 149 | R'man | Thomas Harding | 11 MGS | Corporal No 3 Co 1st Bn. On guard. |
| 150 | R'man | Robert Harling | 9 MGS | Rifleman No 2 Co 1st Bn. |
| 151 | Corp | John Hartley | 10 MGS | Rifleman No 2 Co 3rd Bn. |
| 152 | R'man | Israel Harvey | 8 MGS | Rifleman No 2 Co 1st Bn. |
| 153 | R'man | William Heathcote | 5 MGS | Rifleman No 5 Co 3rd Bn. |

| 154 | R'man | Josiah Heeles | 6 MGS | Rifleman No 6 Co 1st Bn. (Joseph Heels) |
|---|---|---|---|---|
| 155 | Sgt | William Hinde | 11 MGS | Rifleman No 1 Co 1st Bn. |
| 156 | Sgt | Joseph Hindle | 14 MGS | Corporal No 2 Co 3rd Bn. |
| 157 | R'man | James Holden | 8 MGS | Rifleman No 1 Co 2nd Bn. (Holding) |
| 158 | R'man | Thomas Holmes | 10 MGS | Rifleman No 3 Co 1st Bn. |
| 159 | R'man | Elijah Hotley | 9 MGS | Bugler No 5 Co 3rd Bn. |
| 160 | R'man | Patrick Hussey | 10 MGS | Rifleman No 6 Co 1st Bn. |
| 161 | R'man | Robert Hyslop | 3 MGS | Rifleman No 7 Co 1st Bn. (Hayslop) |
| 162 | R'man | Christopher Ingham | 9 MGS | Rifleman No 6 Co 1st Bn. |
| 163 | R'man | John Ireland | 5 MGS | Rifleman No 1 Co 3rd Bn. |
| 164 | R'man | Arthur John | 6 MGS | Rifleman No 3 Co 3rd Bn. |
| 165 | R'man | Charles Jones | 7 MGS | Rifleman No 6 Co 1st Bn. |
| 166 | Corp | John Jones | 9 MGS | Rifleman No 1 Co 1st Bn. |
| 167 | R'man | William Jones | 2 MGS | Rifleman No 2 Co 1st Bn. |
| 168 | R'man | Michael Joyce | 9 MGS | Corporal No 1 Co 1st Bn. |
| 169 | R'man | Samuel Keen | 7 MGS | Corporal No 1 Co 3rd Bn. |
| 170 | R'man | William Kellaugher | 11 MGS | Rifleman No 2 Co 1st Bn. (Kellagher) |
| 171 | R'man | Thomas Kelly | 10 MGS | Rifleman No 1 Co 2nd Bn. |
| 172 | R'man | Alexander Kennedy | 10 MGS | Rifleman No 1 Co 1st Bn. |
| 173 | R'man | Edward Ketchlove | 2 MGS | Rifleman No 2 Co 2nd Bn. |
| 174 | R'man | Thomas Kilaway | 2 MGS | Rifleman No 2 Co 2nd Bn. Wounded. (Killaway) |
| 175 | R'man | Thomas Knight | 6 MGS | Rifleman No 2 Co 2nd Bn. |
| 176 | R'man | John Lamont | 13 MGS | Rifleman No 5 Co 1st Bn. |
| 177 | R'man | Richard Lancaster | 3 MGS | Rifleman No 1 Co 2nd Bn. |
| 178 | R'man | Robert Lane | 7 MGS | Rifleman No 1 Co 2nd Bn. |
| 179 | R'man | Thomas Laurison | 9 MGS | Rifleman No 6 Co 1st Bn. (Lorrison) |
| 180 | R'man | David Law | 11 MGS | Rifleman No 6 Co 1st Bn. |
| 181 | Corp | George Law | 12 MGS | Rifleman No 6 Co 1st Bn. |
| 182 | R'man | Thomas Lawrence | 2 MGS | Rifleman No 6 Co 1st Bn. Wounded. |
| 183 | R'man | James Lennon | 6 MGS | Rifleman No 2 Co 2nd Bn. |
| 184 | R'man | Samuel Long | 4 MGS | Rifleman No 1 Co 3rd Bn. |
| 185 | R'man | James Lord | 11 MGS | Rifleman No 4 Co 3rd Bn. |
| 186 | R'man | Samuel Lovatt | 9 MGS | Rifleman No 5 Co 1st Bn. (Lovett) |
| 187 | Sgt | John Lowe | 8 MGS | Rifleman No 2 Co 2nd Bn. |
| 188 | R'man | Michael Lyons | 9 MGS | Rifleman No 8 Co 1st Bn. |
| 189 | Sgt | William Lyons | 6 MGS | Rifleman No 2 Co 2nd Bn. |
| 190 | R'man | John Maher | 5 MGS | Rifleman No 8 Co 1st Bn. Wounded |
| 191 | R'man | William Mahoney | 10 MGS | Rifleman No 6 Co 1st Bn. |
| 192 | R'man | Peter March | 7 MGS | Rifleman No 1 Co 3rd Bn. |
| 193 | R'man | John Martin | 8 MGS | Rifleman No 4 Co 1st Bn. |
| 194 | Corp | Alexander Masterson | 6 MGS | Rifleman No 1 Co 1st Bn. |
| 195 | R'man | Isaac Maynes | 8 MGS | In General Hospital, not entitled. |
| 196 | R'man | George McCann | 7 MGS | Rifleman No 1 Co 3rd Bn. |
| 197 | Sgt | Thomas McDermid | 8 MGS | Rifleman No 8 Co 1st Bn. Wounded. (McDormott) |
| 198 | R'man | Robert McKay | 5 MGS | Rifleman No 5 Co 3rd Bn. |

| R'man | William McKay | 5 MGS | Rifleman No 3 Co 1st Bn. |
| R'man | John McKelly | 11 MGS | Rifleman No 4 Co 1st Bn. |
| Sgt | Alexander McLeod | 9 MGS | Rifleman No 3 Co 1st Bn. |
| R'man | Hugh McLeod | 6 MGS | Rifleman No 7 Co 1st Bn. |
| Sgt | Charles McPherson | 6 MGS | Sergeant No 8 Co 1st Bn. |
| R'man | Alexander McRae | 8 MGS | Rifleman No 7 Co 1st Bn. |
| R'man | John McUbby | 11 MGS | Rifleman No 2 Co 1st Bn. |
| R'man | George Michelson | 6 MGS | "On command with sick officer," not entitled. |
| R'man | James Miles | 5 MGS | Rifleman No 8 Co 1st Bn. Wounded. |
| R'man | John Montgomery | 3 MGS | Rifleman No 6 Co 1st Bn. Wounded. |
| R'man | Thomas Moore | 6 MGS | Rifleman No 5 Co 3rd Bn. |
| Sgt | John Moran | 11 MGS | Rifleman No 3 Co 1st Bn. |
| R'man | John Mullins | 6 MGS | Rifleman No 3 & 8 Co 1st Bn. (Mullens) |
| Sgt | John Murphy | 7 MGS | Rifleman Corporal No 3 Co 1st Bn. Wexford, Kilhaven, Labourer. |
| Corp | John Murphy | 12 MGS | Rifleman No 3 Co 1st Bn. Tipperary, Cashel, Mason (Two on 1st Bn. paylist) |
| Sgt | John Naughton | 4 MGS | Rifleman No 1 Co 1st Bn. |
| R'man | William Newsham | 6 MGS | Rifleman No 1 Co 3rd Bn. (Newnham) |
| R'man | William Niven | 9 MGS | Sergeant No 1 Co 1st Bn. |
| Sgt | John Norton | 9 MGS | Not on paylists for Badajoz, not entitled. |
| R'man | Martin Oates | 2 MGS | Rifleman No 2 Co 2nd Bn. |
| R'man | James O'Neil | 7 MGS | Rifleman No 1 Co 3rd Bn. (O'Neal) |
| R'man | Charles Ormond | 11 MGS | Rifleman No 2 Co 1st Bn. Wounded. |
| R'man | John Palmer | 12 MGS | Rifleman No 3 Co 1st Bn. Wounded. |
| R'man | Jonathan Palmer | 5 MGS | Bugler No 5 Co 1st Bn. |
| R'man | William Parker | 2 MGS | Rifleman No 3 Co 1st Bn. |
| R'man | William Parkinson | 5 MGS | Rifleman No 5 Co 1st Bn. Wounded. |
| R'man | Oliver Peacock | 9 MGS | Rifleman No 1 Co 1st Bn. Wounded. |
| R'man | Samuel Peters | 11 MGS | Rifleman No 4 Co 1st Bn. |
| R'man | James Petty | 12 MGS | Rifleman No 5 Co 1st Bn. (Pettie) |
| Sgt | George Piper | 8 MGS | Rifleman No 5 Co 1st Bn. |
| R'man | William Poole | 6 MGS | Rifleman No 4 Co 1st Bn. (Pool) |
| R'man | David Powell | 1 MGS | Rifleman No 4 Co 3rd Bn. In Gen. Hosp. not entitled. (David Powell 1& 4 MGS are the same) |
| R'man | Peter Price | 10 MGS | Not on paylists. Not entitled. |
| R'man | Benjamin Pring | 11 MGS | Rifleman No 8 Co 1st Bn. |
| R'man | Samuel Pryke | 7 MGS | Rifleman No 2 Co 2 nd Bn. |
| R'man | James Rawledge | 7 MGS | Rifleman No 6 Co 1st Bn. (Rowledge) |
| R'man | Duncan Reid | 7 MGS | Rifleman No 5 Co 3rd Bn. (Reed) |
| R'man | Henry Reily | 4 MGS | Rifleman No 4 Co 3rd Bn. (Riley) |
| R'man | John Reynolds | 3 MGS | Rifleman No 4 Co 3rd Bn. |
| R'man | William Rhodes | 9 MGS | Rifleman No 5 Co 1st Bn. |
| R'man | Joseph Ripley | 5 MGS | Rifleman No 5 Co 1st Bn. |
| R'man | Alexander Robb | 6 MGS | Rifleman No 1 Co 3rd Bn. |

| 241 | R'man | Thomas Robinson | 4 MGS | Rifleman No 1 Co 1st Bn. |
| 242 | R'man | Thomas Robinson | 8 MGS | Rifleman No 1 Co 1st Bn. |
| 243 | R'man | Thomas Rogers | 7 MGS | Rifleman No 5 Co 1st Bn. (Rodgers) |
| 244 | R'man | James Rolestone | 4 MGS | Rifleman No 7 Co 1st Bn. |
| 245 | Sgt | Charles Ross | 7 MGS | Sergeant No 7 Co 1st Bn. |
| 246 | R'man | John Rostrin | 7 MGS | Rifleman No 2 Co 2nd Bn. Wounded. (Roston) |
| 247 | R'man | John Rouse | 10 MGS | Rifleman No 6 Co 1st Bn. Wounded. |
| 248 | R'man | Richard Rouse | 8 MGS | Rifleman No 6 Co 1st Bn. |
| 249 | R'man | George Rowe | 6 MGS | Rifleman No 1 Co 1st Bn. |
| 250 | Sgt | William Sabin | 10 MGS | Sergeant No 3 Co 3rd Bn. |
| 251 | R'man | James Saunders | 8 MGS | Not on paylists. Not entitled. |
| 252 | R'man | Thomas Sharples | 8 MGS | Rifleman No 2 Co 3rd Bn. |
| 253 | R'man | William Shearman | 4 MGS | Sergeant No 5 Co 3rd Bn. |
| 254 | R'man | John Sheppard | 8 MGS | Rifleman No 2 Co 3rd Bn. |
| 255 | R'man | Benjamin Simons | 6 MGS | Rifleman No 1 Co 3rd Bn. (Simonds) |
| 256 | R'man | Benjamin Slaughter | 2 MGS | Rifleman No 3 Co 1st Bn. |
| 257 | R'man | William Slavin | 8 MGS | Rifleman No 1 Co 3rd Bn. (Slaven) |
| 258 | Corp | Michael Smart | 10 MGS | Rifleman No 3 Co 1st Bn. |
| 259 | R'man | William Smillie | 11 MGS | Rifleman No 7 Co 1st Bn. |
| 260 | Corp | Peter Smith | 3 MGS | Rifleman No 1 Co 1st Bn. |
| 261 | R'man | Thomas Smith | 11 MGS | Rifleman No 4 Co 1st Bn. |
| 262 | R'man | John Smyth | 12 MGS | Rifleman No 6 Co 1st Bn. |
| 263 | R'man | William Solomon | 9 MGS | Rifleman No 2 Co 3rd Bn. |
| 264 | R'man | John Spencer | 4 MGS | Rifleman No 2 Co 2nd Bn. |
| 265 | R'man | Richard Spencer | 7 MGS | Rifleman No 2 Co 2nd Bn. |
| 266 | R'man | George Stephenson | 10 MGS | Rifleman No 2 Co 3rd Bn. Wounded. |
| 267 | R'man | Jonathan Stubbs | 10 MGS | Rifleman No 5 Co 3rd Bn. |
| 268 | R'man | Edward Sutherland | 8 MGS | Rifleman No 2 Co 1st Bn. |
| 269 | R'man | George Sutherland | 9 MGS | Rifleman No 7 Co 1st Bn. |
| 270 | R'man | Matthew Swalwell | 7 MGS | Corporal No 5 Co 1st Bn. On duty. |
| 271 | R'man | John Symington | 11 MGS | Rifleman No 7 Co 1st Bn. Wounded. |
| 272 | Sgt | Thomas Tabbutt | 7 MGS | Rifleman No 2 Co 3rd Bn. (Tebbutt) |
| 273 | R'man | Edward Taggen | 10 MGS | Rifleman No 8 Co 1st Bn. (Teagen) |
| 274 | R'man | James Tate | 7 MGS | Rifleman No 4 Co 3rd Bn. |
| 275 | Sgt | John Tatt | 6 MGS | Corporal No 4 Co 1st Bn. Wounded. |
| 276 | R'man | John Thomas | 4 MGS | Rifleman No 1 Co 1st Bn. |
| 277 | R'man | David Thompson | 2 MGS | Rifleman No 4 Co 3rd Bn. Wounded. |
| 278 | Corp | Edward Tonkinson | 9 MGS | Corporal No 6 Co 1st Bn. |
| 279 | R'man | George Tunnicliffe | 12 MGS | Rifleman No 4 Co 1st Bn. (Toniclift) |
| 280 | R'man | Matthew Turner | 9 MGS | Rifleman No 1 Co 3rd Bn. Wounded. |
| 281 | R'man | Peter Turner | 6 MGS | Rifleman No 2 Co 1st Bn. |
| 282 | R'man | William Usher | 8 MGS | Rifleman No 3 Co 1st Bn. |
| 283 | R'man | George Waine | 4 MGS | Rifleman No 8 Co 1st Bn. |
| 284 | R'man | Abraham Walker | 9 MGS | Rifleman No 5 Co 1st Bn. |
| 285 | Sgt | Thomas Wall | 11 MGS | Sergeant No 3 Co 3rd Bn. |

| 286 | R'man | James Warburton | 8 MGS | Rifleman No 4 Co 1st Bn. Wounded. (Warbutton) |
|---|---|---|---|---|
| 287 | R'man | John Ward | 10 MGS | Rifleman No 4 Co 1st Bn. |
| 288 | Sgt | James Waterson | 10 MGS | Rifleman No 1 Co 3rd Bn. |
| 289 | R'man | Joseph Watniff | 8 MGS | Rifleman No 4 Co 1st Bn. (Watmuff) |
| 290 | R'man | John Wellbelove | 5 MGS | Rifleman No 1 Co 2nd Bn. |
| 291 | R'man | William Wells | 7 MGS | A 2nd Bn. man starting at Salamanca, not entitled. |
| 292 | R'man | William Weston | 7 MGS | Rifleman No 3 Co 1st Bn. |
| 293 | R'man | Thomas Whetstone | 8 MGS | Rifleman No 1 Co 1st Bn. (Whitstone) |
| 294 | R'man | William Whitehead | 7 MGS | Rifleman No 6 Co 1st Bn. |
| 295 | R'man | John Williams | 8 MGS | Rifleman No 1 Co 1st Bn. |
| 296 | R'man | Thomas Wilson | 10 MGS | Rifleman No 7 Co 1st Bn. |
| 297 | R'man | Thomas Wilson | 10 MGS | Rifleman No 3 Co 3rd Bn. Perth, Weaver. |
| 298 | R'man | Joseph Witham | 7 MGS | Rifleman No 2 Co 1st Bn. |
| 299 | R'man | James Woodley | 6 MGS | Rifleman No 1 Co 3rd Bn. |
| 300 | R'man | Henry Wright | 4 MGS | Rifleman No 5 Co 3rd Bn. Wounded. |
| 301 | R'man | William Wright | 10 MGS | Rifleman No 3 Co 1st Bn. |
| 302 | R'man | Richard Young | 6 MGS | Rifleman No 5 Co 3rd Bn. |

## Additional names of MGS men not awarded the clasp for Badajoz:

| Lieut | Walter Bedell | 2 MGS | Lieutenant 2nd Bn. Wounded. |
|---|---|---|---|
| Lieut | Henry Scott | 3 MGS | 2nd Lieutenant 2nd Bn. |
| Corp | Isaac Bagshaw | 2 MGS | Corporal No 8 Co 1st Bn. On duty. |
| R'man | Thomas Bendal | 5 MGS | Rifleman No 3 Co 1st Bn. On guard. (Bandle) |
| R'man | William Brown | 5 MGS | Rifleman No 3 Co 3rd Bn. |
| R'man | James Buckler | 6 MGS | Rifleman No 7 Co 1st Bn. |
| R'man | James Bulcock | 6 MGS | Rifleman No 8 Co 1st Bn. |
| R'man | John Davies | 7 MGS | Rifleman No 5 Co 1st Bn. Carmarthen, Pengboy, Labourer (Six on 1st Bn. paylist) |
| R'man | Thomas Delaroux | 4 MGS | Rifleman No 4 Co 3rd Bn. (Dillerowe) |
| R'man | James Downs | 2 MGS | Rifleman No 2 Co 1st Bn. |
| R'man | Thomas Eastwood | 6 MGS | Rifleman No 2 Co 1st Bn. Wounded. |
| R'man | John Gallagher | 2 MGS | Rifleman No 2 Co 2 Bn. Wounded. (Goulaugher) |
| R'man | John Gastle | 1 MGS | Rifleman No 5 Co 3rd Bn. |
| Sgt | John McDonald | 7 MGS | Sergeant No 1 Co 1st Bn. |
| R'man | John McKitchie | 2 MGS | Sergeant No 5 Co 3rd Bn. (McKeckie) |
| Sgt | John Miller | 1 MGS | Rifleman No 4 Co 1st Bn. |
| Sgt | Robert Nunn | 7 MGS | Corporal No 2 Co 3rd Bn. |
| R'man | John Riddles | 3 MGS | Rifleman No 1 Co 2nd Bn. |
| R'man | James Russell | 4 MGS | Rifleman No 3 Co 1st Bn. |
| R'man | William Sharp | 8 MGS | Rifleman No 5 Co 1st Bn. Wounded. |
| R'man | William Sperry | 9 MGS | Rifleman No 4 Co 1st Bn. Wounded. |

| 22 | R'man | John Standly | 4 MGS | Rifleman No 2 Co 3rd Bn. |
|----|-------|--------------|-------|--------------------------|
| 23 | R'man | James Steele | 6 MGS | Rifleman No 6 Co 1st Bn. |
| 24 | R'man | William Stephenson | 5 MGS | Rifleman No 8 Co 1st Bn. |
| 25 | R'man | John Waterhouse | 4 MGS | Rifleman No 2 Co 2nd Bn. |
| 26 | R'man | William Wilkinson | 2 MGS | Rifleman No 1 Co 1st Bn. |

## MGS Clasp SALAMANCA Battle of Salamanca 22nd July 1812

The battle of Salamanca or Los Arapiles, as it is sometimes called, was a fine victory for Wellington. The 95th Rifles on this occasion were lightly engaged, except towards the end of the conflict. It is the tenth clasp to be awarded to the Rifles who were present in strength with six 1st Battalion, four 2nd Battalion and five 3rd Battalion companies. Officially 308 clasps were given, we have 310 names including Rifleman Richard Young. From this number we have 26 men who we feel are not entitled, together with a further 22 men entitled but not awarded the clasp giving a total of 306 clasps to the Rifles.

We have excluded the following 26 MGS men from the Salamanca clasp:

| 1 | R'man | John Baldwin | Joined from England 26th November 1813. |
|----|-------|--------------|-----------------------------------------|
| 2 | R'man | William Berry | "Sick absent." |
| 3 | R'man | William Boyd | Not on the paylists for Salamanca. |
| 4 | R'man | John Burr | "In General Hospital." |
| 5 | R'man | James Connor | 2nd Bn. Man, who does not appear to be present in the Peninsula. |
| 6 | R'man | James Connor | 2nd Bn. man, who does not appear to be present in the Peninsula. |
| 7 | R'man | John Downs | Joined from England in August 1813. |
| 8 | R'man | John Edwards | "Sick absent." |
| 9 | R'man | Anthony Everitt | Returned to England after Barrosa, not on paylists for Salamanca. |
| 10 | R'man | James Fraser | After Corunna, joined from England 25th July 1812. |
| 11 | R'man | James Futter | "Sick absent." |
| 12 | R'man | William Giddins | Not on paylist for Salamanca. |
| 13 | R'man | Thomas Hooper | Joined from England 25th July 1812. |
| 14 | Corp | John Jones | "General Hospital." |
| 15 | R'man | Daniel Lewen | Not on paylist for Salamanca. |
| 16 | Sgt | John Lowe | "Sick absent." |
| 17 | R'man | George Michelson | "In General Hospital." |
| 18 | Sgt | John Norton | Not on paylist for Salamanca. |
| 19 | R'man | Charles Ormond | "In General Hospital." |
| 20 | R'man | Joseph Piers | Not on paylist for Salamanca. |
| 21 | R'man | Thomas Robinson | "In General Hospital." |
| 22 | R'man | James Saunders | Not on paylist for Salamanca. |

| 23 | R'man | Thomas Sharples | "Sick absent." |
| 24 | Sgt | Alexander Smith | Not on paylist for Salamanca. |
| 25 | R'man | James Swain | Joined from England 25th July 1812. |
| 26 | R'man | William Wellington | Not on paylist for Salamanca. |

## 10th Clasp Salamanca 22nd July 1812

Reference:
1st Bn. WO 12/9523 25 June–24 September 1812.
2nd Bn. WO 12/9583 25 June–24 September 1812.
3rd Bn. WO12/9587 25 June–24 September 1812.
Officers WO 17/217.

### 1st Bn.

| Capt | Hon. J. Stewart | No 1 Co. |
| Capt | J. Leach | No 2 Co. |
| Capt | H. G. Smith | No 5 Co. |
| Capt | J. MacDiarmid | No 6 Co. |
| Capt | W. Balvaird | No 7 Co. |
| Capt | C. Beckwith | No 8 Co. |

### 2nd Bn.

| Capt | S. Mitchell | No 3 Co. |
| Capt | J. Hart | No 6 Co. |
| Capt | J. Duncan | No 8 Co. |
| Capt | D. Fergusson | No 10 Co. |

### 3rd Bn.

| Capt | W. Percival | No 1 Co. |
| Capt | C. Smyth | No 2 Co. |
| Capt | W. Hallen | No 3 Co. |
| Capt | J. Travers | No 4 Co. |
| Capt | J. Kent | No 5 Co. |

| Lieut | William Baldock | 4 MGS | Lieutenant 3rd Bn. |
| Capt | William Balvaird | 6 MGS | Captain 1st Bn. |
| Lieut | Edward Coxen | 10 MGS | Lieutenant 2nd Bn. |
| Lieut | George Drummond | 8 MGS | 2nd Lieutenant 3rd Bn. |
| Lieut | James Gairdner | 9 MGS | Lieutenant 1st Bn. (Gardner) |
| Lieut | William Haggup | 8 MGS | Lieutenant 3rd Bn. (Absent with leave 25th June Portugal.) |
| Sub | William Humbley | 12 MGS | Lieutenant 2nd Bn. |
| Lieut | Loftus Jones | 6 MGS | 2nd Lieutenant 3rd Bn. |
| Asst Surg | William Jones | 12 MGS | Assist Surgeon 1st Bn. |
| Capt | John Kent | 5 MGS | Captain 3rd Bn. |
| Capt | John Kincaid | 9 MGS | Lieutenant 1st Bn. |

| 12 | Lieut | James Kirkman | 8 MGS | Lieutenant 3rd Bn. |
|---|---|---|---|---|
| 13 | Capt | Jonathan Leach | 12 MGS | Captain 1st Bn. |
| 14 | Lieut | John Middleton | 10 MGS | Lieutenant 3rd Bn. |
| 15 | Lieut | Thomas Mitchell | 5 MGS | 2nd Lieutenant 1st Bn. |
| 16 | Lieut | John Molloy | 8 MGS | Lieutenant 1st Bn. |
| 17 | Sub | John Ridgway | 3 MGS | 2nd Lieutenant 2nd Bn. |
| 18 | Lieut | Henry Scott | 3 MGS | Lieutenant 2nd Bn. |
| 19 | Lieut | George Simmons | 8 MGS | Lieutenant 1st Bn. |
| 20 | Lieut | Harry Smith | 12 MGS | 1st Bn. Major of Brigade. |
| 21 | Lieut | Thomas Smith | 10 MGS | Lieutenant 1st Bn. |
| 22 | Lieut | Nicholas Travers | 3 MGS | Lieutenant 2nd Bn. |
| 23 | Lieut | Thomas Worsley | 9 MGS | 2nd Lieutenant 3rd Bn. |
| 24 | R'man | Thomas Alexander | 10 MGS | Rifleman No 4 & 8 Co 1st Bn. |
| 25 | R'man | Charles Allen | 5 MGS | Rifleman No 5 Co 1st Bn. |
| 26 | Sgt | James Anderson | 9 MGS | Corporal No 7 Co 1st Bn. On guard. |
| 27 | R'man | Joseph Arms | 11 MGS | Rifleman No 8 Co 1st Bn. |
| 28 | Sgt | William Armson | 8 MGS | Colour Sergeant No 4 Co 3rd Bn. |
| 29 | Corp | Andrew Ash | 8 MGS | Rifleman No 4 & 5 Co 1st Bn. |
| 30 | R'man | James Ashworth | 7 MGS | Rifleman No 8 Co 1st Bn. |
| 31 | R'man | William Austin | 5 MGS | Rifleman No 8 Co 2nd Bn. |
| 32 | R'man | John Bail | 4 MGS | Rifleman No 2 Co 3rd Bn. |
| 33 | R'man | John Baker | 8 MGS | Rifleman No 3 Co 2nd Bn. |
| 34 | R'man | John Baldwin | 4 MGS | Not on paylists for Salamanca, not entitled. |
| | | | | |
| 35 | Sgt | George Baller | 4 MGS | Sergeant No 3 & 2 Co 1st Bn. |
| 36 | R'man | George Barrett | 7 MGS | Rifleman No 2 Co 1st Bn. |
| 37 | Bugler | William Bashford | 9 MGS | Bugler No 5 Co 3rd Bn. (Bashforth) |
| 38 | R'man | James Bateman | 8 MGS | Rifleman No 6 Co 1st Bn. |
| 39 | R'man | David Beattie | 9 MGS | Rifleman No 3 Co 2nd Bn. |
| 40 | Sgt | Stephen Bedford | 6 MGS | Corporal No 3 Co 2nd Bn. On guard. |
| 41 | R'man | John Bell | 11 MGS | Rifleman No 7 Co 1st Bn. |
| 42 | R'man | Henry Berry | 11 MGS | Rifleman No 4 & 8 Co 1st Bn. On guard. |
| 43 | R'man | William Berry | 2 MGS | Sick absent, not entitled. |
| 44 | R'man | William Berry | 11 MGS | Rifleman No 4 & 8 Co 1st Bn. On guard. |
| 45 | R'man | John Bidwell | 8 MGS | Rifleman No 5 Co 1st Bn. (Bedwell) |
| 46 | R'man | John Bivings | 6 MGS | Rifleman No 8 Co 1st Bn. (Bivens) |
| 47 | R'man | John Bool | 6 MGS | Rifleman No 4 & 5 Co 1st Bn. (Bull) |
| 48 | R'man | Henry Booth | 11 MGS | Rifleman No 4 & 5 Co 1st Bn. |
| 49 | R'man | Edward Bowen | 7 MGS | Rifleman No 5 Co 1st Bn. |
| 50 | Sgt | Joseph Bowley | 10 MGS | Sergeant No 6 Co 2nd Bn. |
| 51 | R'man | William Boyd | 4 MGS | Not on paylists for Salamanca, not entitled. |
| | | | | |
| 52 | Corp | James Britchard | 5 MGS | Rifleman No 2 Co 3rd Bn. |
| 53 | R'man | Richard Broom | 4 MGS | Rifleman No 3 & 2 Co 1st Bn. |
| 54 | R'man | William Brown | 5 MGS | Rifleman No 3 Co 3rd Bn. |
| 55 | R'man | James Bryce | 9 MGS | Rifleman No 7 Co 1st Bn. Lanark, Weaver (Two on 1st Bn. paylist) |

| R'man | James Buckler | 6 MGS | Rifleman No 7 Co 1st Bn. |
|---|---|---|---|
| R'man | William Buckley | 7 MGS | Rifleman No 6 Co 1st Bn. |
| R'man | James Bulcock | 6 MGS | Rifleman No 8 Co 1st Bn. |
| R'man | Philip Bulger | 4 MGS | Rifleman No 4 Co 3rd Bn. |
| R'man | John Burns | 6 MGS | Rifleman No 6 Co 1st Bn. |
| Sgt | Robert Burns | 9 MGS | Rifleman No 5 Co 1st Bn. |
| R'man | William Burns | 7 MGS | Rifleman No 6 Co 1st Bn. |
| R'man | John Burr | 8 MGS | In General Hospital, not entitled. |
| R'man | John Burrows | 8 MGS | Rifleman No 8 Co 1st Bn. |
| R'man | William Burrows | 8 MGS | Rifleman No 4 Co 3rd Bn. |
| R'man | John Cain | 5 MGS | Rifleman No 8 Co 2nd Bn. (Camm) |
| R'man | James Cairns | 12 MGS | Sergeant No 3 Co 2nd Bn. |
| R'man | Thomas Canning | 6 MGS | Sergeant No 3 Co 1st Bn. To England with No 4 Co 25th Aug. |
| Bugler | William Carden | 11 MGS | Bugler No 8 Co 1st Bn. (Carder) |
| R'man | Zachariah Cardy | 8 MGS | Rifleman No 6 Co 1st Bn. |
| Sgt | Andrew Carr | 11 MGS | Rifleman No 3 Co 2nd Bn. |
| R'man | William Carter | 6 MGS | Rifleman No 4 & 5 Co 1st Bn. |
| R'man | Patrick Casey | 3 MGS | Rifleman No 6 Co 2nd Bn. |
| R'man | John Castles | 8 MGS | Rifleman No 2 Co 1st Bn. |
| Sgt | Thomas Chambers | 3 MGS | Corporal No 4 Co 1st Bn. To England with No 4 Co 25th Aug. |
| R'man | Thomas Chapman | 5 MGS | Sick absent, not entitled. |
| R'man | Robert Claxton | 7 MGS | Rifleman No 5 Co 1st Bn. |
| R'man | Edward Clegg | 7 MGS | Rifleman No 10 Co 2nd Bn. |
| R'man | James Coleman | 12 MGS | Rifleman No 3 & 7 Co 1st Bn. |
| R'man | Thomas Coleston | 9 MGS | Rifleman No 4 & 8 Co 1st Bn. |
| R'man | George Coman | 10 MGS | Rifleman No 3 Co 3rd Bn. |
| R'man | Owen Connelly | 12 MGS | Rifleman No 6 & 7 Co 1st Bn. (Conolly) |
| R'man | James Connor | 3 MGS | A 2nd Bn. man, never in the Peninsula, not entitled. |
| R'man | John Conway | 7 MGS | Rifleman No 2 Co 1st Bn. |
| R'man | James Cooke | 13 MGS | Rifleman No 3 & 5 Co 1st Bn. |
| R'man | Thomas Cooper | 5 MGS | Rifleman No 6 Co 2nd Bn. |
| R'man | Thomas Cooper | 9 MGS | Rifleman No 2 Co 1st Bn. |
| Corp | Edward Costello | 11 MGS | Rifleman No 3 & 2 Co 1st Bn. (Costelow) |
| Sgt | Joseph Cowan | 9 MGS | Rifleman No 6 Co 1st Bn. |
| R'man | James Crawley | 3 MGS | Rifleman No 8 Co 2nd Bn. |
| R'man | Edmund Crossley | 9 MGS | Rifleman No 3 Co 3rd Bn. |
| R'man | George Cullumbine | 7 MGS | Rifleman No 10 Co 2nd Bn. |
| Sgt | Major John Dancer | 6 MGS | Sergeant No 4 & 6 Co 1st Bn. |
| R'man | John Davies | 7 MGS | Rifleman No 5 Co 1st Bn. Carmarthen, Pengboy, Labourer (4 on 1st Bn. paylist) |
| R'man | Robert Deacon | 5 MGS | Rifleman No 3 & 2 Co 1st Bn. |
| R'man | Thomas Delaroux | 4 MGS | Rifleman No 4 Co 3rd Bn. (Dillerowe) |
| R'man | George Dempster | 9 MGS | Rifleman No 6 Co 1st Bn. |
| R'man | Thomas Denby | 3 MGS | Corporal No 8 Co 2nd Bn. |

| 99 | R'man | John Dent | 9 MGS | Rifleman No 4 Co 1st Bn. |
|---|---|---|---|---|
| 100 | Sgt | John Dickinson | 4 MGS | Sergeant No 5 Co 3rd Bn. |
| 101 | Sgt | Tobias Digby | 9 MGS | Rifleman No 1 Co 1st Bn. |
| 102 | R'man | John Dixson | 11 MGS | Rifleman No 6 Co 1st Bn. (Dixon) |
| 103 | R'man | Thomas Douglas | 5 MGS | Rifleman No 8 Co 2nd Bn. |
| 104 | R'man | James Downs | 2 MGS | Rifleman No 2 Co 1st Bn. |
| 105 | R'man | John Downs | 6 MGS | Arrived in the Peninsula August 1813. Not entitled. |
| 106 | Sgt | Alexander Eason | 13 MGS | Sergeant No 6 Co 1st Bn. |
| 107 | R'man | Thomas Eastwood | 6 MGS | Rifleman No 2 Co 1st Bn. |
| 108 | R'man | John Edwards | 5 MGS | Sick absent, not entitled. |
| 109 | R'man | Thomas Edwards | 6 MGS | Rifleman No 3 Co 2nd Bn. |
| 110 | R'man | John Edwardstaff | 8 MGS | Rifleman No 4 Co 3rd Bn. |
| 111 | Corp | Thomas Eggarton | 8 MGS | Rifleman No 8 Co 1st Bn. (Thomas Eggington) |
| 112 | R'man | Henry Eldridge | 6 MGS | Rifleman No 3 Co 3rd Bn. |
| 113 | R'man | Anthony Everitt | 3 MGS | After Barrosa returned to England, not on paylists. Not entitled. |
| 114 | Corp | James Ewart | 6 MGS | Rifleman No 7 Co 1st Bn. On guard. |
| 115 | R'man | Bartholomew Fairhurst | 10 MGS | Rifleman No 4 & 8 Co 1st Bn. |
| 116 | R'man | Edward Farmer | 5 MGS | Rifleman No 6 Co 2nd Bn. On guard. |
| 117 | Sgt | James Farmer | 9 MGS | Rifleman No 8 Co 1st Bn. |
| 118 | Bugler | Richard Farmer | 5 MGS | Bugler No 6 Co 2nd Bn. |
| 119 | R'man | James Farnfield | 6 MGS | Rifleman No 8 Co 2nd Bn. |
| 120 | R'man | Edward Fitzsimmons | 7 MGS | Rifleman No 1 Co 1st Bn. |
| 121 | R'man | David Fortune | 8 MGS | Rifleman No 5 Co 1st Bn. (Daniel Fortune) On guard. |
| 122 | R'man | James Fraser | 7 MGS | After Corunna, joined from England 25th July 1812. Not entitled. |
| 123 | Corp | Stephen Frier | 6 MGS | Rifleman No 8 Co 2nd Bn. (Freer) |
| 124 | Sgt | Major William Fry | 9 MGS | Sergeant Major 1st Bn. |
| 125 | R'man | James Futter | 8 MGS | Sick absent, not entitled. |
| 126 | R'man | Daniel Gardner | 6 MGS | Rifleman No 10 Co 2nd Bn. |
| 127 | R'man | John Gardner | 9 MGS | Rifleman No 1 Co 3rd Bn. Ely, Labourer. (Three on 3rd Bn. paylist) |
| 128 | R'man | Edward Gaskell | 5 MGS | Rifleman No 8 Co 2nd Bn. |
| 129 | R'man | Francis Gibbs | 7 MGS | Rifleman No 3 Co 2nd Bn. |
| 130 | R'man | Alexander Gibson | 7 MGS | Rifleman No 3 Co 2nd Bn. |
| 131 | R'man | William Giddins | 5 MGS | Not on paylists. Not entitled. |
| 132 | R'man | Thomas Gilbert | 9 MGS | Rifleman No 4 & 1 Co 1st Bn. |
| 133 | R'man | William Gilbey | 1 MGS | Rifleman No 10 Co 2nd Bn. Invalided to England 25th December 1813. |
| 134 | R'man | Robert Gilchrist | 9 MGS | Rifleman No 3 Co 1st Bn. |
| 135 | R'man | William Gilmore | 9 MGS | Corporal No 5 Co 3rd Bn. |
| 136 | Sgt | Jonathan Glossop | 8 MGS | Corporal No 6 Co 2nd Bn. |
| 137 | R'man | Josiah Goddard | 8 MGS | Rifleman No 4 & 5 Co 1st Bn. (Joshua Goddart) |

| Sgt | William Graham | 6 MGS | Rifleman No 2 Co 1st Bn. On guard. |
|---|---|---|---|
| R'man | Samuel Green | 10 MGS | Rifleman No 3 Co 2nd Bn. |
| R'man | John Griffiths | 6 MGS | Corporal No 5 Co 3rd Bn. |
| R'man | Christopher Grimes | 8 MGS | Rifleman No 4 & 8 Co 1st Bn. On duty. |
| R'man | Joseph Hackett | 3 MGS | Rifleman No 10 Co 2nd Bn. |
| Corp | William Hall | 8 MGS | Rifleman No 5 Co 1st Bn. On guard. |
| Sgt | William Hall | 11 MGS | Sergeant No 8 Co 1st Bn. On duty. |
| R'man | William Hanley | 5 MGS | Sergeant No 4 Co 3rd Bn. |
| R'man | Thomas Harding | 11 MGS | Corporal No 3 & 1 Co 1st Bn. |
| R'man | Robert Harling | 9 MGS | Rifleman No 2 Co 1st Bn. |
| Corp | John Hartley | 10 MGS | Rifleman No 2 Co 3rd Bn. |
| R'man | Israel Harvey | 8 MGS | Rifleman No 2 Co 1st Bn. |
| R'man | William Heathcote | 5 MGS | Rifleman No 5 Co 3rd Bn. |
| R'man | Josiah Heeles | 6 MGS | Rifleman No 6 Co 1st Bn. (Joseph Heels) |
| Sgt | William Hinde | 11 MGS | Rifleman/Corporal No 1 Co 1st Bn. |
| Sgt | Joseph Hindle | 14 MGS | Corporal No 2 Co 3rd Bn. |
| R'man | James Holden | 8 MGS | Rifleman No 3 Co 2nd Bn. |
| R'man | Samuel Holland | 1 MGS | Rifleman No 10 Co 2nd Bn. |
| R'man | Thomas Holmes | 10 MGS | Rifleman No 3 & 7 Co 1st Bn. |
| R'man | Thomas Hooper | 5 MGS | Joined from England 25th July 1812, not entitled. |
| R'man | Elijah Hotley | 9 MGS | Bugler No 5 Co 3rd Bn. |
| R'man | James Hurd | 5 MGS | Rifleman No 8 Co 2nd Bn. (Herd) |
| R'man | Patrick Hussey | 10 MGS | Rifleman No 6 Co 1st Bn. |
| R'man | Robert Hyslop | 3 MGS | Rifleman No 7 Co 1st Bn. (Hayslop) |
| R'man | Christopher Ingham | 9 MGS | Rifleman No 6 Co 1st Bn. |
| R'man | John Ireland | 5 MGS | Rifleman No 1 Co 3rd Bn. |
| R'man | Arthur John | 6 MGS | Rifleman No 3 Co 3rd Bn. |
| R'man | Thomas Johnson | 4 MGS | Rifleman No 8 Co 2nd Bn. |
| Corp | John Jones | 9 MGS | General Hospital, not entitled. |
| R'man | Michael Joyce | 9 MGS | Rifleman No 1 Co 1st Bn. |
| R'man | William Kellaugher | 11 MGS | Rifleman No 1 Co 1st Bn. (Kellagher) |
| R'man | John Kelly | 9 MGS | Sergeant No 1 Co 3rd Bn. |
| R'man | Thomas Kelly | 10 MGS | Rifleman No 3 Co 2nd Bn. |
| R'man | Joseph Kemp | 6 MGS | No 10 Co 2nd Bn. |
| R'man | Alexander Kennedy | 10 MGS | Rifleman No 1 Co 1st Bn. |
| R'man | Thomas Knight | 6 MGS | Rifleman No 6 Co 2nd Bn. On guard. |
| R'man | John Lamont | 13 MGS | Rifleman No 5 Co 1st Bn. |
| R'man | Robert Lane | 7 MGS | Rifleman No 3 Co 2nd Bn. |
| R'man | Thomas Laurison | 9 MGS | Rifleman No 6 Co 1st Bn. (Lorrison) |
| R'man | David Law | 11 MGS | Rifleman No 6 Co 1st Bn. |
| Corp | George Law | 12 MGS | Rifleman No 6 Co 1st Bn. |
| R'man | Jervis Layland | 2 MGS | Rifleman No 8 Co 2nd Bn. (Leyland) |
| R'man | James Lennon | 6 MGS | Rifleman No 6 Co 2nd Bn. |
| R'man | Daniel Lewen | 7 MGS | Not on paylists, not entitled. |
| R'man | Samuel Long | 4 MGS | Rifleman No 1 Co 3rd Bn. Invalided to England 25th March 1813. |

| 183 | R'man | James Lord | 11 MGS | Rifleman No 4 Co 3rd Bn. |
| 184 | R'man | Samuel Lovatt | 9 MGS | Rifleman No 5 Co 1st Bn. (Lovett) |
| 185 | Sgt | John Lowe | 8 MGS | Sick absent, not entitled. |
| 186 | R'man | Michael Lyons | 9 MGS | Rifleman No 8 Co 1st Bn. |
| 187 | Sgt | William Lyons | 6 MGS | Rifleman Corporal No 6 Co 2nd Bn. |
| 188 | R'man | William Mahoney | 10 MGS | Rifleman No 6 Co 1st Bn. On duty. |
| 189 | R'man | Joseph Marriott | 7 MGS | Rifleman No 2 Co 3rd Bn. |
| 190 | R'man | Peter Marsh | 7 MGS | Rifleman No 1 Co 3rd Bn. |
| 191 | R'man | John Martin | 8 MGS | Rifleman No 4 & 5 Co 1st Bn. On duty. |
| 192 | Corp | Alexander Masterson | 6 MGS | Rifleman No 1 Co 1st Bn. |
| 193 | R'man | George McCann | 7 MGS | Rifleman No 1 Co 3rd Bn. |
| 194 | Sgt | Thomas McDermid | 8 MGS | Rifleman No 8 Co 1st Bn. (McDermott) |
| 195 | R'man | Robert McKay | 5 MGS | Rifleman No 5 Co 3rd Bn. |
| 196 | R'man | William McKay | 5 MGS | Rifleman No 3 & 7 Co 1st Bn. |
| 197 | R'man | John McKelly | 11 MGS | Rifleman No 4 & 8 Co 1st Bn. |
| 198 | R'man | Hugh McLeod | 6 MGS | Rifleman No 7 Co 1st Bn. |
| 199 | R'man | Alexander McRae | 8 MGS | Rifleman No 7 Co 1st Bn. |
| 200 | R'man | John McUbby | 11 MGS | Rifleman No 2 Co 1st Bn. |
| 201 | R'man | George Michelson | 6 MGS | General Hospital, not entitled. |
| 202 | R'man | John Miller | 6 MGS | Rifleman No 8 Co 2nd Bn. (Two on 2nd Bn. paylist) |
| 203 | R'man | Daniel Milton | 6 MGS | Rifleman No 10 Co 2nd Bn. |
| 204 | R'man | Hugh Monks | 7 MGS | Rifleman No 3 Co 3rd Bn. |
| 205 | R'man | Thomas Moore | 6 MGS | Rifleman No 5 Co 3rd Bn. |
| 206 | Sgt | John Moran | 11 MGS | Rifleman No 3 & 7 Co 1st Bn. |
| 207 | R'man | John Mullins | 6 MGS | Rifleman No 3 & 8 Co 1st Bn. |
| 208 | Sgt | John Murphy | 7 MGS | Corporal No 3 & 7 Co & Sgt No 1 Co 1st Bn. Wexford, Kilhaven, Labourer. |
| 209 | Corp | John Murphy | 12 MGS | Rifleman No 3 & 6 Co 1st Bn. Tipperary, Cashel, Mason (Two on 1st Bn. paylist) |
| 210 | Sgt | John Naughton | 4 MGS | Rifleman No 1 Co 1st Bn. (Norton) |
| 211 | R'man | William Newsham | 6 MGS | Rifleman No 1 Co 3rd Bn. (Newnham) |
| 212 | R'man | William Niven | 9 MGS | Sergeant No 1 Co 1st Bn. |
| 213 | Sgt | John Norton | 9 MGS | Not on paylists for Salamanca, not entitled. |
| 214 | Sgt | Robert Nunn | 7 MGS | Corporal No 2 Co 3rd Bn. |
| 215 | R'man | James O'Neil | 7 MGS | Rifleman No 1 Co 3rd Bn. (O'Neal) |
| 216 | R'man | Charles Ormond | 11 MGS | General Hospital, not entitled. |
| 217 | R'man | John Palmer | 12 MGS | Rifleman No 3 & 7 Co 1st Bn. |
| 218 | R'man | Jonathan Palmer | 5 MGS | Bugler No 5 Co 1st Bn. |
| 219 | R'man | Samuel Peters | 11 MGS | Rifleman No 4 & 8 Co 1st Bn. |
| 220 | R'man | James Petty | 12 MGS | Rifleman No 5 Co 1st Bn. (Pettie) |
| 221 | R'man | Joseph Piers | 8 MGS | Not on paylists for Salamanca, not entitled. |
| 222 | Sgt | George Piper | 8 MGS | Rifleman No 5 Co 1st Bn. On guard. |
| 223 | R'man | William Poole | 6 MGS | Rifleman No 4 & 8 Co 1st Bn. |
| 224 | R'man | Peter Price | 10 MGS | Rifleman No 6 Co 2nd Bn. |
| 225 | R'man | William Price | 6 MGS | Rifleman No 8 Co 1st Bn. |
| 226 | R'man | Benjamin Pring | 11 MGS | Rifleman No 8 Co 1st Bn. |

| R'man | William Pritchard | 6 MGS | Rifleman No 10 Co 2nd Bn. |
| Sgt | John Reakes | 10 MGS | Rifleman No 6 Co 1st Bn. |
| R'man | Duncan Reid | 7 MGS | Rifleman No 5 Co 3rd Bn. (Reed) |
| R'man | John Reynolds | 3 MGS | Rifleman No 4 Co 3rd Bn. |
| R'man | William Rhodes | 9 MGS | Rifleman No 5 Co 1st Bn. |
| R'man | Joseph Ripley | 5 MGS | Rifleman No 5 Co 1st Bn. |
| R'man | Alexander Robb | 6 MGS | Rifleman No 1 Co 3rd Bn. |
| R'man | Thomas Robinson | 4 MGS | General Hospital, not entitled. |
| R'man | Thomas Robinson | 8 MGS | Rifleman No 1 Co 1st Bn. |
| R'man | Thomas Rogers | 7 MGS | Rifleman No 5 Co 1st Bn. |
| R'man | James Rolestone | 4 MGS | Rifleman No 7 Co 1st Bn. |
| Sgt | Charles Ross | 7 MGS | Sergeant No 7 Co 1st Bn. To England with No 4 Co 25th Aug. |
| R'man | John Rostrin | 7 MGS | Rifleman No 6 Co 2nd Bn. |
| R'man | John Rouse | 10 MGS | Rifleman No 6 Co 1st Bn. |
| R'man | Richard Rouse | 8 MGS | Rifleman No 6 Co 1st Bn. |
| R'man | George Rowe | 6 MGS | Rifleman No 1 Co 1st Bn. |
| R'man | William Russell | 6 MGS | Rifleman No 8 Co 2nd Bn. |
| R'man | Philip Ryan | 5 MGS | Rifleman No 2 Co 1st Bn. |
| Sgt | William Sabin | 10 MGS | Sergeant No 3 Co 3rd Bn. |
| R'man | James Saunders | 8 MGS | Not on paylists, not entitled. |
| R'man | William Sharp | 8 MGS | Rifleman No 5 Co 1st Bn. On guard. |
| R'man | Thomas Sharples | 8 MGS | Sick absent, not entitled. |
| Corp | Adam Shaw | 9 MGS | Rifleman No 1 Co 3rd Bn. |
| R'man | William Shearman | 4 MGS | Sergeant No 4 Co 3rd Bn. |
| R'man | John Sheppard | 8 MGS | Rifleman No 2 Co 3rd Bn. |
| R'man | John Sherrocks | 4 MGS | Rifleman No 10 Co 2nd Bn. |
| R'man | Benjamin Simons | 6 MGS | Rifleman No 1 Co 3rd Bn. (Simonds) |
| R'man | William Slavin | 8 MGS | Rifleman No 1 Co 3rd Bn. |
| Corp | Michael Smart | 10 MGS | Rifleman No 3 & 6 Co 1st Bn. |
| R'man | William Smillie | 11 MGS | Rifleman No 7 Co 1st Bn. |
| Sgt | Alexander Smith | 5 MGS | Not on paylists, not entitled. |
| Sgt | George Smith | 7 MGS | Rifleman No 3 Co 3rd Bn. |
| R'man | Robert Smith | 3 MGS | Rifleman No 10 Co 2nd Bn. |
| R'man | Thomas Smith | 11 MGS | Rifleman No 4 Co & 5 Co 1st Bn. On guard. |
| R'man | John Smyth | 12 MGS | Rifleman No 6 Co 1st Bn. (Smith) On duty. |
| R'man | William Solomon | 9 MGS | Rifleman No 2 Co 3rd Bn. |
| R'man | John Spencer | 4 MGS | Rifleman No 6 Co 2nd Bn. |
| R'man | Richard Spencer | 7 MGS | Rifleman No 6 Co 2nd Bn. |
| R'man | William Sperry | 9 MGS | Rifleman No 4 Co 1st Bn. |
| R'man | John Standly | 4 MGS | Rifleman No 2 Co 3rd Bn. (Stanley) |
| R'man | George Stephenson | 10 MGS | Rifleman No 2 Co 3rd Bn. |
| R'man | William Stephenson | 5 MGS | Rifleman No 8 Co 1st Bn. |
| Bugler | James Stevens | 11 MGS | Bugler No 7 Co 1st Bn. |
| R'man | Jonathan Stubbs | 10 MGS | Rifleman No 2 Co 3rd Bn. |
| R'man | Edward Sutherland | 8 MGS | Rifleman No 2 Co 1st Bn. |
| R'man | George Sutherland | 9 MGS | Rifleman No 7 Co 1st Bn. On guard. |

| 273 | R'man | James Swain | 5 MGS | Joined from England 25th July 1812, not entitled. |
|---|---|---|---|---|
| 274 | R'man | Mathew Swalwell | 7 MGS | Corporal No 5 Co 1st Bn. On guard. |
| 275 | R'man | John Symington | 11 MGS | Rifleman No 7 Co 1st Bn. |
| 276 | Sgt | Thomas Tabbutt | 7 MGS | Rifleman No 2 Co 3rd Bn. (Tebbutt) |
| 277 | R'man | Edward Taggen | 10 MGS | Rifleman No 8 Co 1st Bn. (Teagon) On duty. |
| 278 | R'man | James Tate | 7 MGS | Rifleman No 4 Co 3rd Bn. (Two on 3rd Bn. paylist) |
| 279 | R'man | Benjamin Taylor | 5 MGS | Rifleman No 10 Co 2nd Bn. |
| 280 | R'man | Joseph Taylor | 3 MGS | Rifleman No 8 Co 2nd Bn. (Two on 2nd Bn. paylist) |
| 281 | Corp | Edward Tonkinson | 9 MGS | Corporal No 6 Co 1st Bn. |
| 282 | R'man | George Tunnicliffe | 12 MGS | Rifleman No 4 & 5 Co 1st Bn. (Toniclift) |
| 283 | R'man | Matthew Turner | 9 MGS | Rifleman No 1 Co 3rd Bn. Wounded. |
| 284 | R'man | Peter Turner | 6 MGS | Rifleman No 2 Co 1st Bn. |
| 285 | R'man | William Usher | 8 MGS | Rifleman No 3 & 6 Co 1st Bn. |
| 286 | R'man | George Waine | 4 MGS | Rifleman No 8 Co 1st Bn. |
| 287 | R'man | Abraham Walker | 9 MGS | Rifleman No 5 Co 1st Bn. |
| 288 | Sgt | Thomas Wall | 11 MGS | Sergeant No 3 Co 3rd Bn. |
| 289 | R'man | James Walsh | 5 MGS | Rifleman No 10 Co 2nd Bn. (Welch) |
| 290 | R'man | John Ward | 10 MGS | Rifleman No 4 & 1 Co 1st Bn. |
| 291 | R'man | John Waterhouse | 4 MGS | Rifleman No 6 Co 2nd Bn. |
| 292 | Sgt | James Waterson | 10 MGS | Rifleman No 1 Co 3rd Bn. |
| 293 | R'man | Joseph Watniff | 8 MGS | Rifleman No 4 & 5 Co 1st Bn. (Watmuff) |
| 294 | R'man | John Wellbelove | 5 MGS | Rifleman No 3 Co 2nd Bn. |
| 295 | R'man | William Wellington | 6 MGS | Not on paylists, not entitled. |
| 296 | R'man | William Wells | 7 MGS | Rifleman No 10 Co 2nd Bn. (Wills) |
| 297 | R'man | William Weston | 7 MGS | Rifleman No 3 & 2 Co 1st Bn. |
| 298 | R'man | Thomas Whetstone | 8 MGS | Rifleman No 1 Co 1st Bn. (Whitstone) |
| 299 | R'man | William Whitehead | 7 MGS | Rifleman No 6 Co 1st Bn. |
| 300 | R'man | John Williams | 8 MGS | Rifleman No 1 Co 1st Bn. |
| 301 | R'man | Thomas Wilson | 10 MGS | Rifleman No 7 Co 1st Bn. |
| 302 | R'man | Thomas Wilson | 10 MGS | Rifleman No 3 Co 3rd Bn. |
| 303 | Sgt | William Wilson | 5 MGS | Rifleman No 8 Co 2nd Bn. |
| 304 | R'man | Joseph Witham | 7 MGS | Rifleman No 2 Co 1st Bn. |
| 305 | R'man | William Wood | 6 MGS | Rifleman No 10 Co 2nd Bn. |
| 306 | R'man | James Woodley | 6 MGS | Rifleman No 1 Co 3rd Bn. |
| 307 | R'man | John Wright | 5 MGS | Rifleman No 8 Co 2nd Bn. |
| 308 | R'man | William Wright | 10 MGS | Rifleman No 3 & 2 Co 1st Bn. |
| 309 | Sgt | William Young | 5 MGS | Corporal No 8 Co 1st Bn. |
| 310 | R'man | Richard Young | 6 MGS | Rifleman No 5 Co 3rd Bn. |

## Additional names of MGS men not awarded the clasp for Salamanca:

| Corp | Isaac Bagshaw | 2 MGS | Corporal No 8 Co 1st Bn. On duty. |
|------|---------------|-------|-----------------------------------|
| R'man | Jacob Barlow | 5 MGS | Rifleman No 4 & 8 Co 1st Bn. |
| R'man | Thomas Bendal | 5 MGS | Rifleman No 3 & 2 Co 1st Bn. (Bandle) |
| Corp | James Buckley | 6 MGS | Rifleman No 6 Co 1st Bn. |
| R'man | David Burnet | 6 MGS | Rifleman No 4 & 8 Co 1st Bn. |
| R'man | Andrew Connelly | 5 MGS | Corporal No 4 Co 3rd Bn. |
| R'man | John Gastle | 1 MGS | Rifleman No 5 Co 3rd Bn. |
| R'man | James Hall | 4 MGS | Rifleman No 3 Co 3rd Bn. |
| R'man | Charles Jones | 7 MGS | Rifleman No 6 Co 1st Bn. |
| R'man | Richard Lancaster | 3 MGS | Rifleman No 3 Co 2nd Bn. |
| Sgt | John McDonald | 7 MGS | Sergeant No 1 Co 1st Bn. |
| R'man | John McKitchie | 2 MGS | Sergeant No 5 Co 3rd Bn. (McKeckie) |
| R'man | William Parker | 2 MGS | Rifleman No 3 & 7 Co 1st Bn. |
| R'man | James Rawledge | 7 MGS | Rifleman No 6 Co 1st Bn. (Rowledge) |
| R'man | Henry Reily | 4 MGS | Rifleman No 4 Co 3rd Bn. |
| R'man | John Riddles | 3 MGS | Rifleman No 3 Co 2nd Bn. |
| R'man | James Russell | 4 MGS | Rifleman No 3 & 1 Co 1st Bn. |
| R'man | Benjamin Slaughter | 2 MGS | Rifleman No 3 & 6 Co 1st Bn. |
| Corp | Peter Smith | 3 MGS | Rifleman No 1 Co 1st Bn. |
| R'man | James Steele | 6 MGS | Rifleman No 6 Co 1st Bn. |
| R'man | Thomas Webb | 2 MGS | Rifleman No 6 Co 1st Bn. On duty. |
| R'man | William Wilkinson | 2 MGS | Rifleman No 1 Co 1st Bn. |

## MGS Clasp VITTORIA Battle of Vitoria 21st June 1813

Almost a year after Salamanca the battle of Vitoria marked a great victory for the Allies which led to the beginning of the end for Napoleon's Imperial Army in Spain. Somewhat demoralised by their defeat, their journey now was north towards to the borders of France and, although there are another six MGS clasps to come, within the year it will all be over at Toulouse.

The strength of the Rifles at Vitoria were: six 1st Battalion companies, six 2nd Battalion companies and five 3rd Battalion companies. The 2nd Battalion increasing their four companies to six by the arrival of Captain's D. Cadoux and J. Jenkins from Barrosa.

Officially the Rifles were awarded 403 clasps for Vitoria. We have listed 405 names, excluding Captain William Booth and Rifleman Richard Rogers which research indicates that he and Rifleman Richard Rodgers are the same man. From this number we feel that 12 are not entitled and have located a further 30 men entitled but not awarded the clasp. This makes a total of 423 clasps to the Rifles.

## We have excluded the following 12 MGS men from the Vittoria clasp:

| | | | |
|---|---|---|---|
| 1 | R'man | John Baker | After Barrosa, no trace of in the paylists. |
| 2 | R'man | John Baldwin | Not in the Peninsula until 26th Nov. 1813. |
| 3 | R'man | William Burns | In General Hospital. |
| 4 | R'man | Thomas Carter | In General Hospital. |
| 5 | R'man | James Connor | 2nd Bn. man, who never served in the Peninsula at all. |
| 6 | R'man | John Downs | Not in the Peninsula until August 1813. |
| 7 | R'man | John Kidd | Joins the Peninsula from England 7th May 1814. |
| 8 | Sgt | William Lyons | Sick absent. |
| 9 | R'man | Alexander Moore | Not on the paylists until Nivelle 1813. |
| 10 | R'man | Peter Potter | Sick absent. |
| 11 | R'man | Thomas Smith | In General Hospital. |
| 12 | R'man | William Suthers | Not in the Peninsula until San Sebastian. |

### 11th Clasp Vitoria 21st June 1813

Reference: 1st Bn. WO 12/9524 25 March–24 June 1813.
2nd Bn. WO 12/9584 25 March–24 June 1813.
3rd Bn. WO 12/9588 25 March–24 June 1813.
Officers WO 17/267.

**1st Bn.**
| | | |
|---|---|---|
| Capt | Hon J. Stewart | No 1 Co. |
| Capt | J. Leach | No 2 Co. |
| Capt | C. Smyth | No 5 Co. |
| Capt | C. Beckwith | No 6 Co. |
| Capt | L. Gray | No 7 Co. |
| Capt | W. Johnstone | No 8 Co. |

**2nd Bn.**
| | | |
|---|---|---|
| Capt | D. Cadoux | No 1 Co. |
| Capt | J. Jenkins | No 2 Co. |
| Capt | J. Hart | No 3 Co. |
| Capt | S. Mitchell | No 4 Co. |
| Capt | J. Duncan | No 5 Co. |
| Capt | D. Fergusson | No 6 Co. |

**3rd Bn.**
| | | |
|---|---|---|
| Capt | W. Percival | No 1 Co. |
| Capt | C, G. Gray | No 2 Co. |
| Capt | W. Hallen | No 3 Co. |
| Capt | W. Balvaird | No 4 Co |
| Capt | A. Andrews | No 5 Co. |

| | | | |
|---|---|---|---|
| Capt | Alexander Andrews | 8 MGS | Captain 3rd Bn. |
| Capt | William Booth | 4 MGS | After Corunna in the 15th The King's Light Dragoons. |
| Lieut | John Budgen | 8 MGS | Lieutenant 2nd Bn. |
| Capt | Alexander Cameron | 5 MGS | Captain 1st Bn. Wounded |
| Sub | George Cary | 6 MGS | 2nd Lieutenant 3rd Bn. |
| Lieut | Robert Cochrane | 2 MGS | Lieutenant 3rd Bn. (Doing duty with 2nd Bn) |
| Sub | John Cox | 10 MGS | 2nd Lieutenant 1st Bn. |
| Capt | William Cox | 7 MGS | Lieutenant 1st Bn. Wounded. |
| Lieut | Edward Coxen | 10 MGS | Lieutenant 2nd Bn. |
| Lieut | Charles Cuyler | 2 MGS | Lieutenant 3rd Bn. |
| Vol | Joseph Dornford | 2 MGS | Volunteer in the 1st Bn. |
| Capt | Thomas Drake | 3 MGS | Major (Brevet). On the Staff of the Quarter Master General in the Peninsula. |
| Sub | Charles Eaton | 7 MGS | Lieutenant 2nd Bn. |
| Lieut | John Fitzmaurice | 8 MGS | Lieutenant 1st Bn. |
| Lieut | James Gairdner | 9 MGS | Lieutenant 1st Bn. Wounded. (Garner) |
| Lieut | John Gardiner | 6 MGS | Lieutenant 1st Bn. (Gardner) |
| Lieut | William Hallen | 6 MGS | Captain 3rd Bn. |
| Sub | William Humbley | 12 MGS | Lieutenant 2nd Bn. |
| Lieut | Loftus Jones | 6 MGS | Lieutenant 3rd Bn. (Command at Vitoria) |
| Asst Surg | William Jones | 12 MGS | Assist Surgeon 1st Bn. |
| Capt | John Kincaid | 9 MGS | Lieutenant 1st Bn. |
| Lieut | Thomas Kirkley | 6 MGS | Lieutenant 3rd Bn. |
| Lieut | James Kirkman | 8 MGS | Lieutenant 3rd Bn. |
| Capt | Jonathan Leach | 12 MGS | Captain 1st Bn. |
| Lieut | John Middleton | 10 MGS | Lieutenant 3rd Bn. |
| Lieut | John Molloy | 8 MGS | Lieutenant 1st Bn. Detached to 2nd Bn. |
| Sub | John Ridgway | 3 MGS | Lieutenant 2nd Bn. |
| Lieut | George Simmons | 8 MGS | Lieutenant 1st Bn. |
| Lieut | Joseph Simmons | 3 MGS | 2nd Lieutenant 1st Bn. |
| Lieut | Harry Smith | 12 MGS | 1st Bn. Major of Brigade. |
| Lieut | Thomas Smith | 10 MGS | Lieutenant 1st Bn. |
| Lieut | Nicholas Travers | 3 MGS | Lieutenant 3rd Bn. (Belonging to 2nd Bn) |
| Major | George Wilkins | 2 MGS | Major 2nd Bn. |
| Lieut | Thomas Worsley | 9 MGS | Lieutenant 3rd Bn. |
| R'man | Thomas Alexander | 10 MGS | Rifleman No 8 Co 1st Bn. |
| R'man | George Anderson | 3 MGS | Rifleman No 1 Co 3rd Bn. |
| Sgt | James Anderson | 9 MGS | Sergeant No 7 Co 1st Bn. |
| R'man | Joseph Arms | 11 MGS | Rifleman No 8 Co 1st Bn. Wounded? |
| Sgt | William Armson | 8 MGS | Colour Sergeant No 4 Co 3rd Bn. |
| Corp | Andrew Ash | 8 MGS | Rifleman No 5 Co 1st Bn. |
| R'man | James Ashworth | 7 MGS | Rifleman No 8 Co 1st Bn. Invalided to England. |
| R'man | William Austin | 5 MGS | Rifleman No 5 Co 2nd Bn. Sick absent. (Wounded?) |

| | | | | |
|---|---|---|---|---|
| 42 | R'man | John Baker | 5 MGS | After Barrosa, no trace of in the paylists. Not entitled. |
| 43 | R'man | John Baker | 8 MGS | Rifleman No 4 Co 2nd Bn. Coventry, Labourer. |
| 44 | R'man | John Baldwin | 4 MGS | Rifleman No 1 Co 2nd Bn. Leicester, Framework-knitter. |
| 45 | R'man | John Baldwin | 4 MGS | Not in the Peninsula until 26th Nov. 1813. Not entitled. Middlesex, Carpenter. |
| 46 | R'man | Thomas Ballard | 6 MGS | Rifleman No 3 Co 3rd Bn. |
| 47 | R'man | George Barrett | 7 MGS | Rifleman No 2 Co 1st Bn. |
| 48 | Bugler | William Bashford | 9 MGS | Bugler No 5 Co 3rd Bn. (Bashforth) |
| 49 | R'man | James Bateman | 8 MGS | Rifleman No 5 Co 3rd Bn. (Beatman) From 1st Bn. 25th May. |
| 50 | R'man | David Beattie | 9 MGS | Rifleman No 4 Co 2nd Bn. On guard. |
| 51 | R'man | John Bell | 11 MGS | Rifleman No 7 Co 1st Bn. |
| 52 | R'man | Joseph Bell | 8 MGS | Rifleman No 3 Co 2nd Bn. |
| 53 | R'man | Thomas Bendal | 5 MGS | Rifleman No 2 Co 1st Bn. (Bandle) |
| 54 | R'man | Henry Berry | 11 MGS | Rifleman No 8 Co 1st Bn. |
| 55 | R'man | William Berry | 2 MGS | Rifleman No 5 Co 2nd Bn. |
| 56 | R'man | William Berry | 11 MGS | Rifleman No 8 Co 1st Bn. |
| 57 | R'man | John Bidwell | 8 MGS | Rifleman No 5 Co 1st Bn. (Bedwell) |
| 58 | Corp | Henry Biggs | 5 MGS | Rifleman No 4 Co 3rd Bn. |
| 59 | R'man | Thomas Bills | 6 MGS | Rifleman No 1 Co 2nd Bn. |
| 60 | R'man | John Bivings | 6 MGS | Rifleman No 8 Co 1st Bn. (Bivens) |
| 61 | R'man | John Bool | 6 MGS | Rifleman No 5 Co 1st Bn. (Bull) |
| 62 | R'man | Henry Booth | 11 MGS | Rifleman No 5 Co 1st Bn. |
| 63 | R'man | Edward Bowen | 7 MGS | Rifleman No 5 Co 1st Bn. |
| 64 | Sgt | Joseph Bowley | 10 MGS | Sergeant No 3 Co 2nd Bn. |
| 65 | Corp | James Britchard | 5 MGS | Rifleman No 2 Co 3rd Bn. Wounded, 21st June. |
| 66 | R'man | William Brown | 5 MGS | Rifleman No 3 Co 3rd Bn. (2 on 3rd Bn. paylist) |
| 67 | R'man | James Bryce | 9 MGS | Rifleman No 7 Co 1st Bn. Lanark, Newmunklin, Weaver. (2 on 1st Bn. paylist) |
| 68 | R'man | James Buckler | 6 MGS | Rifleman No 7 Co 1st Bn. On guard. |
| 69 | Corp | James Buckley | 6 MGS | Rifleman No 6 Co 1st Bn. |
| 70 | R'man | James Bulcock | 6 MGS | Rifleman No 8 Co 1st Bn. |
| 71 | R'man | David Burnet | 6 MGS | Rifleman No 8 Co 1st Bn. On duty. |
| 72 | R'man | John Burns | 6 MGS | Rifleman No 6 Co 1st Bn. Gen. Hosp. (Wounded?) |
| 73 | Sgt | Robert Burns | 9 MGS | Rifleman No 5 Co 1st Bn. Gen. Hosp. (Wounded?) |
| 74 | R'man | William Burns | 7 MGS | Rifleman No 6 Co 1st Bn. In reg., div. and Gen. Hosp., not entitled. |
| 75 | R'man | John Burrows | 8 MGS | Rifleman No 8 Co 1st Bn. |
| 76 | R'man | William Burrows | 8 MGS | Rifleman No 4 Co 3rd Bn. |
| 77 | R'man | John Cain | 5 MGS | Rifleman No 5 Co 2nd Bn. (Camm) |

| 8 | R'man | James Cairns | 12 MGS | Sergeant No 4 Co 2nd Bn. |
| 9 | R'man | Neil Cameron | 8 MGS | Rifleman No 4 Co 2nd Bn. |
| 0 | R'man | Daniel Campbell | 2 MGS | Rifleman No 1 Co 3rd Bn. Wounded, 21st June. Sick absent. |
| 1 | Bugler | William Carden | 11 MGS | Bugler No 8 Co 1st Bn. (Carder) |
| 2 | R'man | Zachariah Cardy | 8 MGS | Rifleman No 6 Co 1st Bn. |
| 3 | Sgt | Andrew Carr | 11 MGS | Rifleman No 4 Co 2nd Bn. Sick absent. (Wounded?) |
| 4 | R'man | Thomas Carter | 4 MGS | Rifleman No 5 Co 1st Bn. In General Hospital, not entitled. |
| 5 | R'man | William Carter | 6 MGS | Rifleman No 5 Co 1st Bn. Gen. Hosp. (Wounded?) |
| 6 | R'man | John Castles | 8 MGS | Rifleman No 2 Co 1st Bn. |
| 7 | R'man | Joseph Cawthorn | 5 MGS | Rifleman No 5 Co 1st Bn. |
| 8 | R'man | Thomas Chapman | 5 MGS | Rifleman No 3 Co 2nd Bn. |
| 9 | R'man | Robert Claxton | 7 MGS | Rifleman No 5 Co 1st Bn. Gen. Hosp. (Wounded?) |
| 0 | R'man | Edward Clegg | 7 MGS | Rifleman No 6 Co 2nd Bn. |
| | R'man | James Coleman | 12 MGS | Rifleman No 7 Co 1st Bn. |
| | R'man | Thomas Coleston | 9 MGS | Rifleman No 8 Co 1st Bn. |
| | R'man | Edward Collingham | 5 MGS | Rifleman No 5 Co 2nd Bn. |
| | R'man | George Coman | 10 MGS | Corporal No 3 Co 3rd Bn. |
| | R'man | Andrew Connelly | 5 MGS | Corporal No 4 Co 3rd Bn. |
| | R'man | Owen Connelly | 12 MGS | Rifleman No 7 Co 1st Bn. (Connolly) On guard. |
| | R'man | James Connor | 3 MGS | A 2nd Bn. man, never in the Peninsula, not entitled. |
| | R'man | Patrick Connor | 7 MGS | Rifleman No 5 Co 2nd Bn. Sick absent. (Wounded?) |
| | R'man | John Conway | 7 MGS | Rifleman No 2 Co 1st Bn. |
| | R'man | James Cooke | 13 MGS | Rifleman No 5 Co 1st Bn. |
| | R'man | Thomas Cooper | 9 MGS | Rifleman No 2 Co 1st Bn. |
| | R'man | Edward Cope | 7 MGS | Rifleman No 1 Co 2nd Bn. On guard. |
| | R'man | John Corker | 4 MGS | Rifleman No 2 Co 2nd Bn. (Cocker) |
| | Corp | James Cornish | 3 MGS | Rifleman No 1 Co 2nd Bn. |
| | Corp | Edward Costello | 11 MGS | Rifleman No 2 Co 1st Bn. (Costelow) |
| | Sgt | Joseph Cowan | 9 MGS | Rifleman No 6 Co 1st Bn. Wounded. Divisional Hospital. |
| | R'man | James Crawley | 3 MGS | Rifleman No 5 Co 2nd Bn. On guard. |
| | R'man | James Crooks | 6 MGS | Rifleman No 3 Co 3rd Bn. |
| | R'man | Edmund Crossley | 9 MGS | Rifleman No 3 Co 3rd Bn. (Edward Crossley) |
| | R'man | George Cullumbine | 7 MGS | Rifleman No 6 Co 2nd Bn. |
| | R'man | William Curry | 2 MGS | Rifleman No 5 Co 3rd Bn. |
| | R'man | James Curtis | 5 MGS | Rifleman No 3 Co 3rd Bn. |
| | R'man | John Davies* | 7 MGS | Rifleman No 5 Co 1st Bn. Carmarthen, Pengboy, Labourer. (Four on 1st Bn. paylist) |
| | R'man | George Dawson | 2 MGS | Rifleman No 1 Co 2nd Bn. Provost guard. |

| 115 | R'man | Robert Deacon | 5 MGS | Rifleman No 2 Co 1st Bn. On duty, servant to Lt. W. Gardiner. |
|-----|-------|---------------|-------|---------------------------------------------------------------|
| 116 | R'man | William Deacon | 8 MGS | Rifleman No 3 Co 2nd Bn. |
| 117 | Sgt Major | Thomas Deaman | 6 MGS | Sergeant Major 3rd Bn. (Deamon) |
| 118 | R'man | Thomas Delaroux | 4 MGS | Rifleman No 4 Co 3rd Bn. (Dillerowe) |
| 119 | R'man | George Dempster | 9 MGS | Rifleman No 6 Co 1st Bn. |
| 120 | R'man | Thomas Denby | 3 MGS | Corporal/Rifleman No 5 Co 2nd Bn. |
| 121 | R'man | John Dent | 9 MGS | Rifleman No 1 Co 1st Bn. On guard. |
| 122 | R'man | Thomas Dick | 5 MGS | Rifleman No 3 Co 3rd Bn. Wounded 21st June. Sick absent. |
| 123 | Sgt | Tobias Digby | 9 MGS | Corporal No 1 Co 1st Bn. |
| 124 | Corp | Michael Dillon | 6 MGS | Rifleman No 1 Co 1st Bn. |
| 125 | R'man | John Dixson | 11 MGS | Rifleman No 6 Co 1st Bn. (Dixon) |
| 126 | R'man | Joseph Dodd | 7 MGS | Rifleman No 8 Co 1st Bn. On duty, Vitoria. |
| 127 | R'man | Thomas Douglas | 5 MGS | Rifleman No 5 Co 2nd Bn. On duty. |
| 128 | R'man | James Downs | 2 MGS | Rifleman No 2 Co 1st Bn. |
| 129 | R'man | John Downs | 6 MGS | Not in the Peninsula until August 1813. Not entitled. |
| 130 | R'man | John Dunnage | 4 MGS | Rifleman No 4 Co 3rd Bn. |
| 131 | R'man | William Duty | 3 MGS | Rifleman No 5 Co 3rd Bn. |
| 132 | R'man | John Dyson | 3 MGS | Rifleman No 3 Co 2nd Bn. |
| 133 | Sgt | Alexander Eason | 13 MGS | Sergeant No 6 Co 1st Bn. |
| 134 | R'man | Thomas Eastwood | 6 MGS | Rifleman No 2 Co 1st Bn. |
| 135 | R'man | William Eburn | 3 MGS | Rifleman No 7 Co 1st Bn. (Eaburn) On guard. |
| 136 | R'man | John Edwards | 5 MGS | Rifleman No 5 Co 2nd Bn. On guard. |
| 137 | Corp | John Edwards | 4 MGS | Rifleman No 2 Co 3rd Bn. On command at Vitoria. |
| 138 | R'man | Thomas Edwards | 6 MGS | Rifleman No 4 Co 2nd Bn. |
| 139 | R'man | William Edwards | 8 MGS | Rifleman No 2 Co 2nd Bn. |
| 140 | R'man | John Edwardstaff | 8 MGS | Rifleman No 4 Co 3rd Bn. |
| 141 | Corp | Thomas Eggarton | 8 MGS | Rifleman No 8 Co 1st Bn. (Thomas Eggington) On duty, Vitoria. |
| 142 | R'man | Henry Eldridge | 6 MGS | Rifleman No 3 Co 3rd Bn. |
| 143 | R'man | John Evans | 5 MGS | Rifleman No 2 Co 2nd Bn. |
| 144 | R'man | Robert Evans | 4 MGS | Rifleman No 5 Co 2nd Bn. |
| 145 | Corp | James Ewart | 6 MGS | Rifleman No 7 Co 1st Bn. |
| 146 | R'man | Michael Fagan | 3 MGS | Rifleman No 2 Co 2nd Bn. (Feagan) |
| 147 | R'man | Bartholomew Fairhurst | 10 MGS | Rifleman No 8 Co 1st Bn. On duty, Vitoria. |
| 148 | R'man | John Farlin | 5 MGS | Sergeant/Rifleman No 3 Co 3rd Bn. |
| 149 | R'man | Edward Farmer | 5 MGS | Rifleman No 3 Co 2nd Bn. Wounded. Sick Absent. |
| 150 | Sgt | James Farmer | 9 MGS | Rifleman No 8 Co 1st Bn. |
| 151 | Bugler | Richard Farmer | 5 MGS | Bugler No 3 Co 2nd Bn. Sick absent. (Wounded?) |
| 152 | R'man | James Finch | 4 MGS | Rifleman No 4 Co 3rd Bn. |
| 153 | R'man | Edward Fitzsimmons | 7 MGS | Rifleman No 1 Co 1st Bn. |

| 54 | R'man | David Fortune | 8 MGS | Rifleman No 5 Co 1st Bn. (Daniel Fortune) |
| 55 | R'man | James Fraser | 7 MGS | Sergeant No 1 Co 3rd Bn. |
| 56 | R'man | William Fraser | 6 MGS | Rifleman No 5 Co 3rd Bn. (Frazer) |
| 57 | Corp | Stephen Frier | 6 MGS | Rifleman No 6 Co 2nd Bn. (Freer) |
| 58 | R'man | James Futter | 8 MGS | Corporal No 4 Co 2nd Bn. On guard. |
| 59 | R'man | Thomas Gardiner | 6 MGS | Rifleman No 1 Co 2nd Bn. |
| 60 | R'man | Daniel Gardner | 6 MGS | Rifleman No 6 Co 2nd Bn. |
| 61 | R'man | John Gardner | 9 MGS | Rifleman No 1 Co 3rd Bn. |
| 62 | R'man | Edward Gaskell | 5 MGS | Rifleman No 5 Co 2nd Bn. On command at Vitoria. |
| 63 | R'man | John Gastle | 1 MGS | Rifleman No 5 Co 3rd Bn. |
| 64 | R'man | Francis Gibbs | 7 MGS | Rifleman No 4 Co 2nd Bn. |
| 65 | R'man | Alexander Gibson | 7 MGS | Rifleman No 4 Co 2nd Bn. |
| 66 | R'man | William Giddins | 5 MGS | Rifleman No 1 Co 2nd Bn. Sick absent. (Wounded?) |
| 67 | R'man | Thomas Gilbert | 9 MGS | Rifleman No 2 Co 1st Bn. |
| 68 | R'man | Robert Gilchrist | 9 MGS | Rifleman No 6 Co 1st Bn. Gen. Hosp. (Wounded?) |
| 69 | Corp | William Gillis | 6 MGS | Rifleman No 5 Co 2nd Bn. |
| 0 | R'man | William Gilmore | 9 MGS | Corporal No 5 Co 3rd Bn. |
| 1 | Sgt | Jonathan Glossop | 8 MGS | Corporal No 3 Co 2nd Bn. On guard. |
| 2 | R'man | Josiah Goddard | 8 MGS | Rifleman No 5 Co 1st Bn. (Joshua Goddart) On guard. |
| 3 | R'man | Robert Goulring | 5 MGS | Rifleman No 5 Co 3rd Bn. (Goldring) |
| 4 | R'man | Samuel Green | 10 MGS | Rifleman No 4 Co 2nd Bn. |
| 5 | R'man | William Grierson | 6 MGS | Rifleman No 2 Co 2nd Bn. (Greyson) |
| 6 | R'man | John Griffiths | 6 MGS | Rifleman No 5 Co 3rd Bn. |
| 7 | R'man | Thomas Griffiths | 2 MGS | Rifleman No 7 Co 1st Bn. On guard. |
| 8 | R'man | Thomas Grigson | 3 MGS | Rifleman No 6 Co 2nd Bn. (Greyson) |
| 9 | R'man | Joseph Hackett | 3 MGS | Rifleman No 6 Co 2nd Bn. |
| 0 | R'man | Richard Haines | 5 MGS | Rifleman No 1 Co 2nd Bn. On paylist as Richard Hynds. |
| | Corp | William Haines | 7 MGS | Rifleman No 1 Co 2nd Bn. On Paylist as William Hynds. |
| | Corp | William Hall | 8 MGS | Rifleman No 5 Co 1st Bn. |
| | Sgt | William Hall | 11 MGS | Sergeant No 8 Co 1st Bn. |
| | R'man | William Hanley | 5 MGS | Corporal No 4 Co 3rd Bn. |
| | R'man | Thomas Harding | 11 MGS | Corporal No 1 Co 1st Bn. |
| | R'man | Robert Harling | 9 MGS | Rifleman No 1 Co 1st Bn. On guard. |
| | R'man | Thomas Harris | 1 MGS | Rifleman No 5 Co 2nd Bn. Sick absent. (Wounded?) |
| | Corp | John Hartley | 10 MGS | Rifleman/Corporal No 2 Co 3rd Bn. |
| | R'man | Israel Harvey | 8 MGS | Rifleman No 2 Co 1st Bn. |
| | R'man | John Hatcher | 4 MGS | Rifleman No 2 Co 3rd Bn. On command at Vitoria. |
| | R'man | William Heathcote | 5 MGS | Rifleman No 5 Co 3rd Bn. On command at Vitoria. |

| 192 | R'man | Josiah Heeles | 6 MGS | Rifleman No 6 Co 1st Bn. (Joseph Heels) |
|-----|-------|---------------|-------|------------------------------------------|
| 193 | R'man | Thomas Hill | 2 MGS | Rifleman No 1 Co 3rd Bn. |
| 194 | Sgt | John Himbury | 8 MGS | Rifleman No 2 Co 2nd Bn. (Henbury) |
| 195 | Sgt | William Hinde | 11 MGS | Corporal No 1 Co 1st Bn. |
| 196 | Sgt | Joseph Hindle | 14 MGS | Corporal No 2 Co 3rd Bn. On command at Vitoria. |
| 197 | R'man | James Holden | 8 MGS | Rifleman No 4 Co 2nd Bn. (Holding) |
| 198 | R'man | Thomas Holmes | 10 MGS | Rifleman No 7 Co 1st Bn. |
| 199 | R'man | Thomas Hooper | 5 MGS | Rifleman No 5 Co 3rd Bn. (Hooker) On command at Vitoria. |
| 200 | R'man | Thomas Horner | 4 MGS | Rifleman/Bugler No 5 Co 2nd Bn. |
| 201 | R'man | Peter Horrox | 3 MGS | Rifleman No 5 Co 2nd Bn. "Batman to Gen. Vandeleur." (Horrocks) |
| 202 | R'man | Elijah Hotley | 9 MGS | Bugler No 5 Co 3rd Bn. |
| 203 | R'man | David Hughes | 6 MGS | Rifleman No 2 Co 2nd Bn. On guard. |
| 204 | R'man | James Hurd | 5 MGS | Rifleman No 5 Co 2nd Bn. (Herd) |
| 205 | R'man | Patrick Hussey | 10 MGS | Rifleman No 6 Co 1st Bn. On guard. |
| 206 | R'man | Christopher Ingham | 9 MGS | Rifleman No 6 Co 1st Bn. |
| 207 | R'man | John Ireland | 5 MGS | Rifleman No 1 Co 3rd Bn. |
| 208 | R'man | Arthur John | 6 MGS | Rifleman No 3 Co 3rd Bn. |
| 209 | R'man | Robert Johnson | 5 MGS | Rifleman No 6 Co 2nd Bn. |
| 210 | R'man | Thomas Johnson | 4 MGS | Rifleman No 5 Co 2nd Bn. Sick Absent. (Wounded?) |
| 211 | R'man | Charles Jones | 7 MGS | Rifleman No 6 Co 1st Bn. |
| 212 | Sgt | Job Jones | 5 MGS | Rifleman No 2 Co 2nd Bn. On guard. |
| 213 | Corp | John Jones | 9 MGS | Rifleman No 1 Co 1st Bn. |
| 214 | R'man | Michael Joyce | 9 MGS | Rifleman No 1 Co 1st Bn. |
| 215 | R'man | Samuel Keen | 7 MGS | Corporal No 1 Co 3rd Bn. |
| 216 | R'man | William Kellaugher | 11 MGS | Rifleman No 1 Co 1st Bn. |
| 217 | R'man | John Kelly | 9 MGS | Sergeant No 1 Co 3rd Bn. |
| 218 | R'man | Thomas Kelly | 10 MGS | Rifleman No 4 Co 2nd Bn. |
| 219 | R'man | Joseph Kemp | 6 MGS | Rifleman No 6 Co 2nd Bn. |
| 220 | R'man | Alexander Kennedy | 10 MGS | Rifleman No 1 Co 1st Bn. |
| 221 | R'man | John Kidd | 2 MGS | Joined from England 7th May 1814, not entitled. |
| 222 | R'man | Thomas Knight | 6 MGS | Rifleman No 2 Co 2nd Bn. Commissariat employ. |
| 223 | R'man | Robert Lambert | 6 MGS | Rifleman No 2 Co 3rd Bn. |
| 224 | R'man | John Lamont | 13 MGS | Rifleman No 5 Co 1st Bn. On guard. |
| 225 | R'man | Robert Lane | 7 MGS | Rifleman No 4 Co 2nd Bn. |
| 226 | R'man | Thomas Laurison | 9 MGS | Rifleman No 6 Co 1st Bn. (Lorrison) |
| 227 | R'man | David Law | 11 MGS | Rifleman No 6 Co 1st Bn. |
| 228 | Corp | George Law | 12 MGS | Rifleman No 6 Co 1st Bn. On guard. |
| 229 | R'man | Thomas Lawman | 4 MGS | Rifleman No 2 Co 2nd Bn. |
| 230 | R'man | Jervis Layland | 2 MGS | Rifleman No 5 Co 2nd Bn. (Leyland) Wounded. Sick absent. |
| 231 | R'man | James Lennon | 6 MGS | Rifleman No 3 Co 2nd Bn. |

| | | | |
|---|---|---|---|
| R'man | Daniel Lewen | 7 MGS | Rifleman No 2 Co 3rd Bn. (Leven) |
| R'man | Lewis Lewis | 5 MGS | Rifleman No 7 Co 1st Bn. On guard. |
| R'man | Roderick Lewis | 5 MGS | Rifleman No 5 Co 3rd Bn. (Robert Lewis) |
| R'man | Peter Lisbie | 5 MGS | Rifleman No 1 Co 2nd Bn. |
| R'man | James Lord | 11 MGS | Rifleman No 4 Co 3rd Bn. Wounded 21st June. Sick absent. |
| R'man | Samuel Lovatt | 9 MGS | Rifleman No 5 Co 1st Bn. |
| Sgt | John Lowe | 8 MGS | Rifleman No 3 Co 2nd Bn. |
| R'man | Michael Lyons | 9 MGS | Rifleman No 8 Co 1st Bn. |
| Sgt | William Lyons | 6 MGS | Sick absent, not entitled. |
| Sgt | Angus Mackay | 3 MGS | Sergeant No 4 Co 2nd Bn. |
| R'man | William Mahoney | 10 MGS | Rifleman No 6 Co 1st Bn. |
| Sgt | Michael Malone | 5 MGS | Sergeant No 5 Co 2nd Bn. (Nicholas Malone) On guard. |
| R'man | Joseph Marriott | 7 MGS | Rifleman No 2 Co 3rd Bn. |
| R'man | Peter Marsh | 7 MGS | Rifleman No 1 Co 3rd Bn. |
| Qm Sgt | William Marshall | 6 MGS | Rifleman No 2 Co 3rd Bn. |
| R'man | John Martin | 8 MGS | Rifleman No 5 & 2 Co 1st Bn. |
| R'man | James Mason | 3 MGS | Rifleman No 1 Co 2nd Bn. |
| R'man | Isaac Maynes | 8 MGS | Rifleman No 2 Co 3rd Bn. (Moynes) Wounded 21st June. Sick absent. |
| R'man | George McCann | 7 MGS | Rifleman No 1 Co 3rd Bn. |
| Sgt | Thomas McDermid | 8 MGS | Rifleman No 8 Co 1st Bn. |
| Sgt | John McDonald | 7 MGS | Sergeant No 1 Co 1st Bn. Sick absent. (Wounded?) |
| R'man | Roderick McKay | 6 MGS | Rifleman No 1 Co 3rd Bn. |
| R'man | William McKay | 5 MGS | Rifleman No 7 Co 1st Bn. Sick absent. (Wounded?) |
| R'man | John McKelly | 11 MGS | Rifleman No 8 Co 1st Bn. On duty. |
| R'man | Hugh McLeod | 6 MGS | Rifleman No 7 Co 1st Bn. |
| R'man | Alexander McRae | 8 MGS | Rifleman No 7 Co 1st Bn. |
| R'man | John McUbby | 11 MGS | Rifleman No 2 Co 1st Bn. On guard. |
| R'man | George Michelson | 6 MGS | Rifleman No 4 Co 3rd Bn. (Micherson) |
| R'man | James Miles | 5 MGS | Rifleman No 8 Co 1st Bn. |
| R'man | John Miller | 6 MGS | Rifleman No 5 Co 2nd Bn. (Two on 2nd Bn. paylist) |
| R'man | Daniel Milton | 6 MGS | Rifleman No 6 Co 2nd Bn. |
| Bugle | Major James Mitchell | 8 MGS | Rifleman/Drum Major No 2 Co 2nd Bn. |
| Corp | John Monk | 3 MGS | Rifleman No 1 Co 2nd Bn. |
| R'man | Hugh Monks | 7 MGS | Rifleman No 3 Co 3rd Bn. |
| R'man | John Montgomery | 3 MGS | Rifleman No 6 Co 1st Bn. |
| R'man | Alexander Moore | 1 MGS | Not on the paylists until Nivelle, not entitled. |
| R'man | Thomas Moore | 6 MGS | Rifleman No 5 Co 3rd Bn. |
| Sgt | John Moran | 11 MGS | Rifleman No 7 Co 1st Bn. |
| R'man | Anthony Mullins | 3 MGS | Rifleman No 6 Co 2nd Bn. On duty. |
| R'man | John Mullins | 6 MGS | Rifleman No 8 Co 1st Bn. |

| 272 | R'man | Francis Munns | 2 MGS | Rifleman No 1 Co 2nd Bn. (Muns) |
| 273 | R'man | Charles Murphy | 6 MGS | Rifleman No 1 Co 3rd Bn. |
| 274 | Sgt | John Murphy | 7 MGS | Sergeant No 1 Co 1st Bn. Wexford, Kilhaven, Labourer. MGS man. |
| 275 | Corp | John Murphy | 12 MGS | Rifleman No 6 Co 1st Bn. Tipperary, Cashel, Mason (Two on 1st Bn. paylist) |
| 276 | R'man | William Newsham | 6 MGS | Rifleman No 1 Co 3rd Bn. (Newnham) |
| 277 | R'man | James Nice | 3 MGS | Rifleman No 1 Co 2nd Bn. |
| 278 | R'man | William Niven | 9 MGS | Sergeant No 1 Co 1st Bn. |
| 279 | Sgt | John Norton | 9 MGS | Corporal/Sergeant No 1 Co 2nd Bn. |
| 280 | Sgt | Robert Nunn | 7 MGS | Sergeant No 2 Co 3rd Bn. |
| 281 | R'man | James O'Neil | 7 MGS | Rifleman No 1 Co 3rd Bn. Wounded. Sick absent. |
| 282 | R'man | Charles Ormond | 11 MGS | Rifleman No 2 Co 1st Bn. |
| 283 | R'man | Thomas Osborne | 4 MGS | Rifleman No 2 Co 3rd Bn. Wounded 21st June. Sick absent. |
| 284 | R'man | Bryan Padden | 6 MGS | Corporal/Sergeant No 6 Co 2nd Bn. (Bernard Paddern) |
| 285 | R'man | John Palmer | 12 MGS | Rifleman No 7 Co 1st Bn. On guard. |
| 286 | R'man | Jonathan Palmer | 5 MGS | Bugler No 5 Co 1st Bn. |
| 287 | R'man | William Parker | 2 MGS | Rifleman No 7 Co 1st Bn. On guard. |
| 288 | R'man | John Parry | 5 MGS | Rifleman No 4 Co 3rd Bn. (Perry) |
| 289 | R'man | John Peacock | 5 MGS | Sergeant No 2 Co 2nd Bn. |
| 290 | R'man | Oliver Peacock | 9 MGS | Rifleman No 1 Co 1st Bn. Gen. Hosp. (Wounded?) |
| 291 | R'man | Samuel Peters | 11 MGS | Rifleman No 8 Co 1st Bn. |
| 292 | R'man | James Petty | 12 MGS | Rifleman No 5 Co 1st Bn. (Pettie) |
| 293 | R'man | Joseph Piers | 8 MGS | Rifleman No 2 Co 2nd Bn. (Peers) On guard. |
| 294 | Sgt | George Piper | 8 MGS | Rifleman No 5 Co 1st Bn. On guard. |
| 295 | R'man | Daniel Pointer | 3 MGS | Rifleman No 5 Co 2nd Bn. |
| 296 | R'man | William Poole | 6 MGS | Rifleman No 8 Co 1st Bn. |
| 297 | R'man | Peter Potter | 5 MGS | Sick absent, not entitled. |
| 298 | R'man | William Prestage | 5 MGS | Bugler No 2 Co 2nd Bn. |
| 299 | R'man | Peter Price | 10 MGS | Rifleman No 3 Co 2nd Bn. Sick absent. (Wounded?) |
| 300 | R'man | Thomas Price | 7 MGS | Corporal No 1 Co 2nd Bn. Haverford West, Shoemaker. |
| 301 | R'man | William Price | 6 MGS | Rifleman No 8 Co 1st Bn. On duty. |
| 302 | R'man | Benjamin Pring | 11 MGS | Rifleman No 8 Co 1st Bn. On duty. |
| 303 | R'man | William Pritchard | 6 MGS | Rifleman No 6 Co 2nd Bn. |
| 304 | R'man | Samuel Pryke | 7 MGS | Rifleman No 3 Co 2nd Bn. |
| 305 | R'man | James Rawledge | 7 MGS | Rifleman No 6 Co 1st Bn. (Rowledge) |
| 306 | Sgt | John Reakes | 10 MGS | Corporal No 6 Co 1st Bn. |
| 307 | R'man | Duncan Reid | 7 MGS | Rifleman No 5 Co 3rd Bn. (Reed) |
| 308 | R'man | Thomas Renwick | 5 MGS | Rifleman No 4 Co 3rd Bn. On command at Vitoria. |
| 309 | R'man | William Rhodes | 9 MGS | Rifleman No 5 Co 1st Bn. |

| R'man | William Richards | 2 MGS | Rifleman No 5 Co 3rd Bn. (Two on 3rd Bn. paylist) |
|-------|------------------|-------|---------------------------------------------------|
| R'man | John Riddles | 3 MGS | Rifleman No 4 Co 2nd Bn. On guard. |
| R'man | Alexander Robb | 6 MGS | Rifleman No 1 Co 3rd Bn. |
| R'man | Thomas Robinson | 4 MGS | Rifleman No 1 Co 1st Bn. |
| R'man | Thomas Robinson | 8 MGS | Rifleman No 1 Co 1st Bn. |
| R'man | Richard Rodgers | 6 MGS | Rifleman No 1 Co 1st Bn. |
| R'man | Richard Rogers | 3 MGS | No trace in the paylists, maybe R. Rodgers 6 MGS, as both start at Vitoria. |
| R'man | Thomas Rogers | 7 MGS | Rifleman No 5 Co 1st Bn. |
| R'man | John Rostrin | 7 MGS | Rifleman No 3 Co 2nd Bn. |
| R'man | John Rouse | 10 MGS | Rifleman No 6 Co 1st Bn. |
| R'man | Richard Rouse | 8 MGS | Rifleman No 6 Co 1st Bn. |
| R'man | George Rowe | 6 MGS | Rifleman No 1 Co 1st Bn. |
| R'man | William Russell | 6 MGS | Rifleman No 5 Co 2nd Bn. |
| Sgt | John Rutledge | 8 MGS | Corporal No 2 Co 2nd Bn. |
| R'man | Philip Ryan | 5 MGS | Rifleman No 2 Co 1st Bn. |
| Sgt | William Sabin | 10 MGS | Sergeant No 3 Co 3rd Bn. |
| R'man | James Sell | 5 MGS | Rifleman No 2 Co 2nd Bn. On guard. |
| R'man | William Sharp | 8 MGS | Rifleman No 5 Co 1st Bn. |
| R'man | Thomas Sharples | 8 MGS | Rifleman No 2 Co 3rd Bn. |
| Corp | Adam Shaw | 9 MGS | Rifleman No 1 Co 3rd Bn. |
| Corp | William Shelton | 4 MGS | Rifleman No 3 Co 3rd Bn. (Shilton) |
| R'man | John Sheppard | 8 MGS | Rifleman No 2 Co 3rd Bn. |
| R'man | James Short | 2 MGS | Rifleman No 5 Co 3rd Bn. |
| R'man | Benjamin Simons | 6 MGS | Rifleman No 1 Co 3rd Bn. (Simonds) |
| R'man | William Slavin | 8 MGS | Rifleman No 1 Co 3rd Bn. (Slaven) On command at Vitoria. |
| Corp | Michael Smart | 10 MGS | Rifleman No 6 Co 1st Bn. |
| R'man | William Smillie | 11 MGS | Rifleman No 7 Co 1st Bn. |
| Sgt | Alexander Smith | 5 MGS | Rifleman No 2 Co 2nd Bn. |
| Sgt | George Smith | 7 MGS | Corporal No 2 Co 3rd Bn. |
| Corp | Peter Smith | 3 MGS | Rifleman No 1 Co 1st Bn. |
| R'man | Robert Smith | 3 MGS | Rifleman No 4 Co 2nd Bn. From No 6 Co. |
| R'man | Thomas Smith | 11 MGS | Rifleman No 5 Co 1st Bn. In Gen. Hosp., not entitled. |
| R'man | William Smith | 6 MGS | Rifleman No 1 Co 2nd Bn. Carrick on Shure, Labourer. |
| R'man | William Smithers | 5 MGS | Rifleman No 4 Co 2nd Bn. |
| R'man | John Smyth | 12 MGS | Rifleman No 6 Co 1st Bn. (Smith) |
| R'man | William Solomon | 9 MGS | Rifleman No 2 Co 3rd Bn. |
| R'man | Richard Spencer | 7 MGS | Rifleman No 3 Co 2nd Bn. |
| R'man | William Sperry | 9 MGS | Rifleman No 5 Co 1st Bn. |
| R'man | John Standly | 4 MGS | Rifleman No 1 Co 3rd Bn. (Stanley) |
| R'man | James Steele | 6 MGS | Rifleman No 6 Co 1st Bn. |
| R'man | George Stephenson | 10 MGS | Rifleman No 2 Co 3rd Bn. On command with sick officer. |

| 350 | R'man | William Stephenson | 5 MGS | Rifleman No 8 & 1 Co 1st Bn. |
| 351 | Bugler | James Stevens | 11 MGS | Bugler No 7 Co 1st Bn. Sick absent. (Wounded?) |
| 352 | R'man | Joseph Stringer | 5 MGS | Rifleman No 3 Co 3rd Bn. |
| 353 | R'man | Jonathan Stubbs | 10 MGS | Rifleman No 4 & 5 Co 3rd Bn. |
| 354 | R'man | Edward Sutherland | 8 MGS | Rifleman No 2 Co 1st Bn. |
| 355 | R'man | George Sutherland | 9 MGS | Rifleman No 7 Co 1st Bn. On guard. |
| 356 | R'man | William Suthers | 2 MGS | Not in the Peninsula until San Sebastian, not entitled. |
| 357 | R'man | James Swain | 5 MGS | Rifleman No 2 Co 3rd Bn. Wounded 24th June 1813. Sick absent. |
| 358 | R'man | Mathew Swalwell | 7 MGS | Rifleman No 5 Co 1st Bn. |
| 359 | R'man | John Symington | 11 MGS | Rifleman No 7 Co 1st Bn. |
| 360 | Sgt | Thomas Tabbutt | 7 MGS | Corporal No 5 Co 3rd Bn. Wounded 21st June. Sick absent. |
| 361 | R'man | Edward Taggen | 10 MGS | Rifleman No 8 Co 1st Bn. (Tegan) |
| 362 | R'man | James Tate | 7 MGS | Rifleman No 4 Co 3rd Bn. |
| 363 | R'man | Benjamin Taylor | 5 MGS | Rifleman No 6 Co 2nd Bn. |
| 364 | R'man | Joseph Taylor | 3 MGS | Rifleman No 5 Co 2nd Bn. (Two on 2nd Bn. paylist) |
| 365 | Sgt Major | John Thompson | 5 MGS | Sergeant No 5 Co 1st Bn. |
| 366 | Corp | James Tomlinson | 8 MGS | Rifleman No 5 Co 2nd Bn. |
| 367 | Corp | Edward Tonkinson | 9 MGS | Corporal No 6 Co 1st Bn. |
| 368 | R'man | George Tunnicliffe | 12 MGS | Rifleman No 5 Co 1st Bn. (Tonacliffe) Gen. Hosp. (Wounded?) |
| 369 | R'man | Matthew Turner | 9 MGS | Rifleman No 1 Co 3rd Bn. |
| 370 | R'man | Peter Turner | 6 MGS | Rifleman No 2 Co 1st Bn. |
| 371 | R'man | Richard Underhill | 7 MGS | Rifleman No 2 Co 2nd Bn. On guard |
| 372 | R'man | Thomas Undrill | 3 MGS | Rifleman No 6 Co 2nd Bn. (Underhill) |
| 373 | R'man | William Usher | 8 MGS | Rifleman No 6 Co 1st Bn. On duty, Vitoria. |
| 374 | R'man | John Waghorn | 7 MGS | Rifleman No 5 Co 3rd Bn. |
| 375 | R'man | George Waine | 4 MGS | Rifleman No 8 Co 1st Bn. On duty. |
| 376 | R'man | Abraham Walker | 9 MGS | Rifleman No 5 Co 1st Bn. |
| 377 | R'man | John Walker | 6 MGS | Rifleman No 1 Co 3rd Bn. |
| 378 | Sgt | Thomas Wall | 11 MGS | Sergeant No 3 Co 3rd Bn. On command at Vitoria. |
| 379 | R'man | James Walsh | 5 MGS | Rifleman No 6 Co 2nd Bn. (Welch) |
| 380 | R'man | James Warburton | 8 MGS | Rifleman No 8 Co 1st Bn. Gen. Hosp. (Wounded?) |
| 381 | R'man | John Ward | 10 MGS | Rifleman No 1 & 8 Co 1st Bn. |
| 382 | R'man | John Waterhouse | 4 MGS | Rifleman No 3 Co 2nd Bn. |
| 383 | Sgt | James Waterson | 10 MGS | Rifleman/Corporal No 1 Co 3rd Bn. |
| 384 | R'man | Joseph Watniff | 8 MGS | Rifleman No 5 Co 1st Bn. (Watmiffe) |
| 385 | R'man | Thomas Webb | 2 MGS | Rifleman No 6 Co 1st Bn. |
| 386 | R'man | John Wellbelove | 5 MGS | Rifleman No 4 Co 2nd Bn. On guard. |
| 387 | R'man | William Wellington | 6 MGS | Rifleman No 2 Co 2nd Bn. On guard. |

| R'man | William Wells | 7 MGS | Rifleman No 6 Co 2nd Bn. Sick absent. (Wounded?) |
|---|---|---|---|
| R'man | William Weston | 7 MGS | Rifleman No 2 Co 1st Bn. On duty, Vitoria. |
| R'man | Thomas Whetstone | 8 MGS | Rifleman No 1 Co 1st Bn. (Whitston) On duty, Vitoria. |
| R'man | William Whitehead | 7 MGS | Rifleman No 6 Co 1st Bn. |
| Bugler | Maurice Wildes | 6 MGS | Bugler No 3 Co 2nd Bn. |
| R'man | William Wilkinson | 2 MGS | Rifleman No 1 Co 1st Bn. |
| R'man | John Williams | 8 MGS | Rifleman No 1 Co 1st Bn. |
| R'man | Thomas Wilson | 10 MGS | Rifleman No 7 Co 1st Bn. On guard. |
| R'man | Thomas Wilson | 10 MGS | Rifleman No 3 Co 3rd Bn. (Two on 3rd Bn. paylist) |
| Sgt | William Wilson | 5 MGS | Rifleman No 5 Co 2nd Bn. On guard. |
| R'man | Joseph Witham | 7 MGS | Rifleman No 2 Co 1st Bn. |
| R'man | William Wood | 6 MGS | Rifleman No 6 Co 2nd Bn. |
| R'man | George Woodland | 1 MGS | Rifleman No 2 Co 3rd Bn. Wounded 21st June. Sick absent. |
| R'man | James Woodley | 4 MGS | Rifleman No 4 Co 3rd Bn. Wounded 21st June. Sick absent. |
| R'man | James Woodley | 6 MGS | Rifleman No 1 Co 3rd Bn. |
| R'man | John Wright | 5 MGS | Rifleman No 5 Co 2nd Bn. On guard. |
| R'man | William Wright | 10 MGS | Rifleman No 2 Co 1st Bn. Sick absent. (Wounded?) |
| R'man | David Wylie | 6 MGS | Rifleman No 5 Co 2nd Bn. |

## Additional names of MGS men not awarded the clasp for Vittoria:

| Corp | Isaac Bagshaw | 2 MGS | Corporal No 8 Co 1st Bn. On duty. |
|---|---|---|---|
| R'man | John Bail | 4 MGS | Rifleman No 2 Co 3rd Bn. |
| R'man | Jacob Barlow | 5 MGS | Rifleman No 8 Co 1st Bn. |
| Sgt | Stephen Bedford | 6 MGS | Rifleman No 4 Co 2nd Bn. On guard. |
| R'man | John Burr | 8 MGS | Rifleman No 6 Co 1st Bn. On guard. |
| R'man | Patrick Casey | 3 MGS | Rifleman No 3 Co 2nd Bn. |
| R'man | Thomas Connelly | 2 MGS | Rifleman No 6 Co 1st Bn. On duty, Vitoria. |
| R'man | Thomas Cooper | 5 MGS | Rifleman No 3 Co 2nd Bn. |
| R'man | James Farnfield | 6 MGS | Rifleman No 5 Co 2nd Bn. Sick absent. (Wounded?) |
| Sgt | William Graham | 6 MGS | Rifleman No 2 Co 1st Bn. |
| R'man | Christopher Grimes | 8 MGS | Rifleman No 8 Co 1st Bn. |
| R'man | James Hall | 4 MGS | Rifleman No 3 Co 3rd Bn. |
| R'man | Robert Hyslop | 3 MGS | Rifleman No 7 Co 1st Bn. (Hayslop) |
| R'man | Thomas Jones | 3 MGS | Rifleman No 2 Co 1st Bn. |
| R'man | Richard Lancaster | 3 MGS | Rifleman No 4 Co 2nd Bn. Sick absent. (Wounded?) |
| Corp | Alexander Masterson | 6 MGS | Rifleman No 1 Co 1st Bn. |
| R'man | Robert McKay | 5 MGS | Rifleman No 5 Co 3rd Bn. |

| 18 | R'man | John McKitchie | 2 MGS | Sergeant No 5 Co 3rd Bn. (McKechie) |
|----|-------|----------------|-------|-------------------------------------|
| 19 | R'man | Alexander Mears | 3 MGS | Rifleman No 4 Co 3rd Bn. (Mairs) |
| 20 | R'man | Henry Reily | 4 MGS | Rifleman No 4 Co 3rd Bn. (Riley) |
| 21 | R'man | Joseph Ripley | 5 MGS | Rifleman No 5 Co 1st Bn. On duty, servant to Lieut. Mitchell. |
| 22 | R'man | James Rolestone | 4 MGS | Rifleman No 7 Co 1st Bn. |
| 23 | R'man | James Russell | 4 MGS | Rifleman No 1 Co 1st Bn. |
| 24 | R'man | James Saunders | 8 MGS | Rifleman No 2 Co 2nd Bn. On guard. |
| 25 | R'man | William Shaughnessy | 3 MGS | Rifleman No 1 Co 2nd Bn. On guard. |
| 26 | R'man | John Sherrocks | 4 MGS | Rifleman No 6 Co 2nd Bn. (Shorrocks) |
| 27 | R'man | Benjamin Slaughter | 2 MGS | Rifleman No 6 Co 1st Bn. |
| 28 | R'man | William Taylor | 1 MGS | Bugler No 1 Co 2nd Bn. (Two on 2nd Bn. paylist) |
| 29 | R'man | John Trusssell | 3 MGS | Rifleman No 5 Co 3rd Bn. |
| 30 | R'man | Richard Young | 6 MGS | Rifleman No 5 Co 3rd Bn. |

*John Davies 7 MGS CR, Sal, Vit, Pyr, S/S, Ort and Tou.

With the research to hand it has been somewhat difficult to be precise in identifying John Davies, the 7 MGS man. In the 1st Battalion we have the following men:

1     John Davies Denbigh, Wrexham, Labourer. Present from Bus to Bad (hospital), then no further trace of in the paylists—dead or invalided?

2     John Davies Denbigh, Wrexham, Bricklayer. KIA at Badajoz.

3     John Davies Somerset, Frome, Labourer. Present from Bus to Tou except for CR and Bad.

4     John Davies Carmarthen, Pengboy, Labourer. POW at the Coa, returned 13th May 1814. (Although he is on the paylists from CR to Tou.)

5     John Davis Flint, Holywell, Flaxdresser. Present from Rol to Bad then invalided to England. The 2 MGS man.

6     John Davies Flint, Mold, Weaver. Present from Bus to Tou.

7     John Davies Flint, Mold, Weaver. Present for Sal only then invalided to England.

From the above, number 2 can certainly be eliminated, followed closely by numbers 1 & 7. Number 4 looks straightforward being a POW supposedly until 1814. Although there is no mention of his escaping or returning from the French he appears in the paylists for Ciudad Rodrigo to the end of the war in 1814.

As number 5 John Davis looks suitably to be the 2 MGS man, we are left numbers 3 & 6. The indication against these two men being the MGS man is that both were present at Busaco and Fuentes de Onoro, before Ciudad Rodrigo. Of the two 2nd and one 3rd Battalion men present in the Peninsula none would qualify as MGS men.

# Military General Service medal

## Official entitlement
### and
## actual entitlement

## Volume III

| | MGS | ROL | VIM | COR | TAL | BUS | BAR | F'O | C'R | BAD | SAL | VIT | PYR | S/S | NVL | NIV | ORT | TOU |
|---|---|---|---|---|---|---|---|---|---|---|---|---|---|---|---|---|---|---|
| **MAJOR:** | | | | | | | | | | | | | | | | | | |
| GEORGE WILKINS | 2 MGS | | | | | | | | • | • | GM | VIT | PYR | | | | | |
| | | | | | | | | | | | | VIT | | | | | | |
| **CAPTAINS:** | | | | | | | | | | | | | | | | | | |
| ALEXANDER ANDREWS | 8 MGS | | | | | | | | • | • | • | VIT | PYR | s/s | NVL | NIV | ORT | TOU |
| RECEIVED EGYPT IN 13TH REGT | | | | | | | | | | | | VIT | | | | | | |
| WILLIAM BALVAIRD | 6 MGS | | | | | BUS | | F'O | C'R | BAD | SAL | VIT | PYR | | | | | |
| ALEXANDER CAMERON | 5 MGS | | VIM | COR | | BUS | | F'O | GM | GM | GM | VIT | | | | | | |
| WILLIAM COX | 7 MGS | ROL | VIM | | | | | | • | • | • | VIT | PYR | | NVL | NIV | ORT | |
| THOMAS DRAKE | 3 MGS | | | | | BUS | | F'O | • | • | • | VIT | | | | | | |
| CHARLES GRAY | 7 MGS | | | | | | BAR | | • | BAD | • | VIT | | s/s | NVL | NIV | ORT | TOU |
| JOHN KENT | 5 MGS | ROL | VIM | | | | | | C'R | BAD | SAL | VIT | | | | | | |
| RECEIVED ROL+VIM 50TH REGT | | | | | | | | | C'R | BAD | SAL | VIT | | | | | | |
| JOHN KINCAID | 9 MGS | | | | | | | F'O | C'R | BAD | SAL | VIT | PYR | | NVL | NIV | | TOU |
| JONATHAN LEACH | 12 MGS | ROL | VIM | | | BUS | | F'O | C'R | BAD | SAL | VIT | PYR | | NVL | NIV | | TOU |
| **LIEUTENANTS:** | | | | | | | | | | | | | | | | | | |
| JOSEPH AUSTIN | 1 MGS | | | | | | | | • | BAD | • | • | | | | | | |
| WILLIAM BALDOCK | 4 MGS | | | | | | BAR | | C'R | BAD | SAL | • | | | | | | |
| WALTER BEDELL | 2 MGS | | | | | | | F'O | C'R | BAD | • | • | | | | | | |

KEY: ☐ OFFICIAL  ▨ ACTUAL  • NOT ENTITLED

234

*Table of Military General Service Medal clasps (page rotated). A dot (•) indicates a battle present at without a clasp; an abbreviation indicates a clasp held.*

| Name | MGS | ROL | VIM | COR | TAL | BUS | BAR | F'O | C'R | BAD | SAL | VIT | PYR | S/S | NVL | NIV | ORT | TOU |
|---|---|---|---|---|---|---|---|---|---|---|---|---|---|---|---|---|---|---|
| WILLIAM BOOTH (IN THE 95TH FOR COR ONLY) | 4 MGS | | | COR | | | | | | | | VIT | | | | | ORT | TOU |
| JOHN BUDGEN | 8 MGS | | | COR | | | BAR | | • | • | • | VIT | PYR | | NVL | NIV | ORT | TOU |
| ROBERT COCHRANE | 2 MGS | | | | | | | | • | • | • | • | • | | • | • | ORT | TOU |
| EDWARD COXEN | 10 MGS | | | | | | | F'O | C'R | BAD | SAL | VIT | PYR | | NVL | NIV | ORT | TOU |
| CHARLES CUYLER (AFTER VITORIA IN 69TH FOOT) | 2 MGS | | | | | | | | • | • | SAL | VIT | | | | | | |
| GEORGE DRUMMOND | 8 MGS | | | | | | | | • | BAD | SAL | VIT | PYR | | NVL | NIV | ORT | TOU |
| JOHN FITZMAURICE | 8 MGS | | | | | | | F'O | • | BAD | SAL | VIT | PYR | | NVL | NIV | | TOU |
| JAMES GAIRDNER | 9 MGS | | | | | | | | C'R | BAD | SAL | VIT | PYR | | NVL | NIV | ORT | TOU |
| JOHN GARDINER | 6 MGS | | | | | | | | • | • | • | VIT | PYR | | NVL | NIV | ORT | TOU |
| WILLIAM HAGGUP | 8 MGS | | | | | BUS | | F'O | • | BAD | SAL | VIT | PYR | | NVL | NIV | | TOU |
| WILLIAM HALLEN | 6 MGS | | | COR | | | | | • | • | • | VIT | PYR | | NVL | | ORT | TOU |
| DUDLEY HILL | 4 MGS | ROL | VIM | | | BUS | | | C'R | | | | | | | | | |
| LOFTUS JONES | 6 MGS | | | | | | | | • | • | GM | VIT | PYR | | NVL | | ORT | TOU |
| THOMAS KIRKLEY | 6 MGS | | | | | | | | • | • | • | VIT | PYR | | NVL | NIV | ORT | TOU |
| JAMES KIRKMAN | 8 MGS | | | | | | BAR | | C'R | BAD | SAL | VIT | PYR | | NVL | NIV | | |

235

| Name | | ROL | VIM | COR | TAL | BUS | BAR | F'O | C'R | BAD | SAL | VIT | PYR | S/S | NVL | NIV | ORT | TOU |
|---|---|---|---|---|---|---|---|---|---|---|---|---|---|---|---|---|---|---|
| SAMUEL LAWSON | 4 MGS | | | | | | | | • | BAD | • | • | PYR | | | | ORT | TOU |
| JOHN MIDDLETON | 10 MGS | | | | | | BAR | | C'R | BAD | SAL | VIT | PYR | | NVL | NIV | ORT | TOU |
| THOMAS MITCHELL | 5 MGS | | | | | | | | C'R | BAD | SAL | • | PYR | s/s | | | | |
| JOHN MOLLOY | 8 MGS | ROL | | | | | | | • | • | SAL | VIT | PYR | | NVL | NIV | | TOU |
| HENRY SCOTT | 3 MGS | | | | | | | F'O | • | • | SAL | • | | | NVL | | | |
| GEORGE SIMMONS | 8 MGS | | | | | | | F'O | C'R | BAD | SAL | VIT | PYR | | NVL | | ORT | |
| JOSEPH SIMMONS | 3 MGS | | | | | | | | • | • | • | VIT | | | NVL | NIV | | |
| HARRY SMITH | 12 MGS | | | COR | | BUS | | F'O | C'R | BAD | SAL | VIT | PYR | | NVL | NIV | ORT | TOU |
| THOMAS SMITH | 10 MGS | | | COR | | | | | C'R | BAD | SAL | VIT | PYR | | NVL | NIV | ORT | TOU |
| NICHOLAS TRAVERS | 3 MGS | | | | | | | | • | • | SAL | VIT | PYR | | | | | |
| THOMAS WORSLEY | 9 MGS | | | | | | | | C'R | BAD | SAL | VIT | PYR | | NVL | NIV | ORT | TOU |
| **SUBALTERNS:** | | | | | | | | | | | | | | | | | | |
| GEORGE CARY | 6 MGS | | | | | | | F'O | • | • | • | VIT | PYR | | NVL | NIV | ORT | TOU |
| JOHN COX | 10 MGS | ROL | VIM | | | BUS | | | C'R | • | • | VIT | PYR | | NVL | NIV | ORT | |
| MULLEN GIVES NIV, ORT + TOU | | | | | | | | | | | • | VIT | | | | | | |
| CHARLES EATON | 7 MGS | | | | | | BAR | | • | • | • | VIT | PYR | s/s | NVL | | ORT | TOU |

| | | ROL | VIM | COR | TAL | BUS | BAR | F'O | C'R | BAD | SAL | VIT | PYR | S/S | NVL | NIV | ORT | TOU |
|---|---|---|---|---|---|---|---|---|---|---|---|---|---|---|---|---|---|---|
| WILLIAM HUMBLEY | 12 MGS | ROL | VIM | COR | | BUS | BAR | | • | • | SAL | VIT | PYR | | NVL | NIV | ORT | TOU |
| JOHN RIDGWAY | 3 MGS | | | | | | | | • | • | SAL | VIT | PYR | | | | | |
| **VOLUNTEER:** | | | | | | | | | | | | | | | | | | |
| JOSEPH DORNFORD | 2 MGS | | | | | | | | • | • | • | VIT | PYR | | | | | |
| **ASSISTANT SURGEON:** | | | | | | | | | | | | | | | | | | |
| WILLIAM JONES | 12 MGS | | | COR | | BUS | | F'O | C'R | BAD | SAL | VIT | PYR | | NVL | NIV | ORT | TOU |
| AFTER VITORIA IN 40TH FOOT. | | | | | | | | | | | | | | | | | | |
| **SERGEANT MAJORS:** | | | | | | | | | | | | | | | | | | |
| JOHN DANCER | 6 MGS | | | | | BUS | | F'O | • | BAD | SAL | • | PYR | | | | | TOU |
| THOMAS DEAMAN | 6 MGS | | | | | | | | • | • | SAL | VIT | | | NVL | NIV | ORT | TOU |
| WILLIAM FRY | 9 MGS | | | COR | | | | C'R | | BAD | SAL | • | PYR | | NVL | NIV | ORT | TOU |
| ENSIGN 24TH REGT 14TH OCT. 1812 | | | | | | | | | | | | | | | | | | |
| JOHN THOMPSON | 5 MGS | ROL | VIM | | | BUS | | | • | • | • | VIT | | | | | | TOU |
| **QUARTERMASTER SERGEANTS:** | | | | | | | | | | | | | | | | | | |
| ISAAC BAGSHAW | 2 MGS | | | | | BUS | | F'O | • | • | • | • | | | | | | |
| WILLIAM MARSHALL | 6 MGS | | | | | | | | • | • | • | VIT | PYR | | NVL | NIV | ORT | TOU |

| | | ROL | VIM | COR | TAL | BUS | BAR | F'O | C'R | BAD | SAL | VIT | PYR | S/S | NVL | NIV | ORT | TOU |
|---|---|---|---|---|---|---|---|---|---|---|---|---|---|---|---|---|---|
| **BUGLE MAJOR:** | | | | | | | | | | | | | | | | | | |
| JAMES MITCHELL | 8 MGS | ROL | VIM | | | | | | • | • | • | VIT | PYR | | NVL | NIV | ORT | TOU |
| | | | | | | | | | • | • | • | VIT | | | | | | |
| **COLOUR SERGEANT:** | | | | | | | | | | | | | | | | | | |
| JAMES DAVISON | 7 MGS | | VIM | | | BUS | | | C'R | BAD | • | • | PYR | S/S | | | | TOU |
| | | | | | | | | | • | | | | | | | | | |
| **SERGEANTS:** | | | | | | | | | | | | | | | | | | |
| JAMES ANDERSON | 9 MGS | | VIM | COR | | | | F'O | C'R | BAD | SAL | VIT | PYR | S/S | | | | TOU |
| WILLIAM ARMSON | 8 MGS | | | | | | BAR | | C'R | BAD | SAL | VIT | PYR | | | | ORT | TOU |
| GEORGE BALLER | 4 MGS | | | | | | | F'O | C'R | BAD | SAL | VIT | | | | | | |
| STEPHEN BEDFORD | 6 MGS | | VIM | | | | | | C'R | BAD | SAL | • | | | | | | TOU |
| JOSEPH BOWLEY | 10 MGS | ROL | VIM | COR | | BUS | | | C'R | BAD | SAL | VIT | PYR | | | | | TOU |
| ROBERT BURNS | 9 MGS | | VIM | COR | | BUS | | F'O | C'R | • | • | VIT | | | | | | TOU |
| ANDREW CARR | 11 MGS | | VIM | COR | | BUS | | F'O | C'R | BAD | SAL | VIT | | | NVL | NIV | ORT | TOU |
| THOMAS CHAMBERS | 3 MGS | | | | | | | | C'R | BAD | SAL | • | | | | | | |
| JOSEPH COWAN | 9 MGS | | VIM | COR | | BUS | | | C'R | BAD | SAL | VIT | | | | | ORT | TOU |
| JOHN DICKINSON | 4 MGS | | | | | | BAR | | C'R | BAD | SAL | • | | | | | | |
| TOBIAS DIGBY | 9 MGS | | | COR | | BUS | | | C'R | BAD | SAL | VIT | | | | | ORT | TOU |

| | MGS | ROL | VIM | COR | TAL | BUS | BAR | F'O | C'R | BAD | SAL | VIT | PYR | S/S | NVL | NIV | ORT | TOU |
|---|---|---|---|---|---|---|---|---|---|---|---|---|---|---|---|---|---|---|
| ALEXANDER EASON | 13 MGS | | VIM | COR | | BUS | | F'O | C'R | BAD | SAL | VIT | PYR | | NVL | NIV | ORT | TOU |
| JAMES FARMER | 9 MGS | | VIM | COR | | BUS | | | C'R | BAD | SAL | VIT | PYR | | | | ORT | TOU |
| JONATHAN GLOSSOP | 8 MGS | | | | | BUS | | | • | • | SAL | VIT | PYR | | NVL | NIV | ORT | TOU |
| WILLIAM GRAHAM | 6 MGS | | | COR | | BUS | | F'O | C'R | BAD | SAL | • | | | | | | |
| WILLIAM HALL | 11 MGS | | | COR | | BUS | | F'O | C'R | BAD | SAL | • | PYR | S/S | | | ORT | TOU |
| JOHN HIMBURY | 8 MGS | | | | | | BAR | | • | • | • | VIT | PYR | | NVL | NIV | ORT | TOU |
| WILLIAM HINDE | 11 MGS | | | COR | | | | F'O | C'R | BAD | SAL | VIT | PYR | | NVL | NIV | ORT | TOU |
| JOSEPH HINDLE | 14 MGS | ROL | VIM | COR | | BUS | BAR | F'O | C'R | BAD | SAL | VIT | PYR | S/S | NVL | NIV | ORT | TOU |
| JOB JONES | 5 MGS | | | | | | BAR | | • | • | • | VIT | PYR | | NVL | | | TOU |
| JOHN LOWE | 8 MGS | ROL | VIM | | | | | F'O | C'R | BAD | SAL | VIT | PYR | | | | | |
| WILLIAM LYONS | 6 MGS | | VIM | | | | | | C'R | BAD | SAL | VIT | PYR | S/S | | | | |
| ANGUS MACKAY | 3 MGS | | | | | | | | • | • | • | VIT | PYR | | | | | TOU |
| MICHAEL MALONE | 5 MGS | ROL | VIM | COR | | | | | • | • | • | VIT | PYR | | | | | |
| THOMAS MCDERMID | 8 MGS | | | | | | | | | BAD | SAL | VIT | PYR | | NVL | NIV | ORT | TOU |
| JOHN MCDONALD | 7 MGS | | | COR | | | | F'O | C'R | BAD | • | VIT | | | NVL | NIV | ORT | TOU |

| Name | MGS | ROL | VIM | COR | TAL | BUS | BAR | F'O | C'R | BAD | SAL | VIT | PYR | S/S | NVL | NIV | ORT | TOU |
|------|-----|-----|-----|-----|-----|-----|-----|-----|-----|-----|-----|-----|-----|-----|-----|-----|-----|-----|
| ALEXANDER MCLEOD | 9 MGS | | | | | BUS | | | C'R | BAD | • | • | PYR | S/S | NVL | NIV | ORT | TOU |
| CHARLES MCPHERSON | 6 MGS | ROL | VIM | | | | | F'O | C'R | BAD | • | • | | | | | | |
| JOHN MILLER | 1 MGS | | | | | BUS | | | C'R | BAD | • | • | | | | | | |
| JOHN MORAN | 11 MGS | | VIM | COR | | BUS | | F'O | C'R | BAD | SAL | VIT | PYR | | | NIV | | TOU |
| JOHN MURPHY | 7 MGS | | | COR | | BUS | | F'O | C'R | BAD | SAL | VIT | | | | | | |
| JOHN NAUGHTON | 4 MGS | | | COR | | | | | C'R | BAD | SAL | VIT | | | | | | |
| JOHN NORTON | 9 MGS | | VIM | | TAL | | | | C'R | BAD | SAL | • | PYR | | | | | TOU |
| ROBERT NUNN | 7 MGS | | | COR | | | BAR | | • | • | SAL | VIT | PYR | | | | ORT | TOU |
| GEORGE PIPER | 8 MGS | | | | | | | | C'R | BAD | SAL | VIT | PYR | s/s | | NIV | ORT | TOU |
| JOHN REAKES | 10 MGS | | VIM | COR | | BUS | | F'O | • | • | SAL | VIT | | | NVL | NIV | ORT | TOU |
| CHARLES ROSS | 7 MGS | | VIM | COR | | BUS | | F'O | C'R | BAD | SAL | VIT | | | NVL | NIV | ORT | TOU |
| JOHN RUTLEDGE | 8 MGS | | | COR | | | BAR | | • | • | • | • | PYR | | NVL | NIV | ORT | TOU |
| WILLIAM SABIN | 10 MGS | | | | | | BAR | | C'R | BAD | SAL | VIT | PYR | | NVL | NIV | ORT | TOU |
| ALEXANDER SMITH | 5 MGS | | | | | | BAR | | C'R | | SAL | VIT | PYR | | | | | TOU |
| GEORGE SMITH | 7 MGS | | | | | | | | • | • | SAL | VIT | | | NVL | NIV | ORT | TOU |

| Name | MGS | ROL | VIM | COR | TAL | BUS | BAR | F'O | C'R | BAD | SAL | VIT | PYR | S/S | NVL | NIV | ORT | TOU |
|---|---|---|---|---|---|---|---|---|---|---|---|---|---|---|---|---|---|---|
| THOMAS TABBUTT | 7 MGS | | | | | | BAR | | C'R | BAD | SAL | VIT | PYR | | | | | TOU |
| THOMAS WALL | 11 MGS | | | | | | BAR | | C'R | BAD | SAL | VIT | | | NVL | NIV | ORT | TOU |
| JAMES WATERSON | 10 MGS | | | | | | | F'O | C'R | BAD | SAL | VIT | PYR | S/S | NVL | NIV | ORT | TOU |
| WILLIAM WILSON | 5 MGS | | | | | | | | C'R | BAD | SAL | VIT | PYR | S/S | NVL | NIV | ORT | TOU |
| WILLIAM YOUNG | 5 MGS | | | | | BUS | | F'O | C'R | • | SAL | VIT | | | | | ORT | TOU |
| **CORPORALS:** | | | | | | | | | | | | | | | | | | |
| ANDREW ASH | 8 MGS | | | COR | | | | F'O | • | BAD | SAL | VIT | PYR | | | | | |
| HENRY BIGGS | 5 MGS | | | | | | | | • | BAD | SAL | VIT | | | NVL | NIV | | |
| JAMES BRITCHARD | 5 MGS | | | | | | BAR | | • | BAD | • | VIT | | | | | | TOU |
| JAMES BUCKLEY | 6 MGS | | | | | BUS | | F'O | C'R | BAD | SAL | VIT | PYR | | NVL | NIV | | |
| JAMES CORNISH | 3 MGS | | | | | | BAR | | • | • | • | VIT | | | | | | |
| EDWARD COSTELLO | 11 MGS | | | | | BUS | | | • | • | SAL | VIT | PYR | | NVL | NIV | ORT | TOU |
| MICHAEL DILLON | 6 MGS | | | | | | | | • | BAD | • | VIT | PYR | S/S | | | ORT | TOU |
| JOHN EDWARDS | 4 MGS | | | | | | | | • | BAD | • | VIT | PYR | | | | | TOU |
| THOMAS EGGARTON | 8 MGS | | | | | BUS | | F'O | C'R | BAD | SAL | VIT | PYR | | | | ORT | TOU |
| SHOULD BE EGGINGTON | | | | | | | | | • | BAD | SAL | VIT | | | | | | |

| | ROL | VIM | COR | TAL | BUS | BAR | F'O | C'R | BAD | SAL | VIT | PYR | S/S | NVL | NIV | ORT | TOU |
|---|---|---|---|---|---|---|---|---|---|---|---|---|---|---|---|---|---|
| THOMAS EVERARD — 2 MGS | | | | | | BAR | | C'R | • | • | • | | | | | | |
| JAMES EWART — 6 MGS | | | | | | | | | BAD | SAL | VIT | PYR | | NVL | NIV | | |
| STEPHEN FRIER — 6 MGS | | | | | | | | | • | SAL | VIT | PYR | S/S | | | ORT | TOU |
| WILLIAM GILLIS — 6 MGS | | VIM | COR | | | | | | | | VIT | PYR | | | | ORT | TOU |
| WILLIAM HAINES — 7 MGS | | | | | | BAR | | • | • | • | VIT | PYR | | NVL | NIV | ORT | TOU |
| WILLIAM HALL — 8 MGS | | | COR | | BUS | | | C'R | BAD | SAL | VIT | PYR | | | | | TOU |
| JOHN HARTLEY — 10 MGS | | | | | | BAR | | C'R | BAD | SAL | VIT | PYR | | NVL | NIV | ORT | TOU |
| JOHN JONES — 9 MGS | | | | | BUS | | F'O | C'R | BAD | SAL | VIT | PYR | S/S | | | | TOU |
| GEORGE LAW — 12 MGS | | | COR | | BUS | | F'O | C'R | BAD | SAL | VIT | PYR | S/S | | NIV | ORT | TOU |
| ALEXANDER MASTERSON — 6 MGS | | | | | BUS | | | C'R | BAD | SAL | • | PYR | | | | | TOU |
| JOHN MONK — 3 MGS | | | COR | | | BAR | | • | • | • | VIT | | | | | | |
| JOHN MURPHY — 12 MGS | | | COR | | BUS | | F'O | C'R | BAD | SAL | VIT | PYR | | NVL | NIV | ORT | TOU |
| ADAM SHAW — 9 MGS | | | | | | BAR | | • | BAD | SAL | VIT | PYR | | NVL | NIV | ORT | TOU |
| WILLIAM SHELTON — 4 MGS | | | | | | | | • | • | • | VIT | PYR | | | | ORT | TOU |
| MICHAEL SMART — 10 MGS | | | COR | | BUS | | F'O | C'R | BAD | SAL | VIT | PYR | | NVL | NIV | | |

| | | ROL | VIM | COR | TAL | BUS | BAR | F'O | C'R | BAD | SAL | VIT | PYR | S/S | NVL | NIV | ORT | TOU |
|---|---|---|---|---|---|---|---|---|---|---|---|---|---|---|---|---|---|
| PETER SMITH | 3 MGS | | | | | | | | • | BAD | • | VIT | PYR | | | | | |
| JAMES TOMLINSON | 8 MGS | | | COR | | | | | • | BAD | SAL | VIT | PYR | S/S | NVL | NIV | ORT | TOU |
| EDWARD TONKINSON | 9 MGS | | | COR | | BUS | | F'O | • | • | • | VIT | PYR | | | | | TOU |
| **BUGLERS:** | | | | | | | | | | | | | | | | | | |
| WILLIAM BASHFORD | 9 MGS | | | | | | BAR | | C'R | BAD | SAL | VIT | | | NVL | NIV | ORT | TOU |
| WILLIAM CARDEN | 11 MGS | | | COR | | BUS | | F'O | C'R | BAD | SAL | VIT | PYR | S/S | | | ORT | TOU |
| RICHARD FARMER | 5 MGS | | | | | BUS | | | C'R | BAD | SAL | VIT | | | | | | TOU |
| WILLIAM GREEN | 4 MGS | | | COR | | | | | C'R | BAD | SAL | VIT | | | | | | |
| THOMAS HORNER | 4 MGS | | | | | | | | • | • | • | • | PYR | | | | ORT | TOU |
| ELIJAH HOTLEY | 9 MGS | | | | | | BAR | | • | • | SAL | • | PYR | S/S | | | ORT | TOU |
| JAMES STEVENS | 11 MGS | | | COR | | BUS | | F'O | C'R | BAD | SAL | VIT | PYR | | NVL | NIV | ORT | TOU |
| MAURICE WILDES | 6 MGS | ROL | VIM | | | | | | • | • | • | VIT | PYR | | | | ORT | TOU |
| **RIFLEMEN:** | | | | | | | | | | | | | | | | | | |
| THOMAS ALEXANDER | 10 MGS | | | COR | | BUS | | F'O | C'R | BAD | SAL | • | PYR | | | NIV | ORT | TOU |
| CHARLES ALLEN | 5 MGS | | | | | BUS | | | C'R | BAD | SAL | • | | | | | | |

| | ROL | VIM | COR | TAL | BUS | BAR | F'O | C'R | BAD | SAL | VIT | PYR | S/S | NVL | NIV | ORT | TOU |
|---|---|---|---|---|---|---|---|---|---|---|---|---|---|---|---|---|---|
| JOHN ALLSOP — 2 MGS | | | | | | | | C'R | BAD | • | • | | s/s | | | | |
| GEORGE ANDERSON — 3 MGS | | | | | | | | C'R | BAD | • | • | PYR | | | | | |
| JOSEPH ARMS — 11 MGS | | VIM | COR | | BUS | | F'O | C'R | BAD | SAL | VIT | PYR | | NVL | | ORT | TOU |
| JAMES ASHWORTH — 7 MGS | | | COR | | BUS | | F'O | C'R | BAD | SAL | VIT | | | | | | |
| WILLIAM AUSTIN — 5 MGS | | | | | | | | • | • | SAL | VIT | PYR | | | | ORT | TOU |
| JOHN BAIL — 4 MGS | | | | | | | | C'R | • | SAL | VIT | | s/s | | | | |
| JOHN BAKER — 5 MGS | | | | | | BAR | | C'R | BAD | • | VIT | PYR | | | | ORT | TOU |
| JOHN BAKER — 8 MGS | | | | | | | F'O | C'R | BAD | SAL | VIT | PYR | | | | ORT | TOU |
| JOHN BALDWIN "LEICESTER, KNITTER." — 4 MGS | | | COR | | | BAR | F'O | • | • | • | VIT | PYR | s/s | | | | |
| JOHN BALDWIN "MIDDLESEX, CARPENTER." — 4 MGS | | | | | | | | • | • | SAL | VIT | | | | | | |
| THOMAS BALLARD — 6 MGS | | | | | | | | • | • | • | VIT | PYR | | NVL | NIV | ORT | TOU |
| WILLIAM BARKER — 1 MGS NOT ENTITLED TO MGS MEDAL | | | | | | | | • | BAD | SAL | • | | | | | | |
| JACOB BARLOW — 5 MGS | | | COR | | | | F'O | C'R | BAD | SAL | VIT | | s/s | | | | TOU |
| GEORGE BARRETT — 7 MGS | | | | | BUS | | F'O | C'R | BAD | SAL | VIT | | s/s | | | | |
| JAMES BATEMAN — 8 MGS | | | | | | | F'O | C'R | BAD | SAL | VIT | PYR | | | | ORT | TOU |

| Name | MGS | ROL | VIM | COR | TAL | BUS | BAR | F'O | C'R | BAD | SAL | VIT | PYR | S/S | NVL | NIV | ORT | TOU |
|---|---|---|---|---|---|---|---|---|---|---|---|---|---|---|---|---|---|---|
| DAVID BEATTIE | 9 MGS | ROL | VIM | | | | | F'O | C'R | BAD | SAL | VIT | PYR | | | | | TOU |
| JOHN BELL | 11 MGS | | VIM | COR | | BUS | | | C'R | BAD | SAL | VIT | PYR | | | | ORT | TOU |
| JOSEPH BELL | 8 MGS | ROL | VIM | | | | | F'O | C'R | BAD | SAL | VIT | PYR | | | | ORT | TOU |
| THOMAS BENDAL | 5 MGS | | | | | | | | • | • | • | VIT | PYR | | NVL | NIV | | TOU |
| HENRY BERRY | 11 MGS | | | COR | | BUS | | | C'R | BAD | SAL | VIT | PYR | | NVL | NIV | | TOU |
| WILLIAM BERRY | 2 MGS | | | | | | | | | • | SAL | VIT | | | | | | |
| WILLIAM BERRY | 11 MGS | | | COR | | BUS | | F'O | C'R | BAD | SAL | VIT | PYR | | NVL | NIV | | TOU |
| JOHN BIDWELL | 8 MGS | | | COR | | BUS | | | C'R | BAD | SAL | VIT | PYR | | | | | TOU |
| THOMAS BILLS | 6 MGS | | | | | | | | • | • | • | VIT | PYR | | NVL | NIV | ORT | TOU |
| JOHN BIVINGS | 6 MGS | | | | | BUS | | | • | BAD | SAL | VIT | PYR | | | | | TOU |
| THOMAS BLOOMFIELD | 3 MGS | | | COR | | | | | C'R | BAD | • | • | | | | | | |
| JOHN BOOL | 6 MGS | | | | | BUS | | | C'R | BAD | SAL | VIT | | | | | | TOU |
| HENRY BOOTH | 11 MGS | | | | | BUS | | F'O | C'R | BAD | SAL | VIT | PYR | | NVL | NIV | ORT | TOU |
| EDWARD BOWEN | 7 MGS | | | COR | | | | F'O | C'R | BAD | SAL | VIT | PYR | | | | | |
| WILLIAM BOYD | 4 MGS | | | COR | | | | | • | • | • | • | | | | | | |

NOT ENTITLED TO MGS MEDAL

| Name | Rank | ROL | VIM | COR | TAL | BUS | BAR | F'O | C'R | BAD | SAL | VIT | PYR | S/S | NVL | NIV | ORT | TOU |
|---|---|---|---|---|---|---|---|---|---|---|---|---|---|---|---|---|---|---|
| RICHARD BROOM | 4 MGS | | | COR | | | | | C'R | BAD | SAL | • | | | | | | |
| WILLIAM BROWN | 5 MGS | | | | | | | | C'R | BAD | SAL | • | PYR | | | | ORT | TOU |
| JAMES BRYCE | 9 MGS | | VIM | COR | | | | F'O | C'R | BAD | SAL | VIT | PYR | | NVL | | | |
| JAMES BUCKLER | 6 MGS | | VIM | COR | | | | | C'R | BAD | SAL | VIT | | s/s | | | | |
| WILLIAM BUCKLEY | 7 MGS | | VIM | COR | | BUS | | F'O | C'R | BAD | SAL | VIT | | | | | | |
| JAMES BULCOCK | 6 MGS | | | | | | | | • | • | SAL | VIT | PYR | | NVL | NIV | | TOU |
| PHILIP BULGER | 4 MGS | | | | | | BAR | | • | BAD | SAL | VIT | | | | | | |
| THOMAS BUNTON | 3 MGS | | | | | BUS | | F'O | C'R | BAD | SAL | • | | | | | | |
| DAVID BURNET | 6 MGS | | | COR | | | | F'O | C'R | BAD | • | • | PYR | | | | | |
| JOHN BURNS | 6 MGS | | | | | BUS | | | • | BAD | SAL | VIT | PYR | | | | | TOU |
| NOT ON A. MULLEN'S ROLL | | | | | | | | | | | | | | | | | | |
| WILLIAM BURNS | 7 MGS | | | | | BUS | | F'O | C'R | BAD | SAL | VIT | PYR | | | | | TOU |
| JOHN BURR | 8 MGS | | | COR | | BUS | | | • | BAD | SAL | VIT | PYR | | | | | TOU |
| JOHN BURROWS | 8 MGS | | | COR | | BUS | | | C'R | BAD | SAL | • | | | NVL | NIV | | |
| WILLIAM BURROWS | 8 MGS | | | | | | BAR | | C'R | BAD | SAL | VIT | PYR | | | | ORT | TOU |
| JAMES BYFORD | 5 MGS | | VIM | COR | | | BAR | | C'R | BAD | • | • | | | | | | |

| Name | | ROL | VIM | COR | TAL | BUS | BAR | F'O | C'R | BAD | SAL | VIT | PYR | S/S | NVL | NIV | ORT | TOU |
|---|---|---|---|---|---|---|---|---|---|---|---|---|---|---|---|---|---|---|
| JOHN CAIN | 5 MGS | | | | | | | | • | • | SAL | VIT | PYR | | | | ORT | TOU |
| JAMES CAIRNS | 12 MGS | | VIM | COR | | | | F'O | C'R | BAD | SAL | VIT | PYR | | NVL | NIV | ORT | TOU |
| NEIL CAMERON | 8 MGS | | VIM | COR | | | | | C'R | BAD | SAL | VIT | PYR | | NVL | NIV | ORT | TOU |
| DANIEL CAMPBELL | 2 MGS | | | | | | | | • | • | • | VIT | | | | | | TOU |
| THOMAS CANNING | 6 MGS | | | COR | | BUS | | | C'R | BAD | SAL | • | PYR | | | | | |
| ZACHARIAH CARDY | 8 MGS | | | | TAL | | | | C'R | BAD | SAL | • | | | | | ORT | TOU |
| THOMAS CARTER | 4 MGS | | | | | | | | C'R | BAD | • | VIT | PYR | | | | | |
| WILLIAM CARTER | 6 MGS | | | | | BUS | | | C'R | BAD | • | • | PYR | | | | | |
| SAMSON CARTWRIGHT | 3 MGS | | | | | | BAR | | C'R | • | • | VIT | | | | | | |
| PATRICK CASEY | 3 MGS | | | COR | | | | | • | BAD | SAL | • | | | | | | |
| JOHN CASTLES | 8 MGS | | | | | BUS | | | C'R | BAD | SAL | VIT | PYR | | | | ORT | TOU |
| JOSEPH CAWTHORN | 5 MGS | | | | | | | | C'R | BAD | SAL | • | PYR | | NVL | NIV | ORT | |
| THOMAS CHAPMAN | 5 MGS | | | | | | | | • | • | • | VIT | PYR | | | | | |
| ROBERT CLAXTON | 7 MGS | | | COR | | BUS | | | • | BAD | SAL | VIT | PYR | | NVL | | ORT | TOU |
| EDWARD CLEGG | 7 MGS | | | | | | | | • | • | SAL | VIT | PYR | | NVL | NIV | ORT | TOU |

247

| Name | MGS | ROL | VIM | COR | TAL | BUS | BAR | F'O | C'R | BAD | SAL | VIT | PYR | S/S | NVL | NIV | ORT | TOU |
|---|---|---|---|---|---|---|---|---|---|---|---|---|---|---|---|---|---|---|
| ISAAC COATS | 2 MGS | | | | | | | | C'R | BAD | • | • | | | | | | |
| JAMES COLEMAN | 12 MGS | | VIM | COR | | | | F'O | C'R | BAD | • | • | PYR | | NVL | | ORT | TOU |
| THOMAS COLESTON | 9 MGS | | | | | BUS | | F'O | C'R | BAD | SAL | VIT | PYR | | NVL | | | TOU |
| EDWARD COLLINGHAM | 5 MGS | | | | | | | | C'R | BAD | SAL | VIT | PYR | | NVL | NIV | ORT | TOU |
| GEORGE COMAN | 10 MGS | | | | | | BAR | | • | • | • | VIT | PYR | | NVL | NIV | ORT | TOU |
| ANDREW CONNELLY | 5 MGS | | | | | | BAR | | C'R | • | • | VIT | | | | | ORT | TOU |
| OWEN CONNELLY | 12 MGS | | | COR | | BUS | | F'O | C'R | BAD | SAL | VIT | PYR | | NVL | NIV | ORT | TOU |
| THOMAS CONNELLY | 2 MGS | | | COR | | | BAR | | C'R | BAD | SAL | VIT | | | | | | |
| JAMES CONNOR (NOT ENTITLED TO MGS MEDAL) | 3 MGS | | | | | | | | • | • | SAL | • | | | | | | |
| PATRICK CONNOR | 7 MGS | | | | | BUS | | | • | • | • | VIT | PYR | | NVL | NIV | ORT | TOU |
| JOHN CONWAY | 7 MGS | | | COR | | | | F'O | C'R | BAD | SAL | VIT | | | | | | TOU |
| JAMES COOKE | 13 MGS | | VIM | COR | | BUS | | F'O | C'R | BAD | SAL | VIT | PYR | | NVL | NIV | ORT | TOU |
| THOMAS COOPER | 5 MGS | | | | | | | | C'R | BAD | SAL | • | PYR | | | | | TOU |
| THOMAS COOPER | 9 MGS | | | | | BUS | | F'O | C'R | • | • | VIT | | s/s | NVL | NIV | ORT | TOU |
| EDWARD COPE | 7 MGS | | | COR | | BUS | BAR | | • | • | • | VIT | PYR | | | | ORT | TOU |

| NAME | | ROL | VIM | COR | TAL | BUS | BAR | F'O | C'R | BAD | SAL | VIT | PYR | S/S | NVL | NIV | ORT | TOU |
|---|---|---|---|---|---|---|---|---|---|---|---|---|---|---|---|---|---|---|
| JOHN CORKER | 4 MGS | | | | | | | | • | • | • | VIT | PYR | | | | ORT | TOU |
| WILLIAM COTTON | 3 MGS | | | | | | BAR | | C'R | BAD | • | VIT | | | | | | |
| JAMES CRAWLEY | 3 MGS | | | | | | | | C'R | BAD | | • | | s/s | | | | |
| JAMES CROOKS | 6 MGS | | VIM | | | | BAR | | • | | SAL | VIT | PYR | | | | | TOU |
| EDMUND CROSSLEY | 9 MGS | | | | | | BAR | | C'R | BAD | SAL | VIT | PYR | | NVL | NIV | ORT | TOU |
| GEORGE CULLUMBINE | 7 MGS | | | | | | | | C'R | BAD | SAL | VIT | PYR | | NVL | NIV | ORT | TOU |
| WILLIAM CURRY | 2 MGS | | | | | | | | • | • | SAL | VIT | PYR | | | | | |
| JAMES CURTIS | 5 MGS | | | | | | | | • | • | • | VIT | PYR | s/s | | NIV | ORT | TOU |
| THOMAS DALY | 3 MGS | | | COR | | BUS | | | • | BAD | • | VIT | | | | | | |
| JOHN DAVIES | 7 MGS | | | | | | | | C'R | • | SAL | VIT | PYR | s/s | | | ORT | TOU |
| JOHN DAVIS | 2 MGS | | | | | | | | C'R | BAD | SAL | VIT | | | | | | |
| GEORGE DAWSON | 2 MGS | | | | | | BAR | | C'R | BAD | • | VIT | | | | | | |
| ROBERT DEACON | 5 MGS | | | | | | | | C'R | BAD | SAL | VIT | PYR | | | | | TOU |
| WILLIAM DEACON | 8 MGS | | | | | | | | C'R | BAD | • | VIT | PYR | | NVL | NIV | ORT | TOU |
| THOMAS DELAROUX | 4 MGS | | | | | | | | C'R | BAD | SAL | VIT | | | | | | TOU |

| NAME | Bn | ROL | VIM | COR | TAL | BUS | BAR | F'O | C'R | BAD | SAL | VIT | PYR | S/S | NVL | NIV | ORT | TOU |
|---|---|---|---|---|---|---|---|---|---|---|---|---|---|---|---|---|---|---|
| GEORGE DEMPSTER | 9 MGS | | VIM | COR | | BUS | | F'O | C'R | BAD | SAL | VIT | PYR | | | | | |
| THOMAS DENBY | 3 MGS | | | | | | | | C'R | BAD | SAL | VIT | | | | | | |
| JOHN DENT | 9 MGS | | | | | BUS | | F'O | • | • | SAL | VIT | PYR | | | | ORT | TOU |
| THOMAS DICK | 5 MGS | | | | | | | | • | • | • | VIT | | | NVL | NIV | ORT | TOU |
| JOHN DIXSON | 11 MGS | | | | | BUS | | F'O | C'R | BAD | SAL | VIT | PYR | | NVL | NIV | ORT | TOU |
| JOHN DOBSON | 1 MGS | | | | | | | | • | BAD | • | • | | | | | | |
| JOSEPH DODD | 7 MGS | | | | | | | F'O | C'R | BAD | • | • | PYR | | NVL | | | TOU |
| THOMAS DOUGLAS | 5 MGS | | | | | BUS | | | C'R | BAD | SAL | VIT | PYR | | | | ORT | TOU |
| PATRICK DOWNEY | 3 MGS | | | | | BUS | | | C'R | BAD | SAL | VIT | | | | | | |
| JAMES DOWNS | 2 MGS | | | | | | | | • | BAD | SAL | VIT | | | | | | |
| JOHN DOWNS | 6 MGS | | | | | | | | C'R | BAD | SAL | VIT | PYR | | NVL | NIV | ORT | TOU |
| JOHN DUNNAGE | 4 MGS | | | | | | | | • | • | • | VIT | | | | | | TOU |
| WILLIAM DUTY | 3 MGS | | | | | | | | • | • | • | VIT | PYR | | | | ORT | TOU |
| JOHN DYSON | 3 MGS | | | | | | | | C'R | BAD | SAL | VIT | | | | | | |
| THOMAS EASTWOOD | 6 MGS | | | COR | | BUS | | F'O | C'R | BAD | SAL | VIT | | | | | | |

| Name | | ROL | VIM | COR | TAL | BUS | BAR | F'O | C'R | BAD | SAL | VIT | PYR | S/S | NVL | NIV | ORT | TOU |
|---|---|---|---|---|---|---|---|---|---|---|---|---|---|---|---|---|---|---|
| WILLIAM EBURN | 3 MGS | | | | | | | | • | • | • | VIT | PYR | | NVL | | | |
| JOHN EDWARDS | 5 MGS | | | | | | | | • | • | SAL | VIT | PYR | | | | ORT | TOU |
| THOMAS EDWARDS | 6 MGS | | | | | | | | C'R | BAD | • | VIT | | | | | ORT | TOU |
| WILLIAM EDWARDS | 8 MGS | | | | | | BAR | | • | • | • | VIT | PYR | S/S | NVL | NIV | ORT | TOU |
| JOHN EDWARDSTAFF | 8 MGS | | | | | | BAR | | C'R | • | SAL | VIT | PYR | S/S | | | ORT | TOU |
| HENRY ELDRIDGE | 6 MGS | | | COR | | | BAR | | C'R | BAD | SAL | VIT | | | | | | TOU |
| JOHN EVANS | 5 MGS | | | | | | BAR | | • | BAD | SAL | VIT | PYR | | | | ORT | TOU |
| ROBERT EVANS | 4 MGS | | | | | | | | • | • | • | VIT | PYR | | | | ORT | TOU |
| ANTHONY EVERITT | 3 MGS | | | | | | BAR | | • | | SAL | • | | | | | | TOU |
| MICHAEL FAGAN | 3 MGS | | VIM | | | | | | • | • | • | • | PYR | | | | | |
| BARTHOLOMEW FAIRHURST | 10 MGS | | | COR | | BUS | | | C'R | BAD | SAL | VIT | PYR | | NVL | NIV | ORT | |
| JOHN FARLIN | 5 MGS | | | COR | | | | | C'R | BAD | • | VIT | PYR | | | | ORT | TOU |
| EDWARD FARMER | 5 MGS | | VIM | | | | | | C'R | BAD | SAL | VIT | | | | | | |
| JAMES FARNFIELD | 6 MGS | | | | | | | | • | BAD | SAL | • | PYR | | NVL | | ORT | TOU |
| HUGH FARRELL | 1 MGS | | | | | | | | • | BAD | • | • | | | | | | |

| Name | MGS | ROL | VIM | COR | TAL | BUS | BAR | F'O | C'R | BAD | SAL | VIT | PYR | S/S | NVL | NIV | ORT | TOU |
|---|---|---|---|---|---|---|---|---|---|---|---|---|---|---|---|---|---|---|
| JOSHUA FARRER | 3 MGS | | | | | | BAR | | C'R | BAD | • | • | | | | | | |
| JAMES FINCH | 4 MGS | | | | | | | | • | • | • | VIT | PYR | | | | ORT | TOU |
| PETER FISHER | 4 MGS | | | | | BUS | | F'O | C'R | • | • | VIT | | | | | | |
| JAMES FITZGERALD | 5 MGS | | | COR | | BUS | | F'O | C'R | BAD | • | • | | | | | | |
| EDWARD FITZSIMMONS | 7 MGS | | | | | | | | • | BAD | SAL | VIT | | | NVL | NIV | ORT | TOU |
| DAVID FORTUNE | 8 MGS | | | | | BUS | | F'O | C'R | BAD | SAL | VIT | | | | | ORT | TOU |
| DAVID FOULKES | 2 MGS | | | | | | | F'O | • | BAD | • | • | | | | | | |
| JAMES FRASER | 7 MGS | | VIM | COR | | | | | • | • | SAL | VIT | PYR | | | | ORT | TOU |
| WILLIAM FRASER | 6 MGS | | | | | | | | • | • | • | VIT | PYR | | NVL | NIV | ORT | TOU |
| JOSEPH FULLER | 6 MGS | | VIM | COR | | BUS | | F'O | • | • | • | VIT | PYR | | | | | |
| JAMES FUTTER | 8 MGS | | | | | | | F'O | C'R | BAD | SAL | VIT | PYR | | | | ORT | TOU |
| JOHN GALLAGHER | 2 MGS | | | COR | | | | | • | • | SAL | • | | | | | | |
| THOMAS GARDINER | 6 MGS | | | | | | BAR | | • | • | • | VIT | PYR | | NVL | | ORT | TOU |
| DANIEL GARDNER | 6 MGS | | | | | | | | • | • | SAL | VIT | PYR | S/S | | | ORT | TOU |
| JOHN GARDNER | 9 MGS | | | COR | | | | | C'R | BAD | SAL | VIT | PYR | S/S | | | ORT | TOU |

| NAME | MGS | ROL | VIM | COR | TAL | BUS | BAR | F'O | C'R | BAD | SAL | VIT | PYR | S/S | NVL | NIV | ORT | TOU |
|---|---|---|---|---|---|---|---|---|---|---|---|---|---|---|---|---|---|---|
| EDWARD GASKELL | 5 MGS | | | | | | | | • | • | SAL | VIT | PYR | | | | ORT | TOU |
| JOHN GASTLE | 1 MGS | | | | | | | | • | • | SAL | VIT | | | | | | |
| FRANCIS GIBBS | 7 MGS | | | | | | | | C'R | BAD | • | VIT | PYR | | | | ORT | TOU |
| ALEXANDER GIBSON | 7 MGS | | | | | | | F'O | C'R | BAD | SAL | VIT | PYR | | | | | TOU |
| WILLIAM GIDDINS | 5 MGS | | | | | | | | C'R | BAD | SAL | VIT | | | | | | TOU |
| THOMAS GILBERT | 9 MGS | | | | | | | F'O | C'R | BAD | • | VIT | | | NVL | NIV | | TOU |
| WILLIAM GILBEY | 1 MGS | | | | | | | | • | • | SAL | VIT | | | | | | |
| ROBERT GILCHRIST | 9 MGS | | VIM | COR | | BUS | | F'O | C'R | BAD | SAL | • | | | | | | TOU |
| JOHN GILES | 1 MGS | | | | | | | | • | BAD | • | • | | | | | | |
| WILLIAM GILMORE | 9 MGS | | | | | | BAR | | C'R | BAD | SAL | VIT | PYR | | NVL | | ORT | TOU |
| JOSIAH GODDARD | 8 MGS | | | COR | | BUS | | | C'R | BAD | SAL | VIT | PYR | | | | | TOU |
| DAVID GOODCHILD | 1 MGS | | | | | | | | • | BAD | • | • | | | | | | |
| ROBERT GOULRING | 5 MGS | | | | | | | | • | • | • | VIT | PYR | S/S | | | ORT | TOU |
| JOHN GRANT | 1 MGS | | | | | | | | • | BAD | • | • | | | | | | |
| SAMUEL GREEN | 10 MGS | | | | | | | F'O | C'R | BAD | SAL | VIT | PYR | | NVL | NIV | ORT | TOU |

| Name | | ROL | VIM | COR | TAL | BUS | BAR | F'O | C'R | BAD | SAL | VIT | PYR | S/S | NVL | NIV | ORT | TOU |
|---|---|---|---|---|---|---|---|---|---|---|---|---|---|---|---|---|---|---|
| WILLIAM GRIERSON | 6 MGS | | | | | | | | • | • | • | VIT | PYR | | NVL | NIV | ORT | TOU |
| JOHN GRIFFITHS | 6 MGS | | | | | | BAR | | • | BAD | SAL | VIT | PYR | | | | | TOU |
| THOMAS GRIFFITHS | 2 MGS | | | | | | | | C'R | BAD | SAL | VIT | | s/s | | | | |
| THOMAS GRIGSON | 3 MGS | | | | | | | | • | • | • | VIT | | | | | ORT | TOU |
| CHRISTOPHER GRIMES | 8 MGS | | VIM | | | BUS | | F'O | C'R | BAD | SAL | • | PYR | | | | | TOU |
| JOSEPH HACKETT | 3 MGS | | | | | | | | • | • | SAL | VIT | PYR | | | | | |
| RICHARD HAINES | 5 MGS | | | | | | BAR | | • | • | SAL | VIT | PYR | | | | ORT | TOU |
| JAMES HALL RECEIVED MART + GUAD 25TH REGT | 4 MGS | | | | | | | | C'R | BAD | SAL | • | PYR | | | | | |
| WILLIAM HANLEY | 5 MGS | | | | | | BAR | | C'R | BAD | SAL | VIT | | | | | | |
| THOMAS HARDING | 11 MGS | | | COR | | BUS | | F'O | C'R | BAD | SAL | VIT | PYR | | NVL | NIV | ORT | TOU |
| ROBERT HARLING | 9 MGS | | | COR | | | | | C'R | BAD | SAL | VIT | | | NVL | NIV | ORT | TOU |
| THOMAS HARRIS | 1 MGS | | | | | | | | • | • | • | VIT | | | | | | |
| ISRAEL HARVEY | 8 MGS | | VIM | COR | | | | F'O | C'R | BAD | SAL | VIT | PYR | | | | | |
| JOHN HATCHER | 4 MGS | | | | | | | | • | • | • | VIT | PYR | s/s | | | | TOU |
| WILLIAM HEATHCOTE | 5 MGS | | | | | | BAR | | C'R | BAD | SAL | VIT | | | | | | |

254

| | MGS | ROL | VIM | COR | TAL | BUS | BAR | F'O | C'R | BAD | SAL | VIT | PYR | S/S | NVL | NIV | ORT | TOU |
|---|---|---|---|---|---|---|---|---|---|---|---|---|---|---|---|---|---|---|
| JOSIAH HEELES | 6 MGS | | | | | | | | C'R | BAD | SAL | VIT | PYR | | | | | TOU |
| THOMAS HILL | 2 MGS | | | | | | | | • | • | • | VIT | | | | | ORT | |
| JAMES HOLDEN | 8 MGS | | | | | | | F'O | C'R | BAD | SAL | VIT | PYR | | NVL | NIV | | |
| SAMUEL HOLLAND | 1 MGS | | | | | | | | | • | SAL | VIT | | | | | | |
| THOMAS HOLMES | 10 MGS | | | COR | | BUS | | F'O | C'R | BAD | SAL | VIT | PYR | | | | ORT | TOU |
| THOMAS HOOPER | 5 MGS | | | | | | | | C'R | BAD | SAL | VIT | PYR | | | | ORT | TOU |
| PETER HORROX | 3 MGS | | | | | | | | | • | • | VIT | PYR | | | | | TOU |
| DAVID HUGHES | 6 MGS | | VIM | COR | | | BAR | | | • | • | • | VIT | PYR | | | | | TOU |
| JAMES HURD | 5 MGS | | | | | | | | • | • | SAL | VIT | PYR | | | | ORT | TOU |
| PATRICK HUSSEY | 10 MGS | | VIM | COR | | BUS | | F'O | C'R | BAD | SAL | VIT | PYR | | | | | TOU |
| ROBERT HYSLOP | 3 MGS | | | | | | | | C'R | BAD | SAL | VIT | | | | | | |
| CHRISTOPHER INGHAM | 9 MGS | | | | | BUS | | F'O | C'R | BAD | SAL | VIT | PYR | | | | ORT | TOU |
| JOHN IRELAND | 5 MGS | | | | | | | | C'R | BAD | SAL | VIT | PYR | | | | | TOU |
| ARTHUR JOHN | 6 MGS | | | | | | | | C'R | BAD | SAL | VIT | PYR | | | | | TOU |
| ROBERT JOHNSON | 5 MGS | | | | | | | | • | • | SAL | VIT | PYR | | | NIV | ORT | TOU |

| Name | MGS | ROL | VIM | COR | TAL | BUS | BAR | F'O | C'R | BAD | SAL | VIT | PYR | S/S | NVL | NIV | ORT | TOU |
|---|---|---|---|---|---|---|---|---|---|---|---|---|---|---|---|---|---|---|
| THOMAS JOHNSON | 4 MGS | | | | | | | | • | • | SAL | VIT | PYR | | | | | TOU |
| CHARLES JONES | 7 MGS | | VIM | COR | | | | | C'R | BAD | • | VIT | PYR | | | | | TOU |
| THOMAS JONES | 3 MGS | | | COR | | | | | • | • | • | • | | | | | ORT | TOU |
| WILLIAM JONES | 2 MGS | | | | | | | | C'R | • | • | VIT | | | | | | |
| MICHAEL JOYCE | 9 MGS | | | COR | | BUS | | F'O | C'R | BAD | SAL | VIT | PYR | | | | | TOU |
| SAMUEL KEEN | 7 MGS | | | COR | | | | F'O | C'R | BAD | • | VIT | | | | | ORT | TOU |
| WILLIAM KELLAUGHER | 11 MGS | | | COR | TAL | BUS | | F'O | C'R | BAD | SAL | VIT | PYR | S/S | | | | TOU |
| JOHN KELLY | 9 MGS | | | | | | | F'O | C'R | • | SAL | VIT | PYR | | NVL | NIV | ORT | TOU |
| THOMAS KELLY | 10 MGS | ROL | VIM | COR | | | | F'O | C'R | BAD | SAL | VIT | PYR | | | | | TOU |
| RECEIVED EGYPT OR MAIDA 58TH REGT | | | | | | | | | | | | | | | | | | |
| JOSEPH KEMP | 6 MGS | | | | | | | | | • | SAL | VIT | | | NVL | NIV | ORT | TOU |
| ALEXANDER KENNEDY | 10 MGS | | | | TAL | BUS | | F'O | C'R | BAD | SAL | VIT | | S/S | | | | TOU |
| RECEIVED EGYPT IN 92ND REGT | | | | | | | | | | | | | | | | | | |
| EDWARD KETCHLOVE | 2 MGS | | | | | | | | C'R | BAD | • | • | | | | | | |
| JOHN KIDD | 2 MGS | | | | | | | | • | • | • | VIT | | | | | | |
| NOT ENTITLED TO MGS MEDAL | | | | | | | | | | | | | | | | | | |
| THOMAS KILAWAY | 2 MGS | | | | | | BAR | | C'R | BAD | • | • | | | | | | |
| THOMAS KINSLOW | 3 MGS | | | COR | | | | | C'R | • | | • | | | | | | |

256

| Name | | ROL | VIM | COR | TAL | BUS | BAR | F'O | C'R | BAD | SAL | VIT | PYR | S/S | NVL | NIV | ORT | TOU |
|---|---|---|---|---|---|---|---|---|---|---|---|---|---|---|---|---|---|---|
| THOMAS KNIGHT | 6 MGS | | | | | | | | C'R | BAD | SAL | VIT | | | | | ORT | TOU |
| ROBERT LAMBERT | 6 MGS | | | | | | | | • | • | • | VIT | PYR | | NVL | NIV | ORT | TOU |
| JOHN LAMONT | 13 MGS | | | COR | | BUS | | F'O | C'R | BAD | SAL | VIT | PYR | S/S | NVL | NIV | ORT | TOU |
| RICHARD LANCASTER | 3 MGS | | | | | | | F'O | C'R | | | • | | | | | | |
| ROBERT LANE | 7 MGS | | | | | | | F'O | C'R | BAD | SAL | VIT | PYR | | | | | TOU |
| THOMAS LAURISON | 9 MGS | | VIM | | | BUS | | F'O | C'R | BAD | SAL | VIT | PYR | | | | | TOU |
| DAVID LAW | 11 MGS | | VIM | COR | | | | | C'R | BAD | SAL | VIT | PYR | | NVL | NIV | ORT | TOU |
| THOMAS LAWMAN | 4 MGS | | | | | | BAR | | • | • | • | VIT | | | | | ORT | TOU |
| THOMAS LAWRENCE | 2 MGS | | | | | | | | C'R | BAD | • | • | | | | | | |
| JERVIS LAYLAND | 2 MGS | | | | | | | | • | • | SAL | VIT | | | | | | |
| JAMES LENNON | 6 MGS | | | | | | | | C'R | BAD | SAL | VIT | | | | | ORT | TOU |
| DANIEL LEWEN | 7 MGS | | | | | | | | • | • | SAL | VIT | PYR | S/S | NVL | | ORT | TOU |
| LEWIS LEWIS | 5 MGS | | | | | | | | • | • | • | VIT | PYR | | NVL | NIV | | TOU |
| RODERICK LEWIS | 5 MGS | | | | | | | | • | • | • | VIT | | | NVL | NIV | ORT | TOU |
| PETER LISBIE | 5 MGS | | | | | | BAR | | • | • | • | VIT | PYR | | | | ORT | TOU |

| Name | | ROL | VIM | COR | TAL | BUS | BAR | F'O | C'R | BAD | SAL | VIT | PYR | S/S | NVL | NIV | ORT | TOU |
|---|---|---|---|---|---|---|---|---|---|---|---|---|---|---|---|---|---|---|
| SAMUEL LONG | 4 MGS | | | COR | | | | | C'R | BAD | SAL | • | | | | | | |
| JAMES LORD | 11 MGS | | | | | | BAR | F'O | C'R | BAD | SAL | • | | s/s | NVL | NIV | ORT | TOU |
| SAMUEL LOVATT | 9 MGS | | | COR | | BUS | | | C'R | BAD | SAL | VIT | PYR | | | | ORT | TOU |
| MICHAEL LYONS | 9 MGS | | | | | | | | C'R | BAD | SAL | VIT | PYR | | NVL | NIV | ORT | TOU |
| JOHN MAHER | 5 MGS | | VIM | | | BUS | | F'O | C'R | BAD | SAL | VIT | | | | | | |
| WILLIAM MAHONEY | 10 MGS | | | | | BUS | | | C'R | BAD | • | • | PYR | | NVL | NIV | ORT | TOU |
| JOSEPH MARRIOTT | 7 MGS | | | | | | BAR | | C'R | • | • | VIT | PYR | | | | ORT | TOU |
| PETER MARSH | 7 MGS | | | | | | | | C'R | • | SAL | VIT | PYR | | | NIV | | TOU |
| JOHN MARTIN | 8 MGS | | | COR | | BUS | | F'O | C'R | BAD | SAL | VIT | PYR | | | | | |
| JAMES MASON | 3 MGS | | VIM | | | | BAR | | • | • | • | VIT | | | | | | |
| ISAAC MAYNES | 8 MGS | | | | | | BAR | | C'R | BAD | SAL | VIT | | | NVL | NIV | ORT | TOU |
| GEORGE MCCANN | 7 MGS | | | | | | | F'O | C'R | • | SAL | VIT | PYR | | | | ORT | TOU |
| ROBERT MCKAY | 5 MGS | | | | | | BAR | | C'R | BAD | SAL | • | PYR | | | | | |
| RODERICK MCKAY | 6 MGS | | | | | | | | • | • | • | VIT | PYR | | NVL | NIV | ORT | TOU |
| WILLIAM MCKAY | 5 MGS | | | | | | | | C'R | BAD | SAL | VIT | | | | | | TOU |

| | | ROL | VIM | COR | TAL | BUS | BAR | F'O | C'R | BAD | SAL | VIT | PYR | S/S | NVL | NIV | ORT | TOU |
|---|---|---|---|---|---|---|---|---|---|---|---|---|---|---|---|---|---|---|
| JOHN MCKELLY | 11 MGS | | | | | BUS | | F'O | C'R | BAD | SAL | VIT | PYR | | NVL | NIV | ORT | TOU |
| JOHN MCKITCHIE | 2 MGS | ROL | VIM | | | | | | • | • | • | • | | | | | | |
| HUGH MCLEOD | 6 MGS | | | COR | | | | | C'R | BAD | SAL | VIT | | | | | | TOU |
| ALEXANDER MCRAE | 8 MGS | | VIM | COR | | BUS | | F'O | C'R | BAD | SAL | VIT | | | | | | |
| JOHN MCUBBY | 11 MGS | | | | | BUS | | F'O | C'R | BAD | SAL | VIT | PYR | | NVL | NIV | ORT | TOU |
| ALEXANDER MEARS | 3 MGS | | | | | | | | • | • | • | • | PYR | | | | ORT | TOU |
| GEORGE MICHELSON | 6 MGS | | | | | | BAR | | C'R | BAD | • | VIT | PYR | | | | ORT | |
| JAMES MILES | 5 MGS | | | | | | | | • | BAD | • | VIT | PYR | | | | ORT | TOU |
| JOHN MILLER | 6 MGS | | | | | | | | • | BAD | • | VIT | | | NVL | NIV | ORT | TOU |
| DANIEL MILTON | 6 MGS | | | | | | | | • | BAD | SAL | VIT | PYR | | | | ORT | TOU |
| HUGH MONKS | 7 MGS | | | | | | BAR | | C'R | • | SAL | VIT | PYR | | | | ORT | TOU |
| JOHN MONTGOMERY | 3 MGS | | | | | | | | C'R | BAD | • | VIT | | | | | | |
| ALEXANDER MOORE | 1 MGS | | | | | | | | C'R | BAD | • | • | | | | | | |
| THOMAS MOORE | 6 MGS | | VIM | | | | BAR | | C'R | • | SAL | • | | | | | | TOU |
| ANTHONY MULLINS | 3 MGS | | | COR | | | | | C'R | • | • | VIT | | | | | | |

| | MGS | ROL | VIM | COR | TAL | BUS | BAR | F'O | C'R | BAD | SAL | VIT | PYR | S/S | NVL | NIV | ORT | TOU |
|---|---|---|---|---|---|---|---|---|---|---|---|---|---|---|---|---|---|---|
| JOHN MULLINS | 6 MGS | | | | | | | | • | BAD | SAL | VIT | | | NVL | NIV | | TOU |
| FRANCIS MUNNS | 2 MGS | | | | | | | | • | BAD | SAL | VIT | | | | | | |
| CHARLES MURPHY | 6 MGS | | VIM | COR | | | | | • | • | • | VIT | PYR | | | | ORT | TOU |
| RECEIVED VIM + COR IN 71ST REGT | | | | | | | | • | | | | VIT | | | | | | |
| JAMES NASH | 2 MGS | | | | | | BAR | | C'R | | • | • | | | | | | |
| HENRY NEVIN | I MGS | | | | | | BAR | | • | | • | • | | | | | | |
| WILLIAM NEWSHAM | 6 MGS | | | | | | BAR | | • | BAD | SAL | VIT | | | | NIV | | TOU |
| JAMES NICE | 3 MGS | | | | | | BAR | | • | • | • | VIT | | | | | | TOU |
| WILLIAM NIVEN | 9 MGS | | | COR | | BUS | | F'O | C'R | BAD | SAL | VIT | PYR | | | | | TOU |
| MARTIN OATES | 2 MGS | | | | | | | | C'R | BAD | • | • | | | | | | |
| JAMES O'NEIL | 7 MGS | | | COR | | | | | C'R | BAD | SAL | VIT | PYR | | | | | TOU |
| CHARLES ORMOND | II MGS | | | | | BUS | | F'O | C'R | BAD | SAL | VIT | PYR | S/S | | NIV | ORT | TOU |
| THOMAS OSBORNE | 4 MGS | ROL | VIM | COR | | | | | • | • | • | VIT | | | | | | |
| BRYAN PADDEN | 6 MGS | | | | | | | | • | • | • | VIT | PYR | | NVL | NIV | ORT | TOU |
| JOHN PALMER | 12 MGS | | VIM | COR | | BUS | | F'O | • | BAD | SAL | VIT | PYR | | NVL | NIV | ORT | TOU |
| JONATHAN PALMER | 5 MGS | | | | | | | | • | BAD | SAL | VIT | PYR | | | | | TOU |

| Name | MGS | ROL | VIM | COR | TAL | BUS | BAR | F'O | C'R | BAD | SAL | VIT | PYR | S/S | NVL | NIV | ORT | TOU |
|---|---|---|---|---|---|---|---|---|---|---|---|---|---|---|---|---|---|---|
| WILLIAM PARKER | 2 MGS | | | | | | | | • | BAD | | VIT | | | | | | |
| WILLIAM PARKINSON | 5 MGS | | | COR | | BUS | | F'O | C'R | BAD | SAL | VIT | | | | | | |
| JOHN PARRY | 5 MGS | | | | | | | | C'R | BAD | | VIT | | | NVL | NIV | ORT | TOU |
| JOHN PEACOCK | 5 MGS | | | | | | BAR | | • | • | | VIT | PYR | | | | ORT | TOU |
| OLIVER PEACOCK | 9 MGS | | | COR | | BUS | | F'O | C'R | BAD | • | VIT | PYR | | NVL | | | TOU |
| SAMUEL PETERS | 11 MGS | | | | | BUS | | F'O | C'R | BAD | SAL | VIT | PYR | | NVL | NIV | ORT | TOU |
| JAMES PETTY | 12 MGS | | | COR | | BUS | | F'O | C'R | BAD | SAL | VIT | PYR | | NVL | NIV | ORT | TOU |
| JOSEPH PIERS | 8 MGS | ROL | VIM | | | | BAR | | C'R | • | SAL | VIT | | | | | ORT | TOU |
| DANIEL POINTER | 3 MGS | | | | | | | | • | • | • | VIT | PYR | | | | | TOU |
| WILLIAM POOLE | 6 MGS | | | | | | | | C'R | BAD | SAL | VIT | PYR | | NVL | | | TOU |
| PETER POTTER | 5 MGS | | | | | | | | C'R | BAD | SAL | VIT | | | NVL | NIV | ORT | TOU |
| DAVID POWELL | 1 MGS | | | | | | | | | • | | | | | | | | |
| DAVID POWELL | 4 MGS | | | | | | BAR | | C'R | • | SAL | VIT | PYR | | | | ORT | |
| WILLIAM PRESTAGE | 5 MGS | | | COR | | | BAR | | • | • | SAL | VIT | | | | | | |
| PETER PRICE | 10 MGS | ROL | VIM | COR | | | | | C'R | BAD | SAL | VIT | | | NVL | NIV | ORT | TOU |

"DAVID POWELL I MGS (BAD) AND DAVID POWELL 4 MGS ARE THE SAME MAN, SEE NOTES."

| | | ROL | VIM | COR | TAL | BUS | BAR | F'O | C'R | BAD | SAL | VIT | PYR | S/S | NVL | NIV | ORT | TOU |
|---|---|---|---|---|---|---|---|---|---|---|---|---|---|---|---|---|---|---|
| THOMAS PRICE | 7 MGS | | | | | | BAR | | • | • | • | VIT | PYR | | NVL | NIV | ORT | TOU |
| WILLIAM PRICE | 6 MGS | | | | | BUS | | | • | • | SAL | VIT | PYR | | | | | TOU |
| BENJAMIN PRING | 11 MGS | ROL | VIM | COR | | BUS | | F'O | C'R | BAD | SAL | VIT | PYR | | | | | TOU |
| WILLIAM PRITCHARD | 6 MGS | | | | | | | | • | • | SAL | VIT | PYR | | | NIV | ORT | TOU |
| SAMUEL PRYKE | 7 MGS | | | | | | | | C'R | • | • | VIT | PYR | | NVL | | ORT | TOU |
| JAMES RAWLEDGE | 7 MGS | | | COR | | BUS | | F'O | C'R | • | • | VIT | PYR | | | | | TOU |
| DUNCAN REID | 7 MGS | | | | | | | | C'R | BAD | SAL | VIT | PYR | | | | ORT | TOU |
| HENRY REILY | 4 MGS | | | | | | BAR | | C'R | BAD | • | • | | S/S | | | | |
| THOMAS RENWICK | 5 MGS | | | | | | | | • | • | SAL | VIT | PYR | | | NIV | ORT | TOU |
| JOHN REYNOLDS | 3 MGS | | | | | | | | C'R | BAD | SAL | • | | | | | | |
| WILLIAM RHODES | 9 MGS | | | COR | | BUS | | F'O | C'R | BAD | SAL | VIT | PYR | | | | ORT | TOU |
| WILLIAM RICHARDS | 2 MGS | | | | | | | | • | • | • | VIT | | | | | | |
| JOHN RIDDLES | 3 MGS | | | | | | BAR | | C'R | BAD | SAL | VIT | | | | | | TOU |
| JOSEPH RIPLEY | 5 MGS | | | | | BUS | | | C'R | BAD | SAL | • | VIT | | | | | |
| ALEXANDER ROBB | 6 MGS | | | | | | | F'O | C'R | BAD | SAL | VIT | PYR | | | | | |

| Name | MGS | ROL | VIM | COR | TAL | BUS | BAR | F'O | C'R | BAD | SAL | VIT | PYR | S/S | NVL | NIV | ORT | TOU |
|---|---|---|---|---|---|---|---|---|---|---|---|---|---|---|---|---|---|---|
| THOMAS ROBINSON | 4 MGS | | | | | | | | • | BAD | SAL | VIT | | | | | | TOU |
| THOMAS ROBINSON | 8 MGS | | | | | BUS | | F'O | C'R | BAD | • | VIT | | s/s | | | | TOU |
| RICHARD RODGERS | 6 MGS | | | | | | | | C'R | BAD | SAL | VIT | | | | | ORT | TOU |
| RICHARD ROGERS | 3 MGS | | | | | | | | | | | VIT | | | | | ORT | TOU |
| THOMAS ROGERS | 7 MGS | | | | | BUS | | F'O | • | BAD | SAL | • | | | | | | TOU |
| JAMES ROLESTONE | 4 MGS | | | COR | | | | | • | BAD | SAL | VIT | | s/s | | | | TOU |
| JOHN ROSTRIN | 7 MGS | | | | | | | | C'R | BAD | • | VIT | PYR | | | | ORT | TOU |
| JOHN ROUSE | 10 MGS | | | | | BUS | | F'O | C'R | BAD | SAL | VIT | PYR | | NVL | NIV | | TOU |
| RICHARD ROUSE | 8 MGS | | VIM | COR | | BUS | | | C'R | BAD | SAL | VIT | | | NVL | NIV | | TOU |
| GEORGE ROWE | 6 MGS | | | | | | | F'O | C'R | BAD | SAL | VIT | PYR | | | | | TOU |
| JAMES RUSSELL | 4 MGS | | VIM | COR | | BUS | | F'O | C'R | BAD | SAL | • | | | | | | |
| WILLIAM RUSSELL | 6 MGS | | | COR | | | | | C'R | • | SAL | VIT | PYR | | | | ORT | TOU |
| PHILIP RYAN | 5 MGS | | | | | | | | • | • | SAL | VIT | PYR | s/s | | | | TOU |
| JAMES SAUNDERS | 8 MGS | | | | | | BAR | F'O | • | • | • | VIT | PYR | s/s | NVL | | | TOU |
| JAMES SELL | 5 MGS | | | | | | | | • | • | • | VIT | PYR | | | | ORT | TOU |

"(VIT, ORT &TOU) AND RICHARD RODGERS 6 MGS ARE THE SAME MAN."

Note: "(BAR) AND WILLIAM SEWELL 2 MGS ARE THE SAME MAN, SEE NOTES."

| Name | | ROL | VIM | COR | TAL | BUS | BAR | F'O | C'R | BAD | SAL | VIT | PYR | S/S | NVL | NIV | ORT | TOU |
|---|---|---|---|---|---|---|---|---|---|---|---|---|---|---|---|---|---|---|
| WILLIAM SEWELL | 1 MGS | | | | | | | | | | | | | | | | | |
| WILLIAM SEWELL | 2 MGS | | | | | | BAR | | C'R | | | | | | | NIV | ORT | TOU |
| WILLIAM SHARP | 8 MGS | | | COR | | BUS | | | C'R | BAD | SAL | VIT | PYR | s/s | | | ORT | TOU |
| THOMAS SHARPLES | 8 MGS | | | | | | BAR | | C'R | BAD | SAL | VIT | | | | | ORT | |
| WILLIAM SHAUGHNESSY | 3 MGS | | VIM | COR | | | | | • | • | • | VIT | | | | | ORT | |
| WILLIAM SHEARMAN | 4 MGS | | | | | | BAR | | C'R | BAD | SAL | • | | | | | ORT | TOU |
| JOHN SHEPPARD | 8 MGS | | | | | | BAR | | C'R | BAD | SAL | VIT | PYR | | | | ORT | TOU |
| JOHN SHERROCKS | 4 MGS | | | | | | | | • | • | SAL | VIT | PYR | | | | ORT | TOU |
| JAMES SHORT | 2 MGS | | | | | | | | • | • | SAL | VIT | PYR | | | | | |
| BENJAMIN SIMONS | 6 MGS | | | | | | | | • | BAD | SAL | VIT | PYR | | | | | TOU |
| BENJAMIN SLAUGHTER | 2 MGS | | | COR | | | | | • | BAD | | VIT | | | | | | |
| WILLIAM SLAVIN | 8 MGS | | | | | | | F'O | C'R | BAD | SAL | VIT | PYR | | | | ORT | TOU |
| WILLIAM SMILLIE | 11 MGS | | | | | BUS | | F'O | C'R | BAD | SAL | VIT | PYR | | NVL | NIV | ORT | TOU |
| ROBERT SMITH | 3 MGS | | | | | | | | • | • | SAL | VIT | PYR | | | | | |
| THOMAS SMITH | 11 MGS | ROL | VIM | | | BUS | | | C'R | BAD | SAL | VIT | | s/s | NVL | | ORT | TOU |

| | MGS | ROL | VIM | COR | TAL | BUS | BAR | F'O | C'R | BAD | SAL | VIT | PYR | S/S | NVL | NIV | ORT | TOU |
|---|---|---|---|---|---|---|---|---|---|---|---|---|---|---|---|---|---|---|
| WILLIAM SMITH | 6 MGS | | | COR | | | BAR | | • | • | • | VIT | PYR | | | | | TOU |
| WILLIAM SMITHERS | 5 MGS | | | COR | | | | | • | • | • | VIT | PYR | | | | ORT | TOU |
| JOHN SMYTH | 12 MGS | | VIM | COR | | BUS | | F'O | C'R | BAD | SAL | VIT | | | NVL | NIV | ORT | TOU |
| WILLIAM SOLOMON | 9 MGS | | | | | | BAR | | C'R | BAD | SAL | VIT | PYR | | | NIV | ORT | TOU |
| JOHN SPENCER | 4 MGS | | | | | | | | C'R | BAD | SAL | VIT | | | | | | TOU |
| RICHARD SPENCER | 7 MGS | | | | | | | | C'R | BAD | SAL | VIT | | s/s | | | ORT | TOU |
| WILLIAM SPERRY | 9 MGS | | | COR | | BUS | | F'O | • | • | SAL | VIT | | | NVL | NIV | ORT | TOU |
| JOHN STANDLY | 4 MGS | | | | | | BAR | | C'R | BAD | SAL | VIT | | | | | | |
| JAMES STEELE | 6 MGS | | VIM | COR | | BUS | | | • | • | • | VIT | PYR | | | | | TOU |
| GEORGE STEPHENSON | 10 MGS | | | | | | BAR | | C'R | BAD | SAL | VIT | PYR | | NVL | NIV | ORT | TOU |
| WILLIAM STEPHENSON | 5 MGS | | | | | BUS | | | C'R | BAD | SAL | VIT | | | | | | TOU |
| JOSEPH STRINGER | 5 MGS | | | | | | | | • | • | • | VIT | PYR | | NVL | | | ORT | TOU |
| JONATHAN STUBBS | 10 MGS | ROL | VIM | COR | | BUS | BAR | | C'R | BAD | SAL | VIT | PYR | | | | | |
| EDWARD SUTHERLAND | 8 MGS | | | COR | | BUS | | | C'R | BAD | SAL | VIT | PYR | | | | | TOU |
| GEORGE SUTHERLAND | 9 MGS | | VIM | COR | TAL | BUS | | F'O | C'R | BAD | SAL | VIT | | | | | | |

| Name | MGS | ROL | VIM | COR | TAL | BUS | BAR | F'O | C'R | BAD | SAL | VIT | PYR | S/S | NVL | NIV | ORT | TOU |
|---|---|---|---|---|---|---|---|---|---|---|---|---|---|---|---|---|---|---|
| WILLIAM SUTHERS | 2 MGS | | | | | | | | • | • | • | VIT | | s/s | | | | |
| JAMES SWAIN | 5 MGS | | | | | | | | • | • | SAL | VIT | PYR | | | | ORT | TOU |
| MATTHEW SWALWELL | 7 MGS | | | | | BUS | | F'O | • | BAD | SAL | VIT | | | | | ORT | TOU |
| JOHN SYMINGTON | 11 MGS | | VIM | COR | | BUS | | F'O | C'R | BAD | SAL | VIT | PYR | | NVL | NIV | ORT | |
| SOME MGS LISTS GIVE TAL NOT COR | | | | | | | | | | | | | | | | | | |
| EDWARD TAGGEN | 10 MGS | | | COR | | BUS | | F'O | C'R | BAD | SAL | VIT | PYR | | | | ORT | TOU |
| JAMES TATE | 7 MGS | | | | | | | | C'R | BAD | SAL | VIT | PYR | | | | ORT | TOU |
| JOHN TATT | 6 MGS | ROL | VIM | COR | | | | F'O | C'R | BAD | SAL | VIT | | | | | | |
| BENJAMIN TAYLOR | 5 MGS | | | | | | | | • | • | SAL | VIT | PYR | | | | ORT | TOU |
| JOSEPH TAYLOR | 3 MGS | | | | | | | | • | • | SAL | VIT | PYR | | | | | |
| WILLIAM TAYLOR | 1 MGS | | | COR | | | | | • | • | SAL | VIT | | | | | | |
| JOHN THOMAS | 4 MGS | | VIM | COR | | | | | C'R | BAD | | VIT | | | | | | |
| DAVID THOMPSON | 2 MGS | | | | | | | | C'R | BAD | | VIT | | | | | | |
| JOHN TRUSSELL | 3 MGS | | | | | | | | • | • | • | VIT | PYR | | | | ORT | TOU |
| GEORGE TUNNICLIFFE | 12 MGS | | | | | BUS | | F'O | C'R | BAD | SAL | VIT | PYR | s/s | NVL | NIV | ORT | TOU |
| MATTHEW TURNER | 9 MGS | | | | | | | F'O | C'R | BAD | SAL | VIT | PYR | | NVL | | ORT | TOU |

| Name | MGS | ROL | VIM | COR | TAL | BUS | BAR | F'O | C'R | BAD | SAL | VIT | PYR | S/S | NVL | NIV | ORT | TOU |
|---|---|---|---|---|---|---|---|---|---|---|---|---|---|---|---|---|---|---|
| PETER TURNER | 6 MGS | | | | | BUS | | | C'R | BAD | SAL | VIT | | | | | ORT | |
| RICHARD UNDERHILL | 7 MGS | | | | | | | F'O | C'R | BAD | SAL | VIT | PYR | | NVL | | ORT | TOU |
| THOMAS UNDRILL | 3 MGS | | | | | | BAR | | • | • | • | VIT | PYR | | | | | TOU |
| WILLIAM USHER | 8 MGS | | | COR | | BUS | | | • | BAD | SAL | VIT | PYR | | | | | TOU |
| JOHN WAGHORN | 7 MGS | | | | | | | | C'R | BAD | SAL | VIT | PYR | | | | | TOU |
| GEORGE WAINE | 4 MGS | | | | | | | | • | • | • | VIT | PYR | s/s | NVL | NIV | ORT | TOU |
| ABRAHAM WALKER | 9 MGS | | | | | BUS | | F'O | • | BAD | SAL | VIT | PYR | | NVL | NIV | | TOU |
| JOHN WALKER | 6 MGS | | | | | | | | C'R | BAD | SAL | VIT | PYR | | NVL | NIV | ORT | TOU |
| JAMES WALSH | 5 MGS | | | | | | | | • | • | • | VIT | PYR | | | | | TOU |
| JAMES WARBURTON | 8 MGS | | | COR | | | | F'O | C'R | BAD | SAL | VIT | PYR | | NVL | NIV | ORT | TOU |
| JOHN WARD | 10 MGS | | | COR | | BUS | | F'O | C'R | BAD | • | VIT | PYR | | | | ORT | TOU |
| JOHN WATERHOUSE | 4 MGS | | | | | | | | • | • | SAL | VIT | PYR | | | | | TOU |
| JOSEPH WATNIFF | 8 MGS | | | | | BUS | | F'O | C'R | BAD | SAL | VIT | PYR | | | | | TOU |
| THOMAS WEBB | 2 MGS | | | COR | | | | | • | • | SAL | VIT | | | | | | TOU |
| JOHN WELLBELOVE | 5 MGS | | | | | | | | C'R | BAD | SAL | VIT | | | | | | TOU |

| | ROL | VIM | COR | TAL | BUS | BAR | F'O | C'R | BAD | SAL | VIT | PYR | S/S | NVL | NIV | ORT | TOU |
|---|---|---|---|---|---|---|---|---|---|---|---|---|---|---|---|---|---|
| WILLIAM WELLINGTON — 6 MGS | | | | | | BAR | | • | • | SAL | VIT | | | NVL | | | TOU |
| WILLIAM WELLS — 7 MGS | | | | | | | | • | • | • | VIT | PYR | | | | ORT | TOU |
| WILLIAM WESTON — 7 MGS | | | | TAL | | | | • | • | SAL | VIT | | | | | | TOU |
| THOMAS WHETSTONE — 8 MGS | | | | | BUS | | F'O | C'R | BAD | SAL | VIT | | | NVL | NIV | | |
| WILLIAM WHITEHEAD — 7 MGS | | | | | BUS | | F'O | C'R | BAD | SAL | VIT | | s/s | | | | |
| WILLIAM WILKINSON — 2 MGS | | | COR | | | | | C'R | BAD | • | VIT | | | | | | |
| JOHN WILLIAMS — 8 MGS | | | | | BUS | | F'O | C'R | BAD | SAL | VIT | PYR | | | | | TOU |
| THOMAS WILSON — 10 MGS | | | | | BUS | | F'O | C'R | BAD | SAL | VIT | PYR | | NVL | NIV | | TOU |
| THOMAS WILSON — 10 MGS | | | | | | BAR | | C'R | BAD | SAL | VIT | PYR | | NVL | NIV | ORT | TOU |
| JOSEPH WITHAM — 7 MGS | | | COR | | | | | C'R | BAD | SAL | VIT | PYR | | | | | TOU |
| WILLIAM WOOD — 6 MGS | | | | | | | | • | • | SAL | VIT | PYR | | NVL | | ORT | TOU |
| GEORGE WOODLAND — 1 MGS | | | | | | | | • | • | • | VIT | | | | | | |
| JAMES WOODLEY — 4 MGS | | | | | | | | • | • | • | VIT | PYR | | | | ORT | TOU |
| JAMES WOODLEY — 6 MGS | | | | | | BAR | | C'R | BAD | SAL | VIT | PYR | | | | | TOU |
| HENRY WRIGHT — 4 MGS | | | COR | | | | | C'R | BAD | • | • | | | | | | |

| | MGS | ROL | VIM | COR | TAL | BUS | BAR | F'O | C'R | BAD | SAL | VIT | PYR | S/S | NVL | NIV | ORT | TOU |
|---|---|---|---|---|---|---|---|---|---|---|---|---|---|---|---|---|---|---|
| JOHN WRIGHT | 5 MGS | | | | | | | | • | • | SAL | VIT | PYR | | | | ORT | TOU |
| WILLIAM WRIGHT | 10 MGS | | | COR | | BUS | | | C'R | BAD | SAL | VIT | PYR | | | | ORT | TOU |
| DAVID WYLIE | 6 MGS | ROL | VIM | COR | | | | | C'R | BAD | • | VIT | PYR | s/s | | | | |
| RICHARD YOUNG | 6 MGS | ROL | VIM | | | BUS | | F'O | • | • | SAL | VIT | | | | | | |
| NOT ON MGS LIST | | | | | | | | F'O | C'R | BAD | SAL | VIT | | | | | | TOU |
| | | | | | | | | | 286 | 300 | 308 | 403 | | | | | | |
| | | | | | | | | | 304 | 312 | 306 | 423 | | | | | | |

TOTAL CLASPS TO THE 95TH: 1,297

TRUE TOTAL OF CLASPS: 1,345

| OFFICERS GOLD MEDAL | | C'R | BAD | SAL | VIT |
|---|---|---|---|---|---|
| ANDREW BARNARD | | GM | GM | GM | GM |
| PETER O'HARE | | GM | GM | | |
| JOHN ROSS | | GM | | | GM |

# Footnotes

## Preparation for the Campaign of 1812

1   Lieutenant Sarsfield has been given a poor press in a recent publication on the Rifles, though he might not have been the ideal Rifles' officer he continued to soldier on, and did not quit the service as suggested. He did not resign his commission until around 1819. Norcott gave him praise in the latter part of the Peninsular War.

2   It might be fairer to give the true state of affairs an airing here to clarify what sort of a political climate Wellington was operating under. In 1811 the Prince Regent gave a lavish banquet at Carlton House, no expense spared, to the extent that down the centre of the banquet table some 200 feet long ran an artificial stream, flowing from a silver fountain. The Prince presided over the event from the comfort of a plume backed throne with an illuminated crown and 'GR' cipher. Sir Samuel Romilly contrasted this great extravagance against the starving weavers of Lancashire and Glasgow, the Luddite riots and framework machine breaking in Yorkshire and Nottinghamshire. While Sir Samuel could survive such observations, contrast this with the sentence given to Leigh Hunt the writer in 1813, who was gaoled for two years for describing the Prince as, 'a corpulent man of 50, a violator of his word a libertine over head and ears in disgrace, despiser of domestic ties, the companion of gamblers and demireps, a man who had just closed a half century without one single claim on the gratitude of his country'.

3   In Basil Harvey's *The History of the Rifle Brigade* there is a photograph depicting what is purported to be, 'The Highland Company Pipes'; this is questionable: the pipes shown are either Lowland or Irish, which were played sitting down. The musician used his hand to pump the small wooden bellows as opposed to blowing the air into the bag. It is quite plausible that the Highland Company did have a piper in its ranks, who might have been a member of the regimental band but these pipes were certainly not his. The band did have an Irish musician in its ranks which could account for these particular pipes being erroneously attributed to the Highland Company.

## The Siege and Capture of Ciudad Rodrigo

1   It is interesting to note here that Governor Barrié had only the day before (the 7th) reinforced the garrison in the Renand Redoubt, adding an officer and 50 infantry men, and eight gunners under the command of another officer. Previous to that the Redoubt was garrisoned by ten infantry men and five gunners. For such an important position this has to be a reckless lack of judgement, which was only rectified at the last moment.

2   The strength given for this force varies between 300 and 450 depending on which account you read.

3   Could this be the reason for the discrepancy in the numbers involved? GC/RC

4   The normal manner of getting under arms was by bugle-calls by day and an alarm by night in the same way, with complete silence required the assembly had therefore to be treated differently. The commander of the division had an orderly from each brigade, who carried the order to the brigadier, who again had an orderly for each regiment, the regimental commander likewise had an orderly from each company in this way orders could be sent quickly without any fuss; the company sergeants were also obliged to memorise the roll of their company, that way when called out at night they did not require a light for the purpose. Though these changes might sound trifling they made the division most efficient and only added to its elitist status,

much to the annoyance of the likes of General Picton. Wellington once made the point, 'I gave them an order over night, for a dangerous service, and on the following morning the work was done, and the division on parade as if nothing had happened'. GC/RC

5   At one time in the building trade ladders were used, known as 'fir-pole' ladders, before modern day ladders were produced. A suitable pine tree was felled, all the branches and bark removed, then split down the centre. Rungs were fashioned and fixed to the inner section between the split tree, the rounded sides to the out side. Once completed these ladders were most sturdy but enormously heavy, with the bottom section bearing most of the weight. Therefore, it would be logical to suggest that ladders in the Peninsula were constructed in a similar fashion; it would require quite a number of men to carry them and place them against a fortification. The most obvious mode of carrying them would be heavy end first, so they could be slid straight into a ditch then when required toppled forward and pushed up towards the walls. It is therefore quite laughable to see ladders illustrated in modern books depicting the assaults on Ciudad Rodrigo and Badajoz; with ladders that look as if they had been supplied by the local window cleaner and highly unlikely to carry the weight of a number of men. When camped in an area with an abundance of pine trees it would seem a logical conclusion that they were used to provide the raw materials for the sieges of Ciudad Rodrigo and Badajoz.

6   Handkerchiefs for this period in British history should not be confused with those of the present day, Smith's could have been up to two or three feet square in 1812. GC/RC

7   The same day that Colborne was making a name for himself, back in England two regiments were called out to control the Luddite rising which had broken out in various parts of the country. Lord Byron made his maiden speech in the House of Lords, opposing Lord Liverpool's 'Frame Breaking Bill' which was being introduced to make it a 'Capital Offence!' It is with little wonder therefore when researching individual Riflemen over the years to see that their former occupations was often given as a 'Framework Knitter'. GC/RC

8   Longford, *Wellington Years of the Sword.*

9   *The Autobiography of Sergeant William Lawrence.* London 1886.

10  Sir William Cope in his history of the Rifle Brigade gives a list of second battalion NCOs, who he says were part of the forlorn hope. It is known that at least one of these is a first battalion Rifleman, Fairfoot. As the second battalion only had two companies present it would be rather fool hardy to allow them to volunteer so many men of rank for such a desperate mission! GC/RC.

11  John Cox manuscript journal, Green Jackets archives.

12  FitzMaurice, privately printed memoir.

13  Most of those writing about the Light Division attack are of the same opinion, the Portuguese failed to produce the ladders and hay-sacks on time. That the men at different stages of the assault were able to climb ladders would suggest that they did eventually put in an appearance, unless the main columns in support seeing the problem carried them forward. It is interesting to note that Colonel George Elder, an ex-Rifles' officer in command of the 3rd Caçadores, would have allowed such a dereliction of duty by his regiment one of the best Portuguese regiments in the Light Division.

14  Since the death of Craufurd's personal bugler, who had been in the 95th, as reported in volume two we have found no evidence that supports him ever being replaced. It was important for Craufurd to give commands over distance when an orderly would not be quick enough. However it would have been unlikely that a bugler would have been of much value on the glacis. GC/RC

15  *Recollections of an Old 52nd Man.* Captain Dobbs.

16  Costello was being a little economical with the truth here; Wilkie was not killed at Ciudad Rodrigo, for he was already dead! The musters show that he died on 11th December 1811. It is impossible to second guess Costello's reason for making up this scenario other than in later life in his confusion he mixed up his name with that of another Rifleman? Only one Rifleman in the 1st Battalion was killed in this action. Though as we have shown earlier two are given as having been killed in the musters. GC/RC

17  Around this time Picton rode up to the commanding officer of the 77th Regiment and after talking to him rode off. It was only after this that the 77th moved off to join the 5th Regiment and took part in the storming.
18  It is with constant admiration we have viewed those men wounded during these primitive medical times, especially seeing in modern times when traumatic stress disorders are trotted out in many cases by those who have only witnessed an incident. Contrast this with the likes of Colborne, the ball had taken the end off the bone and then embedded in the bone itself. This meant the surgeons had a long and difficult task of removing it. He put his watch on one side open to observe the time and allowed them to dig at it for five minute intervals.
19  There was much discussion over this through correspondence in the United Service Journal. For a full account see appendix to Oman Volume V. 1811–1812 p589.
20  An officer of the 3rd Division who had been captured and imprisoned in the citadel also obtained a pair of Barrié's pistols as a souvenir.
21  The 77th was the only regiment to take its colours into action at the capture of Ciudad Rodrigo. GC/RC
22  The British Army had taken part in siege warfare under Oliver Cromwell during the Civil War in Ireland. Marlborough with a multi-national army, and the most recent being Seringapatam and Copenhagen. GC/RC
23  Kincaid's, *Adventures in the Rifle Brigade.*
24  *History of the 52nd Regiment.* Moorsom.
25  *The True Story of a Peninsular War Rifleman.* Eileen Hathaway 1997.
26  This has also been attributed to the 88th regiment.
27  A number of historians state that Craufurd was interned inside the actual wall of Ciudad Rodrigo. This is questionable, by the time Craufurd died work was well advanced repairing the breached walls. This would have been a matter of urgency and a main priority. The town had to be made ready to defend against a possible French attack. Gleig states Craufurd's coffin was 'lowered' into his final resting place, which would correspond with a grave being dug near or close to the walls. Gleig's account of Craufurd's funeral has to be viewed with an air of caution as he was not present. His version was either given to him by somebody who was, or he cobbled the account together from various stories. Of course the account could be perfectly genuine actually relating what someone actually witnessed and Gleig wrote it as if he was witnessing the event himself to add weight to the content? GC/RC

### Siege of Badajoz

—

### Assault and Capture of Badajoz

1  If this is correct and the storming party consisted of 300 men they were left with 200 men from which to form the remaining duties. 12 ladders with six men to a ladder and 24 axe/crowbar men left 104 men from which to provide the forlorn hope, rope party and hay bag men though Wellington's orders say all stormers were to have hay bags. GC/RC
2  Oxford dictionary: Forlorn Hope—A body of soldiers selected for some service of especial danger; a desperate enterprise of last resort; A vain hope; from Dutch; Verlorn hoop, 'lost troop'.
3  We have not come across any evidence to suggest the 4th Division had a rope party. It is interesting that after the capture of Badajoz it was suggested that grappling hooks should have been used against the chevaux-de-frise. GC/RC
4  This would seem logical, to have a large number of these items prepared for the task they were required, a small number would not have had much of an impact. One would have expected the forlorn hope to have also carried them. The actual size of these bags is not known, though Green says (small bags) if they had been too large it would have made carrying a ladder rather awkward. GC/RC

5   The bastions of San Vincente, San Jose, and Santiago, had all been strengthened, by demi-lunes, small out works, which previously they didn't have. The whole was then protected by a system of mines under the glacis. From the safety of their counterscarps the French would have been able to set these off should the British Engineers push the siege trenches closer to the walls, which were rather weak at this point in the fortress. Wellington had learned of these preparations from a French Sergeant Major of Sappers who had originally mapped out the works, who having had a severe grievance against his Captain, turned to the British, and gave Wellington his map! This information was to prove of vital importance for it saved much valuable time and no doubt the loss of many lives.

6   Similar to gabions, some five feet in length and 15 inches in diameter, filled with wool.

7   Counterscarp—see illustration/sketch.

8   Chevaux-de-frise: this is French for Friesland horses, Dutch Vresse Ruyters, Frisian horsemen and German, Spanische Reiter, Spanish horsemen. A military obstacle said to originate from the Dutch War of Independence and used to close the breach of a fortress, street, etc. it was often used in field operations as a defence against cavalry; hence the name, the Dutch were weak in the mounted arm and had therefore to check the enemy's cavalry by an artificial obstacle. It consisted of beams in which are fixed a number of spears, sword-blades, etc; with the points projecting outwards on all sides. (Britanica 11th Edition 1911.) It probably came into existence before the 18th century but was not known by this name at the time. (See The British Library, Military Library or journal Vol I, 1798 which states it was used at Gronigen in 1658 and mounted on wheels.)

9   Behind this the French had dug a deep trench which formed another killing zone should the stormers find a way through the chevaux-de-frise.

10  It isn't always appreciated by the reader or some historians the actual size of the bastions at Badajoz. Many who have visited the city in modern times see it from a completely clinical perspective than the one the troops who besieged and stormed it. Though much of the original defences are still standing the approaches to the three breaches for instance are now obscured by trees and gardens, with much of the area levelled and filled in. Therefore a report detailing the fortifications by Colonel Verner of the Rifle Brigade in 1913 is of great interest, and gives a much clearer picture as to how the original defences would have looked. He states that the size of the bastions can easily be imagined by those who have not seen them, by the fact at that time, (1913) one housed a fine cavalry barracks, while the one adjacent to it, occupied a good size bull-ring! Further observations by Verner will be given as the events unfold. GC/RC

11  William Green, *Where duty calls me.*

12  This mode of dress was obviously ordered to counter what was believed to be a shallow trench of water but events proved it to be an unnecessary measure. GC/RC

13  Lieutenant Bell had only arrived in the country in February and this was his first taste of action. GC/RC

14  Lieutenant Gairdner, National Army Museum.

15  It is impossible to come up with a valid reason for Fairfoot being the only man of the 1st Battalion to be in the forlorn hope. GC/RC

16  It is equally strange that one Captain and four Lieutenants from the two 2nd battalion companies were also allowed to volunteer with the storming party. GC/RC

17  The 60th Rifles had a company serving with the 4th, 5th and 3rd Divisions giving them the distinction of being the only unit to have men at all points of the storming! GC/RC

18  This was well thought out for the stormers of the Light and 4th Divisions would have to put their ladders from the counterscarp into this ditch to get down and the depth of this at times was quite a problem for the men. The continuous rain throughout the siege aided the French cause by swelling the water course from the dam right back as far as the Trinidad breach. GC/RC

19  With Cameron's swing on the glacis, it is possible that at least one of the remaining four 1st Battalion Rifle companies was detached to Colonel Elder's Brigade. While the remaining companies could have been put into the 1st Brigade along with the two 2nd Battalion companies, it is also possible that they were also with Elder. This whole scenario is of course only speculation.

20  These were long wooden stakes set into the ground of the covered way or glacis to form a barrier impeding the descent.

21  Private memorial published of Lowe's service.

22  On Colonel Verner viewing the ditch in 1913 from off the top of the ravelin at a point exactly opposite where the curtain wall had been breached, it was quite clear to him due to the new brickwork, the Santa Maria bastion to his left was roughly 60 yards away and to his right the La Trinidad bastion was roughly the same distance, confirming the curtain breach being almost central in the wall linking both bastions. A number of maps show the Trinidad bastion being closer to the curtain breach. It is therefore quite easy to see how the two storming divisions became so mixed in this confined area.

23  We have not been able to corroborate this action or find out who these extra troops were or where they came from though some of the events that took place around this time could be linked to this event. GC/RC

24  Napier, *British Battles and Sieges*.

25  Meabry had been reduced to the ranks from sergeant for defrauding the company's payroll books; as a result he had lost all standing within the regiment. He volunteered for the storming party in the hope of restoring himself to his comrades. He served in the 2nd Battalion and was eventually killed in action. GC/RC

26  See *Rifle Green in the Peninsula Volume II*. p82.

27  It was the natural instinct of the Light Division men to attack the first breach they encountered in the curtain or join the 4th Division against the La Trinidad breach. Safety in numbers springs to mind here! Some men of course had also taken the easy option in the face of such terrifying opposition, and who could blame them, by going to the rear with the wounded. This was the designated job of the Bandsman, with around 15 Bandsmen in each band; the total number of men for this duty for the whole of the Light Division was no more than 45. The 43rd and 52nd Regiments both had bands present but only the 1st Battalion 95th had a band in the Peninsula in 1812. The 2nd Battalion band did not arrive until 1813 and the 3rd Battalion band until 1814, after the fall of Toulouse. GC/RC

28  *Autobiography of Sir Harry Smith* by G. C. Moore Smith London 1903.

### Aftermath of Badajoz

—

### Salamanca

1  Wellington, due to the exertions of his chief code breaker, Colonel George Scovell, was one step ahead of the French high command. Scovell had been labouring for some years gradually deciphering this complicated form of information transfer used by the French spying system. The lesser known success, never much appreciated by British historians, is the important part played by their Spanish allies, who constantly harried and ambushed aides and couriers going to or from Paris with these ciphers. The French were most ingenious at inventing various ways of concealing or disguising them, while at the same time Spanish sympathisers did their best to make their fellow countrymen's task all the harder. Earning their living by vast bribes for passing or taking messages themselves, a most dangerous and deadly occupation, many thought the dangers worth taking. Though this would have soon changed if captured, due to the lengths the Spanish patriots would go in extracting the information from the most stubborn of men! See Mark Urban's book The man who broke Napoleon's codes, which gives a full and fascinating account of Scovell's part in Wellington's victories.

2  The illustration of Captain Kent was probably done around this time, hence his non-regulation trousers.

## Advance to Madrid and Retreat into Portugal

1 Erskine a couple of months later, committed suicide, by throwing himself from a window in a fit of frenzy and broke his neck.

2 *Wellington's Lieutenant, Napoleon's Gaoler, The Peninsula letters & St Helena Diaries of Sir George Ridout Bingham* by Gareth Glover, Pen and Sword 2004.

## Advance to, and Battle of, Vitoria

1 Throughout our research we have often come across the senior Captains' companies being at the forefront of any pending action; we know Leach's company was definitely one of these two, therefore it seems logical to assume the other was Stewart's the next senior Captain. GC/RC

2 Colonel Verner and Sir William Cope in their histories on the regiment state they advanced with Kempt's brigade but later we will see the 3/95th and the two companies of the 1st Battalion had to advance to join up with the rest of the Light Division. GC/RC

3 There is much confusion as to the positioning of the Rifle companies at times during the battle of Vitoria. It would seem in our research that the battalions did not always remain tied to their respective brigades. GC/RC

4 Harry Smith as we seen was Brigade Major to Vandeleur during the battle, not with his company, which would have been under the command of the senior Lieutenant. GC/RC

## Pursuit of the French after Vitoria

—

## The 2nd Battalion 95th Rifles' Companies in Southern Spain

—

# Bibliography

*A British Rifleman.* Major George Simmons, Greenhill Books London 1986.
*A History of the Peninsula War.* C. Oman KBE, Oxford University Press 1911.
*A Soldier of the 71st Regt.* Christpher Hibbert, Leo Cooper 1975.
*Adventures in the Rifle Brigade.* Captain Sir J. Kincaid.
*Autobiography of Harry Smith.* Edited by Moore-Smith MA, London John Murray, single 1903 volume.
*Biographical Sketch.* Major General John Fitzmaurice, private publication Italy 1908.
*Digest of Service 1/Rifle Brigade 1800-1885.* Battalion Press.
*General Craufurd and his Light Division.* Rev. A. H. Craufurd, Ken Trotman 1987.
*History of the 52nd Regiment 1755-1816.* M. S. Moorsom.
*History of the 60th Rifles.*
*History & Campaigns of the Rifle Brigade.* Willoughby Verner, Volumes I & II London.
*History of the Rifle Brigade.* Sir William Cope, London 1877.
*Medal Roll. 1793-1814.* 'A. J. N.'
*MGS Medal Roll 1793-1814.* Lieut. Colonel F. S. S. Brind.
*MGS Medal Roll 1793-1814.* Lieut. Colonel Kingsley Foster.
*MGS Roll.* edited by A. L. T. Mullen, 1990.
*Narrative of Service.* Lieutenant Cooke 43rd Regiment.
*On the Road with Wellington.* A. L. F. Schaumann, Greenhill Books 1999.
*Peninsula Sketches Volumes I & II.* By actors on the scene, edited by W. H. Maxwell, Naval & Military Press.
*Random Shots from a Rifleman.* Captain Sir J. Kincaid.
*Recollections of an Old 52nd Man.* Captain John Dobbs, Spelmount Ltd 2000, 1st published 1863.
*Rifle Green at Waterloo.* Caldwell & Cooper, Bugle Horn Publications 1990.
*Rifle Green in the Peninsula Vol. I.* Caldwell & Cooper, Bugle Horn Publications 1998.
*Rifle Green in the Peninsula Vol. II.* Caldwell & Cooper, Bugle Horn Publications 2006.
*Rough Sketches in the Life of an Old Soldier.* Lieut. Colonel J Leach CB, London 1831.
*The Humble Address of John Lowe.* Arranged & edited by the Rev. F. Newnham 1827.
*The Peninsular and Waterloo Campaigns.* Edward Costello, Longman, Green & Co 1967.
*The Peninsula War 1807–1814.* Michael Glover.
*The Years of the Sword, Wellington.* E. Longford, published Weidenfield & Nicholson 1969.
*Twenty-Five Years in the Rifle Brigade.* William Surtees, F. Muller Ltd London 1973.
*Wellington in the Peninsula 1808–1814.* Jac Weller.
*Wellington Studies.* Volumes I, II & III.

*Wellington's Lieutenant, Napoleon's Gaoler.* Gareth Glover, Pen and Sword 2004.
*Where Duty Calls Me.* Bugler William Green, Synton Books 1975.
*With the Guns in the Peninsula.* 2nd Captain W. Webber RA, Greenhill Books 1991.
*Years of Victory.* Arthur Bryant.

# Index